THE ZONE GARDEN
5·6·7

Books by Charlotte M. Frieze

Social Gardens

The Zone Garden 3 • 4 • 5

The Zone Garden 5 • 6 • 7

The Zone Garden 8 • 9 • 10

THE ZONE GARDEN

5·6·7

A SUREFIRE GUIDE TO GARDENING IN YOUR ZONE

CHARLOTTE M. FRIEZE

Illustrations by Joel Barkley

Photographs by Michael H. Dodge from the White Flower Farm Collection

A High Tide Press Original
A Fireside Book
Published by Simon & Schuster

FIRESIDE
Rockefeller Center
1230 Avenue of the Americas
New York, NY 10020

Designed by Doris Straus

Edited by Lisa MacDonald

Manufactured in Hong Kong

10 9 8 7 6 5 4 3 2 1

Library of Congress Cataloging-in-Publication Data
Frieze, Charlotte M.
The zone garden : a surefire guide to gardening in your zone / Charlotte M. Frieze ;
illustrations by Joel Barkley ; photographs by Michael H. Dodge from the White Flower Farm Collection.
p.   cm.
"A High Tide Press original." "A Fireside book." Includes indexes. Contents: [1] 3-4-5 -- [2] 5-6-7 [3] 8-9-10.
1. Gardening--United States. 2. Plants, Cultivated--United States. 3. Gardening. 4. Plants, Cultivated. I. Title.
SB453.F76 1997
635'.0973--DC20   96-46057
CIP

ISBN 0-684-82560-0

ACKNOWLEDGMENTS

The author wishes to express her gratitude to Doris Straus, who conceived of the idea for this project and designed it brilliantly; to Roger Straus III for his undeviating support; to my editor Lisa MacDonald who always kept the books on track with her intelligence, organization and enthusiasm; to Anne Yarowsky for acquiring this project and bringing it to fruition; to illustrator Joel Barkley, principal photographer Michael H. Dodge, and photographers Peter Cummin, Peter C. Jones, Claudia A. Palmer, Erik Simmons and Roger Straus III for their exquisite images; to Shepherd and Ellen Ogden, Alex and Carol Rosenberg, John Saladino, Richard and Bonnie Reiss and Sally Tappen for sharing their gardens; to Elizabeth Scholtz for her encouragement; to Alexander A. Apanius, Mary Palmer and Hugh Dargan, Niki Ekstrom, Bill Evans, Mike Graham, Doyle Jones, Jack Lieber, Scott Ogden, Greg Piotrowski, and Adam Lifton-Schwerner for their expert advice; to Susan Goldberger for her insightful recommendations; to Mary Dearborn, who made the complicated simple; to Christine S. Shaw, who kept the hard drive spinning; to Sheila White, without whose assistance I would still be writing the first draft; to Lynne Duffy of White Flower Farm for her thorough and thoughtful picture research; to Katherine Powis and The Horticultural Society of New York for their excellent library; to Robert A. M. Stern for his support and the time in which to write these books; to Frank Lipman, who kept me going; to my parents for giving me my first garden; and to my husband, Peter C. Jones, whose love and devotion have carried me through the many challenges of writing these books.

Additional Photography Credits

Peter Cummin: pages 46; 47; 54: top right, bottom; 56: top left, top right, bottom right; 58: top left, center, bottom right; 80: bottom right; 98: center; 136: top left, top right, center; 138: center; 160: bottom right; 162: top left; top right; center; 164: top right, bottom left; *William B. Harris:* page 120 top; *Saxon Holt:* page 193; *Peter C. Jones:* pages 18; 24; 39; 56: bottom left; 58: bottom left; 72: bottom left; 76: top left; 78: bottom left; 96: top left, center; 98: bottom right; 114; 122; 130; 162: bottom; 166-167; 168; 169; 192; 200-201; 203; 206; *Alan Mandell:* pages 44-45; 198; *Claudia A. Palmer:* page 74: top left; *Erik Simmons:* pages 112-113; 160: top left; *Roger Straus III:* pages 140; 141.

TABLE OF CONTENTS

TABLE OF CONTENTS

Michael H. Dodge

1
THE ZONE
GARDEN

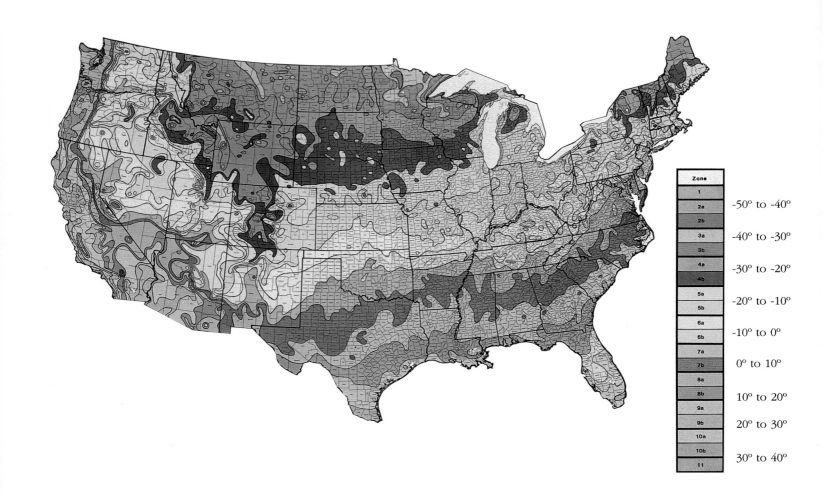

Zone	
1	
2a	-50° to -40°
2b	
3a	-40° to -30°
3b	
4a	-30° to -20°
4b	
5a	-20° to -10°
5b	
6a	-10° to 0°
6b	
7a	0° to 10°
7b	
8a	10° to 20°
8b	
9a	20° to 30°
9b	
10a	30° to 40°
10b	
11	

Agricultural Research Service, USDA

I
THE ZONE GARDEN

Temperature
Altitude
Frost
Snow
Rainfall
Humidity
Sunlight

Iris sibirica

Wind
Soil
Soil Types
Compost
Soil pH
Soil Fertility
Saline Soils

When the plant and seed catalogs arrive in January, the photographs are so beautiful that it's easy to be tempted to buy one of everything. However, like all gardeners, I'm sure you have experienced the disappointment of plants that have inexplicably failed and realize that gardening is about more than selecting plants for color, shape and size.

Climate is at the heart of the garden. By tailoring your gardening practices to where you live, *The Zone Garden* helps takes the guesswork out of plant selection, placement and care. With an understanding of the elements at work in your own backyard, you can choose plants targeted for your unique microclimate to achieve peak performance in your garden.

PLANT HARDINESS AND THE ZONE MAP

For years gardeners have relied on the United States Department of Agriculture's Hardiness Map, which illustrates eleven different climate zones delineated by average minimum annual temperatures. Using this zone system, plants are rated by their ability to survive the winter. For example, a plant rated as hardy to Zone 7 will survive temperatures to 0º Fahrenheit, but not Zone 5's minimum temperature of -20º. Locate your county on the map to determine your zone.

Zone 5 — spring green — minimum temperatures of -20º to -10º
Zone 6 — yellow — minimum temperatures of -10º to 0º
Zone 7 — pink — minimum temperatures to 0º to 10º

Think of the USDA Map as a cold weather survival guide. But survival alone will not lead to a bountiful garden. Instead, use the Zone Map as a starting point to understanding the needs of your plants.

Getting To Know Your Zone

Zones 5, 6 and 7 stretch across the country, beginning in coastal New England, traveling down through New York then crossing through the Midwest and Southwest to northern California, the Pacific Northwest and Alaska.

Gardeners in these zones often enjoy a benevolent sun and generally adequate rainfall. However, many must also contend with a moderate growing season, and surprise periods of severe cold, extreme heat or drought, sometimes all in the same year.

But climatic conditions vary widely within the same zone (Zone 5 runs through parts of Alaska, Arizona, Michigan and Massachusetts), and even in your own backyard. To help your garden flourish, understand your local climate, then zero in on the growing conditions in your own garden.

Zeroing In On Your Microclimate

A microclimate is a small area where growing conditions differ from the overall climate. Microclimates occur when climatic, natural and man-made elements converge; a multitude can exist within your property.

Savvy gardeners in your zones exploit warm pockets to extend the growing season, grow more tender or sun-loving plants, and protect against an unexpectedly brutal winter. Cold pockets are reserved for hardier plants; wet spots for thirsty plants and dry areas for drought-tolerant plants.

Walk around your property during the different seasons. Mark on a plan where you feel warmest in a winter wind and coolest on a blistering hot summer day. Look for late-winter sun traps and low spots of pooling water. Work with the following elements to find the perfect spot for that favorite rose.

HINT: When analyzing your property, take into consideration the unusual weather extremes your climate may experience.

TEMPERATURE

All plants have a minimum temperature below which they can't survive, a maximum temperature above which they can't survive and an optimum temperature. Heat as well as cold control plant growth and influence the following critical plant processes:

PHOTOSYNTHESIS   The process in which leaves, using the sun's energy, convert carbon dioxide from the air and nutrients found in water into carbohydrates.

TRANSPIRATION   The process in which leaves lose water vapor and oxygen through evaporation.

RESPIRATION   The process in which carbohydrates are broken down to create energy, carbon dioxide and water.

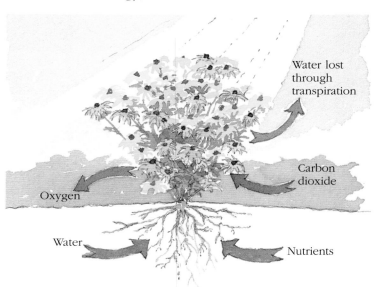

Through photosynthesis, leaves, using the sun's energy, convert carbon dioxide from both air and the nutrients in water, into carbohydrates, which are necessary for plant growth.

The Growing Season

While hardiness zones are based on the average annual minimum temperature in a given zone, the growing season is based on the average number of days above 43° Fahrenheit (the lowest temperature at which grass grows).

Here's how it works. Air temperature controls the soil temperature. Together these temperatures influence dormancy (the slowing down of plant processes and temporary halting of growth), which determines the length of your growing season. The average is as follows:

> Zone 5: 210 days
> Zone 6: 225 days
> Zone 7: 255 days

To determine the growing season in your local area (which may significantly differ from these general guidelines), as well as a record of the first and last days of frost, contact your local Agricultural Cooperative Extension Service (see p.216).

Temperature Moderators And Boosters

The wind on your property can influence the temperature. A garden enclosed by hedges or walls can raise the temperature within the garden by blocking the wind; conversely, wind blowing over the surfaces of pools, ponds and other water features will lower temperatures. Utilizing the microclimates created by these garden factors will allow you to experiment successfully with plants beyond your zone.

Extreme Cold

Gardeners must take precautions for tough, snowless winters, particularly in Zones 5 and 6. Without the snow for protection, devastating cold can cause winterkill unless your plants are properly protected. (See "Winterizing" in each chapter.)

Alternating hard freezes and rapid thaws cause the most damage to plants. Cold temperatures freeze the sap within the plant cells. When the temperature rises, the sap thaws and expands, destroying the cell walls. This thawing damages leaves and flowers alike, and may even split the bark of trees, especially on the northwest side of the trunk.

Extreme Heat

Remember that the dog days of summer can be just as tough on plants as the dead of winter. The harsh summer sun and drought can combine forces, sending plants into false dormancy for survival. Be sure to water thoroughly all summer and select heat-tolerant plants for hot, sunny spots, especially in Zone 7.

ALTITUDE

Altitude can be a major factor in determining your microclimate. For every 250 feet above sea level the temperature drops about one degree Fahrenheit. With only a 10° difference between zones, a high site may well be in the next colder zone. To determine your altitude refer to a local U.S. Geological Survey map or a survey map of your property. The contour numbers represent the altitude in feet.

FROST

An untimely frost can severely damage a garden. In the spring, it can sneak up totally without warning, turning fresh young leaves brown and killing buds before they've had a chance to flower.

Frost is frozen moisture. It forms on plants when air temperatures drop below 32° Fahrenheit and in the soil when ground temperatures drop below freezing. The last day of frost determines the earliest sowing dates for tender plants. The first frost sadly signals the end of the growing season. To familiarize yourself with the frost dates in your area, call your local nursery or contact your Agricultural Cooperative Extension Service, and start to keep a record in your own garden. If you find your garden is prone to late spring frosts, select plants that flower later in the season to prevent frosting of the blooms.

The duration of frost and its depth are important to gardeners. Frozen ground means water is not available to roots. While deep-rooted trees are unaffected by frost, shallow-rooted plants, plants with borderline hardiness, and evergreen shrubs, such as *Rhododendron*, need winter protection. (See "Winterizing" in each chapter.)

Beware of frost pockets, particularly if your home is on a hillside. Cold air naturally flows downhill like water, and if blocked by a hill, wall or building will spread out and up, forming airpools or frost pockets that, like water, can freeze and damage roots. To minimize frost damage, make sure cold air keeps moving through the garden, and avoid planting tender plants in any known frost pockets.

Cold air naturally flows downhill like water, and if blocked by a hill, wall, building or even a tight hedge, it will spread out and up, forming damaging frost pockets.

SNOW

Gardeners welcome a winter blanket of snow as it provides excellent insulation from the often dramatic temperature fluctuations, and, with the spring thaw, the melting snow replenishes the soil's water supply. Snow can also prevent excessive frost heaving, which can push shallow-rooted plants out of the ground. Be sure you have properly winterized your garden prior to the first snowfall. And if you don't have good snow cover, do mulch well to moderate soil temperatures.

Some snows, however, can be damaging. If snow is followed by frigid temperatures, it will freeze on the limbs before it has had a chance to melt or fall off. This can cause severe damage to woody plants, evergreens and hedges. Don't allow snow to accumulate; brush it off as often as necessary.

HINT: Be sure you have lifted tender bulbs and planted new spring bulbs prior to the ground's freezing.

RAINFALL

Water is the lifeblood of plants. Through transpiration, plants draw water and nutrients from the soil up into their leaves where it is then vaporized by the sun. When the water supply is interrupted, plant growth slows down and may even stop.

Farmers worry about rainfall and you should too. If you live near the ocean or the Great Lakes you generally enjoy increased rainfall and a more moderate climate. But for those living further inland, rainfall may be irregular. The July and August thunderstorms in desert areas may be spectacular events but they usually don't add enough water to the soil to satisfy all plants. Dry climate gardeners should select drought-tolerant plants (see "The Drought-tolerant Garden," p.207) or install an irrigation system. In all climates, if you are away from the garden for long periods, make provisions with a neighbor to ensure adequate water should an unexpected hot spell arise. And be sure to water during a dry January thaw. When temperatures rise, plant processes kick in and plants may exhaust their water supply and die.

HINT: If you need to irrigate, the chances are that water should be conserved. Drip irrigation is more efficient than sprinklers, which lose water to evaporation.

Drainage

Adequate drainage is just as important as a steady supply of water. Although deep roots are promoted by a low watertable or by deep watering, too much water, or "waterlogging," decreases the amount of air in the soil. Air provides oxygen and insulation for the roots, but only specialized plants, such as *Eupatorium purpureum* (Joe-Pye weed), can survive long periods without it. A high water table will keep roots up at the surface where they are susceptible to cold; deep roots are well insulated from frost.

Good drainage is especially important for many plants, such as *Asclepias* (butterfly bush), during their winter months of dormancy. They will not survive the winter with "wet feet," but with adequate drainage, they are perfectly hardy.

HINT: Keep an eye out for wet spots in your garden. While roses may hate it, this is a great place for plants that like wet feet, like some Iris *and* Primula.

Xeric Landscaping

Xeric landscaping is a term many people are using to describe water-efficient gardening, which incorporates selecting plants compatible with the microclimate and natural level of rainfall. First, look for natives, as many are naturally adapted to the microclimate and have survival mechanisms, such as deep root systems and leaves with protective wax coating. However, not all native plants are xeric plants. Look also for plants from other areas that are adapted to long periods of drought and poor soils such as *Tithonia* (Mexican sunflower), *Achillea* (yarrow) and *Asclepias.*

Caliche

In the desert there is often a hard layer of an impenetrable, concrete-like material called "caliche" lurking beneath the soil's surface. Caliche is composed of calcium carbonate. It can be as shallow as 6" or as deep as 4'. It causes poor drainage, thereby putting plants at risk of root rot and damaging salt build-ups. Roots and water cannot penetrate caliche, so no matter where it is located, it must be removed when you dig your beds. To test your soil, use a metal rod to probe the soil. If you find caliche, a pickax is the best tool for removing it.

HUMIDITY

Humidity is water vapor in the air and moisture in the soil. Humidity levels are measured as a percentage of total saturation; coastal areas and areas with heavy rainfall will have higher levels. Humidity is beneficial to plants such as ferns, but it can cause severe fungal growth on others, such as *Phlox paniculata* and *Monarda didyma* (bee balm). If your garden is in a humid area, select plants that are adapted to humidity. Mildew-resistant strains of many popular perennials, including *Phlox* and *Monarda* (bee balm), are now available.

HINT: Good air circulation through the garden will help reduce unwanted levels of humidity.

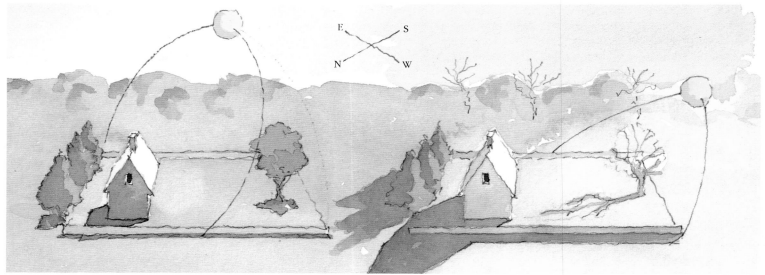

The sun's position changes with the seasons, affecting the amount of shade in your garden. In the summer (left), it is high and creates short shadows. In the winter (right), the sun is low and produces long shadows.

SUNLIGHT

The sun provides the radiant energy and warmth necessary to raise the temperature of both the soil and the air to stimulate plant growth, flower and fruit production. All plants have specific needs for sunlight, which is quantified as follows:

FULL SUN   At least six hours of intense sun between 10 A.M. and 6 P.M.

PARTIAL SHADE   Dappled sun or shade from the hottest sun.

BRIGHT SHADE   Reflected, not direct sunlight.

FULL SHADE   No direct or reflected sunlight.

The intensity of the sun varies at different times of the day. The midday sun is the hottest, followed by the afternoon, then the morning sun. Remember, light requirements may be affected by your zone; a perennial that requires full sun in Zone 5 may perform better in partial shade in Zone 7.

When planning a garden it's important to know where and when the sun hits your yard and for how long each day. Make a map of your yard showing which areas have full sun, partial, bright or full shade at different times of the day. Pay attention to the seasons; the sun's position changes and deciduous trees come into leaf. You may be surprised to find that the corner you thought was so sunny back in February is in partial shade come June. A shady garden requires a vastly different selection of plants than a sunny one.

HINT: When planning your garden site, plan for the growth of shade trees.

Take advantage of protected sunny spots; they may be able to support plants of a higher zone. To extend the growing season, or establish a spring garden, locate it on the south side of the house, but beware of the drying western sun; your soil may require additional water.

The winter sun can also be very hot. It can dehydrate broadleaf evergreens, and even burn the bark, causing "sun scald." And in deciduous trees, unprotected by their seasonal foliage, the hot winter sun can thaw the sap, causing the bark to split.

WIND

We appreciate a cooling breeze on a hot summer day, and plants do too! It disperses their pollen and seeds, prevents pockets of stagnant air in the garden, and dries off the morning dew preventing fungal growth. However, wind can dehydrate leaves just as it dries laundry on a line. A plant on a windy hilltop, on the open plains or along the coast will have to work harder to provide a steady supply of water to the leaves. This may result in diminished growth.

Wind can also lower temperature. If your home is on a windy hillside, your garden may be a Zone 5, while your friend's protected garden down the road may be a Zone 6.

Avoid planting in wind tunnels created by hills, masses of trees or buildings. Trees exposed to continuous winds can become one-sided. Never locate fragile plants such as *Delphinium* in windy spots unless you have a wind barrier. Select only salt-tolerant plants, such as *Rosa rugosa*, for coastal gardens exposed to salt-laden winds.

Storms with high-velocity winds are a gardener's nightmare. High winds can break limbs, defoliate stems, uproot trees and loosen root systems. A gardener's only defense is a good tree maintenance program that includes regular pruning, cabling when necessary and the prompt removal of dead trees. If you do lose one tree located close to another, the chances are good that the root system of the second tree has also been damaged. Be sure to keep an eye on the second tree and take precautions if necessary.

Shelter From The Wind

You may wish to shelter windy locations with a windbreak that can be created by planting a hedge, hedgerow, stand of trees, or by erecting a fence or wall. To prevent strong winds from toppling a windbreak or creating a downdraft on the leeward side, allow 50 percent of the air to flow through the barrier. To reduce a steady wind, a hedge or fence should be 12' high; but in small areas windbreaks need be no higher than the plants requiring protection.

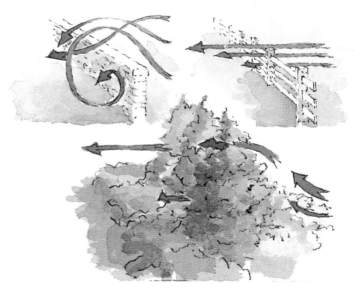

The best windbreaks allow 50 percent of air to pass through. Solid walls can create damaging downdrafts on the leeward side.

Soil: The Common Denominator

A friend once referred to good soil as "black gold" and she's right. Good soil can greatly increase the riches of your garden. Soil is composed of mineral particles, organic matter, air, water and beneficial living organisms such as earthworms, bacteria and fungi. It is divided into three layers: topsoil, which contains most of the nutrients needed to stimulate plant growth; subsoil, which is less fertile; and the lower layer, which is derived from the underlying parent rock. Soil provides plants with anchorage, sustenance and insulation. In each zone there is the possibility of every kind of soil, and it can change right within the bounds of your property. The good news is if you don't have the rich soil you need, you can improve it. But first, know what you have to work with.

SOIL TYPES

Soil type is determined by its texture or the size of the mineral particles. Sand is the largest, followed by silt and then clay. So it follows that the percentage of each particle size in a soil determines its type. For example, if a soil is over 50 percent sand, it is categorized as a sandy soil. The general soil types are as follows:

SANDY OR LIGHT SOIL Coarsely textured with little organic matter.

SILTY SOIL Medium fine textured sediment, medium density.

CLAY OR HEAVY SOIL Finely textured, dense.

LOAM Good mix of about 40 percent sand, 40 percent silt, 20 percent clay.

Soil has many important functions: water percolation and retention, aeration, temperature control, nutrient supply, storage and release. The particle size or soil type influences how these processes function.

At one end of the spectrum is heavy or clay soil, which drains poorly, heats and cools slowly, but is often fertile. In summer, clay soil stays hot longer and can bake the roots; in winter it retains the cold and can freeze the roots. At the other end of the soil spectrum, sandy soil drains quickly, requiring more irrigation and fertilization. However, sandy soil and loam soil (with high organic content) have mini air pockets that insulate the roots from temperature extremes, much like double-paned glass windows.

Loam: The Ideal Soil

Different plants require different kinds of soil. *Cosmos* loves a sandy soil, while roses thrive in soil rich in organic matter. However, the ideal soil for most gardens is a loam soil, which is a mixture of sand, silt and clay with ample amounts of decayed organic material called humus. (See "Compost," below.) Loam is porous, yet spongy enough to retain moisture, and rich in nutrients which encourage soil bacteria activity.

What Kind Of Soil Do You Have?

The percentage of sand, silt and clay determines what type of soil you have. To determine your soil type, try these simple tests:

THE SQUEEZE TEST is the easiest and quickest. Take a handful of moistened soil and squeeze it in your hand. If it feels gritty and falls apart when released, there is a large amount of sand in your soil. If it feels gritty but clings together, it is a loamy sand soil. Clay soil will make a smooth smear, while sandy clay will make a gritty smear.

THE SHAKE TEST takes a little longer. Fill a quart jar about two-thirds full of water. Slowly add soil from one spot in your garden until the jar is almost full. Close the jar and give it a good shake. After several hours different layers will have settled out. Sand weighs the most and will sink to the bottom, silt will settle in the middle with clay on top. Compare the amount of each. The highest percentage determines your soil type.

Amending Soil

Improve your soil with organic soil amendments. Refer to the "Organic Amendments" chart on p.184 for more specific information.

SANDY SOILS Amend with manure, compost and clay-rich soil.
CLAY SOILS Amend with manure, compost and sharp sand (washed and screened quartz sand is best).

In the shake test, the minerals in your soil are seperated out in layers helping you determine your soil type.

COMPOST

Compost is the Cinderella of the garden. What begins as waste products from your kitchen or garden is magically transformed into a garden elixir, rich in nutrients. You can make compost anywhere; a friend makes it in a small bucket on her Brooklyn fire escape.

Make compost by layering organic matter, soil, lime and manure or fertilizer. Use any vegetative kitchen refuse, leaves, faded blossoms and grass clippings. Keep the compost moist, but do cover it in heavy rains, to prevent the leaching out of nutrients. Make sure to turn it every two weeks or so. It's ready for use when the ingredients have broken down and are no longer recognizable. Use compost at the rate of one shovelful to about one square yard.

Add To Your Compost Pile:

Vegetative kitchen refuse such as vegetable and fruit scraps, coffee grounds, tea bags and clean eggshells; garden debris such as leaves, faded blossoms, grass clippings, straw or hay; household waste such as pet fur, human hair, sawdust, shredded newspaper and wood ashes (only if you have acid soil).

Do Not Add To Your Compost Pile:

Woody garden debris and magnolia leaves (take too long to break down); eucalyptus leaves (contain detrimental oils); invasive vines and grasses; noxious weeds; meat, bones, butter, oils, bread or any food derived from grains such as pasta; anything that would attract unwelcome vermin to your garden; used kitty litter or droppings from other carnivorous pets, such as dogs, as they can carry disease.

SOIL pH

Good soil also contains the nutrients necessary for healthy plants. The quantity of nutrients released by the soil and made available to plants depends on the soil's pH, or amount of acidity or alkalinity. The soil pH scale ranges from 1 to 14 as follows:

Acid soil: 1 to 7
Neutral soil: 7
Alkaline: 7 to 14

The amount of calcium (an alkaline element) influences the pH of soils. In areas of heavy rainfall such as the Pacific Northwest and the Northeast, calcium usually leaches out of the soil, resulting in lower pH levels. Soils derived from calcium-rich limestone generally remain alkaline, while sandy soils tend to be more acid.

Although most ornamentals are generally tolerant of a wide pH range, most are happiest around 6.5. Some do, however, require a particular pH for healthy growth. These plants are good indicators of your soil's pH. If you find healthy hemlocks,

Rhododendron or blue hydrangea on your property, you have acid soil. Flourishing beech and ash trees are indicators of alkaline soil. If you plan to grow vegetables, you will maximize production with a neutral pH. For specific pH recommendations, see "Soil" in each chapter.

Testing pH

Determine the pH of your soil with an electronic pH meter or soil testing kit. Or send soil samples to your local Agricultural Extension Service. Be sure to take samples from several spots in the garden as levels may vary. Remember to tailor your soil amendments to the plants in your garden.

Adjusting pH

Amend your soil after you have determined the pH needs of your plants. If your soil is too acid, add lime to neutralize the soil. Good sources of lime include: finely ground Dolomitic limestone, calcium carbonate and mushroom compost. The amount of lime you add depends on the texture of your soil. The heavier the soil, the more that is needed. But do not add lime when adding manure as the combination will produce ammonia, which could hurt your plants.

If your soil is too alkaline, add elemental sulfur or cottonseed meal; otherwise try an acid mulch such as pine needles, sawdust or peat to neutralize the soil.

SOIL FERTILITY

A soil rich in nutrients is like a refrigerator full of healthy food. Plants flourish when properly nourished. Fertility is measured by the levels of nitrogen (N), phosphorous (P) and potassium (K) in a given soil sample. Nitrogen encourages leaf and stem growth; phosphorous, root growth, flowering and fruiting; potassium, overall health.

The secondary nutrients (calcium, magnesium and sulfur)

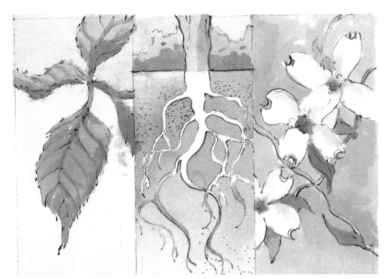

Soil Fertility: (left to right) Nitrogen (N) encourages leaf and stem growth; Phosphorus (P) stimulates root growth; Potassium (K) benefits the plant's overall health.

and micronutrients (boron, chlorine, copper, iron, manganese, molybdenum and zinc) are also important for a plant's health. Commercial fertilizers will provide a great many of these nutrients while seaweed and compost supply them all.

Soil inadequacies can cause leaf discoloration. Look carefully at the leaves. A general yellowing of a plant's leaves indicates a lack of nitrogen. But, if the veins remain green the cause is chlorosis, an iron deficiency possibly brought about by poor drainage, improper pH, or overfertilization. Overfertilization can also weaken a plant.

> HINT: *If you are beginning a new garden, select plants that are compatible with your soil conditions to avoid too much adjusting of your soil.*

Testing For Soil Fertility

This test can be done with a testing kit or by sending a sample of your soil to your local Agricultural Extension Service. The following table will help you read the results of your test:

FERTILITY LEVELS

	Low	Medium	High
N:	0 to 20	20 to 50	over 50
P:	0 to 12	12 to 25	over 25
K:	0 to 50	50 to 100	over 100

If your soil is in the mid range, you're doing everything just right. If levels are low, add nutrients at the recommended rate for your particular plants and soil. If levels are high, do not add more nutrients, but retest later in the season and adjust if necessary. But check your soil regularly as soil amendments do leach out and must be replenished.

SALINE SOIL

Salts normally percolate through the soil, moving away from the root zone where they do the most damage. In dry climates, however, there may not be enough rainfall to leach the salts through the soil. In coastal regions, the culprit is salt spray.

Testing For Salts

Soil laboratories can also test your soil for salt content. This is done with an electrical conductivity test. If the results are:

0 to 2:	Low salt; no damage to plants
2 to 4:	Elevated salts; may affect sensitive plants
4 to 8:	High salt; will kill most plants

If you have elevated levels of salt, select salt-tolerant plants. Correct soil with high salt levels before planting by amending the soil with gypsum or using furrow irrigation, which does not allow the salts to remain near the plant's root systems. Prevent raising salt levels in your garden by using nonsaline de-icers when thawing icy roads, driveways and paths.

Michaël H. Dodge

II
YOUR
GARDEN

II
YOUR GARDEN

Tulipa hybrid

Armed with information — on your zone, microclimates, soil and water — you can now have a beautiful garden with less effort than you think. Even a small amount of planning will help you move toward the garden of your dreams. First take a good look at the big picture. How do you want to use your house and land? What kind of garden do you want? Perhaps an entrance garden to welcome your friends at the front door; a terrace surrounded by colorful flowers on which to entertain; a kitchen garden filled with vegetables and herbs; or even a hedge to hide a neighbor's unsightly addition.

Gardens nurture body and soul. Imagine surrounding yourself with rustling leaves and lovely fragrances. Imagine inviting birds and butterflies with a colorful, mixed perennial and shrub border. Imagine serving your friends vegetables from your own garden. Imagine a lush bed of roses that blooms all summer long. Now, make a wish list.

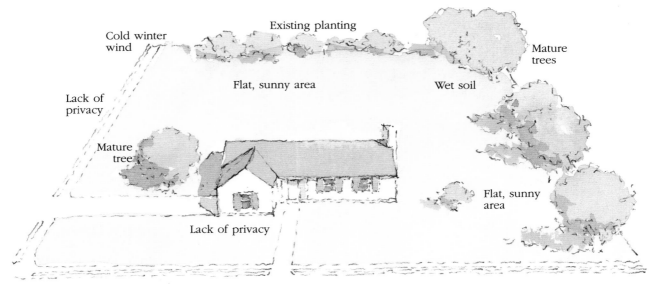

Before you begin, analyze your property for different climatic conditions as well as noise and good and bad views.

Labels in illustration: Cold winter wind · Existing planting · Mature trees · Flat, sunny area · Wet soil · Lack of privacy · Mature tree · Flat, sunny area · Lack of privacy

KNOW YOUR PROPERTY

Before you make your garden dreams a reality, it's time to step back and assess your property. Each site is unique with its own personality, strengths and weaknesses. So before you begin, understand what you have to work with.

Make a sketch of your property, noting the location of your house, property lines and existing conditions, including all microclimate considerations. Add the street, driveway and paths up to and around your house, any terraces or decks, and locate all trees, shrubs, hedges and gardens on the plan.

Look out your windows and walk around your property marking your sketch with different-colored arrows representing the views you want to emphasize or disguise. Look toward the neighboring houses and determine if you need more privacy.

Amend, add or delete items from your wish list according to what you discover from your plan and what you think you can realistically afford.

> *HINT: If you have a new home, you may want to wait and see what comes up in the yard throughout the course of a year.*

LANDSCAPE DESIGN IN A NUTSHELL

Good design is at the heart of every successful landscape. While planting a beautiful garden is a source of great pride, the design of your property is just as important. Consider the following concepts when working with your landscape:

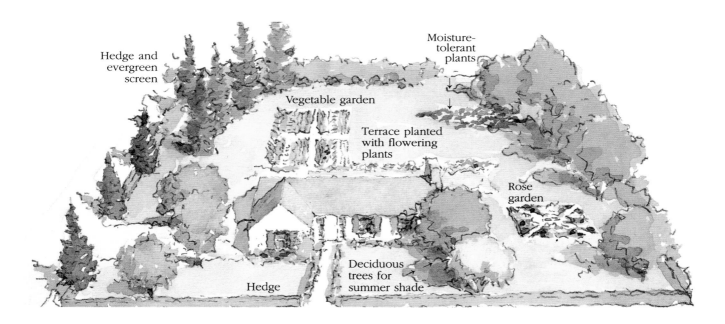

Hedge and evergreen screen

Moisture-tolerant plants

Vegetable garden

Terrace planted with flowering plants

Rose garden

Deciduous trees for summer shade

Hedge

UNITY   To create harmony, all elements of the landscape should feel part of a larger whole. The repetition of elements, such as shrubs or trees, or the enclosure of spaces with walls, hedges or fences can create a unified landscape.

SCALE   The comparative size of plants is integral to creating a pleasing sense of proportion. Plantings should be designed in scale with the overall landscape.

BALANCE   Like a seesaw, a balanced garden can be achieved in more than one way: the symmetry of a formal planting can come from the repetition of similar plants, while a large tree in an informal planting can be offset by a mass of shrubs.

MASS   Similar plants planted in large masses form a bold, uncluttered statement in the landscape.

CHOOSING A SITE

Examine your sketch and look for the best location for each item on your list. You will find some instant answers. There may be only one flat, sunny area big enough for a vegetable garden and you may find that the corner set aside for a shade garden receives hot, western afternoon sun. Remember, while it is essential to meet the climatic needs of the plants, the impact of the garden on your overall landscape is equally important.

HINT: In a small property it is best to use one planting style to create a unified garden.

Site Planning At A Glance

When choosing a site, there are many things to consider:

- Orientation (north, south, east and west)
- Location of property lines, utility lines, septic fields and water source
- Microclimate considerations:
  - Sun/shade map of your site
  - Drainage problems and wet spots
  - Frost pockets
  - Windy spots
- Slope (both flat and steep areas)
- Circulation for people, pets and cars
- Views: both good and bad
- Need for sun/shade
- Need for buffers: privacy, sound, wind or dust
- Local building codes (if you plan on building any structures)
- Energy and water conservation
- Fire hazard considerations
- Impact on overall landscape

The resulting master plan will give you a garden agenda that you can implement and modify over time. Having a plan will prevent you from making frustrating mistakes like erecting a swing set in the perfect spot for a rose garden. If you have a difficult property or find yourself completely perplexed, you may wish to consider hiring a design professional.

START SMALL

With your master plan in hand, decide on a project. But start small! Once you figure out how much time your new garden requires, you can determine how much more you can handle. Don't be overly ambitious. Nothing is more frustrating than seeing a once carefully tended garden engulfed in weeds.

DESIGNING YOUR GARDEN

The best design for your garden complements the architecture, develops from an understanding of the natural character of the land, works with the climate and reflects you! The choice of garden styles is endless. A garden can be rustic or formal; modern or classical. As Zones 5, 6, and 7 span the country, you might find gardens in oriental or contemporary styles in Oregon; French or English gardens in Ohio; colonial gardens in Virginia. Look around your neighborhood; notice the plant selections and how they work with the different styles of architecture. What will look best with your home?

Think of your own garden as a garden room. The ceiling can be of tree branches, wood, or canvas; the floor of grass, groundcovers, decking, stone or brick. Form the enclosure with shrubs, trees, stone walls or fences. Decorate it with flowering plants. Furnish it, light it and control the sound in it just as you would your living room.

> HINT: A general rule of thumb for determining how large a garden you can handle is to decide what you want and cut it in half.

CHOOSING PLANTS

Slender and elegant, short or round, some raise their branches high, while others swoop down to touch the ground. Work horses, like *Cornus alba* 'Siberica' (red-twig dogwood), look best when massed together, while others are so beautiful they can stand alone. Plant color, size, need for sun, shade and water, time of bloom . . . so many things to consider, it really is the great challenge of gardening. But it is also the most fun. Don't feel you have to use every plant right from the start. Half the fun is seeing how the garden grows and fine-tuning it from season to season. Remember, gardens don't happen overnight; they evolve.

Plant Design In A Nutshell

FORM The plant's mature shape. A tree may be vase-shaped or rounded, shrubs upright or spreading. A perennial may produce mounds of flowers or a glorious single, tall stem.

SIZE   Plant, leaf and flower size are essential ingredients for scale and balance.

COLOR Leaf color as well as flower color are useful in altering space and mood. When selecting colors, think first of the purpose of the garden. Pick up the red from your front door or plant soft lavenders, pinks and whites in front of a weathered shingled house.

TEXTURE Leaf as well as flower texture create the personality of the plant. Leaves can be rounded or sword-like, feathery, coarse or needle-like. Fine-textured plants soften hard surfaces; large-leafed plants add a bold accent.

Remember, leaves are just as important as flowers in planting design. For a lush look, include lots of greenery and vary the leaf textures for visual excitement. Emphasize a choice specimen by contrasting it with plants of a different color, texture or form. But, above all, when selecting plants, think climate, climate, climate!

Climate Considerations

Your garden will flourish with the least amount of effort if you match the plant's needs to your site and microclimate. So, gather information. . Peruse catalogs for plants hardy to your zone.   Try calling your local Agricultural Cooperative Extension Service and consider joining a horticultural society or garden club. Visit nurseries and nearby gardens. See what thrives and what struggles. Take advantage of your neighbors' successes, while avoiding their failures.

Generally, gardeners in Zones 5, 6 and 7 have a lot to work with. They have the best of both worlds: cold winters, nec-essary for many perennials, and a long, warm growing season. Naturally there are many exceptions to the rule: Zone 7's summer temperatures are too hot for some perennials and Zone 5's growing season is too short for others to bloom. Gardeners in hot humid areas should avoid dry Mediterranean climate plants such as *Lavandula* (lavender) and *Santolina sempervirens*. Happily, there are roses that thrive in nearly all areas of Zones 5, 6 and 7. For a full, colorful garden with many months of interest, consider using evergreen shrubs such as *Buxus* spp. (boxwood) and *Taxus cuspidata* (yew) to form the backbone of the garden, then fill in with annuals and perennials for seasonal color. For help selecting plants for your microclimate, see the plant lists in each chapter.

Genus, Species, Varieties And Cultivars

Plants have two different types of names: a botanical name, which is in Latin and universally accepted, and a common name, which may differ from region to region. The Latin name consists of two words. The first is the genus; the second the species. As a species is a subdivision of the genus, you'll find that all plants of a certain genus share common characteristics but differ in at least one habit. For instance, *Lilium auratum* is a gold band lily and *Lilium candidum* is a Madonna lily. While the Latin names may seem daunting at first, they are more accurate and will soon become second nature.

Today there are thousands of cultivars from which to choose. Although they retain most of the characteristics of the species, they may differ slightly in their drought or temperature tolerance, disease resistance, color or fruit size. Some are open pollinated and reproduce by means of the wind or animals (such as birds and bees); these are never exactly alike. Many heirloom plants are reproduced this way. Breeders simply select the best plants from the crop. Hybrids are man-made forms and have more consistent qualities. Have fun choosing your plants. Experiment! You're likely to find one that's just right for your climate.

Environmental Considerations
Planting design is more than just a pretty picture. It is a means with which to conserve our natural resources and, in especially dry climates, reduce fire hazard.

To lower energy consumption:
- Position deciduous shade trees on the south side of the house to cool it and provide shelter from summer heat.
- Locate evergreen trees and hedges on the north side to block cold winter winds.

To reduce water evaporation and conserve water:
- Group plants of similar water needs together to prevent water waste.
- On windswept or hot, dry sites use native plants, which are better adapted to the existing conditions.
- Design garden enclosures to reduce evaporation due to wind.
- Select drought-tolerant plants (see "The Drought-tolerant Garden," p.207).

To reduce risk of fires:
- Plant buffers of low-growing, fire-retardant plants around the perimeter of your property.

Garden Design Checklist
- Style of your house
- Purpose of the garden
- Style, shape and size of the garden
- Microclimate
- Soil
- Water supply
- Local plant palette
- Mature plant size, color, texture and form
- Year-round interest
- Bloom sequence
- Energy and water conservation
- Fire safety in dry microclimates

ESSENTIAL TOOLS
Just as an artist prepares the canvas before applying the paint, you should carefully prepare your site before planting. If you don't have the basic tools, it's time to outfit yourself. Select the right tools and make sure you buy good ones! Using the right tool for the job will make difficult garden tasks easier and leave you with more time to smell the flowers.

To get your plants into the ground as soon as possible, be sure that you are fully equipped, and that the planting beds are dug, soil amended and mulch available, before bringing your plants home from the nursery.

HINT: Remember, you can always rent rarely used equipment such as rototillers and shredders.

Digging And Planting
SPADE for straight-sided holes; cuts easily through sod and is ideal for edging and transplanting.

ROUND-POINT SHOVEL for digging and mixing soil, compost and fertilizer.

TROWEL for hand digging; all gardeners need more than one trowel. Be sure to vary the blade widths so you won't be frustrated on small jobs.

HINT: If your back isn't what it used to be, buy tools with long handles to reduce bending.

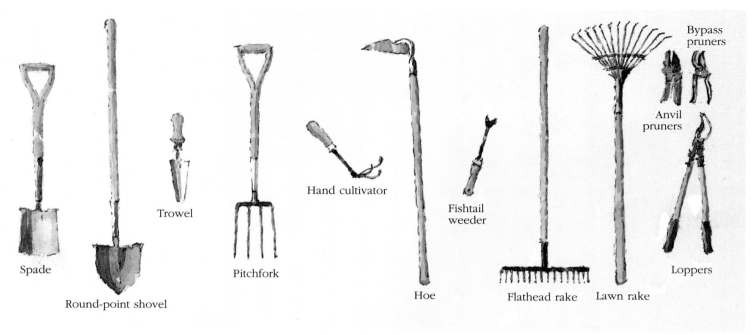

Spade

Round-point shovel

Trowel

Pitchfork

Hand cultivator

Fishtail weeder

Hoe

Flathead rake

Lawn rake

Bypass pruners

Anvil pruners

Loppers

Good tools make working in the garden a pleasure.

Cultivating And Lifting

PITCHFORK for working heavy soil, lifting root vegetables, dividing perennials and turning over the compost pile.

HAND FORK for loosening soil in tight spaces and lifting small plants.

HAND CULTIVATOR for loosening the soil and weeding. (Less precise for weeding than a fishtail weeder or trowel, but often faster.)

Raking

FLATHEAD RAKE for removing debris; breaking up and leveling soil and gravel. (Twelve teeth are standard; sixteen are good for vegetable gardens and gravel terraces.)

LAWN RAKE for gathering fallen leaves, twigs, grass clippings and debris.

HINT: For tough weeds, don't hesitate to use a trowel.

Weeding

HOES for surface weeding, aerating and hilling up soil.

FISHTAIL WEEDER (also known as an asparagus fork or dandelion weeder) for deeply rooted weeds.

Pruning

PRUNERS for cutting herbaceous stems, rose or berry canes, woody twigs and branches up to 1/2". (Bypass pruners have two sharp blades and a scissors-like action, which make a clean, precise cut; anvil pruners have a sharp upper blade, which cuts against a flat, lower anvil.)

LONG-HANDLED LOPPERS for cutting thick or high branches.

PRUNING SAWS for cutting branches over 1" thick.

HEDGE SHEARS for shaping hedges or topiaries and cutting back herbaceous plants.

GRASS SHEARS for trimming grass and plants with soft stems.

HINT: Pruners with bright handles won't get lost in the foliage. Some gardeners prefer bright blue handles as they stand out against colorful fall leaves.

If you're left-handed, pruners made especially for you are now available through catalogs and garden centers. And if you have arthritis or would like to reduce hand stress, select hand pruners with rotating handles or ratchet pruners (with each squeeze of the handles, the ratchet moves up a notch, while maintaining pressure on the branch, until the blades cut cleanly through the wood).

Hauling

BARROW a basket on wheels for collecting weeds and carrying light loads.

WHEELBARROW a one-wheeled cart for hauling heavier loads; great to use along narrow paths.

TWO-WHEELED CART for hauling large or heavy loads. Easier to maneuver than a wheelbarrow.

BUYING TOOLS

This is not the place to skimp, but don't worry, good tools are not always the most expensive. Tools are a personal decision, so test them out before buying them. First grasp the handle. Does it feel comfortable in your hand? A good tool should feel solid and well balanced. Pruners must be sharp, well aligned and securely bolted; shafts on digging tools must be strong enough to defeat the inevitable rock.

High-end stainless steel tools, available through catalogs and garden centers, are strong, durable and rust resistant and make digging easier because soil doesn't stick to the working surface. Carbon steel tools, usually found at the hardware store, are much less expensive, but are subject to rust and therefore require more care. Avoid stamped sheet metal tools, which can bend or break under pressure.

MAINTAINING TOOLS

Good tools that are well cared for can last a lifetime. So, whenever possible, clean tools after use. For carbon steel tools, use an oiled rag to prevent rusting. Experienced gardeners keep a bucket of sand saturated with a quart of motor oil in the garden shed to clean and oil tools simultaneously. Remember to lubricate all movable metal parts and sharpen blades regularly. Remove sap from pruners with steel wool and oil.

HINT: Keep anvil pruners sharp so they cut through the stems instead of crushing them.

GARDEN LAYOUT

Laying out the planting beds can be a very satisfying task. If you haven't yet determined the shape, decide what is appropriate for your garden: rectangular, circular or free-form. For geometric beds, you will need heavy string, stakes, a 50' to 100' long metal tape measure and a hammer. Pound stakes into the corners of rectangular beds and stretch the string between them. For circles, drive a stake at the center, attach a string to the stake, and use it as a compass to mark the edge. The easiest way to lay out a free-form curve is with a garden hose. When you have finalized the shape of the bed, go around its edge nicking out a line of sod with a spade. This will set the guidelines for digging the bed.

HINT: When digging out the planting beds, protect the lawn by placing the soil on a dropcloth.

REMOVING SOD

If you are digging a new bed in a lawn area, it will be necessary to eradicate the grass roots completely, and this takes time. Grass, especially perennial quack grass, can be deep-rooted. Use an environmentally safe herbicide or strip the sod, then till the soil repeatedly at two- to three-week intervals until the soil is free of grass shoots. Prior to sowing seed or planting, level and rake the soil until it is finely pulverized. If you do opt to use an herbicide like Roundup, allow three weeks in your gardening schedule between the last application and planting or seeding. Take special care in selecting your herbicide; some may "sterilize" the soil for up to a year.

PLANTING BEDS

Ideally, planting beds should be prepared the previous fall, which gives them time to settle over the winter and gives you a head start in the spring. If this is not possible, prepare the beds in the spring just prior to planting.

First, check the condition of your soil. If the soil is too wet, it will stick to your tools, making digging extra hard. You also risk compacting it with your footsteps, damaging the soil's texture. On the other hand, if it is too dry, it will be difficult to get a spade into the ground.

The preparation of planting beds varies depending on what is to be planted. Annuals are shallow rooted and require less preparation than perennials. A shrub border requires more depth to accommodate the large root balls. Vegetable, herb and rose gardens require excellent drainage. For specific planting preparations, see "Bed Preparation" in each chapter.

DIGGING THE BED

Time to dig the bed! There are three different types of digging, each requiring more work than the previous: simple, single and double digging. How you dig depends on how particular you are about the results. The better the beds are prepared, the better your plants will perform. But don't go in for overkill; there's no sense double digging an annual garden. For specific depth recommendations, see "Bed Preparation" in each chapter.

SIMPLE DIGGING Best for working in established or irregularly shaped beds. Lift each spadeful of soil and turn it over before returning it to the hole, bringing the bottom layer of soil to the top. Break up all lumps and remove all rocks, weeds or debris. Work in organic matter, soil amendments and fertilizers as required.

SINGLE DIGGING An efficient and effective method for most new beds. Mark your bed in 1' strips along its width. Dig a trench 1' wide, removing the soil and setting it aside. With a fork loosen the soil in the bottom of the trench and add soil amendments. Remove the soil from the next strip and turn it into the first trench. Continue this process until you reach the end, then amend and fill the last trench with the soil previously set aside.

Double digging shifts the soil in a perennial bed, improving drainage and soil structure to get perennials off to the best start.

DOUBLE DIGGING Double digging is a lot of work but some gardeners believe the results make the extra effort well worth their while, especially for herbaceous and perennial borders. This method improves drainage but is only possible in deep soils as the trenches are dug two spade blades, or "spits," deep.

Divide your planting area into 1' strips along its width. In the first strip, make a trench by removing the soil from the upper and bottom spits and set it aside in separate identifiable piles. (If your topsoil is shallow, it is especially important to keep soil from the upper and lower spits separate.) Then remove the soil from the top of the second strip and set it aside. Transfer the soil from the bottom spit of the second trench into the bottom of the first and cover it with the top spit from the third trench. Continue this process until the end and use the soil from the first to fill in the last two.

TILLING

Tilling, or working the soil, provides aeration, improves soil structure and drainage, and is critical for a successful garden. For large areas, it is often necessary to use a rototiller, but in small areas you can work to a greater depth by tilling by hand. Spades and forks are the best tools for tilling the soil. To dig efficiently, push the spade or fork into the ground for the entire length of the blade maintaining a 90° angle, then lift and turn the blade over. Thoroughly till annual beds and vegetable gardens in the fall or before planting.

RAISED BEDS

Raised beds are your best bet in areas with inadequate drainage, poor or shallow soils. By raising the soil level above the existing grade with amended soil, you will improve the texture and fertility of the soil while also increasing its depth and drainage. But raised beds are not for every garden. In dry climates they dry out more quickly, requiring additional watering.

PLANTING TIMES

When it comes to gardening, timing is everything. In temperate climates most perennials, roses and trees are planted while they are dormant in the spring and fall. Deciduous and evergreen shrubs, especially *Rhododendron*, are best planted in the early spring to give them a chance to set new roots before the heat of summer. However, if you move into a new house in the fall and are eager to get started, planting of all shrubs except broadleaf evergreens can be successful if completed by mid-October. Fall-flowering bulbs are planted in the early autumn; spring-flowering bulbs are planted in the fall. Plant summer-blooming annuals as soon as the ground is warm and the nights are frost free.

PLANTING
For specific planting recommendations, see "Planting" in each chapter.

MAINTENANCE
A well-maintained garden allows plants to flourish. When you plan your garden, consider how much time you can spend each week tending it. Weeding, fertilizing and watering continue throughout the gardening year. Deadheading, pruning, and mulching are seasonal. If you have a flower or vegetable garden, picking is not only time consuming but essential for a healthy garden.

TIME AND ENERGY SAVERS
1. Select the right plants for your microclimate.
2. Select disease-resistant plants.
3. Avoid high-maintenance plants.
4. Avoid thirsty plants in dry climates.
5. Use groundcovers, not grass, in shade, on slopes or in other difficult spots.
6. Use edging to keep grass and groundcovers in place.
7. Use high-quality tools.
8. Use good irrigation equipment, especially drip irrigation.
9. Mulch to reduce weeding and watering.
10. Mow more frequently so you don't have to pick up the clippings.
11. Keep an eye out for insects and diseases. The faster they're controlled, the less work it is battling them.

WATERING
Water the garden when it is dry! If your mulch is concealing the soil, look at your plants. They will tell you when they're thirsty. Look for these signs:

WILTING The most obvious sign. But be sure to check the soil as wilting can also be a symptom of too much water or a response to root damage. Dig down into the soil around the root zone. If it is dry, water! If it is wet, wait and let it dry out before watering again.

FOLDING OR CUPPING Plants like *Impatiens wallerana* will fold their leaves when they're dry for self-preservation. Less exposed leaf surface means less evaporation.

COLOR CHANGES When plants are dry, leaves loose their rich color and become dull.

> *HINT: Wind is just as drying as sun. If your garden is on an exposed site, you may have to water more often.*

There are several things to keep in mind when you water your garden:

Watering in the morning is preferable. It provides plants with a good reserve to make it through hot summer days and allows excess water to evaporate before nightfall. Evening watering allows water to sit on the leaves, encouraging mildew and disease. But, if your plants are desperate, water them immediately no matter what time of day. In a dry spell, it may be necessary to water twice a day.

Water deeply to encourage deep root growth. Soak the soil thoroughly, then allow it to dry moderately before watering again. In this way you will encourage your plants' roots to grow downward toward the moist soil. The deeper the roots, the less susceptible they are to drought.

Water the soil, not the foliage or blossoms. Use a watering wand on the end of your hose to get in under the foliage. Use drip irrigation or soaker hoses for flower beds to prevent damage to the blossoms from overhead sprinklers.

> *HINT: If you live in an area prone to freezing temperatures, don't leave your hose or sprinklers outside. Water remaining in the hose can freeze and expand, bursting the hose.*

Conserving Water

Water conservation is critical in dry climates and a good practice for all gardeners. To conserve water in the garden:

- Use irrigation appropriate for each kind of plant: trees, shrubs, flowers, vegetables.
- Use drip irrigation whenever possible. Remember, sprinklers lose water to evaporation; drip irrigation is more efficient.
- Mulch to prevent the soil from drying out.

WEEDING

A weed is any plant that is not meant to be in the planting bed. A maple seedling may be welcome in the woods, but is an eyesore in your perennial border or rose garden. Weeds always seem out of place, diluting the desired impact of the design. In dry climates it's especially important to remove these interlopers as they compete intensely with garden plants for water and nutrients.

> *HINT: If you are removing nettles, be sure to wear gloves. The sting can last for hours.*

I like to weed by hand first thing in the morning, while the sun is still cool and the soil is slightly moist. When the soil is very wet it sticks to the roots, making extra work. If the soil is so dry it has become hard, you risk breaking the stems off the weeds, leaving the roots behind. Cultivate large areas with a hoe when the soil is dry, but loose.

You can pull many weeds by hand, but never break off the weed in the process! Like pinched seedlings, weeds will bound back stronger and bushier than ever. A fishtail weeder is a real help for stubborn, deep-rooted weeds like dandelions or weeds in tight spaces. Position the fork right next to the weed, push it straight into the soil, then push the fork handle away from the weed to lever it out of the ground. Be sure to go as deep as you can to remove as much root as possible, but stay well clear of the roots of your garden plants.

Weed the beds at least once a week. Annual weeds are easily removed when they are seedlings, and you certainly don't want them to go to seed! There's a lot of truth in the old farmer's adage: "One year's seeding makes seven years' weeding."

> *HINT: Weeding can loosen the soil around your plants so after weeding, give the garden a good watering to settle the soil.*

MULCH

Mulch is the soil's protective blanket and invaluable to a successful garden. It can be organic (composted leaf mold, bark, sawdust, woodchips, composted grass clippings, buckwheat or cocoa hulls, spent hops from breweries, composted salt marsh hay, seaweed, straw, corn cobs, evergreen boughs, pine needles or cones) or inorganic (gravel, washed stones, oyster shells or black polyethylene plastic). Mulch varies in texture and color. Carefully match the mulch to the garden setting.

Use mulch to:

- Protect plants from temperature fluctuations.
- Protect plants from temperature extremes.
- Reduce weeds.
- Conserve soil moisture.
- Reduce soil erosion and runoff on slopes due to wind and rain.
- Reduce soil compaction from intense rains.
- Improve soil structure and fertility.
- Prevent seed from washing away during heavy spring rains (light mulch).
- Prevent seed such as grass or wildflowers from blowing away (light mulch).
- Create garden paths.
- Prevent fungi from splashing up on plant leaves.

Never use mulch when:

- Your soil is waterlogged.
- Young seedlings are smaller than the mulch is thick.

Special Hints

PINE BARK MULCH IS AVAILABLE IN TWO SIZES. Use the finely textured pine bark mulch, no larger than 3/4", to amend the soil. Use 3" bark nuggets as a top dressing around trees and shrubs on windy sites.

IF YOU WANT TO USE MAPLE LEAVES AS A MULCH, be sure to shred them first. Maple leaves are big and flat and tend to mat together allowing little water to penetrate.

IN HIGH FIRE RISK AREAS, select mulch with great care. Avoid highly flammable mulches such as dried pine needles and straw and never place them near wooden walls or fences. Apply mulch 2" to 4" thick and augment as necessary.

IF YOU USE PINE BOUGHS AS A WINTER MULCH, don't put them down too early. Small critters won't be able to resist building their nests in your garden.

Black Plastic Mulch

Black plastic can be an effective mulch in out-of-the-way places, such as vegetable gardens. It should be overlapped 4" to 6" to prevent weeds from sneaking up through the seams.

Use black plastic mulch:

- Away from the entertaining areas in your garden, where it would be an eyesore.
- Only in areas with good drainage, since it inhibits evaporation.
- To smother weeds in areas intended for future gardens.
- In vegetable gardens to lengthen the season by warming the soil in spring and fall.

HINT: In the summer, the black plastic can become too hot. Cover it with straw or another light colored mulch to reflect the radiant energy.

LEAF REMOVAL

Most fallen leaves make excellent mulch, especially in shrub beds, but in humid and very dry areas leaves should be removed. In humid climates, fallen leaves can promote disease. All leaves should be removed from the beds and added to the compost pile. However, diseased leaves should be discarded altogether.

In dry climates the accumulation of fallen leaves can present a fire hazard in late summer and early fall. If you live in a fire hazard zone, the clearing of potential fire fuels such as brush and dry fallen leaves should be part of your annual maintenance program.

COLD WEATHER IN THE GARDEN

Surprise Frosts

Surprise frosts can be devastating in any garden. A gentle sprinkling of water in the early morning to wash the frost off the leaves can help prevent damage caused by the rapid drying and burning of leaves when morning sun hits full force. Keep an old sheet or a roll of plastic handy to protect favorite tender plants from unusually cold winter nights. But don't forget to remove the plastic when the day warms up. Unlike burlap or sheets, it will magnify the heat and burn the leaves.

Preparing For Winter Temperatures

One never knows what to expect come winter: record warm temperatures; brutal, deep freezes; lots of snow or none at all. In the Midwest and West, midwinter thaws followed by severe cold temperatures leave gardens with little snow for protection. Next to snow, mulch is a gardener's best defense. Mulch your plants well to protect them from the cold and fluctuating temperatures. For appropriate winterizing techniques, see "Winterizing" in each chapter.

Assessing Damage From A Late Freeze

An unexpected deep freeze in late spring, after plants have begun to grow, can wreak havoc on a garden. But never prune or discard a plant until it has had a chance to make a comeback. The following guidelines will help you assess the damage:

ASSESSING FOLIAGE DAMAGE:

Slimy brown foliage: Remove and discard foliage.

Bronzed or brown-edged foliage: Allow to drop off naturally; new ones will grow back.

Crispy, brown leaves: Very little hope for recovery.

ASSESSING WOOD DAMAGE:

Do a scrape test. If the scraping reveals green tissue beneath, you have reason to be optimistic.

Split bark: Prune the limb back in late February to an inch below the split.

Pests And Intruders

Your garden is a prime target for inconsiderate, hungry pests who dig, munch and crunch with abandon. They come from all angles: chipmunks and voles come from below; squirrels dig down from above; rabbits and deer waltz right in on ground level while birds zoom in from the sky. It's easy to feel defenseless, but there are ways to protect your garden.

Deer

In some areas of Zones 5, 6 and 7, deer have gone from being a beloved wild animal to a gardener's greatest enemy. Where gardeners once erected decorative deer statues in the garden, they now install deer fencing! Deer populations have outgrown their bounds, and they have begun looking to greener gardens for their dinners. Deer generally prefer a bland diet, staying away from the stronger, more pungent plants with lemon, mint or sage-like aromas (see "The Deer-resistant Garden," p.211). But remember, if deer are starving they will nibble at anything! The best defense is often an electric fence.

Electric fencing can now be done with electric tape. Three strips attached to 9' posts will do the job. Paint strips black to make them blend into the setting. Police the fence for several weeks looking for breakage; deer will soon become familiar with the location and stay away.

Chewing Pests

Caterpillars and cutworms munch on leaves during the day while slugs and snails are more discreet; they do their damage in the dark of night. Nematodes, small eel-like worms, work underground on the root systems of plants. To prevent damage, rotate vegetables with nonsusceptible plants or control them with plants, such as *Tagetes* (marigold), which have roots that entrap nematodes. Always destroy infected plants.

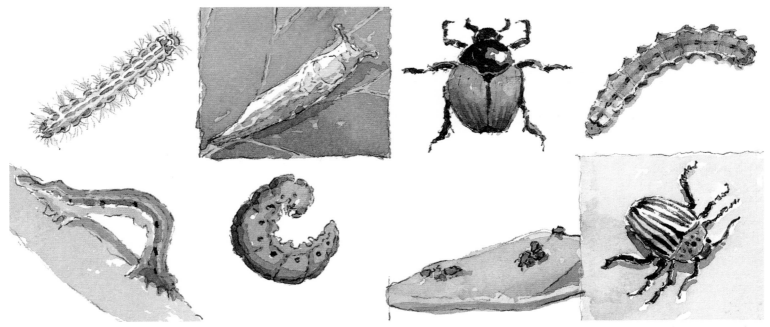

Pests can quickly destroy your garden by chewing or sucking the sap out of plants. (Clockwise from top left) Tent caterpillar, slug, Japanese beetle, corn earworm, Colorado potato beetle, aphid, cutworm and cabbage looper.

Sucking Pests

Sucking pests include aphids, leaf miners, mealy bugs, spider mites, whiteflies, thrips and scale. As voracious as chewing pests, they suck the sap and cell contents from plants, leaving behind a trail of yellow leaves or deformed foliage, buds, flowers and fruit. To reduce damage, sucking pests such as spider mites can be removed by spraying the undersides of leaves with cold water. Mealy bugs can be removed with alcohol. Whiteflies and aphids are attracted to and trapped by oil applied to painted yellow boards laid in the garden.

Disease

There are three causes of plant disease: fungi, bacteria and viruses. Your best bet in preventing the occurrence of bacteria and viruses is the use of resistant plants. Fungi flourishes during rainy summers. Some of the most common and easiest to control fungal diseases include:

BLACKSPOT Black spots appear on plant leaves, gradually growing together, killing the leaf and defoliating the plant. The best prevention is good air circulation: keep the interiors of plants thinned out and do not crowd plants. Discard or burn all infected leaves to control its spread.

Safe pest control includes introducing natural predators into the garden (Clockwise from top) Praying mantid, lady bug, trichogramma wasp and green lacewing.

DAMPING OFF   The rotting at soil level of young seedlings and cuttings. Prevention is the best control. When propagating new plants, use sterilized soil, treat seeds with a fungicide, provide good air circulation and avoid overwatering.

DOWNY MILDEW The development of powdery, white, mold-like fungus on leaves, buds and stems. To prevent downy mildew, buy mildew-resistant cultivars, do not overcrowd plants, avoid overhead irrigation and provide good air circulation and drainage.

What Is Integrated Pest Management?

Integrated Pest Management (IPM), although it may include selective use of toxic sprays, advocates the following methods of safe pest control: natural predators, hand-picking insects, crop rotation, using insect diseases and traps, and the release of sterile male insects to mate but not reproduce.

HINT: If your neighbor uses toxic sprays, suggest safe alternatives and that they spray on windless days.

SOME SAFE ALTERNATIVES AND PRECAUTIONS

When Planning Your Garden

- Select disease-resistant plants.
- Consider interplanting or companion planting: The planting of plants that repel insects among the plants the insects find most attractive. Especially effective in vegetable gardens.
- Rotate your crops.
- Be sure your garden has good air circulation.
- If moles or gophers are a problem, use raised beds and line the beds with 1/2" wire before filling them with top soil. For shrubs, line the planting hole.

Keep A Clean Garden

- Keep weeds under control.
- To prevent the spread of disease, immediately remove and discard all diseased leaves and plants.
- Keep your garden tools clean.
- Wipe your pruners with alcohol before moving to a new species to avoid the spread of disease.

Invite Good Predators

- Invite beneficial predators such as birds and bats into your garden for twenty-four-hour insect patrol.
- Place martin houses in sunny, open areas in early March prior to arrival of the scout birds, who fly ahead of the migrating colonies.
- Place bat houses, which can accommodate twenty to fifty bats, near the garden. Although you may think bats are scary, remember a single bat can eat up to five hundred mosquitoes an hour.
- Encourage beneficial insects such as ladybugs, lacewings and praying mantids.

HINT: If you invite birds to your garden, be sure to protect your ripening berries with netting, mylar streamers or other deterrents.

Create Barriers

- Use barriers such as paper cups set into the soil to protect seedlings from cutworms.
- Wrap aluminum foil around the base of your plants to deter spider mites, Mexican bean beetles, striped cucumber beetles, leafhoppers and squash bugs.
- Protect the bases of tree trunks from rabbits and mice with plastic shields or hardware cloth.
- Cover the soil's surface with sharp-edged diatomaceous earth to deter soft-bodied slugs and cabbage worms.
- Enclose your garden with chicken wire that extends 12" below grade to frustrate rabbits, gophers and other small critters.
- Install an electric fence or electric tape at raccoon height, 18" high, around your vegetable garden; at 9' high or more around your yard to deter deer.

If You Find Pests

- Place low containers of beer set in the soil to lure slugs to their death.
- Pick off bugs, such as Japanese beetles, and drop them in a jar of kerosene or soapy water.
- Destroy the nests of insects, such as tent caterpillars.
- To rid your garden of ants, pour a kettle full of hot water down ant hills.
- Some gardeners use traps containing pheromones (sex attractants) to lure insects to their deaths. These do attract insects and should be placed away from the garden.

- To control aphids and spider mites, use a garden hose adjusted to have enough force to knock insects off plants without damaging the leaf structure. Don't forget to spray the undersides of the leaves, too!
- Use homemade sprays made of water and garlic or hot pepper puree to deter pests.
- Sprinkle garlic powder around your plants — said to deter deer from roses.
- Place mothballs around but not touching your plants to discourage chipmunks. Replace as they lose their smell.
- To deter rabbits, tuck clumps of dog fur under leaves and out of sight.
- Spray a solution of one tablespoon of baking soda with a few drops of horticultural oil in one gallon of water to control mildew.
- Control the reproduction of apple maggots by hanging a sticky red, apple-like ball in your apple trees. The maggot eggs laid on it won't hatch.

In An Emergency

- Use horticultural oils, which smother rather than poison insects such as aphids, scale, spider mites, and whiteflies.
- Use commercially available insecticidal soaps to control aphids, earwigs, leaf miners and leaf rollers.
- Apply natural organic poisons such as Neem, Pyrethrum and Rotenone. While they are not toxic to humans, some organic poisons can be harmful to beneficial insects and fish. Always apply with great care.
- Homemade "bug spray" is unappetizing to make but quite successful. Pick abnormal and normal caterpillars off your plants, pulverize them in a blender with a cup of nonchlorinated tepid water, add more water, let sit several days and then dilute again and spray on plants. You will have spread the infection carried by the abnor-

mal caterpillars and curtailed their munching.
- Use biological pesticides to control bagworms, cabbage worms, gypsy moths, tent caterpillars among others. BT (*Bacillus thuringiensis*), commercially available as Dipel and Thuricide, is a naturally occurring bacterium. Read the instructions carefully and apply it at the right time for maximum effect.

And don't forget, not all insects are detrimental to the garden. Some insects actually eat the bad guys, but insecticides don't discriminate. Try to steer clear of toxic sprays and dusts, choosing Integrated Pest Management, a safer means of pest control. Yes, a flower or head of lettuce is more attractive without little holes nibbled out of it, but the long term damage done by pesticides can be far reaching. In the end, the decision to use pesticides is yours, but first seek the advice of your nurseryman or local Agricultural Cooperative Extension Service, and only use toxins with the greatest of care.

Allan Mandell

III
THE
FLOWERS

Annuals
Perennials
Roses
Bulbs, Etc.

Peter Cummin

ANNUALS

Tagetes erecta 'Discovery'

Temperature
Sun/Shade
Soil
Water
Bed Preparation
Seeds Or Plants?
Seeds
Plants
Fertilizing

Cultivating
Mulch
Thinning
Pinching
Deadheading
Cut Flowers
Fall Cleanup
Best Bets For Your Garden

Annuals are plants that complete their life cycle in one season. With little care, many grow quickly from seed sown in the late spring, producing a profusion of flowers from midsummer until frost. Available in a wide variety of colors, shapes and sizes, annuals are wonderfully diverse flowers. Some grow tall, while others climb and trail. Some thrive in hot, dry sunny areas while others are at home in the cool shade. But to me, the greatest advantage of annuals is their impermanence. You can change your color schemes from year to year, and even season to season. A handful of annual seed packets is like having a box of Crayolas to color your garden. And, unlike perennials, the more you pick or pinch them, the more flowers they produce.

Both beautiful and practical, annuals are the perfect flowers with which to decorate house and garden. In the garden, large masses of annuals can be focal points, or fillers in borders after the perennials have passed. As cut flowers, they are cheerful, plentiful and often fragrant. Annuals can come to your rescue when you have new plantings and need to cover the soil between plants. A container of colorful annuals will brighten your terrace or deck; low annuals will beautifully edge a path. For every spot in the garden or home, there's an annual to suit your needs.

Grow Annuals:
- In beds for quick, long-lasting color
- As accents in borders against a fence, wall or hedge
- As fillers in mixed borders
- To edge a path
- To hide yellowing bulb foliage
- To fill in bare spots
- For temporary splashes of color
- To brighten dark corners
- To add color to shrub borders
- To fill in around young shrubs, tying the mass together
- In your cutting garden
- In pots and planters

TEMPERATURE

Cold weather usually signals the end of an annual's life cycle. Annuals are extremely sensitive to climatic conditions and are categorized by their cold and heat tolerance, so be sure to keep both in mind when making your selections. The different types of annuals are:

HARDY ANNUALS Can survive some frost. Are successful when sown directly outdoors, even while cool temperatures prevail. Include *Lathyrus odoratus* (sweet pea), *Consolida ambigua* (annual larkspur), *Lobularia maritima* (sweet alyssum).

HALF-HARDY ANNUALS Will take some frost, but not as much as hardy annuals. Include *Cleome hasslerana* (spiderflower) and *Petunia* x *hybrida*.

TENDER ANNUALS Cannot tolerate frost. Many tender annuals need several weeks in order to reach flowering size, and thus, should be sown early indoors, in cold frames, or outdoors as soon as the danger of frost has past. They can also be purchased as greenhouse-grown seedlings or rooted cuttings. Include *Ageratum houstonianum*, *Salvia* and *Zinnia*.

WARM-SEASON ANNUALS Half-hardy or tender annuals that prefer warm temperatures and warm soil. They may show no growth until the soil warms sufficiently. Include *Portulaca* and *Helianthus* (sunflower).

COOL-SEASON ANNUALS Hardy annuals and some half-hardy annuals that can tolerate cool weather. Include *Viola* x *wittrockiana* (pansy), *Brassica oleracea* (ornamental cabbage), *Antirrhinum majus* (snapdragon) and *Matthiola incana* (stock).

Consider the following when choosing annuals:
- The last date of frost in the spring
- The first date of frost in the fall
- The highest expected temperatures in the summer

In your moderate climate, include annuals that are described as hardy or half-hardy. If you live in an area with extremely hot summers, look for warm-season annuals.

SUN/SHADE

Most annuals thrive in full sun. Thankfully, there are a number of lovely annuals that prefer shade including *Impatiens*, *Begonia* and *Coleus*.

SOIL

A good garden loam with a pH ranging from 5.5 to 7.0 is excellent for most annuals. However, some native annuals, such as *Eschscholzia californica* (California poppy), are tolerant of varying soil conditions.

WATER

If your garden is in the high desert, on a windswept site or in an area prone to seasonal droughts, your annuals will be fuller and more floriferous with additional water. And remember, freshly sown seed and seedlings should be kept moist until they are established.

BED PREPARATION

Good bed preparation always pays off with an abundance of flowers. As annuals have shallow roots, the beds need only be prepared to a depth of 8"-12". They bloom so prolifically, however, that they require a healthy plant system to nourish them. Enrich the soil with compost or well-rotted manure in the fall or early spring to promote the early growth of healthy plants.

SEEDS OR PLANTS?

Consider the growth rate of the annuals that you have selected. With your growing season, most annuals do well grown from seed, but others need a jump on the season and are best planted as seedlings or larger plants. And remember, if you opt for a bed of just annual seeds, the gardening season will be well under way before the annuals begin to bloom.

> HINT: If you have clay soil that is slow to warm up in the spring, use seedlings instead of seed whenever possible for earlier bloom.

SEEDS
Buying Seeds

Annual seeds can be purchased from your local garden center or from a variety of mail-order sources (see "Sources"). They are available as loose seeds in seed packets or in a more limited selection, as seed tapes. Seed tapes are actually soluble tapes with seeds imbedded in them for perfect planting in rows!

Growing from seed is more work, but there are advantages. There is an enormous selection of annuals, including many improved and old-fashioned varieties, available through mail-order catalogs. Look for All-American selections that will work well within your growing season. When buying seedlings, you often have to buy mixed colors, while with seeds you can grow a particular color. But perhaps the greatest advantage of all is price! Seeds are the best bargain in the garden.

Time To Sow

Get the best results possible by planting annual seeds at the right time and right temperature:

HARDY ANNUALS Sow outside from mid- to late spring when the soil temperature has risen to 45° Fahrenheit. Some seeds like wildflowers can be sown in the fall.

HALF-HARDY ANNUALS Sow indoors in containers in the spring maintaining a temperature range of 55° to 70° Fahrenheit or sow outdoors from mid- to late spring.

TENDER ANNUALS Sow indoors in containers in the spring maintaining temperature of 55° to 70° Fahrenheit or sow outdoors after all threat of frost.

Germination

Seeds need warmth, water, oxygen and light to germinate. Sow seeds indoors in flats or plastic trays filled with a sterile, lightweight soil mix. Soilless mixes containing vermiculite and peat moss also provide excellent results. Place them in a warm sunny location or under fluorescent lights. Most seeds will respond within a few days. To speed up seeds with hard shells, such as *Lathyrus odoratus* (sweet pea) and *Ipomea purpurea* (morning glory), chip or soak them before sowing. This allows moisture to penetrate the surface, stimulating growth. When the seedlings have developed two sets of leaves, carefully "prick out," or transplant, to larger containers.

Damping Off

During germination, seedlings are susceptible to "damping off," a soil-borne disease that causes them to wilt. It spreads most easily in warm, moist conditions with poor air circulation. *To avoid damping off:*

- Use clean pots or trays.
- Use sterilized potting soil.
- Keep seeds moist, but do not overwater.
- Do not crowd seeds; thin them out as necessary.

Hardening Off Seedlings

Before transplanting seedlings into the garden, they must be gradually acclimated or "hardened off." Harden off seedlings by first moving them to a cold frame (a box with a light-permeable cover that can be opened and closed depending on the temperature), or a shady, protected spot outdoors for a few hours. Gradually increase the time outdoors to build up their tolerance. When the temperature is right, transplant them into the garden.

Sowing Outdoors

To plant in rows, first stretch a string between two stakes marking the center of the row. Use the corner of a hoe to form deep furrows directly beneath the string. For shallow furrows use the tip of a trowel. Distribute the seeds evenly, then firm the soil over the furrow using the flat side of a rake. Gently sprinkle the beds taking care not to wash the seeds away. Keep the soil moist, but not waterlogged, until the seeds sprout.

When seeding a large area, broadcasting is your best bet. Broadcast the seeds, using a drop or rotary spreader, first in one direction across the entire area then repeat it, walking in a direction perpendicular to the first. This will give you the most even results.

HINT: If the seeds are very small and difficult to see, line the furrow with tissue paper before distributing the seed. Once covered with soil and watered, the tissue will quickly decompose.

PLANTS
Buying Plants

Buying annual plants is an easy way to have instant color in the garden. Plants are usually available in flats, cell-packs and individual pots as follows:

Seedling Packs: (clockwise from top left) Seedlings are available in flats, individual pots and cell-packs.

SEEDLING FLATS Seedlings sold in a large box or flat. Roots tend to be intertangled so not the best choice.
CELL-PACKS Four to twelve seedlings in individually molded plastic container. Minimal transplant shock since plants are grown individually.
INDIVIDUALLY POTTED Transplants sold in 2" to 6" pots. Plants retain all roots so are easily re-established in your garden. Larger plants give you a head start on the growing season, provide a big splash fast, and require less pampering.

When buying seedlings or larger plants, look for:
- Plants that are pest free.
- Plants that have a good shape with healthy leaves.

and avoid:
- Plants that are leggy or have yellow leaves.
- Plants that are potbound. (Check to see if roots are growing out of the bottom of the pot.)

> *HINT: Be ready to plant when you bring your annuals home from the nursery. If you can't plant right away, put your plants in a shady spot and give them lots of water.*

Time To Plant

Many annuals are killed by frost, so no matter how eager you are to get the plants in the ground, be cautious. Some guidelines:
HARDY ANNUALS Plant early spring through midsummer.
HALF-HARDY ANNUALS Plant from early to late spring.
TENDER ANNUALS Plant in late spring (when temperatures are reliably warm and all threat of frost has passed) through midsummer.

Planting

Dig a hole slightly bigger than the root ball, and set the plant in the hole at the same level as it was growing in the container. Gently replace the soil around the roots, and tamp down carefully to remove all air pockets and allow the roots to make good contact with the soil.

When you remove a plant from a container, you inevitably injure a few roots, which may cause a slight setback in plant growth. Your goal when planting is to reduce stress. Here are some suggestions:
- Transplant on a cloudy day or in the early morning before the heat of the day.
- Water the seedlings before transplanting, gently spraying the leaves to reduce wilting.
- Water transplants thoroughly after planting.
- Shade plants if necessary.
- Pinch back to reduce surface area of leaves and to promote branching.

FERTILIZING

Most sun-loving annuals benefit from an application of liquid fertilizer two weeks after seed germination or planting and monthly thereafter. Fertilize shade annuals, such as *Impatiens*, less frequently. To encourage flowering, use a complete fertilizer with a high middle number, representing phosphorous, such as 5-10-10. Avoid high nitrogen fertilizers for annuals, such as *Tagetes* (marigold) and *Ipomea purpurea* (morning glory); high nitrogen produces an abundance of leaves and no flowers. But if you are growing annuals such as *Coleus* for their foliage, you'll get good results using an equally balanced fertilizer, such as 8-8-8. In areas with high rainfall and sandy soils, try controlled-release fertilizers, which don't leach through the soil as quickly.

> *HINT: Some annuals do better without fertilizer, including* Tropaeolum *(nasturtium),* Cosmos, *and* Cleome *(spiderflower).*

CULTIVATING

Breaking up the soil to encourage air and moisture penetration is called cultivation. Soil should never be allowed to form a hard crust! If your annuals are planted in rows, cultivate them using a hoe to loosen the soil around the base of the plants, being careful not to break the stems or injure the roots. A three-pronged fork is excellent for hand-cultivating small areas. Begin prior to mulching, once the seedlings are a few inches high. Cultivate weekly, if you do not mulch.

MULCH

Mulch annual beds when the seedlings are several inches high. Spread a 2"-3" layer of a light mulch, such as shredded leaves, spent hops, buckwheat or cocoa hulls.

To avoid damaging your more fragile plants, first spread the mulch, then insert the small plants in it. If you are mulching just one or two tender transplants, cover them with an upturned pot and spread the mulch. When the pot is removed the mulch will gently fall into place around, but not on, the small plants.

THINNING

When sowing, seeds are often so small it's difficult to space them just right. Several seeds may begin to develop right next to each other. To develop into a full, healthy plant, a seedling needs enough space in which to grow. Look over your seedlings. Decide which look the most vigorous, then make room for them by thinning out, or pulling out, the less vigorous plants. To prevent disturbance to the remaining seedling, press down on the soil around it with your fingers, while simultaneously pulling out the other. The general rule of thumb for spacing annuals is to allow one half their mature height between plants. Look at the seed packets for more specific directions.

> *HINT: Thin out your seedlings on a cloudy day or early in the morning when the soil is moist. This will protect the seedlings' disturbed roots from exposure to the sun and loss of water.*

PINCHING

Most annuals grow naturally into a full, bushy plant or tall spire. Other annuals, such as *Viola* (pansy), *Petunia* x *hybrida* and *Antirrhinum* (snapdragon), need a little help developing into pleasing and productive shapes. "Pinching back" prevents the

Pinching, the removal of the growing tip (left), encourages bushy, new growth (right).

plants from becoming leggy and encourages them to fill out. To pinch back a plant, remove the terminal bud or tip of the plant after several sets of leaves have developed along the main stem. It is sometimes necessary to pinch back the side shoots as well. Two or more branches will grow from each pinched stem.

DEADHEADING

Deadheading is the wonderfully descriptive term for the removal of faded flowers. Use pruning clippers or your fingers to deadhead. Use shears to deadhead large masses of flowers with upward growing blossoms like *Tagetes* (marigold) or *Iberis umbellata* (candytuft). Be sure to make a clean cut and don't tear the stem.

Deadhead after flowering to:
- Maintain the appearance of the flower bed
- Discourage disease
- Prolong flower production by preventing annuals from going to seed

HINT: Save time in the garden; plant flowers that naturally drop their petals such as: Begonia, Impatiens, Lobularia *(sweet alyssum),* Ageratum, Lobelia, Salvia, *and* Catharanthus roseus *(annual vinca).*

CUT FLOWERS

There are few things more satisfying than walking out to the garden early in the morning to pick flowers for your home or friends. But annuals come on later in the spring and die back early in the fall, so to extend your cutting garden, do consider including perennials.

HINT: Growing your own flowers from seed gives you control over the selection.

Picking Annuals

1. Cut flowers early in the morning when they are most turgid.
2. Cut stems at an angle using a sharp knife or oriental shears.
3. Take as long a stem as possible without removing future flower buds.
4. Plunge freshly cut flowers immediately into a bucket of warm water you've carried into the garden.

To Prolong The Life Of Cut Annuals:

1. Recut the stems under water and place them in deep, warm water for at least ten minutes.
2. Remove all leaves below the water level.
3. Keep the vase filled with water.

4. Change the water in the vase daily to prevent buildup of bacteria in the water.
5. Mist the flowers and foliage to prevent wilting.
6. To restore wilted flowers, give the stems a clean cut and place them in a mixture of a half a cup of vinegar to one quart of cold water.

Special Hints

CALLISTEPHUS CHINENSIS (CHINA ASTER) To make flower heads stand upright, soak stems in a solution of one teaspoon sugar to one quart water.

CHRYSANTHEMUM (DAISY) AND *TAGETES* (MARIGOLD) Add several drops of peppermint oil to water. Also prevents water from smelling.

CONSOLIDA (ANNUAL LARKSPUR) Crush stems and plunge into solution of one-half teaspoon peppermint oil to one quart water.

LATHYRUS ODORATUS (SWEET PEA) Place in solution of one tablespoon alcohol to one quart of water.

HELIANTHUS (SUNFLOWER) Freshly cut sunflowers emit oil into the vase water, causing an unpleasant smell. To neutralize the oil and control the smell, fill the vase three-quarters full with water, add household bleach until you can just smell it, then add water to fill the vase.

HINT: To restore wilted flowers, give the stems a clean cut and place them in a mixture of a half a cup of vinegar to one quart of cold water.

FALL CLEANUP

As annuals perform for only one season, they should be removed as soon as they have been killed by the frost and added to your compost pile.

Annuals

Best Bets For Your Garden

above left: Canna x *generalis* 'Bounty'

above right: Callistephus chinensis

left: Calendula officinalis

below: Catharanthus roseus 'Rose Carpet'

Botanical Name Common Name	Color	Height Spacing	Sun/ Shade	
Ageratum houstonianum Ageratum	White, pink, blue	6-18" *6-12"*	○	
Antirrhinum majus Snapdragon	White, pink, red, orange, yellow, reddish-purple	1-3' *15"*	○	
Begonia x *semperflorens* Wax begonia	White, pink, rose, red	8-18" *12"*	◑ ●	
Brassica oleracea Ornamental cabbage	White, yellow	12" *12"*	○	
Calendula officinalis Pot marigold	Orange, yellow	12-15" *12"*	○	
Callistephus chinensis China aster	White, pink, red, purple, lavender	10-36" *12"*	○	
Canna x *generalis* Canna	White, pink, red, orange, yellow	1 1/2-6' *18-30"*	○	
Catharanthus roseus Annual vinca	White, pink, rose, light purple	6-18" *10"*	○ ◑	
Centaurea cyanus Bachelor's button	White, pink, blue, purple	24-30" *2'*	○	
Cleome hasslerana Spiderflower	White, pink, light purple	3-4' *15"*	○	
Consolida spp. Annual larkspur	White, pink, blue, lilac	2-3' *6"*	○	
Cosmos bipinnatus Mexican aster	White, pink, rose	3-5' *18-24"*	○	
Cynoglossum amabile Chinese forget-me-not	White, pink, blue	18" *8"*	○	
Dahlia hybrids Dahlia hybrids	Many colors, except blue	1-5' *3-4'*	○ ◑	

Annual Key: Hardy (HA); Half-hardy (HH); Tender (T)

Microclimate	Planting Time / Bloom Time	Comments
HH to T; warm-season; drought- and seashore-tolerant	Sow or plant after frost *Summer until frost*	Edging, cut flowers; attracts butterflies; self-seeding, but not always true from seed; rich, well-drained soil; alkaline-tolerant; deer-resistant
HA to HH; cool-season	Late spring *Summer - fall*	Borders, cut flowers; attracts butterflies; pinch out terminal bud when transplanting; deadhead to prolong bloom; rich, well-drained soil; alkaline-tolerant; deer-resistant
HH; warm-season; seashore-tolerant	Anytime after frost *Summer until frost*	Bedding, hanging baskets, containers; well-drained soil; deer-resistant
HA; cool-season; freeze-resistant	Summer *Fall*	Borders, bedding; good for fall color; rich, well-drained soil, alkaline-tolerant
HA; cool-season; best in areas with cool summers; resists light frost; seashore-tolerant	Sow in early spring *Summer*	Borders, containers; any well-drained soil; tolerates poor, sandy, moist and alkaline soils; deer-resistant
HH; warm-season	Late spring - summer *Summer*	Bedding, cut flowers; water during drought; rich, well-drained soil; alkaline-tolerant
T; warm summers	Spring *Summer until frost*	Tender perennial grown as an annual; rhizome; bedding, foliage, cut flowers; rich, moist soil; alkaline-tolerant; lift in fall
HH; warm-season; drought-, humidity-, and heat-tolerant	Late spring *Summer until frost*	Bedding, edging, containers; rich, well-drained soil
HA; cool-season	Sow fall - spring *Summer*	Borders, cut flowers; thin for larger plants and flowers; sow every 2 weeks for continuous bloom; any well-drained soil; tolerant of poor soils
HH; warm-season; drought-tolerant	Late spring - summer *Summer until frost*	Borders, cut flowers; easy to grow; rich, well-drained soil
HA; cool-season	Sow in fall or early spring *Summer*	Bedding, cut flowers; will reseed; fertilize frequently; rich, well-drained soil; deer-resistant; 12" in humid climates
HH; warm-season; drought-tolerant; good air circulation	Sow after last frost *Early summer until frost*	Borders, cut flowers; attracts butterflies; self-sows; well-drained soil; tolerant of poor, sandy and alkaline soils
HA; warm-season; heat-tolerant	Sow in fall or early spring *Late spring - early fall*	Biennial grown as hardy annual; borders, cut flowers; rich soil; deer-resistant
T; warm-season	Late spring *Summer until frost*	Perennial grown as annual; tuber; borders, cut flowers; pinch early for bushier, stronger plant; fertilize regularly; well-drained soil; plant 6-8" deep; lift/store annually

Annuals

Best Bets For Your Garden

above left: Eschscholzia califor-nica

above right: Gomphrena glo-bosa 'Strawberry Fields'

left: Salvia coccinea 'Lady in Red'

below left: Helianthus annuus

below right: Impatiens wallerana

Botanical Name / Common Name	Color	Height / Spacing	Sun/ Shade
Eschscholzia californica California poppy	Pink, red, orange, yellow, pink, red	12" *8"*	○
Gaillardia pulchella Blanket flower	Cream, orange, yellow	12-18" *12"*	○
Gomphrena globosa Globe amaranth	White, pink, rose, reddish purple	10-18" *6-10"*	○
Helianthus annuus Sunflower	Yellow, gold	3-7' *12"*	○
Iberis umbellata Candytuft (annual)	White, red, lilac	12-18" *12"*	○
Impatiens wallerana Impatiens	White, pink, red, salmon, magenta, lilac	12-18" *18"*	●
Ipomea alba Moonflower	White	20-30' *8-12"*	○
Ipomea purpurea Morning glory	White, pink, blue, purple	10-15' *8-12"*	○
Lathyrus odoratus Sweet pea	White, pink, blue, lavender	4-6' *12"*	○
Lavatera trimestris Annual mallow	White, pink, rose, red	12" *18"*	○
Lobelia erinus Lobelia	Blue	4-10" *4-6"*	○
Lobularia maritima Sweet alyssum	White, lilac	2-6" *6"*	○ ◑
Matthiola incana Stock	White, pink, yellow, purple	15-30" *15"*	○
Nicotiana alata Flowering tobacco	White, yellowish green, pink, rose, scarlet	12-18" *18-24"*	○ ◑

Annual Key: Hardy (HA); Half-hardy (HH); Tender (T)

Microclimate	Planting Time Bloom Time	Comments
HA; cool-season	Sow in fall or early spring *Summer - early fall*	Best for naturalizing; transplants poorly; tolerates alkaline and poor, sandy soils
HH; warm-season; drought- and seashore-tolerant	Early spring *Summer*	Cut flowers; attracts butterflies; dry, sandy soil; alkaline-tolerant
HH; warm-season; drought-tolerant	Sow in early spring *Summer*	Cut or dried flowers; rich, well-drained soil; tolerates alkaline and clay soils
HA; warm-season; drought-tolerant	Sow in early spring *Late summer*	Cut flowers; well-drained soil; tolerant of poor, sandy and clay soils
T; cool-season	Early spring *Spring*	Cut flowers; rock gardens; well-drained soil; deer-resistant
HH; warm-season	After frost *Summer until frost*	Perennial treated as annual; bedding; containers, hanging baskets; cut back to 6" if leggy; moist soil; deer-resistant
T; warm-season	Sow after frost *Midsummer until frost*	Twining vine; quick shade; good in containers; fragrant; night blooming; rich, well-drained soil; tolerates clay soil; deer-resistant
HA; warm-season	Sow after frost *Summer - fall*	Twining vine; perennial grown as annual; rich, well-drained soil; tolerates clay soil; deer-resistant
HA; cool-season	Sow in early spring *Summer*	Bush or tendril climber; cut flowers; fragrant; rich, well-drained soil
HA; cool-season; drought-tolerant	Sow 2 weeks before last frost *Summer - early fall*	Borders; fast-growing; dry, moderately rich soil
HA; cool-season; dry climates; seashore-tolerant	Spring *Summer until frost*	Bedding, edging, containers; sandy soil; deer-resistant
HH; prefers cool-season; seashore-tolerant	Sow early spring or plant in spring *Spring - early fall*	Borders, hanging baskets; fragrant; tolerant of poor, sandy and alkaline soils; keep spent flowers removed by shearing for succession of bloom; deer-resistant
HH; cool-season; seashore-tolerant	Sow in early spring *Summer*	Cut flowers, bedding; fragrant; sow thickly and do not thin to force early bloom; loamy soil; tolerates moist and alkaline soil; deer-resistant
HH; warm-season; seashore-tolerant	Plant after last frost *Summer until frost*	Borders; fragrant; attracts butterflies; moist, alkaline soil

Annuals

Best Bets For Your Garden

above left: Zinnia elegans

above right: Nigella damascena

left: Tithonia rotundifolia

below left: Petunia x hybrida

below right: Thunbergia alata

Botanical Name Common Name	Color	Height Spacing	Sun/ Shade
Nigella damascena Love-in-a-mist	White, pink, blue	18" *8"*	○
Pelargonium spp. Geranium	White, pink, red, salmon, light purple	12-15" *12"*	○
Petunia x *hybrida* Petunia	White, pink, red, yel- low, purple	12-18" *12"*	○
Phlox drummondii Annual phlox	White, pink, crimson, blue	10-20" *18"*	○
Portulaca grandiflora Portulaca	Many colors, except blue	4-6" *4-6"*	○
Salvia spp. Salvia	Red, blue	10-24" *15-20"*	○
Scabiosa atropurpurea Sweet scabious	White, pink, purple	18-24" *8-12"*	○
Tagetes spp. Marigold	Orange, yellow, brown, many shades	6-36" *6-12"*	○
Thunbergia alata Black-eyed Susan vine	Orange-yellow	10' *8-12"*	○
Tithonia rotundifolia Mexican sunflower	Orange, yellow	4-6' *12"*	○
Tropaeolum majus Nasturtium	Shades of yellow, orange, red, mahogany	1-12' *15"*	○
Verbena x *hybrida* Verbena	Pink, red, blue, lilac	8-18" *18"*	○
Viola x *wittkrokiana* Pansy	White, pink, red, orange, yellow, blue, purple, black	6" *6-8"*	○ ◑
Zinnia elegans Zinnia	White, pink, red, orange, yellow	12-36" *12"*	○

Annual Key: Hardy (HA); Half-hardy (HH); Tender (T)

Microclimate	Planting Time Bloom Time	Comments
HA; cool-season	Fall or spring *Summer*	Borders, cut and dried flowers; fast-growing; use peat pots if starting indoors; does not like transplanting; deadhead to extend bloom; average, well-drained soil
HH; intolerant of high humidity; seashore-tolerant	Plant outdoors after frost *Late spring until frost*	Can bring indoors for winter; do not overfertilize; well-drained soil, neutral to alkaline pH
HH; warm-season	Plant outdoors after frost *Late spring until frost*	Borders, containers; water often in hot weather; feed and pinch regularly; rich, moist soil; deer-resistant
HA; cool-season; best with good air circulation; seashore-tolerant	Sow in early spring *Summer - early fall*	Bedding; cut flowers; rich, moist, well-drained soil; alkaline-tolerant
T; warm-season; thrives in hot, dry conditions; seashore-tolerant	Late spring - midsummer *Summer until frost*	Dry banks and rock gardens; sandy, well-drained soil
T; warm-season; seashore-tolerant	Late spring - midsummer *Summer until frost*	Perennial grown as annual; good bedding; thrives in hot but not dry conditions; rich, well-drained soil; deer-resistant
HH; warm-season; seashore-tolerant	Sow in spring/plant after frost *Summer - early fall*	Borders, cut flowers; attracts butterflies; average soil
HH; warm-season; seashore-tolerant	Late spring or summer *Summer until frost*	Bedding, edging; attracts butterflies; used in companion planting to dissuade pests; all soils; tolerant of poor, sandy and alkaline soils; deer-resistant
T; warm-season	Sow indoors; plant after frost *Early summer - early fall*	Perennial grown as annual; twining vine; hanging baskets, window boxes, trellises; rich, well-drained soil
HH; warm-season; drought-, heat- and seashore-tolerant	Sow late spring *Midsummer until frost*	Borders; attracts butterflies; best in rich, well-drained soil; tolerant of poor, sandy and alkaline soils; deadhead regularly; deer-resistant
HA; cool-season	Sow or plant after frost *Summer*	Bush or vine; bedding, containers, cut flowers; train on poles; prefers poor soil; poor flowering in rich soil; do not overfertilize
HH; warm-season; heat- and seashore-tolerant	Late spring *Summer - early fall*	Borders, containers, cut flowers; fragrant; attracts butterflies; compact and spreading varieties; rich, well-drained soil; tolerant of poor, sandy soils
HH; cool-season; in warm areas plant in shade to prolong bloom	Late spring *Late spring - early fall*	Biennial grown as annual; borders, containers; fragrant; pick frequently; feed every two weeks; rich, moist soil
HH; warm-season, thrives in heat with water; intolerant of humidity*	Sow/plant late spring into summer	Cut flowers; attracts butterflies; sow every 2 weeks for continuous bloom; well-drained soil; alkaline-tolerant; *avoid wetting leaves to prevent mildew

PERENNIALS

Chrysanthemum x *superbum*

Perennials are plants you can depend on year after year to bring life to your garden. Although perennial foliage usually dies back in the fall, their roots carry them through the winter, enabling them to make a reappearance each spring. Many families have become so attached to their perennials that they are handed down from generation to generation or transplanted when the family moves. As most can be propagated by division, many gardeners take great pleasure in sharing their favorites with friends.

Perennials are grown for their decorative foliage as well as their colorful blooms. They are traditionally grown in borders, cottage gardens, mass plantings, as groundcovers and for cutting. The English have made perennials famous with their exquisite, beautifully choreographed perennial borders. Try them with bulbs in the spring garden, under shrubs and trees, along the edge of a pond or in a shade garden. Plant perennials at the base of a vine to cool its roots or edge a rose bed with perennials such as *Nepeta* x *faassenii* (catmint). With so many to choose from, there's a perennial for any location in your garden.

PERENNIALS VS. ANNUALS

To help you determine whether perennials are right for your garden, consider some of the differences between perennials and annuals:

ANNUALS CAN BLOOM ALL SEASON LONG. Some perennials, such as *Scabiosa* 'Butterfly Blue,' bloom for up to four months, while others, such as *Astilbe*, often bloom for just a few weeks each year.

ANNUALS REQUIRE WARM TEMPERATURES TO BLOOM; many perennials thrive in cooler temperatures. With carefully selected perennials your garden can begin blooming early in the spring and continue into the late fall.

ANNUALS MUST BE REPLANTED EVERY YEAR, which is fun for variety, but time consuming.

PERENNIALS REQUIRE MORE MAINTENANCE THAN ANNUALS. A perennial must be healthy and vigorous to persist from year to year.

Grow Perennials:

- In herbaceous borders against a fence, wall or hedge
- In mixed perennial and shrub borders
- In mass plantings
- In shade, rock or water gardens
- As groundcovers
- To edge rose gardens
- To hide yellowing bulb foliage
- To fill in bare spots between shrubs
- To fill in around young shrubs, tying the mass together
- To brighten dark corners
- In your cutting garden
- In pots and planters

HINT: A garden all in white will glow in the moonlight.

TEMPERATURE

Perennials are sensitive to both cold and warm temperatures. Look for plants that are cold hardy in your zone. And, if you experience very hot summers, opt for heat-tolerant perennials, such as *Gaura lindheimeri* and *Gaillardia grandiflora* (blanket flower). With many favorites, you will find the hotter the summer, the shorter the bloom period. When making your selection, consider the following:

- First and last dates of frost
- The coldest expected winter temperature
- The highest expected summer temperature

SUN/SHADE

Although most perennials prefer a sunny location, there are perennials, such as *Astilbe*, *Aquilegia* (columbine) and *Hemerocallis* (daylily), which grow in light shade. *Dicentra* (bleeding heart), *Viola odorata* (violet) and *Convallaria majalis* (lily-of-the-valley) grow well in full shade.

HINT: Don't grow sun-loving plants in the shade; they will become leggy and require staking.

SOIL

Most perennials require a humus-rich, well-drained, but moist soil. Soil with a good balance of clay, sand and silt will provide the necessary drainage, yet retain moisture. If you have sandy or clay soil, amend your soil or select perennials that tolerate your conditions. A slightly acid soil, with a pH of 5.5-6.6, will suit most perennials.

WATER

Regular moisture is important for most perennials during the growing season. If your summers bring hot winds and drought, be sure to monitor your soil carefully. When the top

2" have dried out and rain is not on the horizon, it's time to water. And, when planting new perennials, always water deeply and thoroughly. Avoid using sprinklers; they will damage the blossoms and wet the leaves, attracting mildew in humid microclimates. Don't stop watering in winter; if the soil is dry, but not frozen, your perennials may need additional moisture.

HINT: To control mildew on Phlox paniculata, *spray the foliage with Wilt Pruf during the growing season.*

PLANNING A PERENNIAL BORDER

Planning a perennial border is like composing a symphony. Perennials, like violins, trumpets and drums, perform at specific times to create an harmonious whole. As each instrument contributes a different sound to the orchestra, each perennial offers the garden a different form, silhouette, color and texture.

The Planting Bed

First set the stage. If possible, locate your border on either side of a walk, or in a garden enclosed by walls, fences or hedges. Flowers show off to their best advantage against a solid background. If you do site your bed in front of a solid background, make a narrow path behind the bed. This will provide easy access for tending the plants and prevent you from compacting the planting bed with your footsteps.

The border should be in scale and proportion to its location in your landscape. Small perennial borders should be at least 5' to 6' wide; 10' to 12' is an ideal depth for long beds. Stay clear of any trees that may have invasive roots.

HINT: To extend the season of perennials in areas with hot summers, locate your perennial border out of the heat of the afternoon sun.

The Plant List

Next, decide whether the border will be devoted solely to perennials or whether it will be mixed, including bulbs, annuals, biennials and roses or other shrubs. If you use only perennials, place spring-, summer- and fall-blooming plants in groups, forming a set pattern of bloom through the border. If it is a mixed border, fill in the blooming gaps with flowering bulbs and annuals. In either design, be sure to include many perennials with long blooming periods for continuity.

Bloom Sequence

As perennials bloom for defined periods, timing the sequence of bloom in a perennial border is very important. When making your plant selection, choose perennials that are early-, mid- and late-season bloomers. Then use tracing paper to plan your sequence of bloom and color. Use a different sheet for each month and lay them on top of each other to see how one blends into the next. Don't be concerned if you don't get the results you want the first year. It's very hard to plan for the *exact* time of bloom, until you see how the plants perform in your microclimate. And next season, you can always move the plants! When you do get it right, the show is well worth the effort.

Mass Plantings

For maximum impact, group the plants together in masses of from three to a dozen. Remember, the smaller the plant, the more you need to make an impression. Smaller groups will look all right in small gardens; large gardens can support bold masses of color. Some bushy plants such as *Paeonia* (peony) or *Gypsophila* (baby's breath) can stand alone.

Plant Placement

The plant masses should mesh together from front to back and side to side. Form irregularly shaped masses of each perennial so plant masses can weave together. Consider the horizontal and vertical relationship of the plants as well as the texture of the foliage. Remember, the foliage will be there all season, while the blooms may not! Position short masses in front and tall in back. But add some variety and surprises so the garden is not monotonous. Vary the height in the back row and pull some of the tall and medium height plants forward into the shorter masses.

Spacing

Perennial plants look so small when you first plant them you can't believe they'll ever fill the 12" or larger gap that is recommended. But believe me they do. As perennials send up new shoots every year, they'll fill in in no time, and you'll be digging up and dividing your plants sooner than you would like. See the spacing recommendations in "Best Bets For Your Garden" and follow them!

PLANNING AT A GLANCE:

- Microclimate
- Soil
- Water
- Height and width
- Plant form and silhouette
- Flower texture and color
- Leaf texture and color
- Spacing
- Time and length of bloom
- Life cycle of the plants: growth, bloom and decline

BED PREPARATION

Perennials have the potential to grow in the same place for many years, even decades! The better the bed preparation, the happier the perennials, the longer the life. Prepare the beds in the fall to a depth of 12" (minimum) to 24" (ideal) by single or double digging (see "Digging the Bed," p.33). If your planting plan includes shrubs or roses, I urge you to dig the full 24" depth. Add soil amendments as required, and let the beds settle over the winter before planting in the spring. If this is not possible, prepare them as soon as the soil is workable in the spring and water well to settle the soil before planting.

> *HINT: If you were unable to prepare the beds in advance, plant the perennials slightly deeper to accommodate for the soil's settling.*

SEEDS OR PLANTS?

Although perennials reproduce by seed as well as by sending up new shoots, most perennials are purchased as plants. Perennials grown from seeds take longer to reach flowering than annuals and often do not grow true in color and habit. Container-grown perennials are available from catalogs or your local nursery; bare-root plants are most often purchased by mail.

BUYING PERENNIALS

If you are buying your plants from a local nursery, you will have the opportunity to pick and choose.

To select a healthy plant, look for:

- Plants that are pest free.
- Plants that have healthy, new growth.

and avoid:

- Plants with yellow leaves or dieback.
- Plants that are potbound. (Check to see if roots are growing out of the bottom of pot.)
- Plants with underdeveloped root systems. (Check to see if plant is loose in pot.)
- Plants that are leggy.

PLANTING

Now that you've prepared the bed, it's time to make your perennials feel at home. If possible, install your plants as soon as they arrive. If this isn't possible, be sure to keep them well watered and in the shade. For information on digging the beds and amending the soil, see the index.

Container Plants

1. Set the containers out on the bed according to your garden plan. Now, fine-tune your design. Water the containers, then begin to plant one at a time.
2. Dig a hole one-and-a-half times wider and deeper than the container
3. Holding one hand over the top of the container, turn the container over and remove the plant. If the plant is pot-bound, you may need to loosen the plant by tapping the sides with a trowel. Do not pull the plant out by the stem; it may break! If the plant has an underdeveloped root system, and the root ball begins to crumble, retain as much soil around the root ball as possible.
4. Next, carefully scrape any weeds that may be growing from the top surface of the root ball, then gently loosen the roots along the sides and bottom to encourage their growth out into their new home.
5. Adjust the plant in the hole. Most perennials should be planted with their crowns at the same level as the surrounding soil.
6. Fill the hole with soil, gently firm the soil around the plant, then water thoroughly to settle the soil around the roots.

Bare-root Plants

Plant bare-root plants as soon as possible. The roots will be brittle so remove any protective covering with great care, then rehydrate the roots by soaking them in a bucket of water with a couple of drops of liquid dish detergent for at least an hour. This will make the roots more pliable and less prone to damage.

1. Cut off any dead or damaged roots using sharp scissor pruners or a knife that has been cleaned with alcohol.
2. Dig a hole ample enough to avoid crowding the plant and form a mound of soil in the bottom.
3. Next, gently spread the roots over the mound so the base of the crown rests on the mound, yet is level with the surrounding soil. (The base of the crown is where the roots meet the stems.)
4. Fill the hole with soil. Be careful not to cover the crown!
5. Gently firm the soil and water in well.

FERTILIZING

If you have prepared your perennial beds well, there should be little need for much fertilizing. An annual top dressing of a balanced slow-release fertilizer and compost in the early spring should be enough. But established beds and beds with heavy feeders such as *Paeonia* (peony) and *Phlox* may need a little help. But do not apply fertilizer on top of your mulch. Remove the mulch, spread the fertilizer, then replace.

HINT: Do not add fertilizer to the planting hole. You risk burning the roots.

Some Signs Of Nutrient Deficiency

You will see signs when your plants are suffering from nutrient deficiency:

- Small leaves or blossoms
- Yellow leaves
- Yellow leaves with dark veins
- Plants are weak and wilted (although well-watered)
- Lateral buds die before blooming
- Small blossoms

MULCH

Apply a light mulch, such as buckwheat hulls, ground-up leaf mold or spent hops, 2" thick. Bark chips are too large and clumsy looking in a flower bed. Since some are prone to crown rot, don't mound the mulch around the crowns of perennials. Reapply as necessary.

WEEDING

Keep an eye out for annual weeds, but if you've prepared your beds well and applied your mulch, weeding should be minimal. But keep on top of it!

PINCHING

"Pinching back" prevents the plants from becoming leggy and encourages them to develop into more compact, bushy plants. Pinching often delays flowering time, but produces more flowers, although they may be smaller in size. Perennials that benefit from a pinch here and there include: *Artemisia* (wormwood), *Aster, Boltonia asteroides, Lobelia, Monarda* (bee balm), and *Salvia. Helenium autumnale* (sneezeweed) and many species of *Chrysanthemum* actually require pinching to fill out and flourish!

To pinch back a plant, remove the tips of the stems. The best time to start is in the late spring or early summer just as the perennials begin to grow. Two branches will grow from each pinched stem. Stop pinching when the flower buds are set. (See the Pinching Illustration on p.52.)

STAKING

Whether or not to stake is just as personal a decision as the design of the garden and the plant selection. Some people feel that stakes detract from the beauty of the flowers, while others think of them as a necessity. Some prefer a casual cottage garden look, others a formal garden. Whichever your view, there are some flowers that cannot stand alone. The first heavy rain or wind storm will flatten the tall spikes of *Delphinium* and the heavy flowers of double *Paeonia* (peony). The type of staking you use depends on the habit of the plant.

> *HINT: If staking is not to your liking, select lower-growing plants and plants with lighter flower heads.*

Tall Spiked Flowers Such As Delphinium

Use a tall green bamboo cane long enough to go deep into the ground and rise to within 6" of the anticipated height of the flower stalk. Being careful not to disturb the plant's crown, push the stake in as close to the flower stalk as possible. Loop a piece of soft green twine around the stem, then loosely tie it to the stake and trim off the ends. Add more ties as the flower stalk grows.

Medium Spike Flowers Such As Lilium (Lily)

Stake as for tall spike flowers or use metal single stem supports that curl around the stalk.

For Bushy Plants Such As Paeonia (Peony)

There are several approaches to bushy plants; choose from the following:

CIRCULAR METAL FRAMES Place above the plants in early spring to allow the stems to grow up through them. Some stems will need to be guided into the circle. Conspicuous until hidden by the plants.

ZIGZAG SUPPORTS Available in different heights and lengths, these green metal supports are easily placed after the plants, such as *Achillea* (yarrow), have begun to grow. They lift plants up without totally restraining them.

LINKED STAKES Green metal stakes installed around plants, such as *Monarda* (bee balm), as they near maturity, but before they are at risk of flopping. The late installation will prevent your garden from looking like a sea of green metal early in the season.

BAMBOO STAKES   Evenly space green bamboo stakes around clumps of perennials, such as *Chrysanthemum*, and run dark green twine between them to support the flower stems. These can be installed after the plants have filled out, but before they are top-heavy.

Airy Plants Such As Achillea (Yarrow)

BRUSH STAKES   Stick a branch from a twiggy bush in the ground next to perennials such as *Gypsophila paniculata* (baby's breath) and *Coreopsis* in the spring. The plant will grow up through and eventually hide the branch. The only drawback is — your garden will look like a mass of twigs in early summer until the perennials have filled out.

Some of the most picturesque plant supports can be found right in your garden. Look around. Perhaps you'll find a strong grapevine that curves in just the right direction or a birch stem that's just the right height.

DISBUDDING

While you pinch back for a bushier plant, you disbud for a bigger flower. Locate the terminal bud on perennials such as *Paeonia* (peony) and *Dahlia*. Pinch out the smaller side buds growing at the base of its stem. The resulting blossom will be extra-large. Do not disbud perennials with spiked blooms such as *Delphinium*.

DEADHEADING

Behead your faded flowers! Use pruning clippers or your fingers to deadhead. For large masses of flowers with upward growing blossoms such as *Lavandula* (lavender), *Achillea*

(From top left clockwise) Bamboo cane; circular metal frame; natural brush stakes, metal zigzag supports.

(yarrow), *Nepeta* x *faassenii* (catmint) and *Iberis sempervirens* (candytuft), use shears. But be sure to make a clean cut and don't tear the stems. On perennials, such as *Hemerocallis* (daylily) and *Monarda* (bee balm), which have several blooms per stem, remove the individual spent bloom only.

If a perennial's foliage is out of control, you can trim it back at the same time. But remember, perennials bloom for a limited time; the foliage lingers to fill the gaps. Allow the spent flowerheads of showy *Sedum* and *Rudbeckia* (black-eyed Susan) to dry on the plants; they look wonderful all winter long.

Deadhead after flowering to:
- Maintain the appearance of the flower bed.
- Discourage disease.
- Prevent seed formation and extend the bloom.

CUT FLOWERS

With their foliage and blooms, perennials can make lovely, long-lasting cut flowers. But remember, many perennials, unlike annuals, have one short blooming season. If you plan to cut your perennials, it is best to grow them in a separate cutting garden so your borders will look full and not ratty or moth-eaten.

When Picking Perennials

1. Cut flowers early in the morning when they are most turgid.
2. Cut stems at an angle using a sharp knife or oriental shears.
3. Take as long a stem as possible without removing future flower buds.
4. Plunge freshly cut flowers immediately into a bucket of warm water you've carried into the garden.

To Prolong The Life Of Cut Perennials:
- Cut flowers before they are fully open.
- Keep the vase filled with water!

- Change the water daily to prevent buildup of bacteria.
- Mist the flowers and foliage to prevent wilting.
- Keep the vase cool whenever possible.

Special Hints

FOR FLOWERS WITH SAP SUCH AS *PAPAVER* (POPPY) Cut stems to desired length, then burn tips of stems in a flame or dip in boiling water for one minute. If stems are re-cut, repeat process.

FOR FLOWERS WITH HOLLOW STEMS SUCH AS *DELPHINIUM* Fill stems with water and plug up with cotton balls or Oasis.

FOR *CHRYSANTHEMUM* Crush or burn stems. Soak flowers up to their necks in a solution of eight drops of peppermint oil to two quarts of water.

FOR *PAEONIA* (PEONY) Cut when in bud. Crush stems four inches up and place in deep, cold water.

DIVIDING

Dividing perennials may sound like a lot of work, but it's well worth it. Not only can you rejuvenate older plants, but you will have many new plants to keep or to give away to friends. Divide your plants when they are overcrowded or when flower production is down.

FIBROUS-ROOTED PLANTS Dig up plants like *Galium odoratum* (sweet woodruff) and gently pull the plants apart.

PLANTS WITH SOLID CROWNS OR RHIZOMES Use a sharp knife to divide solid crowned plants like *Paeonia* (peony) and *Astilbe* or rhizomes like *Iris*. Dust with fungicide.

PLANTS THAT BECOME WOODY As some perennials such as *Aster* and *Artemisia* age, the parent plants become woody and produce fewer blooms, but their side shoots may show great potential. Dig all around the clump with a spade and lift

Dividing (clockwise from left). For large clumps: Dig up the plant, lift and insert two digging forks back to back in the center of the clump and pry apart. For plants that become woody: Cut off the young side shoots with a spade and discard the woody parent plant. For plants with solid crowns or rhizomes: Divide with a sharp knife. For fibrous-rooted plants: Gently pull the plants apart.

up the whole colony. Cut off the young side shoots and replant them. Discard the parent plant.

LARGE CLUMPS   Heavy-crowned plants like *Hemerocallis* (daylily) need a little more effort. Dig all around the clump with a spade, then lift the plant. Shake off excess soil so you can see the roots and set the clump to the side of the bed. Insert two digging forks back to back in the center of the clump. Pressing the handles together, pry the clump apart. Divide into as many smaller clumps as necessary and replant.

Time To Divide

Most perennials can be divided and transplanted in the fall when the foliage begins to die back. A general rule of thumb: If it blooms in the spring, divide it in the fall. If it blooms in the fall, divide it in the spring. More specifically, divide plants that bloom from midsummer to fall in the early spring. *Papaver* (poppy) should be divided in August when they have begun to produce new foliage.

TRANSPLANTING

Remember to prepare a planting bed for the newly divided plants prior to getting started because you don't want any delays getting them back into the ground. If you are incorporating new divisions into existing beds, amend the soil in the individual holes at planting time. Before planting, cut back the foliage by one-half to ensure that most of the plant's energy goes to the roots. The foliage on spring-planted divisions will be small and most likely will not need to be reduced. In newly prepared beds, plant the divisions deeper than their original level as the soil is bound to settle. Thoroughly water all transplants. New plantings are in danger of losing too much water from transpiring moisture through their leaves before new roots have formed to take up additional water.

WINTERIZING

Most plantings, but especially all first-year plantings, should be carefully winterized in Zones 5, 6 and 7. The first step to preparing for winter is a good fall cleanup. Look over the garden after the plants have died back. Save any plants that will add winter interest such as *Sedum spectabile* (showy sedum) or *Rudbeckia* (black-eyed Susan) and cut back all others to the ground. When the ground is frozen, spread a 2" layer of compost and in Zone 5 cover the garden with evergreen boughs, salt hay or straw, which will hold the snow for additional insulation. But do not rake leaves into the bed; they will flatten down and prevent water from penetrating the surface. Add them to your compost pile instead.

SPRING CLEANUP

When the weather starts to warm up and the early spring bulbs are in bloom, you know it's time to begin removing the winter mulch. If you leave the mulch on too late in the spring; it will slow down the growth of the young shoots. To give young shoots a chance to adjust to the sunlight, begin removing the mulch on a cloudy day. If you layered your mulch, remove it gradually a few boughs or a layer of hay at a time. When all the winter protection is removed, work the compost evenly over the bed.

Early spring is the time to cut back all perennials left standing through the winter. Using scissor pruners, remove the stems down to the crown, taking care not to damage any young shoots.

Biennials

Digitalis purpurea

Biennials complete their life cycles within a two-year period. The first year, the plants produce leaves; the second, they bloom, set seed and die. If left alone, biennials self-sow, so some plants will be in bloom every year. However, biennials can't be counted on to return each year as perennials do, so gardeners often steer clear of them. But there are so many beautiful flowers within their ranks, they deserve consideration.

Much-loved biennials such as *Dianthus barbatus* (Sweet William) and *Campanula medium* (Canterbury bells) are a wonderful addition to herbaceous borders and cottage gardens; *Digitalis* spp. (foxglove) makes an impressive display naturalized in a woodland setting; *Myosotis* (forget-me-not) is an all-time favorite planted with spring-flowering bulbs. Some treat biennials as annuals, while others treat them like perennials, reserving a special place for them in the garden.

Biennials have dual personalities. Plants raised from seeds the first year winter over just like perennials. Yet in their second season they behave like annuals, leaving behind their seed to repeat the cycle the next year. Since annual beds are tilled every year, biennials in Zones 5, 6 and 7 find a safer home in the perennial border.

Biennials are easily grown from seeds. However, since they take two years to bloom from seeds, many prefer to buy plants. To grow biennials from seeds, follow instructions in the annuals section under "Sowing."

Biennials are readily available as container-grown plants from your local garden centers or through mail-order catalogs. Plant them as you would perennials. (See p.65.) For bloom every year, grow plants on alternate cycles.

Perennials

Best Bets For Your Garden

above left: Achillea 'Moonshine'

above right: Campanula persicifolia 'Telham Beauty'

left: Aster novae-angliae 'Hella Lacy'

below left: Alchemilla mollis

below right: Astilbe x arendsii 'Bridal Veil'

Botanical Name / Common Name	Color	Height / Spacing	Sun/ Shade
Achillea spp. / Yarrow	Yellow	18-24" / *12-18"*	○
Alchemilla mollis / Lady's mantle	Yellow	1-2' / *18"*	○ ◑
Anemone x *hybrida* / Japanese anemone	White, pink, rose	3-5' / *2'*	○ ◑
Aquilegia spp. / Columbine	Many colors	18" / *8-12"*	◑
Artemisia ludoviciana / Artemisia	Silver gray foliage	24-42" / *12-18"*	○
Asclepias tuberosa / Butterfly weed	Orange	18"-3' / *1-2'*	○
Aster x *frikartii* / Frikart's aster	Lavender	2-3' / *18"*	○ ◑
Aster novae-angliae / New England aster	Pink, crimson, rose, purple, lavender	1-6' / *2'*	○
Aster novi-belgi / New York aster	Pink, rose, crimson, purple, lavender	1-6' / *18-24"*	○
Astilbe x *arendsii* / Astilbe	White, pink, red	18-30" / *18-24"*	◑
Baileya multiradiata / Desert marigold	Yellow	18" / *12-18"*	○
Boltonia asteroides / Boltonia	White, pink, lilac	4-7' / *2'*	○ ◑
Campanula persicifolia / Bellflower	White, blue	2-3' / *12-18"*	○ ◑
Centranthus ruber / Red valerian	Pink, red	18-30" / *12-18"*	○ ◑

Microclimate	Planting Time / Bloom Time	Comments
Very hardy; tolerates hot sun, dry and humid microclimates; seashore-tolerant	Spring or fall *Summer*	Borders, cut flowers; well-drained soil; tolerates alkaline soil; attracts butterflies; try 'Moonshine'
Hardy	Spring or fall *Late spring - early summer*	Borders, cut flowers; groundcover; most well-drained, moist soils; deer-resistant
Hardy to Zone 6, with winter protection in Zone 5	Spring *Late summer - fall*	Borders, cut flowers; humus-rich, well-drained soil; low-maintenance
Hardy	Early spring or fall *Early spring - early summer*	Borders; well-drained, moist soil; tolerates alkaline soil; deer-resistant
Hardy; heat- and seashore-tolerant	Spring or fall *Summer*	Borders, edging; aromatic foliage; moist, well-drained soil
Very hardy; heat-, humidity- and drought-tolerant	Spring *Summer*	Borders; cut flowers; easily grown from seeds; dry, sandy soil; tolerates clay soil; attracts butterflies; deer-resistant
Hardy; protect in winter; heat-tolerant	Spring *Summer - fall*	Borders, cut flowers; moist, rich, well-drained soil; in Zone 5 may die out in winter but too nice to omit; try 'Monch'
Hardy; tolerant of wet soils	Spring or late summer *Summer - fall*	Borders, cut flowers; moist, rich soil; attracts butterflies; deer-resistant
Hardy; tolerant of wet soils	Spring or late summer *Summer - fall*	Borders, cut flowers; moist, rich soil; attracts butterflies; deer-resistant
Very hardy; prefers cold weather	Spring or fall *Early summer*	Bedding, borders, woodland gardens; moist soil, tolerates clay soil; deer-resistant; many cultivars
Hardy to Zones 6 and 7; heat, drought- and humidity-tolerant	Spring or fall *Spring - fall*	Borders; silver-grey, woolly foliage; daisy-like flower; well-drained, sandy soil; water every week or two to prolong bloom
Hardy; humidity-tolerant	Spring or fall *Late summer - fall*	Back of border, naturalizing; cultivars are better behaved; regular water; does not require staking; tolerant of most soils; deer-resistant; try 'Snowbank'
Hardy	Spring or fall *Spring - summer*	Borders, cut flowers; well-drained, rich, neutral to alkaline soil; try 'Telham Beauty'
Hardy; drought-tolerant	Spring *Spring - summer*	Border; cut flowers; fragrant; cut back for second bloom; well-drained average soil; tolerates alkaline soil; attracts butterflies; deer-resistant

Perennials

Best Bets For Your Garden

above left: Delphinium elatum

above right: Echinacea purpurea

left: Coreopsis verticillata 'Zagreb'

below: Gypsophila paniculata 'Pink Fairy'

Botanical Name / Common Name	Color	Height / Spacing	Sun/ Shade
Ceratostigma plumbaginoides / False plumbago	Blue	6-10" / *18"*	○ ◐
Chrysanthemum x *superbum* / (C. maximum) Shasta daisy	White	1-2' / *18"*	○
Coreopsis verticillata / Threadleaf coreopsis	Yellow	1-3' / *2'*	○
Delphinium elatum / Delphinium hybrids	White, blue, lavender	3-8' / *2-3'*	○
Dianthus x *allwoodii* / Cottage pink	White, pink	12-18" / *18"*	○
Dicentra spectabilis / Bleeding heart	White, pink	2-3' / *1-5'*	◐ ●
Echinacea purpurea / Purple coneflower	White, purple	2-3' / *18"*	○
Echinops humilis / Globe thistle	Lavender	4-6' / *2'*	○
Gaillardia x *grandiflora* / Blanket flower	Red, orange, yellow	2-3' / *18"*	○
Gaura lindheimeri / Gaura	White	3-4' / *1-2'*	○
Geranium spp. / Cranesbill	Pink, rose, blue, purple	18-24" / *18-24"*	○ ◐
Geum quellyon / Geum	Red	1-2' / *12"*	○ ◐
Gypsophila paniculata / Baby's breath	White, pink	18-48" / *4'*	○
Helenium autumnale / Sneezeweed	Yellow	4-5' / *18"*	○

Microclimate	Planting Time / Bloom Time	Comments
Hardy; drought- and seashore-tolerant	Spring *Late summer - fall*	Borders; well-drained soil; tolerates alkaline soil; cut back at end of season; attracts butterflies
Hardy; seashore-tolerant	Spring or fall *Early summer - fall*	Borders; cut flowers; rich, well-drained soil; tolerates clay and alkaline soil; deadhead for rebloom; cut back at end of season; deer-resistant
Very hardy; drought-, seashore- and humidity-tolerant	Spring or fall *Summer*	Borders; cut flowers; average, well-drained soil; tolerates alkaline soil; attracts butterflies; deer-resistant
Very hardy; heat-intolerant; prefers cold winters	Spring *Summer*	Borders, cut flowers; rich, well-drained soil; most require staking; requires more care
Hardy	Spring *Summer*	Borders, edging; fragrant; neutral, humus-rich, very well-drained soil; tolerates alkaline soil; deer-resistant
Hardy	Early spring or fall *Spring - late spring*	Borders, cottage gardens; humus-rich, well-drained soil; tolerates alkaline soil; dies back in summer
Very hardy; seashore- and humidity-tolerant	Spring *Summer*	Borders; cut flowers; rich, moist soil; tolerates clay and alkaline soil; attracts butterflies; deer-resistant
Very hardy; seashore- and drought-tolerant	Spring *Midsummer - fall*	Borders; cut flowers; light, well-drained soil; attracts butterflies
Very hardy; heat- drought-, and seashore-tolerant	Spring *Summer*	Borders, cut flowers; light, well-drained soil; short-lived
Hardy to Zone 6; drought-, heat-, seashore- and humidity-tolerant	Spring *Summer - fall*	Borders, cut flowers; light, well-drained soil; long-lived in the Southwest
Hardy; part shade in the heat	Spring or fall *Late spring - summer*	Borders, rock gardens, all well-drained soils; deadhead for rebloom; deer-resistant
Hardy; provide shade in hot climates	Spring or fall *Summer*	Rhizome; borders, cut flowers; long bloom; deer-resistant
Hardy; seashore-tolerant	Spring *Summer*	Borders, cut or dried flowers; rich, moist, well-drained neutral to alkaline soil; select smaller cultivars to avoid staking
Very hardy; heat-tolerant	Spring or fall *Summer - early fall*	Informal plantings; moist soil; tolerates alkaline soil; deadhead for more blooms; attracts butterflies; deer-resistant

Perennials

Best Bets For Your Garden

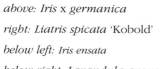

above: Iris x *germanica*

right: Liatris spicata 'Kobold'

below left: Iris ensata

below right: Lavandula angustifolia 'Dwarf White'

Botanical Name / Common Name	Color	Height / Spacing	Sun/ Shade
Helianthemum nummularium Sun rose	White, pink, red, yellow	8-12" *2-3'*	○
Heliopsis helianthoides False sunflower	Orange, yellow	5' *2'*	○
Hemerocallis x *hybrida* Daylily	Shades of orange, pink, red, yellow	2-3' *18"*	○ ◑
Hesperis matronalis Sweet rocket	Purple	1-3' *18"*	○ ◑
Heuchera x *brizoides* Coralbells	White, pink, red	12-18" *12-18"*	Morning sun only
Hibiscus moscheutos Rose mallow	White, pink, red	4-6' *30-36"*	○ ◑
Iberis sempervirens Candytuft	White	6-9" *12"*	○ ◑
Iris x *germanica* Bearded iris	Many	10-36" *12"*	○
Iris ensata Japanese iris	Many	24-30" *12"*	○ ●
Iris pseudacorus Yellow flag	Yellow	3-4' *15"*	○ ◑
Iris sibirica Siberian iris	White, blue, purple	2-4' *2'*	○
Lavandula angustifolia English lavender	Lavender, pinkish white	1-2' *12-18"*	○
Liatris spicata Gayfeather	White, purple	3-4' *12"*	○
Limonium latifolium Sea lavender	Bluish white	2' *18"*	○

Microclimate	Planting Time / Bloom Time	Comments
Hardy; heat-tolerant	Early spring / *Spring - summer*	Containers, rock gardens, dry banks, neutral to alkaline, very well-drained soil; prune lightly after bloom
Hardy; drought- and seashore-tolerant	Spring or fall / *Summer*	Back of border; disease-resistant; any well-drained soil, tolerates poor soils; deadhead to extend bloom
Very hardy; seashore- and humidity-tolerant	Early spring or fall / *Spring - fall*	Borders, bedding; any soil; water regularly when blooming; 'Happy Returns' blooms over a long period
Hardy; protect from strong sun	Early spring / *Late spring - summer*	Borders; fragrant; self-seeds; well-drained, moist soil, tolerant of poor soil; deadhead to force second bloom; attracts butterflies
Hardy; seashore-tolerant	Early spring or fall / *Spring*	Edging; borders; rich, well-drained, moist soil; tolerates alkaline soil
Hardy; seashore- and humidity-tolerant; protect from wind	Spring / *Summer*	Borders; moist soil; fertilize regularly; deer-resistant
Very hardy; prefers cool nights; drought- and humidity-tolerant	Spring / *Spring - early summer*	Evergreen border; well-drained soil; tolerates alkaline soil; deer-resistant
Hardy; some resent heat, others thrive; seashore-tolerant	Fall / *Spring*	Rhizome; many hybrids; alkaline, well-drained soil; plant high to prevent crown rot; divide every 3-4 years; cut seed pods as they form; deer-resistant
Hardy; seashore- and heat-tolerant	Spring or fall / *Summer*	Rhizome; moist, acid to neutral soil; deer-resistant
Hardy; prefers moist, boggy soils	Spring or fall / *Midspring*	Rhizome; moist, acid soil; thrive in shallow water; deer-resistant
Hardy; seashore-tolerant	Spring / *Early spring*	Rhizome; prefers moist, neutral to acid soil; tolerant of many soils; deer-resistant
Hardy; intolerant of wet or severe winters	Spring / *Summer*	Borders, edging, dried flowers; woody; fragrant foliage; must have light, well-drained, neutral to slightly alkaline soil; many cultivars
Very hardy; drought- and humidity-tolerant	Spring / *Mid - late summer*	Borders; cut flowers; well-drained, moist soil; attracts butterflies
Very hardy; heat-, drought- and seashore-tolerant	Spring / *Summer - early fall*	Borders, cut and dried flowers; well-drained soil

Perennials
Best Bets For Your Garden

above left: Monarda didyma 'Raspberry Wine'

above right: Salvia nemerosa 'Rose Wine'

left: Nepeta x faassenii

below left: Malva moschata

below right: Perovskia atriplicifolia

Botanical Name / Common Name	Color	Height / Spacing	Sun/Shade
Macleaya cordata / Plume poppy	White	6-8' / 2-3'	○ ◑
Malva moschata / Musk mallow	White, pink	2-3' / 2'	○
Monarda didyma / Bee balm	White, pink, red, lavender	30-40" / 18"	○ ◑
Myosotis sylvatica / Forget-me-not	Blue	6-8" / 10"	○ ◑
Nepeta x *faassenii* / Catmint	Lavender	1-2' / 18"	○
Oenothera spp. / Evening primrose	Pink, yellow	9-24" / 1-2'	○
Paeonia lactiflora / Peony	White, pink, red	24-42" / 2-3'	○
Perovskia spp. / Russian sage	Lavender	3-5' / 18-24"	○
Phlox paniculata / Border phlox	White, pink, red	2-4' / 12"	○ ◑
Physotegia virginiana / False dragonhead	White, lavender	2-5' / 18"	○ ◑
Platycodon grandiflorus / Balloon flower	White, pink, blue	18-30" / 12"	○ ◑
Primula japonica / Japanese primrose	Many colors	12-30" / 12"	◑
Rudbeckia spp. / Black-eyed Susan	Yellow, gold, mahogany	2-3' / 18"	○
Salvia spp. / Perennial salvia	Blue	2-3' / 18-24"	○

Microclimate	Planting Time / Bloom Time	Comments
Hardy	Spring / *Summer*	Back of border; average soil; deer-resistant
Hardy; seashore-tolerant	Spring / *Summer - fall*	Borders; easy to grow; bloom over long season
Hardy; heat-tolerant	Spring / *Summer*	Borders; fragrant foliage; moist soil; tolerates clay soil; attracts butterflies; deer-resistant
Hardy; wet soils	Spring or fall / *Spring - summer*	Borders, water's edge; moist soil; spreads rapidly
Very hardy; seashore- and drought-tolerant	Spring / *Early summer*	Borders, edging, herb gardens; fragrant; well-drained soil; shear for second bloom
Hardy; some drought-tolerant; seashore-tolerant	Spring / *Summer*	Borders, rock garden; fragrant; well-drained, thin soils
Very hardy; prefers long, cold winters; provide shade in areas with hot summers	Fall / *Spring - early summer*	Borders; fragrant; deep soil, enriched with compost and lime; deer-resistant
Hardy; seashore-, heat- and drought-tolerant	Spring or fall / *Summer - late summer*	Borders, cut flowers; well-drained soil; deer-resistant
Very hardy	Spring / *Summer*	Borders; fragrant; well-drained soil; attracts butterflies; deer-resistant
Very hardy	Spring / *Late summer - fall*	Borders, cut flowers; sandy soil; invasive in moist, light soil; attracts butterflies
Hardy; seashore-tolerant	Spring or fall / *Summer*	Borders, cut flowers; easy to grow; tolerant of most moist soils; many cultivars
Hardy; drought-intolerant	Spring / *Late spring*	Woodland, stream gardens; among easiest to grow; self-seeds, creating colonies, especially in wet places
Very hardy; seashore-, drought- and humidity-tolerant	Spring or fall / *Summer - fall*	Borders, cut flowers; any well-drained soil; cut to encourage bloom; attracts butterflies; deer-resistant
Hardy; drought- and humidity-tolerant	Spring or fall / *Summer*	Borders, mass plantings, cut flowers; any well-drained soil; deer-resistant

Perennials

Best Bets For Your Garden

above left: Stokesia laevis 'Blue Danube'

above right: Sedum spectabile 'Meteor'

below left: Digitalis purpurea 'Excelsior hybrids'

below right: Bellis perennis

Botanical Name Common Name	Color	Height Spacing	Sun/ Shade
Scabiosa caucasica Scabiosa	White, lavender	18-30" 1-2'	○
Sedum spectabile Showy stonecrop	Pink, red	18-24" 18-24'	○ ◑
Solidago hybrids Goldenrod	Light to deep yellow	18-36" 12-18"	○ ◑
Stokesia laevis Stokes' aster	White, pink, blue	1-2' 12"	○ ◑
Veronica spicata Speedwell	White, pink, blue	12-18" 12"	○ ◑
Viola odorata Violet	White, purple	6" 6"	◑
Yucca filamentosa Adam's needle	White	4-6' 2-3'	○
BIENNIALS 5, 6, 7			
Bellis perennis English daisy	White, pink	6" 8"	○ ◑
Campanula medium Canterbury bells	White, pink, blue, lilac	2' 12"	○
Dianthus barbatus Sweet William	Pink, rose, red, salmon	8-18" 9"	○
Digitalis purpurea Foxglove	Many colors	1-2' 12"	○ ◑
Myosotis 'Blue Ball' Forget-me-not	Blue	8" 6"	◑
Papaver nudicaule Iceland poppy	White, red, yellow	8-12" 8"	○

Microclimate	Planting Time / Bloom Time	Comments
Very hardy	Spring or fall *Summer*	Borders; cut flowers; rich, well-drained, alkaline soil; moderate water; attracts butterflies; try 'Butterfly Blue' for long bloom
Hardy; drought-tolerant	Spring *Late summer - early fall*	Borders, rock gardens; average soil; in South requires good winter drainage; attracts butterflies; deer-resistant
Very hardy; seashore- and drought-tolerant	Spring or fall *Late summer - fall*	Borders, cut flowers; all well-drained soils, tolerates clay soil; attracts butterflies; deer-resistant
Hardy; drought- and humidity-tolerant	Spring *Early summer*	Borders, cut flowers; light, sandy soil
Hardy; seashore-tolerant	Spring or fall *Summer*	Borders; edging; well-drained soil; tolerates alkaline soil; long-blooming; deer-resistant
Hardy	Spring or fall *Spring*	Edging; fragrant; rich, moist soil; fertilize with bone meal; deer-resistant
Hardy; drought-, heat-, seashore- and humidity-tolerant	Spring *Summer*	Evergreen; fast-draining soil; plants may not bloom annually
Hardy	Fall *Spring - early summer*	Edging, cut flowers, companions to bulbs; perennial treated as biennial
Hardy; winter protection in Zone 5	Spring or fall *Spring - early summer*	Borders, cut flowers; any rich, well-drained soil; can be transplanted in full flower and removed after bloom
Hardy; seashore-tolerant	Sow in early summer *Spring*	Borders, cut flowers, containers; well-drained, slightly alkaline soil
Hardy	Fall *Early summer*	Borders, cut flowers; reseeds; moist soil; tolerates clay soil; deer-resistant
Hardy	Sow in fall *Spring*	Woodland and spring gardens; lovely with bulbs, cut flowers; rich, moist, well-drained soil; deer-resistant
Hardy	Sow in fall *Early summer*	Borders, cut flowers; colorful dainty blossoms; many soils

Michael H. Dodge

ROSES

Rosa 'Heritage,' English rose

Roses are among the most loved and beautiful plants in the garden. Yet many gardeners are afraid to include them in their gardens for fear they won't grow. But roses have survived many centuries in varying climates, so there's bound to be one that's just right for your garden.

Gardeners everywhere are discovering that roses are among the most elegant yet versatile plants in the garden. Ranging from white to deep burgundy, yellow and orange, roses come in all shapes and sizes. Some climb while others crawl; some grow stiff and upright while others sprawl. Roses can be single or double, have many petals or just a few, have blossoms 4" across or as tiny as a thimble. Some grow alone on straight stems while others grow in full, showy clusters. There are hardy roses, roses that tolerate shade, and roses that bloom all summer long. For years of immeasurable pleasure, select the right rose for your garden.

flat

rounded

cupped

rosette

pointed

quartered

urn-shaped

pompom

Rose flower shapes: Rose blossoms are either single with four to seven petals; semidouble with eight to fourteen petals; double with fifteen to thirty petals or fully double with over thirty petals. While single roses may be either flat or cupped; the many-petaled roses come in a variety of shapes.

Plant a rose beside a walk, around a terrace or beneath a window where its lovely fragrance will ride the wind, delighting everyone in its path. Grow roses as standards (tree roses) to bring the fragrance up to nose level or give height to the garden. Train climbing roses up pillars and along chains, over arbors and trellises; let them soften the hard lines of a fence or sprawl over a wall. Add a touch of romance to an orchard by encouraging a rose to climb up into the gnarled branches of an old apple tree. Use groundcover roses in mass plantings and to cover a slope. Plant shrub roses close together to form an impenetrable hedge. Plan a formal rose garden or find a spot for them with your perennials. Everyone loves a bouquet of roses, and as potpourri, rose petals are hard to beat.

Grow Roses:
- In formal beds and borders
- In informal mass plantings
- To climb over walls, fences and arbors
- To edge a path
- As flowering hedges
- As flowering groundcovers
- As accents in the perennial or shrub border
- In your cutting garden
- In pots and planters

ROSE ROUNDUP
Roses are categorized into three basic groups: Species, Old and Modern. Climbers span all three.

Species Roses
The original roses, found in the wild, are the hardiest roses, tolerant of poor soil and shade and resistant to salt spray, pollution and disease. Species roses require very little care and can grow like wildfire.

RUGOSA ROSES Grown on their own roots, indisputably the hardiest, and most successful in cold, difficult conditions. These large, dense, fragrant shrubs with handsome crinkled foliage withstand the abuses of wind and salt beautifully. Ranging in color from white to red and pink, their large hips and colorful fall color put on a show over a long period.

Today there are many notable hybrid rugosas. 'Hansa,' a very hardy, vigorous rugosa with fragrant, double magenta blooms, is an all-time favorite. 'Frau Dagmar Hastrup,' a single pink, is very fragrant and tolerates saline soil, salt air, wind and drought. 'Blanc Double de Coubert,' a vigorous, double white, is disease resistant, but definitely does not like wet feet. (*Up to 8' high*)

HINT: If you have very sandy soil, try rugosa roses.

SPECIES ROSES Found growing naturally, they have fragrant, simple blossoms reminiscent of apple blossoms. Spring-blooming, they require little care to succeed. *Rosa acicularis*, a native of the Colorado plains, has medium pink blooms and is drought-tolerant. The foliage of *Rosa eglanteria* has a lovely apple-and-spice fragrance. For a good display of hips that lasts through the winter, try *Rosa virginiana*. (*Up to 6' high*)

Old Roses

Defined as roses in existence prior to the 1867 recognition of hybrid tea roses. Often very fragrant, these decorative roses may bring back memories of your grandmother's garden. Look for a full burst of bloom in the late spring.

ALBA ROSES Not all albas are white! Hardy to Zone 4, they have healthy blue-green foliage. The pink to white blooms are nonrecurrent, usually opening in June in Zones 6 and 7 and July in Zone 5. Albas range from the full cabbage type to almost single. In damp climates the double blossoms of 'Maiden's Blush' may rot before fully opening. *Rosa* x *alba semi-plena*, with its semidouble blooms, long arching canes and red hips, is wonderfully fragrant. (*Up to 5' high*)

BOURBONS Vigorous shrubs, most are hardy to Zone 6 yet can withstand summer's high temperatures. They put on a fabulous display of large, incredibly fragrant blooms in late spring with fewer but even bigger blooms later in the summer. They are more susceptible to blackspot, but many think the blooms are so incredible, it is worth it. Try the double white 'Boule de Neige,' which is less prone to blackspot, or 'Honorine de Brabant,' one of the hardier Bourbons. (*Up to 8' high*)

DAMASK ROSES Very old garden roses with extraordinary fragrance. Most are strong growers with double blooms in colors from crimson to white. Blooms are loose and open, borne in bunches, but usually bloom only once. Beware the blossoms of damasks; they can be messy on hot days. The many-petaled 'Madame Hardy' is an exquisite white with a distinctive green eye. 'Hebe's Lip' has fragrant, semidouble, cream blooms edged in rose with apple-scented foliage. (*Up to 4' high*)

GALLICA ROSES The oldest of the cultivated roses, most have an old-fashioned, many-petaled bloom. Gallicas are winter hardy to Zone 4, very fragrant and available in a palette of crimsons, lavender, mauve and purple. They tolerate poor and sandy soils and form a bushy, compact shrub. Most are one-time bloomers, so can tolerate some shade later in the summer. The many-petaled varieties such as 'Belle Isis' prefer drier weather to open properly. 'Charles de Mills,' one of the most vigorous gallicas, flourishes in Zone 5. Its large, double and quartered blooms are a wonderful mix of deep crimson, purple and mauve. (*Up to 4' high*)

HINT: Old roses are more tolerant of alkaline soil.

Modern Roses

The fascination with modern roses began in 1867 with the introduction of 'La France,' which is accepted as the first hybrid tea. It was the first rose to combine the fragrant, large flowers of hybrid perpetuals, the most popular rose of the mid-1800's, with the long stems and everblooming habit of the tea rose. Elegant in the formal garden and excellent as a cut flower, it was a hybridizer's dream come true and marked the beginning of the craze for new roses.

FLORIBUNDAS Hardy and disease-resistant, floribundas come in shades from white and yellow to pink and carmine. Free-flowering with multiple blooms per stem, a mass of floribundas adds a big splash of color to the garden. New varieties are so easy to grow, 'French Lace' is growing in Times Square! Among the most fragrant are the yellow 'Sunsprite' and the elegant blush-white 'Margaret Merril.' Flesh pink 'Gruss an Aachen' does very well in light shade. 'Europeana' is an excellent ruby red floribunda. Floribundas need extra winter protection in Zone 5. *(Up to 4' high)*

GRANDIFLORAS Grandifloras have blooms similar to hybrid teas, but in clusters. The buds open quickly and bloom repeatedly, making them a good choice for mass plantings. 'Queen Elizabeth,' a delicate pink, deserves a place in any rose garden. 'Gold Medal' retains its color in hot weather. *(Up to 6' high)*

HYBRID TEA ROSES The excellent cut flowers we're all familiar with from the florist's, they generally have one bloom per long stem and come in a wide range of colors. Narrow and upright in habit, hybrid tea roses are repeat flowering, but most have little fragrance. Hybrid tea roses do require more care than most other roses. 'Friendship,' a floriferous pink, is recommended for a humid environment, while coral red 'Fragrant Cloud' is one of the more disease-resistant and easy to grow. *(Up to 4' high)*

> HINT: *To combat fungi on hybrid tea roses, it may be necessary to apply a weekly fungicide.*

MINIATURE ROSES Miniature roses are like hybrid teas and floribundas in every way but size! Growing only 10"-24" high, there are shrub types as well as climbers, trailers and cascading miniatures. They are perfect for planting in containers and as low hedges in the garden. Plant 'Red Cascade' in a hanging basket for a steady stream of crimson flowers. For a hybrid tea form, try the orange-red 'Starina.' *(Up to 2' high)*

POLYANTHAS Hardy and low-growing, polyanthas produce profuse clusters of small flowers. Many bloom continuously! 'The Fairy,' a hardy pink polyantha, is resistant to blackspot and excellent for bedding and low hedges. Pale white 'Marie Pavie' is thornless. *(Up to 2' high)*

Shrub Roses

Shrub roses are easily grown tall shrubs and groundcovers developed for hardiness, disease resistance and low maintenance. Unlike hybrid tea roses, which are grown primarily for the flower, modern shrub roses are grown for the masses of continuous color and overall beauty of the bush. They are often referred to as landscape roses in mail-order catalogs.

SHRUB ROSES Growing naturally broad and high, shrub roses create a dramatic effect in the landscape, and are a welcome addition to the mixed border. Look for David Austin's English Roses, such as 'Heritage,' for their old-fashioned shapes and lovely fragrances. The Meilland roses from France perform well in hedges and mass plantings. 'Bonica' and 'Carefree Wonder' will produce spectacular pink blooms from early spring until frost. *(Up to 6' high)*

GROUNDCOVER ROSES Groundcover roses expand wide, yet remain low. They are an excellent choice for adding low masses of color to the garden. Meilland's 'Alba Meidiland' blooms profusely, is weed-smothering and self-cleaning (does not need deadheading!). 'Red Meidiland' and 'Augusta,' a peach Towne and Country rose, flowers from the ground up. A medium-low spreader, 'Sea Foam' billows with pale pink, double blossoms. *(Up to 2 1/2' high)*

Climbing Roses

Climbing roses don't truly climb! Having no tendrils, they need our help to train them up walls and over supports. These long caned roses are categorized as either climbing or rambling, depending on the flexibility of their canes.

CLIMBING ROSES Climbing roses are long, stiff-caned roses of various parentage. Both single and clustered, most climbers bloom more than once a season. 'New Dawn,' hardy and disease-resistant, is a beautiful, light pink climber that blooms right up to frost. Select 'Golden Showers' for a profusion of perfect yellow blooms from early summer until fall or 'Rhonda' for a summer-long show of double, mid-pink with coral blossoms. (Up to 20' high)

RAMBLING ROSES Most often one-time bloomers, ramblers are commonly distinguished from climbers by their flexible canes, which are ideal for training on arbors, pillars and chains. Ramblers produce smaller leaves than climbers, and the blossoms are usually borne in clusters. 'Seven Sisters,' an old, soft pink rambler hardy to Zone 4, tolerates poor soils and partial sun, yet blooms late in the summer. The extremely hardy and vigorous, red-blossomed 'Chevy Chase' has been known to grow 15' in one year. 'The Garland' has blush-white blooms that fill the air with a heavy orange perfume. (Up to 15' high)

HINT: Don't use wood preservatives near roses.

ROSES IN YOUR MICROCLIMATE

Roses grown in ideal conditions will bring the gardener years of joy, while roses in less favorable conditions will require much more time and energy to succeed. An understanding of your microclimate and a careful selection of the roses for your garden will help reduce the amount of maintenance required for a beautiful display.

TEMPERATURE

In Zones 5, 6 and 7, rose gardeners must be prepared for surprise cold spells as well as weeks of staggering heat. Select roses hardy to your zone and carefully winterize to protect them from freezing soils and winter winds. (See "Winterizing" in this chapter.) In Zone 5 avoid roses that are frost sensitive, yet bud out early. Late spring frosts may burn the tender early growth, causing severe dieback.

Warm temperatures encourage blooming. With hybrid tea roses, the warmer the climate, the bigger the blooms. However, for some roses, scorching heat is another story. Hot temperatures force some single blooms to open too quickly; others wilt yet remain on the bush where they look messy. Some rose bushes drop their leaves altogether to conserve water. There are few things worse than a denuded rose in the midst of an otherwise verdant garden. Water your roses well during long periods of intense heat.

Enjoy the perfume of your roses in the early summer. As the temperature rises, the fragrance will fade. But don't despair; the fragrance will return for an encore in late summer and early fall.

SUN/SHADE

For roses, the type of sunlight is just as important as the amount. Most roses require at least six hours of sunlight a day to produce healthy plants with good blooms, although there are a few that tolerate some shade, including 'Gruss an Aachen,' a floribunda.

Roses flourish in the morning sun; it is cooler and dries the nighttime dew off the leaves, discouraging pests and disease. Hot midday and afternoon sunlight can affect the quality of the blooms by causing their color to fade. Red roses are especially sensitive; their petals can turn blue, called "bluing," when exposed to the summer sun's scorching rays. In warmer areas, afternoon shade helps the blooms retain their color longer. If your roses are growing in sandy soil, try to provide high mid-day shade to counter the loss of water, thus prolonging the life of the bloom and preventing bluing.

WATER

Roses have deep roots. Water thoroughly so water penetrates down through the soil to the *entire* root system. Give roses at least 1" of water per week. If you are irrigating with overhead sprinklers, early morning watering is best; it gives the leaves time to dry off before nightfall. Soaker hoses and water breakers can be used to moisten the soil but not the foliage. For large rose gardens consider installing an irrigation system. Drip systems are best because they keep the leaves dry. If you prefer spray heads, install the heads at a low level.

Don't be surprised if growth and blooming slow down in a drought; the rose is just reserving its supplies. Continue to water your roses until the ground freezes.

HUMIDITY

Careful consideration of the humidity in your microclimate can make or break your rose garden. High levels of humidity can lead to disease and rotting buds. If your garden receives damp ocean winds or coastal fog, put roses that open quickly and are resistant to blackspot and mildew at the top of your list. If your garden is in the interior and less prone to dampness, try the very beautiful, full roses with closely rolled petals. In all microclimates be sure your rose garden has good air circulation so moisture won't settle on the leaves.

SOIL

The ideal soil for roses is a well-balanced garden loam rich in organic matter. Organic matter is critical to the success of your roses. If you have heavy clay or sandy soils, amend the soil well with lots of compost and well-rotted manure. While roses can grow in moist soil, it must be well-drained; they cannot tolerate

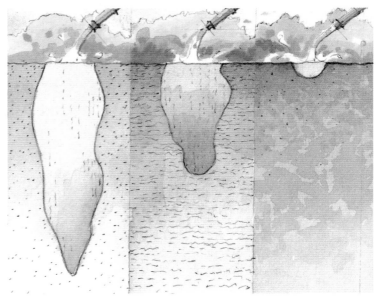

Water penetrates soil at varying rates depending on its composition. Water drains quickly through sandy soil; loam retains water for roots to absorb at their leisure; heavy clay soil is so dense that only a drenching rain will fully penetrate to deep roots.

waterlogged soils. Although roses aren't particular about pH, they do prefer slightly acid soils with a pH of 6.0 to 6.6.

Recipe For Ideal Soil In The Rose Garden

> 60 percent sandy top soil
> 30 percent leaf mold
> 10 percent peat moss

Rose-sick Soil

Rose-sick soil is soil in which roses have been growing for many years. A rose bed suffers from "rose sickness" when young plants added to it grow less vigorously than those previously growing in the same place. Many believe the cause to be soil depletion and possibly disease. Others think the soil structure breaks down over time.

If your home has an existing rose garden, replace the soil in the planting holes prior to adding new roses. If you are planting a lot of new rose bushes, it might be best to change the location of the bed altogether.

PLANNING THE ROSE GARDEN
When planning the rose garden, match the natural habit of the rose to the type of garden. Hybrid teas, floribundas, polyanthas and climbing roses, for instance, fit wonderfully into a formal setting. Large, sprawling roses like species roses are best reserved for informal shrub plantings.

Form the enclosure with a low fence, trellis or posts with chains on which to grow climbing roses. Lay the beds out in a formal, geometric design. Beds that are 5' wide accommodate four rows of hybrid teas set 18" apart with easy access for maintenance. Add accents of evergreen topiary, rose standards or arches to give the garden height.

Spacing
Each type of rose has its own natural growth habits that determine the spacing between plants. In microclimates with high humidity, space the bushes 6" further apart to allow for better air circulation, which will reduce the incidence of mildew. But in general, space as follows:

Hybrid Teas, Floribundas, Grandifloras: 2' apart; up to 3' in humid microclimates
Large Shrubs: 4'-6' apart
Climbing Roses: 6' apart
Miniature Roses: 12" apart
*Hedge*s: Large shrub roses: 3'-4' apart in a line; modern bush roses: 18"-24" in two staggered rows.

Rose Companions
Some of my favorite companions in the rose garden include:

Artemisia	*Campanula* (bellflower)
Clematis	*Dianthus*
Digitalis (foxglove)	*Gypsophila* (baby's breath)
Iris	*Lavandula* (lavender)
Nepeta x *faassenii* (catmint)	*Paeonia* (peony)
Salvia	

PLANNING AT A GLANCE
Consider the following when you select your roses:
- Microclimate
- Soil
- Water supply
- Natural habit of roses: compact, upright, sprawling or climbing
- Height and width
- Spacing
- Period of bloom: one-time, repeat or everblooming
- Color of blooms and leaves
- Significance of rose hips
- Roses that tolerate late spring frosts
- In areas with hot summers, slow-opening roses
- In damp microclimates, quick-opening single roses with fewer petals, and roses resistant to blackspot and mildew
- Amount of maintenance required
- Companion plants

BED PREPARATION
Good drainage and deep, rich soil are essential in the rose garden. Prepare the beds to a depth of 24" by single or double digging (see "Digging the Bed," Chapter 2). If the soil is waterlogged, raise the beds to gain 24" of well-drained soil, and install the necessary drainage beneath the bed. Or find another sunny site.

BUYING ROSES

Your goal when buying roses is to buy strong, healthy plants, appropriate for your climate. Roses are grown either on their own roots or are grafted onto a different root stock. (The joint is known as a bud union.) They are sold either bare-root (dormant, with no soil around the roots) or planted in containers.

> HINT: *Protect your roses from shrubs and trees with invasive roots. Roses are heavy feeders and can't stand competition.*

Bare-root Roses

Mail-order catalogs provide a large selection of bare-root roses, both old and new. Buy from a reputable supplier known to ship well-packed roses with at least three canes, and roots that are in proportion to the top growth. See "Sources" for a list of suppliers and remember to place your order early as supplies are limited. Bare-root roses are usually shipped at the appropriate planting time for your area, and should be planted immediately. If this isn't possible, heel them into the garden or store them in a cool, dark place. Don't be concerned if the roses are coming from another part of the country, such as Texas. If the rose you have selected is compatible with your conditions, it will settle right in, often more quickly than container-grown plants.

> HINT: *Read the directions on the package and never leave bare-root roses unwrapped.*

Container Roses

Your local nursery may have a good selection of roses in containers. Nurseries get a headstart by potting up bare-root roses in mid-winter for sale in the spring. Container-grown roses are graded as follows:

Number 1: The best quality with sound roots and three or four vigorous canes.

Number 1-1/2: Fewer canes and intermediate quality.

Number 2: The least developed, will need more care to establish.

For plants with the best root development, buy roses growing in at least a two-gallon, or preferably a five-gallon, container. Don't be surprised if your container-grown roses take longer to become established in your garden. Their roots have been confined and may not spread out into the surrounding soil as quickly as bare-root plants. Container-grown roses can be planted any time the ground isn't frozen.

When buying container-grown roses, look for:
- "All American Rose Selections"
- Number 1 container-grown plants
- Healthy, vigorous plants with three to five canes
- Roses that are pest free
- Climbers with vigorous canes at least 1' high
- Plants with developed root systems in two- or preferably five-gallon containers; the bigger, the better!

and avoid:
- Plants with yellow leaves or blackspot
- Plants that are potbound (Check to see if roots are growing out of the bottom of the pot)

PLANTING

Planting your roses with care will give them the strength they need to survive in your climate. The best times to plant in Zones 5, 6 and 7 are March to May or October and November. However, if you will be planting in May, you should only plant container-grown roses, not bare-root. Planting in fall just as the roses are heading into dormancy can lessen the shock of transplanting. In Zone 5, spring planting allows roses to become established before the winter sets in.

> HINT: *Don't spread fireplace ashes on desert rosebeds. Ashes are very alkaline as are desert soils.*

Prior To Planting

For bare-root roses, soak the roots in a bucket of muddy water for a few hours to make them less brittle and more pliable. The mud will adhere to the roots and protect them from drying out. Prune off any damaged or broken roots or canes.

HINT: Never plant a dried-out rose bush. Bury the entire bush, canes and all, for several days to resuscitate the canes before planting.

The Planting Hole

Dig each hole 18"-24" deep and 18" wide; if you have a drainage problem, go 6" deeper to accommodate gravel and perforated pipe. Mix a spade of compost and a spade of well-rotted manure into the hole and add the soil you've set aside.

FOR BARE-ROOT ROSES, make a mound with your soil mix in the bottom of the hole. Gently fan the roots over it in a natural pattern.

FOR CONTAINER ROSES, first prune off any blooms or buds to channel all the plant's energy into establishing new roots, then gently remove the plant, retaining as much of the soil around the roots as possible and place in the hole without delay.

HINT: Some gardeners assure me that placing a medium-size fish head in the bottom of the hole and covering it with an inch of soil will give a rose an extra boost.

The Depth

Roses on their own roots should be planted at the depth that they were grown in the nursery. The amount of freezing weather you can expect determines the depth for grafted roses. In Zones 5, 6 and 7, position the bud union 1"-2" below the surface to protect it from freeze-thaw cycles.

HINT: Don't use straight chicken manure; it is too hot and will burn your plant's roots.

In your moderate zone, plant budded roses with the bud union 1" to 2" deep. Plant roses grown on their own roots at the same depth as they were growing in the container.

The Coverup

Hold the rose in place and gradually fill the hole with soil mix. Work the soil around the roots and gently tamp it to eliminate any air pockets. Water the bush in thoroughly. If the soil has compacted further, add more of your soil mix until it is level with the surrounding grade. Mound mulch high around the canes to prevent them from drying out due to the effects of sun and spring winds. Gradually break down the mound in the spring as new growth becomes evident. If planting in the fall, leave the mound for winter protection.

FERTILIZING

Do not fertilize roses when you first plant them. Wait for the first blooming, then apply monthly. If you plant with manure, fertilize after the second flush. For established roses, apply granular 10-6-4 fertilizer when first growth begins in the spring, after the first blooming period, then monthly until August. Roses need a chance to harden off before they face the winter. Epsom salts contain magnesium, which promotes healthy foliage, roots and canes. Using a hand fork, work two table-spoons into the soil around the base of each plant after the first blooming and a month before your first frost date.

Foliar feeding is liquid fertilizer that is sprayed on the leaves; it gives roses an extra push, particularly roses in planters. Applied in addition to granular fertilizer, it is easily absorbed by the leaves, giving them good color and encouraging flowering. Use liquid seaweed or fish emulsion and spray it on your roses every ten days.

If leaves look light with dark veins, your rose is most likely suffering from iron deficiency. Apply a foliar feeding of chelated iron.

HINT: Manure tea (one part manure to five parts water) is also an excellent fertilizer for roses.

MULCH

Use a light mulch that breaks down readily, such as well-rotted manure, shredded leaf mold, or licorice root. Avoid buckwheat or other seed hulls, which decompose slowly, or bark chips, which cause water to splash up on the leaves.

TRAINING CLIMBING ROSES

Climbing roses are perfect for adorning bare walls and fences. Because climbers bloom on laterals, it is important to train climbers in a horizontal position to encourage the development of laterals. The more laterals, the more blooms.

Since roses do not have tendrils with which to grab hold, it is necessary to provide support with wires and masonry hooks. Space horizontal wires 15" to 18" apart and 3" from the surface to allow for air circulation. If growing climbing roses against a painted fence or wall, attach galvanized wire mesh over the surface and train roses on mesh. When it comes time to repaint, just fold the wire down. Use jute or cotton string to attach climbers and ramblers to wires or structures.

If training roses against a house, note the drip line of the eaves. Plant roses about 18" out to avoid the dry area beneath the eaves and the runoff from water draining off the eaves. Dig an extra wide hole for the rose, position it at a 45° angle leaning toward the wall with its roots aiming out toward the moist soil. Spread climbers out in a fan shape so the canes are horizontal.

As ramblers have more flexible canes than climbers, they are your best choice for training on arches, pillars or chains. At the beginning of the growing season, remove all but two or three healthy canes and wrap them around the structure. In this way you gain the maximum horizontal exposure.

PRUNING

There's a great stigma surrounding the pruning of roses. Don't let it scare you. Pruning isn't a case of life or death for you or your roses. You are simply pruning them to improve their performance, appearance, longevity and hardiness.

Don't prune bushes back to the ground. This will waste all the nourishment stored in the canes, forcing the plants to draw on reserves in the roots to support new growth. The reserves in the roots are best used to sustain the canes until the leaves can take over.

HINT: Even with daily pruning, a wide-growing rose will never look well in a small space.

Pruning Goals:

- To remove dead and diseased wood. (Injured wood is dark colored.)
- To remove unproductive, weak and twiggy growth. Cut the oldest canes back to the base of the plant.
- To remove all crossing canes.
- To open up the center of the bush to improve air circulation. Make sure all growth buds are facing away from the center.
- To shape bush to give it a pleasing appearance.
- To encourage repeat bloom.
- To remove suckers, which may grow up at the base of grafted roses.

Pruning Tools

Bypass pruners: For canes up to 1/2" in diameter
Loppers: For canes 1"-2" in diameter
Small hand saw: For any canes over 2"

> *HINT: Sealing the cuts with a dab of white glue or wax keeps out insects and disease.*

PRUNING BUSH ROSES
Where To Cut

Cut at a 45° angle 1/4" above a healthy bud that is pointing away from the center of the bush. Be sure not to cut too close to the bud, which could dry out from exposure, or too far away, which would leave an expanse of dead wood above the bud.

When To Prune

Pruning begins in the early to late spring, when the leaf buds have begun to swell but not grow. Some gardeners adhere to the rule of thumb: "Prune when the forsythia is in bloom," but this is not right for all roses. To determine when to prune, look for your roses in the following list:

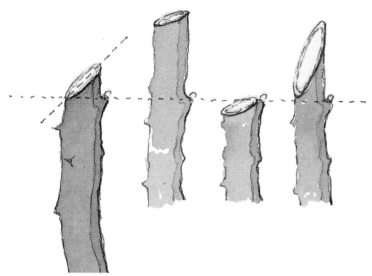

Pruning: (Left to right) A perfect cut; a cut too far away from the bud; a cut too close to the bud; too sharply angled a cut.

SPECIES ROSES Most species roses flower on the second year's growth, so prune to remove dead and diseased wood, thin out crowded stems or to rejuvenate overgrown plants.

RUGOSA ROSES Don't prune for the first three years to establish a basic framework, then prune as for the species or to shape the plant.

GALLICAS, DAMASKS, ALBAS Give these roses a few years of unpruned growth to create a substantial, shapely plant. During these first years remove dead, diseased or crowded canes. Once established, some canes may be removed after flowering, to be replaced by new-growing canes. Deadhead after flowering. Once new canes reach mature length, shape them by trimming back if necessary.

MODERN SHRUB ROSES Prune as for rugosa roses. Keep deadheaded as many will rebloom if this is done.

HYBRID TEA ROSES, GRANDIFLORAS, FLORIBUNDAS, POLYANTHAS, MINIATURES Prune in early spring to remove dead, diseased or crossing canes and to shape the plant. First, remove all dead wood. After severe winters, this can be substantial, leaving only 4"-8" canes, but typically you can expect 12" canes after pruning, 6" on miniatures. During mild winters in these zones, very little damage may occur, allowing for taller plants if desired. Prune off discolored wood, twiggy growth and canes that rub against each other. Remember, you want to keep the center of the rose bush open to allow better air circulation and sun penetration to help reduce disease and promote better growth. Floribundas, polyanthas and miniatures typically have twiggy growth that should only be removed if crowding the center.

PRUNING CLIMBING ROSES

Climbers bloom on laterals, small branches growing off the main canes. Prune climbing roses to control growth, to promote the development of the laterals and to increase bloom.

Where To Cut

Prune as on shrub roses at a 45° angle.

What To Cut

Prevent climbing roses from becoming too dense by removing about one-third of the old canes. To encourage more bloom on repeat-blooming climbers, shorten the tips of the laterals by two-thirds. Cut back the laterals of ramblers and one-time bloomers after they bloom and only if they don't produce rose hips.

> HINT: If growing climbers over structures, prune them more often to keep them under control so they won't grab people walking by.

Keep climbers vigorous by removing one-third of the old canes, and all crossing, weak, dead or diseased canes. Shorten the tips of the laterals by two-thirds.

When To Prune

To rejuvenate climbers, prune them in the early spring at the beginning of the growing season, before the leaves hide the branching habit. Since climbers bloom on year-old wood, flowers will be sacrificed, but often this is necessary. Continue to cut back the laterals of everblooming climbers between periods of bloom throughout the summer. Prune ramblers after they have bloomed.

DISBUDDING

Hybrid teas often produce two or more buds per stem. As one bloom at the end of the stem is preferable for cut flowers, the side buds should be removed. This is called "disbudding." Disbudding eliminates the competition, allowing the single bloom to flourish.

However, if color in the garden is your goal you may prefer not to disbud, for you will have a longer season of bloom.

Disbud your roses when the secondary buds are large enough to hold between two fingers and break off. To disbud, grasp the bud and pull it down and sideways so it snaps off close to the stem. Do not use your fingernails as you will leave a stub behind. Be sure to disbud early! You want all the energy to go to the chosen bloom.

CUT FLOWERS
Roses are among everyone's favorite cut flowers. Cut them early in the morning while the petals are still turgid and place them immediately in water. Remember, when you pick a rose, you are in fact pruning the bush.

Where To Cut
Cut the stem 1/4" above an outward facing leaf with five leaflets, leaving at least two leaf buds between the cut and where the branch joins the main cane.

Cutting Hybrid Teas
Conserve foliage on your hybrid teas. Cut only as much stem as you will need and try not to cut too many long-stemmed flowers on young plants. You will leave them with too little foliage to sustain good growth. The fewer blooms cut the first year the better for the bush.

To Prolong The Life Of Cut Roses
Here are several methods from which to select:
- Hold the stems in boiling water for a minute, then plunge them in a deep container of cold water for several hours before arranging.
- Hammer the ends of the stems and place in warm water.
- Give freshly picked roses a clean cut. Burn the tip of the stem. Plunge the stem into a solution of one tablespoon of alum to one quart of water.
- To salvage drooping blooms, give the stems a fresh cut in deep warm water. This will force the air bubbles out of the stem.

DEADHEADING
"Deadheading" is the removal of flowers well past their prime. On repeat bloomers, remove all faded roses before the petals have fallen. (See "Where To Cut.") This will channel all energy to producing new blossoms, not seed. Only let rose hips develop on one-time bloomers and at the end of the season on modern roses so that they will harden off — the slowing down of their metabolism to prepare them for the cold of fall and winter.

HINT: Do not deadhead albas or rugosas; most set red hips.

WINTERIZING
Protect your roses from low temperatures and damaging freeze-thaw cycles with good winterizing. Begin just before the surface soil starts to freeze after the first heavy frost in the fall. Start by removing all the leaves that have fallen around your plants. Then form a mound of soil (from a source other than the rose bed), compost with some aged manure mixed in or a mix of all three 10"-12" high around their crowns. Be sure you use more soil than organic matter, which holds moisture and could cause rot at the base of the canes. As the ground begins to freeze the soil mound will "knit" with the surface soil, creating greater insulation. Place loose mulch that will not hold moisture, such as salt hay or straw, around the canes of more tender roses to give them extra protection from winter winds and fluctuating temperatures. Remember, no amount of winterizing will protect a weak rose; a healthy plant is the best defense against a cold winter.

Roses

Best Bets For Your Garden

above left: Rosa virginiana, *species*

above right: Rosa 'Hansa,' *hybrid rugosa*

left: Rosa 'Madame Hardy,' *damask*

below: Rosa 'Frau Dagmar Hastrup,' *hybrid rugosa*

Botanical Name/ Common Name	Color	Bloom	Size
SPECIES			
Rosa acicularis	Medium pink	Single	6'x5'
Rosa setigera 'Serena' Prairie rose	Bright pink	Medium single	3-5'
Rosa virginiana Virginia rose	Silvery pink	Single	4'x4'
RUGOSA ROSES			
'Blanc Double de Coubert'	White	Semidouble	5'x4'
'Frau Dagmar Hastrup'	Baby pink	Single	4'x4'
'Hansa'	Mauve	Large double	5'x4'
'Sarah van Fleet'	Clear pink	Large semidouble	7'
GALLICA ROSES			
'Belle Isis'	Light pink	Cupped double	4'x3'
'Complicata'	Rose-pink	Large single	5'x6'
'Tuscany Superb'	Deep crimson	Loosely double	4'x3'
DAMASK ROSES			
'Hebe's Lip'	Cream edged w/rose	Semidouble	5'x3'
'Madame Hardy'	White w/green eye	Double	5'x4'
ALBA ROSES			
x *alba semi-plena*	White	Single	6'x5'
'Celestial'	Clear pink	Double	6'x4'
'Maiden's Blush'	Clear blush	Loosely double	5'x4'
BOURBONS			
'Boule de Neige'	White	Round, double	4-8'
'Honorine de Brabant'	Pinkish white striped w/ violet	Large, cupped and quartered	4'-5'

Microclimate	Bloom Time	Comments
Hardy; drought-tolerant	Late spring; no repeat	Informal screen; arching canes; bright red hips; native of Colorado Plains
Hardy	Late spring	Screen; long, graceful canes; clusters; no fragrance; red foliage and orange hips in fall; long-lasting blooms; disease-resistant; native to north Texas
Hardy	Early - midsummer	Screen; airy; handsome, glossy foliage; holds hips through winter
Hardy; seashore- and wind-tolerant	Repeat	Hedges, screen, mass plantings; heavy fragrance; dark green foliage
Hardy; seashore-, wind-, drought-tolerant	Early summer; deadhead for repeat	Hedges, screen, mass plantings; very fragrant; vigorous; tolerates saline soil
Hardy; seashore-tolerant	Early summer; fall repeat	Hedges, screen, mass plantings; very fragrant; large hips; vase-shaped habit
Hardy; seashore-tolerant	Continuous bloom	Hedges, screen, mass plantings; clusters; fragrant; dense shrub; thorny; leathery foliage; needs space
Very hardy	Early summer; no repeat	Hedges, mixed borders; compact; grey-green foliage; very fragrant
Very hardy; shade-tolerant	Early summer; no repeat	Hedges, mixed borders; blooms have lighter eye, golden stamens; fragrant; arching canes; grey-green foliage; tolerates poor soil
Very hardy	Midseason; no repeat	Mixed borders; upright, rounded; bright golden stamens; fragrant; wavy petals; few thorns; dark green foliage
Hardy	Early summer; no repeat	Borders, fences; lovely fragrance; apple-scented leaves; flowers in clusters
Hardy	Early summer; no repeat	Borders, fences; light lemon fragrance; dark green foliage
Very hardy	Early summer	Hedges, back of border; prominent yellow stamens; very fragrant; grey-green foliage; good hips
Very hardy; shade-tolerant	Early summer	Hedges, back of border; dark green foliage; sweet fragrance; tolerant of shade and poor soils
Very hardy	Early summer	Back of border; very lovely bush; sweet fragrance; deep blue-green foliage
Hardy to Zone 6; heat- and drought-tolerant	Midseason; repeats throughout summer	Mass plantings, borders; blooms single and in clusters; intensely fragrant; dark green foliage; not prone to blackspot
Hardy to Zone 6 (5*); heat- and drought-tolerant	Profuse in early summer; lighter repeat	Mass plantings, specimen; distinctive; striping is darker in cool climates; fragrant; vigorous; few thorns; one of the hardiest Bourbons; *with protection

Roses

Best Bets For Your Garden

above left: Rosa 'Fragrant Cloud,' hybrid tea

above right: Rosa 'Queen Elizabeth,' grandiflora

left: Rosa 'Iceberg,' floribunda

below right: Rosa 'Sunsprite,' floribunda

below left: Rosa 'The Fairy,' polyantha

Botanical Name/ Common Name	Color	Bloom	Size
'La Reine Victoria'	Rich pink	Large, cupped	4-6'
HYBRID TEA ROSES			
'Fragrant Cloud'	Coral red	Large double	Medium
'Friendship'	Pink	Large full	Tall
'Mister Lincoln'	Deep red	Large double	Tall
'Sheer Bliss'	Light pink	Medium double	Tall
GRANDIFLORAS			
'Gold Medal'	Gold/orange	Medium double	Tall
'Mount Shasta'	White	Large double	Medium to tall
'Queen Elizabeth'	Clear pink	Large	Tall
'Tournament of Roses'	Pinky beige	Large	Medium
FLORIBUNDA			
'Europeana'	Dark red	Medium double	Low to medium
'French Lace'	Peach-ivory	Large	Small
'Iceberg'	White	Medium double	Medium
'Simplicity'	Mid-pink	Semidouble, flat	Medium
'Sunsprite'	Yellow	Medium	Medium
'Margaret Merril'	Blush white	Large	Medium to tall
POLYANTHAS			
'The Fairy'	Shell pink	Small double	Low
'Marie Pavie'	Pale white	Small	Low

Microclimate	Bloom Time	Comments
Hardy to Zone 6; heat- and drought-tolerant	Midseason; lighter repeat	Cut flowers, mass plantings, specimen; long-lasting; slender bush; clusters; fragrant; soft green foliage; disease-resistant
Hardy; tolerant of cool summers	Summer until frost	Cut flowers; heavy tea fragrance; dark, glossy foliage; easy to grow; disease-resistant
Hardy; humidity-tolerant	Summer until frost	Cut flowers, mass plantings; bushy; fragrant; very floriferous
Hardy; tolerant of cool summers	Summer until frost	Cut flowers, hedge, mass plantings; upright; fragrant; excellent red
Hardy; humidity-tolerant	Summer until frost	Cut flowers, mass plantings; upright; very fragrant; long stems; floriferous
Hardy; tolerant of hot, dry climates; warm, humid climates; cool summers	Summer until frost	Cut flowers, mass plantings; upright; fragrant; free-flowering; lighter bloom in Zone 5; color doesn't fade in hot weather
Hardy	Summer until frost	Cut flowers; upright; light fragrance; leathery leaves; disease-resistant
Hardy; tolerant of hot, dry climates; warm, humid climates; cool summers	Summer until frost	Cut flowers, mass plantings; broad; fragrant; long stems; dark green foliage; all-time favorite; disease-resistant
Hardy; tolerant of hot, dry climates; warm, humid climates; cool summers	Summer until frost	Cut flowers, mass plantings; clusters of blooms; light fragrance; glossy, dark green foliage; disease-resistant
Hardy; tolerant of cool summers	Summer - fall	Mass plantings, hedges; broad; light fragrance; clusters of blooms; low and spreading; disease-resistant
Hardy	Summer - fall	Cut flowers, hedges; graceful bush; dainty bloom; small, dark green leaves; disease-resistant
Hardy; tolerant of cool summers	Summer - fall	Mass plantings, hedges; bushy; fragrant; vigorous and floriferous
Hardy; tolerant of cool summers	Summer - fall	Cut flowers, hedges; dense and upright; produces sprays of blooms; floriferous
Hardy; tolerant of cool summers	Summer - fall	Cut flowers, mass plantings; compact; very fragrant; nonfading; disease-resistant
Hardy	Summer - fall	Cut flowers, hedges; wonderfully fragrant; dark green foliage
Hardy	Summer until frost	Front of border, low hedge, mass plantings; spreading; easy to grow; glossy foliage; prolific and continuous bloom; disease-resistant
Very hardy	Summer until frost	Low hedge, mass plantings; pink centers with golden stamens; thornless, dark foliage; fragrant

Roses

Best Bets For Your Garden

above left: Rosa 'Graham Thomas,' English rose

above right: Rosa 'Carefree Wonder,' shrub

left: Rosa 'Blaze Improved,' climber

below left: Rosa 'New Dawn,' climber

below right: Rosa 'Red Cascade,' climbing miniature

Botanical Name/ Common Name	Color	Bloom	Size
MINIATURE			
'Red Cascade'	Crimson	Small	Low
SHRUB ROSES			
'Bonica'	Light pink	Double	5'x5'
'Carefree Wonder'	Pink/cream reverse	Semidouble	4'x3'
'Graham Thomas'	Rich yellow	Medium, cupped	6'x5'
'Heritage'	Shell pink	Medium, cupped	4'x4'
'Nearly Wild'	Rosy red	Single	3'x3'
GROUNDCOVERS			
'Alba Meidiland'	White	Small	2 1/2'x6'
'Augusta'	Peach	Medium	2'x5'
'Red Meidiland'	Red	Medium single	1 1/2'x5'
'Seafoam'	Pinkish white	Medium double	3'x7'
CLIMBING			
'Blaze Improved'	Red	Large semi-double	Up to 15'
'Golden Showers'	Yellow	Large	Up to 8'
'New Dawn'	Shell pink	Medium double	Up to 10'
'White Cap'	White	Large, cupped	Up to 10'
RAMBLING			
'Chevy Chase'	Red	Small	Up to 15'
'The Garland'	Blush white	Small	15'x10'
'Seven Sisters'	Deep to soft pink	Double	8'
'Veilchenblau'	Violet w/ white streaks	Small semidouble	12'x4'

Microclimate	Bloom Time	Comments
Hardy	Spring until frost	Hanging baskets, miniature climber, groundcover; cascading; blooms best when plant is full size; bright green foliage
Hardy	Late spring until frost	Borders, screen, hedges, mass plantings; clusters; floriferous; orange-red hips; easy care; disease-resistant
Hardy	Late spring until frost	Borders, hedges, screen, mass plantings; compact; floriferous; medium green foliage; orange hips; easy care; disease-resistant
Hardy to Zone 6; heat-tolerant	Summer until frost	Borders, hedges, screen; upright; fragrant; vigorous; reputedly the best of the English roses
Hardy to Zone 6; heat-tolerant	Summer until frost	Borders, mass plantings; bushy; strong fragrance; sprays; dark leathery leaves; a favorite English rose
Hardy	Summer until frost	Borders, mass plantings; bushy; compact; fragrant; wild rose look
Hardy	Late spring until frost	Groundcover; mass plantings; mounding; graceful; clusters; light fragrance; easy care; disease-resistant
Hardy	Summer until frost	Groundcover, mass plantings; uniform; blooms from ground up; disease-resistant
Hardy to Zone 4	Summer until frost	Mass plantings; mounding; vigorous; graceful
Hardy; heat-tolerant	Summer until frost	Groundcover, mass plantings; vigorous; floriferous; impenetrable; disease-resistant
Hardy	All summer	Clusters; light fragrance; vigorous; fast-growing; easy to train; dark, leathery leaves
Hardy; tolerant of cool summers and humidity	Spring to late fall	Trains easily; fragrant; floriferous; glossy foliage
Hardy	Early summer; repeats until frost	Rampant; slight fragrance; floriferous; glossy foliage
Hardy	All summer	Many petaled; fragrant; dark green foliage; easy care
Hardy	Early summer; no repeat	Large clusters; grey-green foliage; vigorous; not susceptible to mildew
Hardy	Early summer; no repeat	Heavy orange fragrance; masses of blooms; dark green foliage; vigorous
Hardy	Late summer; no repeat	Old rambler; large clusters; opens deep pink and fades to almost white; tolerates poor soil and part shade
Hardy	Late season; no repeat	Clusters of small blooms; vigorous

Michael H. Dodge

BULBS, ETC.

Muscari armeniacum

When the first snowdrops poke their little heads out of the snow you know you have reason to be optimistic. Spring is definitely on the way. Bulbous plants are fleeting beauties that make a short and often spectacular appearance before going dormant for the balance of the year. Given good conditions, spring-flowering bulbs such as *Galanthus nivalis* (snowdrop) and *Narcissus* spp. will multiply quickly, forming impressive sweeps of color. For some gardeners, planting spring-flowering bulbs each fall has become a family ritual.

Bulbous plants aren't for springtime alone; there are bulbous plants for every season and every location in the garden. They make a wonderful show in herbaceous borders, en masse in formal beds, naturalized under shrubs and trees or as drifts in the lawn. Create an early spring garden in a warm spot near the house or have a container of bulbs to add a bright splash of color to the porch or terrace. Force bulbs for a cheerful display indoors in the middle of winter.

Bulb Cycle: (From left to right) 1) In dormancy the flower bud is surrounded by stored food. 2) Roots form and absorb water, which stimulates leaf growth. 3) The flower blooms while, through photosynthesis, the leaves replenish food supplies in the bulb. 4) After the flower fades, the leaves continue to store food. 5) After the leaves die back, new bulbets form.

WHAT ARE BULBOUS PLANTS?

Bulbous plants gather food from their leaves and store the nutrients in their swollen bases for future plant growth. There are five different categories of bulbous plants:

BULBS (*Tulipa* and *Narcissus*) have an underground stem made up of fleshy scale-like leaves tightly packed around a bud at the center of the bulb. The bulb is attached to a basal plate, has a growing point at its apex and is wrapped in a papery covering called a tunic.

CORMS (*Crocus* and *Gladiolus*) are formed from the swollen bases of stems, often covered with fibrous tunics. Unlike bulbs, corms have distinct nodes and internodes.

TUBEROUS ROOTS (*Dahlia*) have thickened horizontal underground roots.

TUBERS (*Anemone blanda*) are swollen stems that function as storage organs.

RHIZOMES (*Canna* and some *Iris*) have tuber-like stems that store food and produce roots along their length.

TEMPERATURE

Temperature is critical to the success of many bulbous plants. Narcissus and tulips require a cold period to bloom, while tender plants such as *Dahlia* and *Gladiolus* must be protected from freezing temperatures. For specific recommendations, see "Best Bets for Your Garden," p.110.

HINT: Species tulips or select cultivars are longer lasting than hybrids.

SUN/SHADE

Most bulbs prefer full sun to light shade. This isn't a problem for spring-flowering bulbs since they generally bloom and begin to go dormant before the trees have fully leafed out. Plant summer-flowering *Dahlia* and *Gladiolus* in sunny flower beds. Bulbs that grow naturally in the woods, such as *Galanthus nivalis* (snowdrop), *Scilla* spp. and certain species of *Lilium* (lily) are perfect for shade locations.

> *HINT: To extend your spring bulb blooming season, use your microclimates! Plant bulbs in sun pockets for early bloom and cool areas for later bloom.*

SOIL

Well-drained soil is the key to success for all bulbous plants. A bulb planted in a low, overly moist site will most likely rot. If your soil is soggy, try planting your bulbs in raised beds. In clay soil, the addition of organic matter will improve drainage. In sandy soil, add organic matter, such as compost, to help retain moisture. Spring- and fall-flowering bulbs can grow in most types of soil, while summer-flowering bulbs are more particular. The soil in these planting beds should be moderately fertile with a pH of between 6.0 and 7.2.

WATER

Bulbous plants require water during the growing season. Water regularly and deeply until the leaves die back. However, when it comes to water, the dormant season of bulbs is even more important. Spring- and fall-flowering bulbs are dormant during the summer and should not receive too much water during those months. Be especially careful that summer-flowering bulbs do not become waterlogged while dormant during the winter.

> *HINT: If naturalizing bulbs, try to avoid areas with lots of roots that might compete for water and nutrients.*

PLANNING AT A GLANCE

- Microclimate
- Soil
- Water
- Time of bloom
- Color
- Height
- How to disguise the yellowing leaves

> *HINT: Plant quick-growing annuals around bulbs to disguise their fading leaves.*

BUYING BULBS, ETC.

Bulbs are usually sold dry, but occasionally some such as *Lilium* and *Dahlia* are sold in moistened wood shavings or peat moss. They can be sold individually or prepackaged in mesh. Bulbs are available through mail-order catalogs and from local nurseries and hardware stores.

If you're ordering your bulbs through the mail, buy them from a reputable bulb importer (see "Sources"). If you're going to pick them up from a local garden center you will be able to pick and choose. Some tips for selecting healthy bulbs follow:

When buying dry bulbs, look for:

- The largest bulbs: "double-nosed," "top size," "jumbo."
- Bulbs that are firm and dry. As in buying a head of garlic, look for bulbs that feel heavy, not light and dried-out.
- Strong growing points.
- Solid basal plates.
- Tunics that are intact.

and avoid:

- Moldy or rotten bulbs.
- Bulbs with signs of disease, insects or mildew.

When buying other bulbous plants, look for:
- Firm, plump tubers.
- Woodland bulbs that are in moist peat or packing materials.
- Strong growing points on corms.

Mail-order bulbs usually arrive at the correct planting time for your zone. If you're buying bulbs locally, buy them when you are ready to plant. If you do need to store them temporarily, keep them in a cool, dark, dry place.

TIME TO PLANT
Spring-flowering bulbs use the fall to prepare for their early spring performance. They set their roots in the fall, opening up the flow of nutrients, which will ensure a spectacular show. The soil temperature 6" below the soil should be 60º Fahrenheit before you plant, but can be planted any time before the soil freezes. To be their best, many spring-flowering bulbs like *Narcissus* and *Tulipa* must be exposed to a long period of cold. Pot-grown bulbs can be planted any time during the season.

Spring Bulbs
Plant spring bulbs in late September to early October in Zone 5; October to early November in Zones 6 and 7.

Summer Bulbs, Corms And Tubers
DAHLIA Tubers and clumps can be planted one to two weeks before the last frost date. Container plants in leaf should be planted after threat of frost.
GLADIOLUS AND TENDER SUMMER-FLOWERING BULBS Plant *Gladiolus* corms and tender bulbs after all threat of frost.

Fall Bulbs
Plant in late summer to early fall as they become available.

PLANTING DEPTH
The size of the bulb determines its planting depth: the bigger the bulb, the deeper it's planted. A general rule of thumb is to plant at a depth three to five times the height of the bulb. In Zone 5, plant spring-flowering bulbs a little deeper to avoid damage from heaving or the cold. For specific requirements, see the Planting Depth Illustration on the next page.

HINT: For better support, plant tall varieties of Gladiolus *a little deeper than the specified 4".*

SPACING
Spacing should be two to three times the width of the bulb. See "Best Bets For Your Garden" for specific requirements.

PLANTING BULBS AND CORMS
Bulbs and corms are fleshy and damage easily. Take great care not to bruise them when planting. Use a trowel or garden fork for planting small bulbs; a spade, bulb planter or bulb drill for larger bulbs. Bulbs make a great display when clustered together.

Planting Single Bulbs In Beds
Using a trowel, dig a hole to the required depth that is several times wider than the bulb. Place bulb growing point up in the hole, cover with soil and gently tamp with your hands.

Planting Many Bulbs Together In Beds
In well-prepared beds, dig a hole to the required depth large enough to accommodate the number of bulbs. Smooth the bottom of the hole. Place bulbs right side up and carefully cover with soil. Using the flat end of a rake, gently tamp soil. Do not stamp on them with your feet.

HINT: For a natural look, avoid planting in rows.

Bulb Planting Depth: Planting your bulbs at the correct depth in well-prepared soil gets them off to a good start and rewards you with beautiful blooms at the right time.

Planting Single Large Bulbs In A Grassy Area

Consider using a bulb planter or bulb drill for larger bulbs such as *Narcissus*. However, bulb drills won't work in very rocky soil; instead, try a spade. For one or two bulbs, simply insert the spade at a 90º angle as deep as required for the bulb, then push the handle away from you, opening up the soil. Toss in a little bulb fertilizer, place the bulbs, then gently release the soil and tamp it in place.

> *HINT: If you can't tell which side of the bulb is up, plant it sideways. Bulbs will naturally right themselves.*

Planting Many Small Bulbs In A Grassy Area

Use an edger to outline the area, then cut a line down the middle. Using a spade, undercut the sod and gently fold back both sides like opening shutters. Work the exposed soil with a hand fork to the required depth, mix in bulb fertilizer, then gently press the bulbs into the loose soil. Score the back of the sod with a hand fork to loosen the roots, then carefully fold it back into place, working the edges together. Tamp to ensure good root contact.

For very small bulbs, use a garden fork to puncture the sod, pour a little bulb fertilizer in the holes and place a bulb in each hole. Fill the holes with soil.

Planting Bulbs In Layers

Dig the hole to the depth required for the largest bulb, place bulb in hole and cover up to depth for next bulb and continue for the desired number of layers.

PLANTING TUBERS

Dig a hole that provides for the required depth plus room for the roots. The hole should be wide enough for the roots to comfortably spread out. Fill the hole with soil and gently tamp down.

PLANTING TUBEROUS ROOTS

Dig a hole 6" to 8" deep and a good 9" wide. Plant tuberous roots such as *Dahlia* horizontally. Cover with soil. Insert a stake for later support.

PLANTING RHIZOMES

Rhizomes are propagated by division and are planted in much the same way as perennials. To prevent crown rot, plant new divisions or container plants at a slightly higher depth than they were growing. Be sure to spread out the roots of new divisions. Fill hole with soil, water well and let settle. Add more soil to top if needed.

FERTILIZING

Add a covering of compost, manure or 10-10-10 fertilizer in the spring when the leaf tips first appear and again after blooming.

If your perennial bulbs such as *Narcissus* spp. have stopped blooming or produce more leaves than flowers, they are in need of fertilizer, preferably a bulb fertilizer. If you still can't get them to bloom, dig them up and divide them.

> *HINT: Spraying leaves with foliar fertilizer every ten days during the growing season can encourage newly developed offset bulbs to grow to flowering size more quickly.*

DISBUDDING DAHLIA

Dahlia respond beautifully to disbudding. If your goal is one large, glorious flower for arranging, locate the terminal bud and pinch out the buds to the side. This will channel all the energy to developing a larger terminal blossom. Do not disbud if you prefer a full, colorful display in the garden.

CUT FLOWERS

Use sharp scissors to cut flowers right down at base of stems. Place in water immediately.

Special Hints

DAHLIA Place stem ends in boiling water, then arrange in tall vase with a little sugar and an aspirin in the water.

GLADIOLUS Place in solution of one tablespoon alcohol to one quart water.

HYACINTHUS Squeeze slippery substance out of stem, then plunge immediately into cold water.

IRIS Burn tip of stem and immediately plunge in cold water.

NARCISSUS Daffodils and jonquils last longer when "broken," not cut. Grasp the stem at its base where it emerges from the ground and snap it off. In this way the hollow stem is not exposed; the solid stem lasts longer in water. Arrange in low containers; never place in deep water.

DEADHEADING

Deadhead flowering bulbs to prevent seed production. This will direct all the plant's energy into food storage instead of seed production.

CUTTING BACK THE FOLIAGE

Allow the foliage to turn yellow prior to removing it. The longer it remains, the more nutrients it can direct to the bulbs. When the foliage has turned yellow, it can be cut off using hand clippers or scissors, but be careful not to damage the bulbs.

> *HINT: Never tie or braid the foliage. While it may look neat and stylish, it reduces the surface area thereby reducing the amount of food produced.*

DIVIDING BULBS

Small bulbs can be left to multiply indefinitely, but large bulbs such as *Narcissus,* which have not been naturalized, should be divided every five years or so. Lift them after the leaves have yellowed in the late spring. Shake off the soil and pull clumps apart discarding any which show signs of rot. Replant the remaining bulbs, leaving the leaves to nourish the newly divided bulbs.

Tulipa and *Hyacinthus* tend not to multiply in your climate. For continued bloom, they must be replaced.

WINTERIZING

Be sure to dig up tender bulbs before freezing temperatures arrive. For hardy bulbs, apply a light mulch to planting beds.

Lifting And Storing Tender Bulbs

Tender bulbs such as *Gladiolus* and *Dahlia* make excellent cut flowers, while *Caladium* and *Zantedischia* (calla lily) add an exotic touch to containers and herbaceous borders. Potted bulbs must be brought indoors for winter. In the garden, after frost, cut the foliage of tender bulbs to ground level. Lift and clean the clumps. Discard any bulbs with signs of disease or rot. Dust the remaining bulbs with fungicide and store them indoors in a cool (45 to 50º Fahrenheit), dark location in mesh bags or wire-bottomed trays. And don't forget to label them with name *and* color!

Storing Dahlia And Gladiolus

DAHLIA Let the soil dry on the tubers. If you have the space, store them as is; if not, gently knock off the soil, treat with fungicide and place the tubers in perlite or vermiculite in plastic bags with holes in them. Keep an eye on the tubers. If they begin to wither, sprinkle them with water. In the spring, inspect the tubers carefully, discard any that are withered, then cut the clumps into pieces allowing one eye per piece.

GLADIOLUS Remove all the foliage and gently shake off all the soil. Separate and discard the old corm. Hang the new corms in a mesh bag in a dry area with good air circulation.

> *HINT: Do not store bulbs in airtight plastic bags. Moisture can collect and cause the bulbs to rot.*

Bulbs, Etc.

Best Bets For Your Garden

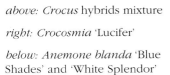

above: Crocus hybrids mixture

right: Crocosmia 'Lucifer'

below: Anemone blanda 'Blue Shades' and 'White Splendor'

Botanical Name Common Name	Key	Color	Height	Spacing	Depth
Allium giganteum Flowering onion	B	Lavender	to 6'	12-14"	8"
Anemone blanda Windflower	T	White, pink, blue, lavender	2-4"	4-6"	3"
Chionodoxa luciliae Glory-of-the-snow	B	Blue	6-8"	3"	2"
Crocosmia spp. Montbretia	C	Orange, yellow, red	18-24"	2-3"	3"
Crocus spp. Crocus	C	White, yellow, purple	2-6"	2-3"	2-3"
Galanthus nivalis Snowdrop	B	White	3-8"	3"	3"
Gladiolus spp. Gladiolus	C	Many colors except blue, bicolor blends	1-3'	6-8"	3-6"
Hyacinthus orientalis Dutch hyacinth	B	White, pink, blue, purple	8-15"	6-8"	6"
Lilium spp. Lily hybrids	B	All except blue	3-6'	8-12"	6-8"
Lycoris squamigera Spider lily	B	Rose pink	15-18"	6-9"	5"
Muscari armeniacum Grape hyacinth	B	Blue	6-12"	3-4"	3-4"
Narcissus spp. Daffodil	B	White, orange, yellow or tricolor	8-20"	3-6"	3-6"
Scilla siberica Siberian squill	B	Dark blue	4-6"	6"	3-4"
Tulipa spp. Tulip	B	All colors, except blue	6-30"	6"	6"

Key: Bulb (B); Corm (C); Tuber (T)

Sun/Shade	Microclimate	Planting Time / Bloom Time	Comments
○ ◐	Hardy; seashore-tolerant	Spring or fall *Summer*	Borders, cut flowers; light, moist, well-drained soil; attracts butterflies; deer-resistant
○	Hardy; seashore-tolerant; mulch in Zone 5	Fall *Early spring*	Naturalizes well
○ ◐	Hardy; seashore-tolerant	Fall *Early - midspring*	Naturalizes in woodlands, rock gardens; deer-resistant
○	Hardy to Zone 6, lift annually in Zone 5	Early spring *Early fall*	Cut flowers, borders; well-drained soil
○	Hardy; seashore-tolerant	Fall *Early - midspring*	Mass plantings; naturalizes well; well-drained soil; deer-resistant
○ ◐	Very hardy; seashore-tolerant	Fall *Early - midspring*	Naturalizes well; deer-resistant
○	Frost to half-hardy; lift half-hardy bulbs annually in early fall	Spring *Summer until frost*	Cut flowers; plant at 10-day intervals to extend blooming season; rich, moist, well-drained soil; many hybrids
○	Hardy, prefers cold winters	Fall *Early - midspring*	Bedding, containers; fragrant
○ ●	Hardy	Fall or early spring *Spring and summer*	Borders, cut flowers; fragrant; deep, loamy, well-drained soil; deep mulch; divide in fall only when bulbs become overcrowded; fertilize in spring; attracts butterflies
◐	Hardy to Zone 6	Fall *Late summer*	Borders, cut flowers; fragrant; well-drained, rich soil; tolerates alkaline soil
○ ◐	Hardy; seashore-tolerant	Fall *Mid - late spring*	Naturalizes well; plant in large numbers for best effect; deer-resistant
○ ◐	Hardy; seashore-tolerant	Fall *Mid - late spring*	Mass plantings, cut flowers; fragrant; naturalizes well; tolerates alkaline soil; deer-resistant
○ ◐	Very hardy; seashore-tolerant	Fall *Mid - late spring*	Mass plantings; naturalizes well; mulch in fall; deer-resistant
○ ◐	Hardy; seashore-tolerant	Midwinter *Mid - late spring*	Borders, beds, cut flowers; rich sandy soil; replant annually; plant 12" deep for more years of blooms

For additional bulbous plants, refer to the Annual and Perennial plant lists.

Erik Simmons

IV

GREENSCAPES

Vines
Ornamental Grasses
Groundcovers
Shrubs

VINES

Hedera helix 'Baltica'

Vines are the "garnish" of the garden. They are excellent for softening the hard lines of fences or posts, house corners and entrances, and are often perfect for hiding an architect's mistakes! With their often lush foliage, showy fruit and fragrant flowers, vines add a touch of romance to the garden, and in nonblooming trees, vines add a splash of color. A wisteria-covered pergola is a refreshing destination on hot summer days. As vines take up little planting space — only 6" — vines are also a small garden's best ally.

Whatever the requirements of your garden, there's a vine for you. Some are annuals, others perennials or evergreen; some are herbaceous, others are woody; some are blooming, others are not; some have large, exotic leaves, others have small leaflets. What all vines do have in common is that although they like to climb, they do require support to continue their upward growth.

Vines climb by different means: (Clockwise from top left) Twining stems wrap around their supports; tendrils spiral around anything they touch; disks and rootlets hold fast to stone and wood vertical surfaces.

HOW VINES CLIMB

Vines are categorized by the means by which they climb: twining, tendrils, or clinging rootlets. Twining vines, such as *Akebia quinata* (five-leaf akebia), *Polygonum aubertii* (silver lace vine) and *Wisteria*, climb by stems that twine around their supports. Others, such as *Parthenocissus quinquefolia* (Virginia creeper) and *Lathyrus latifolius* (everlasting sweet peas), have tendrils, which twist around supports to climb. Clinging vines have two kinds of rootlets that attach to surfaces: hair-like and disks. *Hedera helix* (English ivy), *Euonymus fortunei radicans* (wintercreeper) and *Campsis radicans* (trumpet vine) are aerial root climbers with hairlike rootlets. *Parthenocissus tricuspidata* 'Veitchii' (Boston ivy) and *Hydrangea anomala petiolaris* (climbing hydrangea) cling to surfaces by means of adhesive disks.

Grow Vines:
- To provide vertical interest in your garden
- To soften hard lines of fences and garden walls
- To obscure unattractive structures (like chainlink fences)
- To provide temporary shade in the summer
- To add interest to blank building walls
- To frame an entranceway
- To add colorful height to small gardens
- To bring fragrance up to nose level
- On fences, pillars, posts, pergolas, arbors and in trees

SUN/SHADE

Most flowering vines prefer sun, although some, like *Lathyrus latifolius* (everlasting sweet pea), *Lonicera japonica* 'Halliana' (Hall's honeysuckle), *Lonicera sempervirens* (trumpet honeysuckle) and *Polygonum aubertii* (silver lace vine) can withstand partial shade, although the flowering may not be as prolific. Most of the vines that thrive in shade are nonflowering, such as *Hedera helix* (English ivy), *Parthenocissus tricuspidata* (Boston ivy), *Euonymus fortunei radicans* (wintercreeper) and *Parthenocissus quinquefolia* (Virginia creeper), with the exception of *Akebia quinata* (five-leaf akebia). *Akebia quinata* is also a good choice for east- or north-facing locations.

TEMPERATURE

Vines are sensitive to heat and cold. Most require warm weather to grow and bloom, then go dormant with the arrival of cold weather. The amount of cold determines whether a vine is deciduous or evergreen. *Lonicera japonica* 'Halliana' (Hall's honeysuckle), which is evergreen in warm-winter areas, is semievergreen in Zone 5.

HUMIDITY

Good air circulation is critical if you live in a humid area. If you would like to grow vines against a wall, be sure the supports or wires are raised a few inches from the surface to allow for air circulation behind the vine.

SOIL
Since vines can grow up to 50' long in one season, they need vigorous root systems to provide them with nonstop nourishment. Rich, deep, well-drained soil will help your vines flourish. Most vines are pH adaptable, but some, such as *Campsis radicans* (trumpet vine), are especially tolerant of alkaline soils. *Actinidia kolomitka* (Arctic beauty kiwi) has less variegation in its leaves in acid soil.

WATER
All vines require ample water until they are established and most prefer regular water to thrive. A few, such as *Parthenocissus quinquefolia* (Virginia creeper), *Parthenocissus tricuspidata* (Boston ivy) and *Polygonum aubertii* (silver lace vine), tolerate drought conditions. Vines grown against western walls, which receive hot afternoon sun, will require additional water.

PLANNING FOR VINES
Leaf texture, flower, fragrance, season of bloom, growth rate and whether a vine is deciduous or evergreen are all primary considerations when selecting vines. Vines chosen incorrectly can be disappointing or get out of hand, becoming more of a nuisance than a pleasure.

When selecting vines for your garden, first ask yourself what the vine's purpose will be. This will help you select the one that best suits your needs. As rampant growers, such as *Lonicera* (honeysuckle) and *Polygonum aubertii* (silver lace vine) have a tendency to take over, they are not the best choice for small gardens. *Clematis* would be a better choice. The delicate foliage of *Akebia* works well on small arbors, while the large leaves of *Wisteria* look good against large structures. Beware of training tendril climbers such as *Parthenocissus*

quinquefolia (Virginia creeper) on shingle siding as they tend to creep under shingles and hold on voraciously. Ivies, such as *Parthenocissis quinquefolia* 'Saint-Paulii' and *Parthenocissus tricuspidata* 'Veitchii' (Boston ivy), are equipped with strong gripping discs and grow extremely well on stone surfaces.

SPACING
Most vines should be planted 3' to 5' apart. Vigorous growers such as *Wisteria* and *Campsis* (trumpet vine) should be planted 6' to 10' feet apart.

PLANNING AT A GLANCE
- Microclimate
- Sun/shade
- Soil
- Water
- Use of vine
- Evergreen or deciduous
- Ultimate size
- Growth rate
- Spacing
- Means of attachment
- Foliage size and texture
- Flower color and time of bloom
- Fruit color and season

BED PREPARATION
For perennial vines, dig a hole 1' to 2' deep and 1-1/2' to 2' wide and amend the soil as necessary. See "Soil" in the appropriate chapter.

BUYING VINES
Most vines are sold in containers, although some deciduous vines are also available as bare-root plants. To select a healthy plant, refer to "Buying Perennials" on p.64 and do look for vigorous plants with several healthy stems.

PLANTING

Spring is the best time to plant woody perennial vines as it allows enough time for them to become established prior to the summer heat. For planting bare-root or container plants, see "Planting" in "Perennials," p.65.

TRAINING VINES

How you train a vine is determined by how it grows. Vines with aerial roots and adhesive discs need just a bit of encouragement to climb on their own, while scramblers require tying. As long as there are supports nearby, twining and tendril climbing vines need only be pointed in the right direction.

Use soft twine, green plastic ribbon or plastic clips to attach vines to their supports, taking care not to constrict the stems. If you plan to leave a tie on for more than one growing season, be sure it is loose enough to accommodate future growth. To train vines on brick walls, glue on masonry hooks, which have wires to bend around the stems.

Twining vines naturally twine in either a clockwise or counterclockwise direction. If you are training a twining vine in a set direction, be sure to determine which way it naturally twines before planting it.

Use twining vines on fence posts, pillars, or anything with a small diameter that is strong enough to support the vine. Train tendril climbing vines on wire, lattice or shrubs. Vines with rootlets are best used for covering masonry walls.

FERTILIZING

You can use fertilizer like a gas pedal to control the growth of vines. If you feed a vine regularly, it will grow more quickly; if you hold off on the fertilizer, plant growth will slow down.

Vines that are grown for foliage and flower are generally fertilized in early spring and again in early summer. Fertilize flowering and fruiting vines with a balanced fertilizer such as 12-12-12. Spring-flowering vines will also benefit from a high-phosphorous fertilizer such as 10-20-10 in early fall. Foliage vines prefer a high-nitrogen fertilizer such as 16-4-8 or 15-5-10. Always thoroughly water after fertilizing.

Fertilizing Wisteria

Wisteria has a habit of slowing down flower production, sometimes coming to a complete stop altogether. If your wisteria vines are producing lush foliage but few blooms, withhold nitrogen fertilizers for a summer to channel the plant's energy from producing leafy growth into the formation of flower buds.

MULCH

Vines, like other perennials, benefit from a 2" layer of light mulch. Some, such as *Clematis*, actually require mulch to keep their roots moist during the summer. Renew the mulch in the fall to moderate the soil's temperature during the cold winter months and to prevent frost heaving.

PRUNING

How you prune a vine is determined by both your pruning goals and the vine's flowering habit. To train most vines, flowering or nonflowering, you will want to prune them in late winter or early spring and then again in the late fall. To increase flower production, prune vines that bloom on the previous year's growth after they have flowered; prune vines that bloom on the current season's growth in the early spring.

While tip pruning (the removal of the ends of the branches) will provide temporary shaping for moderate growers, vigorous vines require regular removal of entire stems to avoid the inevitable tangled mess. If the stems are intricately entwined, cut the stem you wish to remove in several places to untangle it. And remember, pruning encourages new growth. Avoid stimulating new, tender growth by pruning heavily in the early fall when plants should be slowing down in preparation for the winter.

When starting with young plants, you may have to wait two to three years for them to grow enough to establish a framework. Just a light pruning may be all that's necessary to shape and direct their growth.

Pruning Vines

AT INSTALLATION AND TO ENCOURAGE DENSE BRANCHING AT GROUND Locate the two or three healthiest stems and cut them back by one-half.

BLOOMERS ON THE CURRENT SEASON'S GROWTH To maintain an established vine, determine the framework for the vine's growth and cut it back to this framework each winter.

BLOOMERS ON THE PREVIOUS SEASON'S GROWTH To maintain an established vine, after flowering in the spring, remove all shoots that have flowered. Cut back other shoots to just above start of new growth. As new shoots grow, thin them, retaining just enough to fill the framework.

FOR REJUVENATION Locate two or three easily traceable stems and prune out all other growth. Cut back the laterals, leaving two or three buds on each.

Pruning Goals:

- To train
- To control a vigorous grower
- To renew shape
- To increase flower production
- To encourage dense branching close to the ground
- To rejuvenate a plant

Pruning Clematis

SPRING BLOOMERS Minimal or selective pruning in February or March to remove dead wood and oldest growth as they flower on old wood, which must be preserved and maintained.

SUMMER AND FALL BLOOMERS In early spring (February or March) cut stems back to a pair of strong buds; remove dead growth.

REJUVENATION PRUNING Every three to five years in early spring (February or March) prune stems to 1' from ground. This encourages new growth from the base and prevents unattractive bare stems.

Pruning Wisteria

Wisteria can grow to be so large that it is best to begin training it immediately. Remember that *Wisteria sinensis* (Chinese wisteria) grows clockwise, while *Wisteria floribunda* (Japanese wisteria) grows counterclockwise. First determine the framework for growth, then decide whether the vine should be single or multistemmed. Plan ahead for the size and weight of wisteria trunks. A well-established, healthy trunk can be the size of a tree trunk!

TO TRAIN A NEW MULTISTEMMED *WISTERIA* Select as many vigorous stems as needed to fill your framework. Prune out all other stems. Pinch back side stems and streamers.

ANNUAL PRUNING *Wisteria* responds enthusiastically to severe annual pruning. Reduce the main stems by one-half each summer and side stems to three or four flower buds in late winter. Remove any suckers that may grow up at the base of the vine.

HINT: To train a new single-stemmed Wisteria, *remove all buds along the single stem and keep streamers pruned during the growing season.*

WINTERIZING

When selected carefully for climate and location, hardy vines need little care in the winter. When putting the rest of the garden to bed, simply renew the mulch and securely tie any wayward stems.

Vines

Best Bets For Your Garden

above: *Clematis panic-*
ulata

left: *Hydrangea*
anomala petiolaris

below: *Wisteria sinensis*

Botanical Name Common Name	Key	Bloom Color	Height	Sun/ Shade
Actinidia kolomitka (Male) Arctic beauty kiwi	D	White	15-20'	○
Akebia quinata Five-leaf akebia	D to Semi E	Purple	30-40'	○ ●
Campsis x *tagliabuana* 'Madame Galen' Trumpet vine	D	Salmon red	40'	○ ◑
Clematis x *jackmanii* Jackman clematis	D	Purple, white, pink	10'	○
Clematis paniculata Sweet autumn clematis	D	White	30'	○
Hedera helix English ivy	E	Foliage	30-50'	◑ ●
Hydrangea anomala petiolaris Climbing hydrangea	D	White	50-75'	○
Lathyrus latifolius Everlasting sweet pea	D	Pink to purple	6'	○ ◑
Lonicera x *brownii* 'Dropmore Scarlet'	E	Orange to red	12'	○ ◑
Lonicera x *heckrotti* Gold flame honeysuckle	E	Pink and orange	15'	○
Parthenocissus quinquefolia Virginia creeper	D	Foliage	50'	○ ●
Parthenocissus tricuspidata 'Veitchii' Boston ivy	D	Foliage	60'	○ ●
Polygonum aubertii Silver lace vine	D	White	20-40'	○ ●
Wisteria floribunda Japanese wisteria	D	Lilac, white	25'	○

KEY: Deciduous (D); Evergreen (E)

Microclimate	Bloom Time	Comments
Hardy	Early summer	Vigorous, twining climber; foliage pink and white variegated, more so on male; less pronounced variegation in acid soil; small, cup-shaped flowers; moist, well-drained soil
Hardy	Late spring - early summer	Vigorous twining climber; dark blue-green foliage; small, vanilla-scented flowers; sausage-shaped fruit; well-drained soil; tolerates east- or north-facing location; deer-resistant
Hardy; seashore-tolerant	Summer	Climbs by aerial roots; trumpet-shaped blossoms in clusters; fertile, moist, well-drained soil; tolerates alkaline soil; prune in early spring to encourage flowering
Hardy; seashore-tolerant	Summer	Cultivars; twining climber; velvety, single, 3-4" blossoms; rich, well-drained soil; shade roots from hot sun; can prune in early spring as flowers on current growth; deer-resistant
Hardy; seashore-tolerant	Late summer	Twining climber; profusion of small, fragrant blossoms; dense, glossy foliage; rich, well-drained soil; shade roots from hot sun; prune out old wood annually; blooms on new wood; deer-resistant
Hardy; moderately drought-tolerant	NA	Fast-growing, aerial root climber; dull, dark green leaves; not as tolerant of sun; moist, well-drained alkaline soil; variegated varieties prefer more light; will grow on north wall; deer-resistant
Hardy; seashore-tolerant	Early summer	Clinging, root climber; lateral branches up to 3'; glossy dark green foliage, gold in fall; fragrant, large, flat flower clusters; fertile, moist, well-drained soil
Hardy; seashore-tolerant	Summer - fall	Tendril climber; medium green foliage; sweet pea-like blossoms; humus-rich, well-drained soil
Hardy; seashore-tolerant	Summer	Twining climber; blue-green leaves; fragrant trumpet-shaped flowers; any fertile, well-drained soil
Hardy; seashore-tolerant	Summer	Woody, twining climber; leaves green above, bluish below; fragrant orange-throated pink blossoms; any fertile, well-drained soil; prune and fertilize for continuous bloom
Hardy; drought- and seashore-tolerant	NA	Vigorous, woody, tendril climber; five-toothed, dull green leaflets; crimson fall color; blue-black berries; well-drained soil; deer-resistant
Hardy; drought- and seashore-tolerant	NA	Vigorous, woody, tendril climber with adhesive disks; glossy, dark green maple-like foliage; crimson fall color; blue-black berries; well-drained soil; one of·best for clinging to stone
Hardy; drought- and seashore-tolerant	Late spring - fall	Vigorous, twining climber; heart-shaped leaves; frothy, fragrant flowers; pinkish fruits; most well-drained soils; deer-resistant; also known as Chinese fleece vine
Hardy; drought- and seashore-tolerant	Early summer	Woody, twining climber; fragrant pea-like flowers in long clusters after leaves appear; fertile, well-drained soil; prune after flowering and in late winter; buy cutting-grown, grafted or budded *Wisteria*, not seedlings; many varieties; also try *Wisteria sinensis*

Peter G. Jones

ORNAMENTAL GRASSES

Pennisetum alopecuroides

Ornamental grasses are the great showmen in the landscape, putting on a continuous performance as they progress through their life cycles, developing and producing showy flowerheads and seed. They change color through the season, sway in the wind and add a gentle rustling sound to the garden. When bathed in sunlight, the foliage sparkles; when backlit, some glow. The flamboyant plumes and seedheads challenge the imaginations of the best costume designers. And during the winter they add color, structure and drama to the sleeping garden.

Ornamental grasses comprise a wonderfully diverse group of low-maintenance plants that grow everywhere and at almost every elevation. Short and compact like a pincushion, open and spreading like a waterfall or tall and columnar, they range in color from blue-green to yellow-green, red or variegated. Some are rampant spreaders while others are clump forming and better controlled. Graceful and beautiful, ornamental grasses can add a sense of mystery, magic or even a wild feeling to the home landscape.

Ornamental grasses are grown for their fine foliage as well as their dramatic inflorescences. Combine them with annuals and perennials or use them as softening contrasts with shrubs in the border for year-round interest. As solitary, sculptural elements, large grasses can stand majestically in the lawn. Low-growing, running grasses make quick-spreading groundcovers that can control dust and erosion. Tall grasses make excellent hedges and screens. Plant ornamental grasses near the seashore where their plumes will move with the wind or in an intimate garden to obscure irritating ambient sounds. With their contrasting life cycles, grasses and bulbs are excellent companions. Grasses begin to grow just as bulbs are coming into bloom; as grasses expand, their blades conceal the dying bulb foliage. Grasses are always marvelous additions to fresh and dried flower arrangements.

Grow Ornamental Grasses:
- In herbaceous, mixed perennial and shrub borders
- In mass plantings
- In seashore gardens
- As specimens and accents
- As groundcovers
- As edging
- As screens and hedges
- As background plantings
- As bulb companions
- In dried arrangements
- To control dust and erosion
- To add a touch of the wild, fun or mystery to the garden
- For dramatic inflorescences
- For color and texture
- For the rustling sound

HOW ORNAMENTAL GRASSES GROW
Ornamental grasses are classified by how they grow:
CLUMPING GRASSES grow as individual tufts that gradually get fatter and fatter. *Calamagrostis acutiflora* 'Stricta' (feather reed grass) is a tall, erect clumper; *Carex morrowii* (Japanese sedge) is short and turf-like.

SPREADING (OR RUNNING) GRASSES spread by rhizomes (underground stems) such as *Elymus arenarius* 'Glaucus' (blue lyme grass), or by stolons (above-ground stems). Due to their spreading habit running grasses can cover an area very quickly. But watch out, they can be invasive!

TEMPERATURE
As most ornamental grasses are either annuals or perennials, temperature is an important factor in their life cycles. Warm weather signals the beginning of an annual's cycle; cold weather, the end. Perennials go into dormancy with the arrival of cold weather, but return year after year. But all perennial grasses have their own tolerance to cold, so select those that are hardy to your zone. *Pennisetum alopecuroides* (rose fountain grass), for example, is particularly sensitive to temperature; a fountain grass that is perennial in Zone 8 may grow as an annual in Zone 5. When selecting ornamental grasses for your garden, be sure to consider the coldest expected temperatures.

SUN/SHADE
Most grasses prefer full sun; however, others, such as *Calamagrostis acutiflora* 'Stricta' (feather reed grass), *Carex morrowii* 'Variegata' (variegated Japanese sedge), *Chasmanthium latifolium* (inland sea oats) and *Miscanthus sinensis* 'Variegatus' (variegated Japanese silver grass) can tolerate partial shade, particularly in Zone 7.

SOIL
Ornamental grasses tolerate most moderately fertile, well-drained soils with an average pH. If you have clay soil, amend it to improve drainage. See "Soil," p.18.

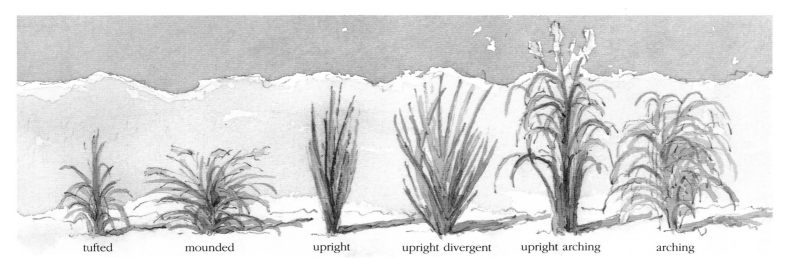

tufted   mounded   upright   upright divergent   upright arching   arching

Ornamental grasses come in many shapes and sizes, so there's bound to be one that's just right for your garden.

WATER

All grasses respond well to water, especially when newly planted, but in moderation. Too much water or sitting water will rot their roots. This is particularly true of blue grasses, such as *Elymus arenarius* 'Glaucus' (blue lyme grass), which are coated with a protective blue-gray wax to reduce water loss. In hot summer climates, water regulates plant growth. The less grasses are watered, the less they grow.

PLANNING FOR ORNAMENTAL GRASSES

Ornamental grasses offer the gardener lots of shapes and sizes from which to choose. Their foliage can be tufted, like *Carex morrowii* (Japanese sedge); mounded, like *Pennisetum alopecuroides* (rose fountain grass); upright, upright divergent, upright arching, like *Calamagrostis acutiflora* 'Stricta' (feather reed grass); or arching, like *Miscanthus sinensis* 'Zebrinus' (zebra grass).

If sound is your goal, plant tall grasses such as *Cortaderia selloana* (pampas grass) where they will catch the breeze. For strong winds, use low, narrow-leafed grasses that would not be bent by the force of the wind. For a shimmering effect, plant *Miscanthus sinensis* (Japanese silver grass) where sunlight will reflect off its leaves; to capture the full drama of showy inflorescences, such as those of *Miscanthus sinensis* 'Gracillimus' (maiden grass), plant them against a dark background such as a fence, wall or hedge. When planting grasses with perennials, do not use vigorous runners or aggressive seeders; they would soon disrupt the balance. Rampant runners are best reserved for stabilizing steep slopes or covering large areas.

Ornamental Grass Companions
- *Aster*
- *Narcissus*
- *Eupatorium*
- *Rudbeckia*
- *Sedum*

Ornamental Grasses For Strong Winds

- *Calamagrostis acutiflora* 'Stricta' (feather reed grass)
- *Panicum virgatum* (switch grass)
- *Schizachyrium scoparium* (little bluestem)

SPACING

How an ornamental grass grows is integral to its use in the garden. Clumping grasses spaced far apart will give a hummocky look; those planted close together will soon meld into a solid mass. A good rule of thumb for all ornamental grasses is to plant them as far apart as their ultimate height. If you want a massed effect or would like to see faster results, space plants closer together.

PLANNING AT A GLANCE

- Microclimate
- Warm- or cool-season
- Sun/shade
- Soil
- Water
- Evergreen or deciduous
- Plant size and shape
- Foliage color and texture
- Plant inflorescence or seedhead color
- Time of display
- Seasonal appearance
- Year-round interest
- Plant spacing
- Grass's growth and spreading habits

BED PREPARATION

Ornamental grasses are prone to root rot so good drainage is the goal when preparing the bed. Dig beds a minimum of 12". For larger grasses, such as *Miscanthus*, dig the bed 24". If you have clay soils, dig the beds deeper and amend the soil to improve drainage.

BUYING GRASSES

Although ornamental grasses reproduce by seed as well as runners, most are purchased as plants. Container-grown grasses are available from catalogs or your local nursery; bare-root plants are most often purchased by mail. Many grasses don't bloom until the second year, so buy the largest plant possible. See "Buying Perennials" on p.64 for suggestions on selecting a healthy plant.

Bare-root Plants

Bare-root plants are shipped dormant. Be forewarned — dormant grasses are not an appealing bunch. Although they show no signs of their future glory, they should respond enthusiastically to careful planting and regular water when purchased from a reputable source. But remember, roots dry quickly, so plant them as soon as possible.

PLANTING

To plant container-grown and bare-root plants, see "Planting" in "Perennials," p.65. Remember, water is critical for the success of newly planted grasses. To reduce transpiration, keep plants cut back by one-third until they are well established. If scorching should occur, simply cut back the plants. With water, new growth should quickly appear.

DIVIDING

Divide and multiply! Not only does dividing rejuvenate your older, overcrowded plants but it also provides you with many young, new plants to spread around your garden. When you see your older plants begin to take over the garden or flop over, you know the time has come to brace yourself and bring out the heavy artillery: an axe, saw and spade. Divide ornamental grasses just as new growth begins to show in late winter or early spring; fall-divided grasses rarely winter well.

Begin by cutting back the existing foliage by about one-third to reduce the loss of moisture through transpiration during dividing and transplanting. Dig all around the clump with a spade, then lift the plant. If your grasses are very large, ask a friend to help you. Next, using the appropriate tool for the size of your grass, cut the plant into substantial chunks. For stoloniferous or rhizomateous plants, cut off the runners, keeping as much soil on the roots as soon as possible, and replant right away. If plants must be out of the ground for a while, keep them moist and out of direct sunlight.

FERTILIZING
Grasses grow in direct relation to soil fertility. Grasses given a diet of very fertile soil and regular water will take off; those that are starved will stand still.

Most grasses excel with an application of slow-release, low-nitrogen fertilizer in spring. Too much nitrogen weakens them — particularly important on exposed sites where the wind would bend the foliage.

MULCH
Keep them mulched! Apply 2" to 3" at the time of installation and renew regularly. See "Mulch," p.36.

WEEDING
Once grasses are established as groundcovers, weeding is over because grasses outgrow the weeds! However, beware of planting invasive runners or self-sowing grasses in perennial beds; you will have a continual battle.

STAKING
Staking should not be necessary for healthy grasses. If the need does arise, see "Staking" in "Perennials," p.66. Brush stakes often work well for smaller grasses.

HINT: If your grasses are flopping over, they may be suffering from overfertilization, too much nitrogen, or insufficient light.

CUTTING BACK
Once a year, cut back ornamental grasses to remove thick, old or dried-out leaves. To avoid damaging new shoots, the best time to cut plants back is in late winter just before growth begins. Those who like to enjoy the winter foliage and feathery plumes to their fullest can hold off pruning until the new green shoots begin to appear in the spring. But spring pruning does have its consequences. Grasses become very brittle as they dry over the winter and may break up into thousands of little pieces when cut. Before pruning, surround the grasses with a tarp to easily collect the clippings. Some ornamental grasses such as *Elymus arenarius* 'Glaucus' (blue lyme grass) benefit from an additional shearing in midseason to force new, blue foliage.

Hand pruners will do the job for most ornamental grasses, but to save time, use weed trimmers on mass plantings of tall perennial grasses.

DEADHEADING
The plumes of ornamental grasses are so attractive you may want to leave them as long as possible. However, if they get broken or no longer look attractive, cut their stems back to below the foliage.

WINTERIZING
Look over your ornamental grasses. Leave any that are elegant, sculptural or evergreen, such as *Carex morrowii* (Japanese sedge) for winter interest in the garden; cut back those that are less attractive (see above). In late winter before any signs of new growth, cut back all grasses that were left standing.

Ornamental Grasses

Best Bets For Your Garden

above: Miscanthus floridulus and *Miscanthus sinensis* 'Gracillimus'

right: Calamagrostis acutiflora 'Stricta'

below: Carex morrowii 'Variegata'

Botanical Name / Common Name	Height	Spacing	Sun/ Shade
Calamagrostis acutiflora 'Stricta' / Feather reed grass	4 1/2-7'	2'	○ ◑
Carex morrowii 'Variegata' / Variegated Japanese sedge	12"	8"	◑
Chasmanthium latifolium / Inland sea oats	3'	2'	○ ◑
Cortaderia selloana 'Pumila' / Dwarf pampas grass	4-6'	4-5'	○
Elymus arenarius 'Glaucus' / Blue lyme grass	3-4'	3-4'	○
Imperata cylindrica 'Red Baron' / Japanese bloodgrass	12-18"	12-18"	○ ◑
Miscanthus sinensis / Japanese silver grass	5-6'	3-4'	○
Miscanthus sinensis 'Gracillimus' / Maiden grass	4-5'	3-4'	○
Molinia caerulea subsp. *arundinacea* 'Windspiel' / Windplay tall moor grass	6-7'	3'-4'	○ ◑
Panicum virgatum / Switch grass	5'	4'	○
Panicum virgatum 'Haense Herms' / Red switch grass	3-4'	2-3'	○
Pennisetum alopecuroides / Rose fountain grass	4'	3'	○
Schizachyrium scoparium / Little bluestem	3'	1'	○
Sesleria autumnalis / Autumn moor grass	12-18"	18"	○ ◑

Microclimate	Planting Time	Comments
Hardy; warm-season; drought-tolerant	Spring or fall	Deciduous; background, massing; course, narrowly erect; upright panicles in early summer, persist through winter; growth begins early in spring
Hardy; heat- and drought-tolerant	Spring	Semievergreen; groundcover or accent; green leaves with white margins; very tolerant but prefers cool, moist soil
Hardy; warm-season; seashore-tolerant	Spring	Accent, massing; clumper; bamboo-like; dangling seed heads from summer to fall; most soils; protect from wind
Hardy to Zones 5 and 6; warm-season; heat-tolerant	Spring	Screening, accent; clumper; sharp-edged leaves; large, silvery plumes in autumn; well-drained soil
Hardy; warm-season; drought-tolerant	Spring or fall	Accent, groundcover; runner; blue-grey foliage; very aggressive
Hardy; warm-season	Spring	Accent, groundcover; runner; red foliage becoming brilliant in fall; moist, well-drained soil; slow to become established
Hardy; warm-season	Spring	Accent; screen; clumper; all *Miscanthus sinensis* have white midribs; Japanese silver grass has broad blades and medium texture, magenta plumes, outstanding winter color; moist, well-drained soil; many cultivars
Hardy; warm-season	Spring	Fine-textured foliage; elegant; bronze-red inflorescence turning silver
Hardy; warm-season	Spring	Accent; clumper; fine blue-green foliage; elegant, transparent flower stalks sway in the wind; moist, acid, well-drained soil
Hardy; warm-season; seashore-tolerant	Spring or fall	Accent, groundcover; runner; fine blue-green foliage; most soils
Very hardy; warm-season; drought-tolerant	Spring or fall	Foliage turns reddish in fall; airy reddish inflorescence
Hardy; warm-season	Spring	Outstanding accent, groundcover; clumper; fine texture; lovely mauve plumes
Very hardy; warm-season; drought-tolerant	Spring or fall	Groundcover, massing, accent in low groundcover, erosion control; clumper; erect; light green, narrow foliage; fluffy plumes in late summer; bronze to orange in fall; any well-drained soil
Hardy; warm-season; extremely drought-tolerant	Spring or fall	Accent, groundcover, rock gardens; clumper; yellow-green foliage; yellow fall color; silvery panicles; alkaline, well-drained soil

Peter C. Jones

GROUNDCOVERS

Sun/Shade
Temperature
Humidity
Soil
Water
Spacing
Planning At A Glance
Bed Preparation

Sedum kamtschaticum

Buying Groundcovers
Time To Plant
Planting
Fertilizing
Mulch
Deadheading And Shearing
Winterizing
Best Bets For Your Garden

Groundcovers are the carpets of the garden. Although usually selected for their foliage, many flowering plants also make great groundcovers, so you have an array to choose from including low-growing shrubs, roses, perennials, succulents or vines. The only prerequisite — that they cover the ground quickly and thoroughly.

For the best effect, groundcovers should be perennial, low maintenance, long lasting and provide year-round visual interest. The best choices for areas with little snow cover are hardy evergreens, which bring a little color and texture to an otherwise monotone winter landscape.

Groundcovers usually spread by means of trailing branches, underground roots or above-ground runners. There is a happy medium, however, between plants that are vigorous spreaders and those that are invasive. Avoid invasive vines such as *Celastrus scandens* (bittersweet) no matter how tempting they may be. You will be pulling shoots out of your garden for years on end.

Use groundcovers as the transition between your lawn areas and taller shrubs or in places where grass refuses to grow. Plant groundcovers to reduce weeding or even mowing! Fill in between the stones of a path or plant them along the edge. For the best erosion control on slopes too steep to mow, select vigorous growers that have deep roots to hold the soil. If you use vines as groundcovers, remember that almost all vines like to climb. To avoid unnecessary maintenance beneath shrubs and trees, choose groundcovers that prefer to hug the ground.

Grow Groundcovers:

- To carpet the floor of the garden
- To control dust
- To reduce weeding
- To keep the soil cool and reduce evaporation
- To reduce lawn area
- To unify planting areas visually
- To edge a path
- To fill in between stones in a path
- To edge lawn areas with color and texture
- As a transition between the lawn and taller shrubs
- To obscure fading bulb foliage
- To prevent erosion from wind and rain
- On slopes too steep to mow
- As fire retardants

SUN/SHADE

Most groundcovers require at least four to six hours of sunlight daily, preferably in the morning. Fortunately, there are groundcovers that grow in difficult areas in the landscape. In deep shade try *Hedera helix* (ivy), *Vinca minor* (periwinkle) or *Pachysandra terminalis*; in sunny spots try *Ajuga reptans*, *Liriope spicata*, or *Sedum acre*.

TEMPERATURE

Many groundcovers flourish in your moderate climate. But, if you regularly experience hot, sunny summers, it is essential that the plants you select are heat-tolerant. And if your Zone 5 garden is chilled by stormy blasts from the north, select cold-hardy plants. Groundcovers have the potential to grow for many years in the garden, so make the right choice in the beginning and watch them grow! Select evergreen groundcovers, such as *Euonymus fortunei radicans* (wintercreeper) and *Vinca*, that look well year-round, yet stand up to snowless cold winters. Flowering and fragrant groundcovers, such as *Hemerocallis* (daylily) and *Convallaria majalis* (lily-of-the-valley), thrive in areas with hot summers and cold winters.

HUMIDITY

Humidity can be a problem for groundcovers — especially in coastal areas. They grow close to the ground where low light levels, high humidity and poor air circulation provide the perfect conditions for mold and mildew. In humid areas, such as the Chesapeake Bay, avoid dry heat- and sun-loving groundcovers like *Artemisia*. Look instead for plants more tolerant of humidity, such as *Liriope muscari,* and in light shade try *Hemerocallis* x *hybrida* (daylily) or *Ophiopogon japonicus* (mondo grass). Increase air circulation in and around the garden by removing any obstacles to the natural airflow and with proper spacing of your plants.

SOIL

Good preparation of the soil is essential to quick growth as groundcovers spread by underground rhizomes, rapid multiplication or by sending out stems that root wherever they touch down. Most groundcovers prefer loose, rich, well-drained soil with an average pH. However, some, such as *Adiantum pedatum* (maidenhair fern), do well in alkaline soils; *Arctostaphylos uva-ursi* (bearberry), in acid soils. Groundcovers must thrive to cover an area solidly, so be sure the groundcover you select is compatible with your soil's pH.

> *HINT: Once groundcovers are established, it's practically impossible to work the soil, so the soil must be well prepared before you plant.*

WATER

Although most groundcovers prefer humus rich soil and regular water, they generally do not like wet feet. In areas with low rainfall and water restrictions, there are many drought-tolerant plants to chose from including many succulents, *Cerastium tomentosum* (snow-in-summer) and *Ajuga reptans*. But even drought-tolerant plants need water until they are established. If water supplies permit, drip irrigation is very helpful in establishing groundcovers, especially on slopes. Be sure to install it prior to planting.

> *HINT: If you live in a fire-prone area, keep groundcovers near the house well watered to maintain a high moisture content. Plants that are dried out are extremely flammable.*

SPACING

Buying enough plants is always a concern when it comes to groundcovers. The quantities are so large, you always think you've gone overboard only to find you haven't bought enough. To make an accurate count, measure your planting area carefully, then calculate the number of square feet. The recommended spacing you leave between plants will determine how many will be necessary to cover the area. Use the chart below to help you.

Spacing	Area 64 Plants Will Cover	Area 100 Plants Will Cover
4"	7 Square Feet	11 Square Feet
6	16	25
8	28	44
10	45	70
12	64	100
15	100	156
18	144	225
24	256	400

PLANNING AT A GLANCE

- Microclimate
- Sun/shade
- Soil
- Water
- Evergreen or deciduous
- Plant form and texture
- Flower color and time of bloom
- Fruit color and season
- Plant spread and spacing

> *HINT: Although groundcovers are the "carpet" of the garden, they do not appreciate being walked on. Provide a path or stepping stones if you think people will be tempted to tiptoe through your groundcovers.*

BED PREPARATION

When planting large areas of groundcovers, weeds can be a nightmare. Once the groundcover has covered the area, it's very difficult to reach the base of a weed to pull it out properly, roots and all. Your best defense is to eradicate weeds and grasses, especially perennial quack grass, several weeks prior to installation. (See "Removing Sod," p.33.) Prepare the beds to a depth of 10"-12" by single digging (see "Digging The Bed," p.33), adding amendments as necessary. If you can, allow the soil to settle for a few weeks, then rake the bed smooth.

BUYING GROUNDCOVERS

Groundcovers can be succulents, vines, shrubs, perennials or grasses, so you will find them available in many different types of containers, ranging from flats of seedlings to 2" pots and gallon containers. Vines, such as *Vinca* (periwinkle) and *Hedera* (ivy), can be purchased as bare-root plants, usually through mail-order catalogs.

To select a healthy plant, look for:

- Plants that are vigorous (those that fill the pot or flat).
- Plants that are pest free.
- Plants that have several healthy stems and abundant new growth.

and avoid:

- Plants with smaller new growth.
- Plants with yellow leaves or dieback.
- Plants that are potbound. (Check to see if roots are growing out of the bottom of the pot.)
- Plants with underdeveloped root systems. (Check to see if plant is loose in the pot.)
- Plants in containers with low soil levels or hard-packed soil.
- Plants with broken stems or twigs.

HINT: When purchasing groundcovers, buy the largest size possible. Larger plants are more vigorous and will rapidly cover an area, quickly restricting the ability of weeds to take hold.

TIME TO PLANT

In warm areas of Zone 7, most groundcovers are planted in the fall to give them several cool months to adjust prior to the onset of summer's heat. However, in Zone 5 plant your groundcovers in the spring to give roots a chance to establish prior to the winter's damaging freeze/thaw cycles, which have a tendency to heave young plants out of the ground. For more specific planting recommendations, see "Planting" in the appropriate chapter.

PLANTING

Plant your groundcovers in either straight or staggered rows. If you are planting on a slope, staggered rows will help prevent soil erosion. For additional information, see "Planting" in the appropriate chapter.

HINT: To maintain a clean edge between the lawn area and your groundcovers, install a metal, plastic, brick or wood garden edge that is deep enough to thwart the progress of spreading underground roots.

Planting On Steep Slopes

When planting groundcovers on steep slopes in areas with below-average rainfall, create flat terraces for each plant. "Terracing" interrupts the flow of water down the slope, thereby increasing the amount of water that goes to the plant's roots. It will also raise the plant up to help prevent it from being buried by soil washing down the slope.

Planting on a slope: (Left) On gentle slopes, use the guidelines for planting perennials, vines or shrubs. (Right) On steep slopes, plant groundcovers on individual terraces, which interrupt and capture water for the plants. But be sure the root balls are not exposed.

To plant on a terrace, dig a hole in the middle of the terrace that is about two-thirds as deep as the container. Place the plant in the hole and mound soil over it. The crown of the plant will be high, forming a basin between it and the slope. Water will collect in the basin and percolate down into the soil instead of running down the slope.

FERTILIZING

Fertilize your new transplants with a balanced fertilizer two to three weeks after installation. For more specific fertilizing recommendations, see "Fertilizing" in the appropriate chapter.

MULCH

It will take time for newly planted groundcovers to cover the given area, so remember to mulch them well to inhibit weed growth. Mulch will also moderate the soil temperature, protecting your plants from extreme cold and heat and the temperature fluctuations of the freeze/thaw cycles, which can heave your plants out of the ground in winter. Some gardeners prefer spreading the mulch before planting. This prevents damage to the seedlings and ensures a solid defense against invading weeds.

DEADHEADING AND SHEARING

As groundcovers often span very large areas, it is best to select plants that are self-cleaning and require little pruning. But do prune out stray branches that have turned brown. If you want a formal look or want to revitalize the plants, you may wish to shear groundcovers, such as *Euonymus fortunei radicans* (wintercreeper), *Iberis sempervirens* (candytuft) and *Artemisia*. *Liriope* actually benefits from an early spring mowing!

WINTERIZING

Well-chosen groundcovers should require little winterizing once they are established. For specific winterizing recommendations see "Winterizing" in the appropriate chapter.

Groundcovers

Best Bets For Your Garden

above left: Ajuga reptans

above right: Artemisia abrotanum

left: Dennstaedtia punctilobula

below: Cerastium tomentosum

Botanical Name Common Name	Key	Bloom Color	Height	Spacing
Adiantum pedatum Maidenhair fern	D, SE	Foliage	18"	12-18"
Ajuga reptans Bugleweed	E	Purple	2"	8-12"
Artemisia abrotanum Southernwood	E	Yellowish white	3-4'	12-15"
Asarum caudatum British Columbia wild ginger	E	Reddish brown	6-10"	8-12"
Athyrium filix-femina Lady fern	D	Foliage	2-4'	1-3'
Cerastium tomentosum Snow-in-summer	D	White	6-12"	2'
Convallaria majalis Lily-of-the-valley	D	White	8"	12"
Dennstaedtia punctilobula Hay-scented fern	D	Foliage	12"	12"
Epimedium x *versicolor* 'Sulphureum' Bishop's hats	D	Yellow	12"	12"
Euonymus fortunei radicans 'Coloratus' Wintercreeper	E	Inconspicuous green	4-6"	18-24"
Galium odoratum Sweet woodruff	E	White	3-4"	6"
Hosta spp. Plantain lily	D	White, blue, lavender	16-24"	1-2' or more
Hypericum calycinum Creeping Saint John's-wort	SE	Yellow	12-18"	3-4'

KEY: Deciduous (D); Evergreen (E); Semievergreen (SE)

Sun	Microclimate	Bloom Time	Comments
◐	Hardy	NA	Under trees, borders, woodlands; dainty, divided, medium green fronds; dark brown stems; moist, neutral to alkaline soil
○ ●	Hardy; drought- and salt-intolerant	Early summer	Under trees, on slopes, edging; dark green foliage; spike bloom; spreads rapidly; any well-drained soil; nematode-sensitive; deer-resistant
○	Hardy to Zones 6 and 7; drought-tolerant	Summer	Massing; lemon-scented, grey-green foliage; prune to maintain shape
◐ ●	Drought-intolerant	NA	Under trees; shiny, heart-shaped leaves; rich soil; water well; Pacific Northwest
●	Hardy	NA	Under trees, borders, woodlands; delicate, lance-shaped, divided, arching, pale green fronds; humus-rich, moist soil; remove fading fronds regularly
○	Hardy; drought- and seashore-tolerant	Spring - early summer	Slopes, rock gardens, walls, borders, edging, between stepping stones; prostrate; silvery foliage; clusters of star-shaped flowers; aggressive; must have well-drained soil; tolerant of pure sand; good for mountains, coast or desert; deer-resistant
◐ ●	Hardy	Spring	Under trees; rhizomes; vigorous roots allow little else to grow near it; very fragrant, bell-shaped flowers; pairs of leaves wrap around stems; leaves turn brown in late summer; humus-rich soil; divide when crowded; deer-resistant
●	Hardy	NA	Under trees, borders, woodlands; oval to triangular, much-divided, lacelike, green fronds; humus-rich, moist soil
◐ ●	Hardy	Spring	Under trees, borders; steady spreader; dainty flowers in clusters on wiry stems; heart-shaped leaves, good fall color; cut back old foliage in late winter; deer-resistant
○ ●	Hardy; seashore-tolerant	Summer	Under trees, slopes; creeper and prostrate or climbing by aerial roots; dark green, glossy leaves turn reddish-purple in winter; inconspicuous flowers; intolerant of wet soil; rapid grower
●	Hardy; drought-intolerant	Late spring	Under trees, edging; hay-scented foliage when dried; moist, acid soil; self-sows freely; divide in spring or fall; deer-resistant
●	Hardy	Summer	Under trees, borders; prefers moist, rich soil but tolerates all moist soils; some tolerate clay soil; good drainage in winter; apply super phosphate in late summer; keep a look-out for slugs
○ ◐	Hardy to Zone 6; seashore-tolerant	Midsummer - fall	Semievergreen in Zone 7; groundcover, slopes, under trees; tough, dense, spreading; medium green short-stalked leaves; big, bright flowers; tolerates poor soils

Groundcovers

Best Bets For Your Garden

above left: Lamium maculatum

above right: Phlox stolonifera
'Bruce's White'

left: Pachysandra terminalis

below: Vinca minor

Botanical Name Common Name	Key	Bloom Color	Height	Spacing	
Lamiastrum galeobdolon 'Variegatum' Variegated yellow archangel	D to E	Yellow	1-2'	2'	
Lamium maculatum Dead nettle	D	White, pink	8-24"	12"	
Liriope muscari Big blue lily turf 'Silvery Sunproof'	E	Dark violet Lilac	12"	12"	
Lysimachia nummularia Creeping Jenny	D	Yellow	1-2'	6-12"	
Ophiopogon japonicus Mondo, Monkey grass	E	Lilac	6"	4-6"	
Pachysandra terminalis Japanese pachysandra	E	White	4"	5"	
Phalaris arundinacea 'Picta' Ribbon grass 'Luteo-Picta' Golden ribbon grass	D or E	White	24-30"	12"	
Phlox stolonifera Creeping phlox	E	White, pale blue	6-12"	6"	
Polystichum acrostichoides Christmas fern	E	Foliage	2'	18"	
Sedum acre Gold moss sedum	E	Yellow	3-6"	6"	
Thymus serpyllum Mother-of-thyme	E	Purplish white	1-2"	8"	
Vinca minor Common periwinkle	E	Purple, light blue, white	5-8"	8-12"	

KEY: Deciduous (D); Evergreen (E)

Sun	Microclimate	Bloom Time	Comments
◐ ●	Hardy	Summer	Under trees; silver-dappled foliage; moist, well-drained soil; keep a lookout for slugs
◐ ●	Hardy; heat-tolerant	Spring - late summer	Evergreen in Zones 6 and 7; blunt leaves with white stripe up midrib; small flowers; tolerates most soils; easy to grow; spreads vigorously; shear in midsummer for compact growth; deer-resistant; many cultivars
○ ●	Hardy; heat- and drought-tolerant	Summer	Under trees, slopes, edging; spike flowers; turf-like foliage; sand or loamy soil; intolerant of foot traffic, mow in spring prior to new growth
○	More sun-tolerant		Gold-striped foliage
○ ◐	Hardy	Summer	Rock gardens, between terrace stones; mat-forming; small flowers; small, round, light green leaves; moist, well-drained soil
○ ◐	Hardy to Zone 7; drought-tolerant	Early summer	Under trees, slopes, open areas; spike flowers; dark green foliage; blue berries; fertile, well-drained soil; look out for slugs; foliage may yellow with extended frosts
◐ ○	Hardy	Early summer	Under trees, slopes, edging; small spike flower; leathery leaves clustered at stem tips; all moist soils; deer-resistant
○	Very hardy	Summer	Under trees, slopes, open areas; evergreen in milder climates; long narrow leaves with white stripe turn all white with frost; showy white flower above foliage; spreads quickly; poor gravelly soils or moist soils
			Pale golden-yellow variegated foliage turns beige with frost; white flower in early summer
○ ◐	Hardy	Early summer	Under trees, borders; flowers in loose clusters; oblong to oval leaves; moist, acid, peaty soil; try 'Bruce's White'
◐	Hardy	NA	Under trees, borders; slender, lance-shaped, dark green fronds; rich, moist, well-drained soil
○	Hardy, drought-tolerant	Summer	Open areas, between stones; starlike flowers; small, fleshy, light green leaves; any well-drained soil; easy to grow; deer-resistant
○ ◐	Hardy	Summer	Open areas, between stones; flowers in clusters; fragrant dark green foliage; light foot traffic; light, well-drained soil
○ ●	Hardy	Spring - early summer	Under trees, slopes; glossy, dark green leaves; any soil but prefers rich, moist soil; deer-resistant

SHRUBS

Rhododendron hybrid

Shrubs are a gardener's best friend. Human in scale, they are the multiple-stemmed woody plants that help make the transition between tall trees and groundcovers in the landscape. Evergreen or deciduous, large or small, spreading, rounded, upright or vase-shaped, shrubs are the workhorses of the garden. Not only can you fill a space faster with shrubs than any other type of plant, but you can use them to create the structure or "backbone" of the garden.

Use mass plantings of shrubs to divide the lawn into smaller garden spaces or plant a single flowering shrub, such as a *Magnolia stellata* (star magnolia), to make an impressive accent in your lawn or in a bed of low-growing groundcovers. Fragrant shrubs surround a terrace or deck with their sweet perfume, while flowering shrubs add variety to your perennial border. Use shrubs as hedges or screens to increase your privacy or obscure a view. A thorny hedge will provide protection from unwanted visitors; evergreen shrubs will hide an unattractive foundation.

Juniperus is among the most versatile evergreen shrubs, growing naturally in many different shapes and hues of green.

In Borders

With their height, leaf color and texture, shrubs add a bold accent to mixed perennial and shrub borders. On a large scale, shrub borders can give shape to a lawn by defining the edges; on a smaller scale they can elegantly enclose a terrace. Evergreen and topiary shrubs, such as *Juniperus* spp. (juniper), *Taxus cuspidata* (yew) and *Buxus* spp. (boxwood), planted at regular intervals within the perennial border impart rhythm and order to the design. With their height, shrubs such as *Viburnum* x *burkwoodii* (Burkwood viburnum) bring the color and fragrance of the border up to nose level. But remember, shrubs grow vigorously, so place them where they will enhance, not overwhelm, the neighboring perennials.

At The Front Entrance

Shrubs can create a welcoming approach to your front door, frame the entrance and link the house with the surrounding landscape. To have your front entry look inviting year-round, select shrubs such as azaleas, *Ilex* (holly), and *Mahonia aquifolium* (Oregon grape holly) for flower, fragrance and fall color. Use shrubs in a foundation planting to obscure unattractive concrete.

HINT: Consider the scale of your house and the ultimate size of the shrubs when making your selection. Your shrub planting should frame, not hide, your front door.

Hedges

Hedges are one of the most popular uses for shrubs and an excellent way to organize your garden spaces. Formal or informal, hedges are comprised of shrubs planted closely together, to create a solid line in the landscape. Evergreen shrubs provide year-round interest and are an excellent choice. Their leaves can be broad and leathery, like *Ilex* (holly), or narrow, scale-like or needled, like *Juniperus* (juniper), *Taxus* (yew) and *Thuja occidentalis* (arborvitae).

Select shrubs such as *Buxus* (boxwood) or *Ilex crenata* 'Microphylla' (Japanese holly) for their glossy leaves, *Viburnum* for its showy flowers, *Ilex* for its fruit. To create a protective barrier use thorny shrubs, such as *Berberis thun-bergii* (barberry); to frame flower beds and herb gardens use low boxwood or *Santolina*. To build a private garden room, select shrubs that respond well to pruning, such as *Ligustrum* (privet), *Thuja occidentalis* and x *Cupressocyparis leylandii* (Leyland cypress — hardy to Zone 6). Hedges hide unattractive pool or tennis court fencing with ease and are a friendly way to enclose a child's play area. A tall evergreen hedge makes the perfect backdrop for a perennial border.

HINT: For privacy, select shrubs that will grow as a solid mass to above eye level.

Screens

Shrubs massed together in an informal way create a soft, friendly visual block or screen that can hide almost anything. For the best effect, use evergreen and deciduous shrubs of varying heights and combine them with flowering shrubs, such as *Rhododendron*, *Viburnum* and *Syringa* (lilac). Remember, to block noise, a screen planting must be solid and deep.

Windbreaks

To provide a windbreak, plant shrubs in conjunction with trees to the north and west of your home. Planted close together they form a green mass that allows at least 50 percent of the wind to pass through its branches. The branches not only reduce the force of the damaging winds, but also act as a filter, trapping airborne particulate matter and causing it to fall harmlessly to the ground.

On A Hillside

If your home is on a steep hillside, erosion control is of primary importance. Use deep-rooted shrubs such as *Cotoneaster*, *Mahonia* (Oregon grape holly) and *Rhus* (sumac). For variety in height, plant them with groundcovers, such as *Hedera* (ivy) and *Euonymus fortunei radicans* (wintercreeper).

Grow Shrubs:
- For their form, color, foliage, flower and fruit
- For fragrance
- To provide structure in the garden
- As hedges or screens
- As a thorny, protective hedge
- As windbreaks
- To reduce erosion
- As low edging around perennial, herb or rose gardens
- In borders to shape your garden spaces
- In foundation plantings
- In mixed perennial and shrub borders
- In mass plantings
- To frame an entrance

SUN/SHADE

There are shrubs for all levels of light. Understory shrubs, such as *Clethra alnifolia* (sweet pepper bush), thrive in the shade. *Skimmia japonica* (Japanese skimmia) prefers partial shade, and others, such as *Rhus* (sumac), *Buddleia* (butterfly bush), and *Syringa* (lilac) prefer direct sunlight. Some versatile shrubs, like *Spiraea x vanhouttei* and *Calycanthus floridus* (sweetshrub), thrive in sun or shade.

On cold, windy sites in Zones 5 and 6, protect broadleaved evergreens such as *Rhododendron* and *Ilex* (holly), from the drying effects of late winter and early spring sun by planting them in a north- or east-facing location. Warm south or west sun combined with strong winds can cause "winter injury," the burning (or browning) of the foliage.

TEMPERATURE

Cold hardiness, heat tolerance and resilience are important considerations in your moderate climate where temperatures can drop from 90° to 40° Fahrenheit within a twenty-four-hour period. Flowering shrubs such as *Hibiscus syriacus* (rose-of-Sharon) and *Hydrangea* thrive in summer's warm temperatures. But when cold weather arrives, deciduous shrubs drop their leaves and the leaves of some broadleaf evergreens, such as *Rhododendron*, actually curl up for self protection in the bitter cold. As shrubs are the mainstay of the landscape, select shrubs that thrive in hot summers and are tough enough to survive cold winters with little snow.

Consider the following when selecting shrubs:
- The highest expected summer temperatures
- The coldest expected winter temperatures

SOIL

Most shrubs prefer well-drained soil and although they are not as particular as perennials, they do develop better in a soil rich in nutrients. Many shrubs are pH adaptable. For example, *Potentilla* spp. (cinquefoil), *Buxus microphylla* (littleleaf box) and *Ilex vomitoria* (yaupon holly) will tolerate alkaline soils. The flowers of *Hydrangea macrophylla* (big leaf hydrangea) actually change color in direct response to the soil pH as follows:

FOR BLUE *HYDRANGEA* apply aluminum sulfate (acid).
FOR PINK *HYDRANGEA* apply lime or superphosphate (alkaline).

Others, such as azaleas, *Fothergilla*, *Clethra alnifolia* (sweet pepper bush) and *Camellia* must have acid soil to thrive.

WATER

Most shrubs require regular water and well-drained soils. If you live in an area prone to drought, select drought-tolerant shrubs. But all shrubs, including your drought-tolerant shrubs, need water thoroughly after planting. Continue to provide regular water for two to three years until they are established. Then water thoroughly whenever the soil becomes dry, particularly during the growing season. Even drought-tolerant shrubs will look better with a little water. Well-watered plants can survive greater extremes of temperature.

HUMIDITY

In humid areas, it is always a good practice to provide good air circulation in the garden. Don't overcrowd your shrubs; it can lead to poor air circulation, which opens plants up to disease. Whenever possible, select humidity-tolerant plants and avoid daily light watering, which can also promote fungal growth on your shrubs.

SNOW AND ICE

Light snow provides the garden with welcome insulation in winter. However, the weight of wet snow or ice can break the branches of woody plants. If wet snows are common in your area, avoid flat-topped hedges, which hold the snow, and choose instead rounded or pointed tops with angled sides which allow the snow to slide off. If you opt for a hedge of *Thuja occidentalis* (arborvitae), select a single leader variety such as 'Wintergreen,' as those with multiple leaders are prone to snow damage — the snow settles down, opening the shrubs up between the leaders. Don't allow snow to accumulate; brush it off as often as necessary. But be careful of ice-covered branches; they will be especially brittle.

WINTER INJURY

Evergreens are prone to "winter injury," the burning (or browning) of evergreen foliage due to excessive moisture loss during the winter. Evergreens continue to transpire throughout the winter although the ground may be frozen and water unavailable from the soil. For survival, the shrub will resort to tapping living tissue to replace moisture. The drained living tissue will then turn brown, causing winter injury. Drought-stressed plants are most susceptible to winter injury, so water your evergreen shrubs regularly during dry autumns to help prepare them for winter. And avoid planting evergreens in windy areas with intense southern or western exposure. Strong winds and intense sun are an especially lethal combination for susceptible evergreens as they increase transpiration.

> *HINT: Avoid planting shrubs directly under the drip line of the roof to avoid damage from snow sliding off the roof.*

PLANNING A SHRUB BORDER

Planning a shrub border can be as much fun as planning a perennial border and the results just as visually exciting. Select shrubs for the style of your garden — their leaf color and texture, flower and time of bloom as well as height and shape.

When planning the shrub border, first consider the theme or concept. Will it be a foliage border in varying textures and shades of green or a flowering border that blooms from spring to late fall? Will the flowers be all white or graduated shades of pink? Don't forget to consider the bloom time and color of your flowering trees. Select shrubs for contrast or repeat the color of the trees.

For maximum impact, group shrubs in masses of three or more plants. The smaller the shrub, the more you will need to make an impact. Small groups of shrubs will be in scale with a small garden; large shrub masses make an impact in large landscapes.

Consider the horizontal and vertical lines of the border. Place the shrub masses in relation to vertical elements such as your existing trees. Use shorter shrubs, such as low-growing azaleas and *Ilex crenata* 'Helleri' (Heller holly), in front of the border to create a visually smooth transition from lawn to shrubs to surrounding trees. Irregularly shaped masses will weave together. In general, place shorter shrubs in front and taller in back, but don't be afraid to break the rules. Vary the height by bringing some taller shrubs toward the front.

SPACING

Shrubs always look small in their containers, but with proper care, they will grow to their mature size faster than you think. Always consider the ultimate height, width and shape of the shrub before digging the hole. A general rule of thumb is to space small shrubs a minimum of 2' apart; larger shrubs, 5' apart.

Hedge spacing is critical to the success of a formal hedge. For narrow hedges, plant in a single row; for wider hedges, plant in a double staggered row.

Spacing Hedges

For hedges, the general rule of thumb is to plant shrubs tip to tip. Space narrow plants, such as *Ligustrum* (privet), 18" apart; larger plants, such as x *Cupressocyparis leylandii* (Leyland cypress), 24" to 36" apart. Hedges can be planted in single straight rows or two staggered rows, which will provide a more solid block immediately. When staggering the rows, the plants should be equidistant in both directions.

PLANNING AT A GLANCE
- Microclimate
- Sun/shade
- Soil
- Water

- Goal; i.e. privacy, windblock
- Evergreen or deciduous
- Spacing
- Ultimate size
- Growth rate
- Spacing
- Growth habit, form or shape
- Foliage size, color and texture
- Flower color, fragrance and time of bloom
- Fruit color, season, edibility, persistance
- Fall leaf color
- Winter interest: bark color, branching
- Garden style; i.e., natural, informal, formal

BED PREPARATION

Most shrubs will prosper in the same place for many years, so it's important to start them off right with good bed preparation which stimulates new root growth, and encourages healthy, vigorous shrubs. Prepare the shrub beds to a depth of 12"-24", amending the soil as necessary. (See "Soil," p.18.) Water the beds well and allow them to settle for as long as possible. Fill in any sink holes and rake the bed smooth before planting.

BUYING SHRUBS

Shrubs can be purchased as container-grown, balled-and-burlapped (B-and-B), or bare-root as follows:

Container-grown Shrubs

Most shrubs, but especially broadleaf evergreens, are grown in containers of varying sizes. The container size you select depends on your budget and your patience. If you want immediate satisfaction, buy the five-gallon size. If you are patient, a one-gallon size shrub will catch up to a five-gallon size plant in about three years.

Balled-and-burlapped Shrubs

Many deciduous shrubs, evergreen shrubs, and conifers are available as balled-and-burlapped plants. They are grown in the field and will not tolerate bare-root transplanting. Instead, they are dug with a solid ball of soil to protect their roots. The root ball is then wrapped in burlap and tied with biodegradable twine to keep the ball intact. Once you have placed the shrub in its planting hole, remove the burlap and all nonbiodegradable materials from around the trunk and stems, but leave the burlap intact around the root ball. B-and-B plants must be treated with great care to prevent the soil from loosening around the roots. While it is tempting to pick up B-and-B plants by their trunks or stems, never do so. Carry them with good support under the root ball and put them down gently. Dropping a B-and-B plant could shatter the root ball, damaging the roots.

When buying container-grown or B-and-B shrubs look for:
- Plants held in a partly shaded area.
- Healthy, vigorous plants.
- Well-shaped, densely branched plants.
- Dense foliage on evergreens.
- Plants that are in proportion to their containers.
- Firm, moist root balls if plants are B-and-B.
- Biodegradable twine around B-and-B plants.
- Wire baskets around B-and-B plants grown in sandy soil.

and avoid shrubs that:
- Are stressed from being held in the sun.
- Are weak or unhealthy.
- Are poorly formed.
- Have scarred or cracked branches or trunks.
- Have leaves of abnormal size.
- Have yellowing foliage.
- Are loose in the container (gently lift the shrub by its stem).

- Are potbound (examine the container for roots emerging from the bottom).
- Have "girdling" roots (roots wrapped around the trunk) if plants are in containers.
- Are tied with plastic twine if plants are B-and-B.
- Have broken or cracked root balls if plants are B-and-B.

HINT: If your shrub is in a straight-sided, metal can, ask the nursery to cut the sides to facilitate planting.

Bare-root Shrubs

Generally a good buy, bare-root shrubs are available in winter and late spring at local nurseries and through mail-order catalogs. See "Sources," p.218. Bare-root shrubs bring no soil with them and grow in only one type of soil: yours. This allows them to adjust more quickly than container-grown or B-and-B shrubs. Buy bare-root plants with many healthy, thick, brown roots growing in different directions and be sure to keep them moist. Buy and plant them before they leaf out.

HINT: Use bare-root plants for the least expensive installation of a privet hedge.

TIME TO PLANT

In Zones 5, 6 and 7 most shrubs can be planted in spring or fall. In parts of Zone 7 with stressful, hot summers, fall planting will give shrubs a better opportunity to become established prior to the onset of heat and/or drought. In Zone 5 avoid planting in the very late fall; spring planting will give shrubs a chance to become established prior to the stresses of winter. *Rhododendron* is best planted in the spring. If you choose to plant shrubs in the fall, do so before October 15 to encourage new root growth prior to the ground's freezing.

But how you purchase your shrubs will also determine the planting time. Bare-root shrubs are best planted while they are dormant in the spring to give them the many months they may need to become established before the cold of winter. Balled-and-burlapped shrubs can be planted when the soil is workable in all but the hottest months. Plant container-grown shrubs whenever the soil is workable and there is an ample supply of water.

Plants lose moisture through transpiration and through their roots when they are out of the ground. To reduce stress, install your shrubs on cool, cloudy days as soon as possible after they arrive. If there are unforeseen delays, be sure to keep them well watered and in a cool, shady spot. Always water the shrubs in well, apply mulch, then water regularly during the growing season.

PLANTING
Transplanting Container-grown Shrubs

If you are planting more than one shrub, set your plants out on the bed according to your garden plan. Step back and take a good look. Fine-tune the design as necessary, then begin to plant one by one.

1. Dig a hole twice as wide and 12" deeper than the root ball.
2. Carefully "knock" plants out of their containers.
3. To loosen the roots (which may be potbound), spray the root ball with water to get rid of the soil on the outer edge of the root ball; tease the roots loose with your hands; or make vertical cuts down the sides of the root ball with a sharp knife.
4. Return enough soil to the bottom of the hole for the top of the root ball to be 1"-2" above the surrounding soil. Never plant lower than the surrounding soil.
5. Spread the roots at the bottom of the hole (if they are loose) and gradually fill the hole with soil mix, watering midway to remove air pockets.
6. Form a soil rim above the existing grade to contain water around the plant.

7. Water thoroughly, but gently, so as not to break through the rim.
8. In two to three weeks break down the soil rim and mulch.

Transplanting Balled-and-burlapped Shrubs

B-and-B plants are generally grown in heavy or clay soils that hold together, forming sturdy root balls. If your soil is similar in texture, it will not be necessary to add amendments to change your soil's texture. If your soil is lighter than that of the root ball, the B-and-B plant won't be able to absorb water at the same rate as the surrounding soil and may have trouble adjusting. To prevent the root ball from drying out, equalize the soils by adding water-retentive, organic amendments to the backfill, and carefully puncture the root ball with a narrow, pointed instrument such as a planting stake. The holes will allow additional water penetration and help prevent dehydration. (See "Soil," p.18.)

1. Prepare the hole as for container-grown plants.
2. Set the shrub in the hole with the top of the root ball 1"- 2" above existing grade.
3. Untie the burlap, removing all synthetic twine, and fold it back to expose the top half of the root ball. (If burlap is synthetic, it should be removed entirely.)
4. Backfill to level of existing grade and firm soil.
5. Form a soil rim above the existing grade to contain water around the plant.
6. In two to three weeks break down the soil rim and mulch.

Planting Bare-root Shrubs

Unlike container-grown plants that can be planted year-round, bare-root shrubs must be planted during their dormancy. If you can't plant them immediately upon their arrival, heel them in and keep them moist.

(From the top) Plant bare-root shrubs while they are dormant; container-grown shrubs can be planted whenever the soil is workable; balled-and-burlapped shrubs should be planted soon after they are dug in the spring or fall.

1. Prior to planting, soak the roots in a bucket of muddy water for a few hours to make them less brittle and more pliable. The mud will adhere to the roots during planting, protecting them from dryness.
2. Prune off any damaged or broken roots or branches.
3. Prepare the hole as for container-grown shrubs.
4. Make a mound with your soil mix in the bottom of the hole. Gently fan the roots over the mound in a natural pattern, keeping the shrub at the same depth or slightly higher than it was growing in the field.
5. Replace the soil mix nearly to the top, and gently firm the soil with your hands so as not to damage roots.
6. Water thoroughly, allow soil to settle around roots, then continue to fill to grade level.
7. When the shrub begins to grow, form a watering basin and water regularly.
8. Mulch during the summer to conserve moisture.

Like moving into a new neighborhood, it takes time for new shrubs to become established in the garden. They arrive packed full of stored nutrients that nourish them through the first year while they spread out their roots and get settled into their new soil. If you've planted the shrubs well, they will flourish the second year in their new community.

FERTILIZING

The type and amount of fertilizer required depends on both the type of shrub you are planting and the soil. A soil fertility test (see "Soil," p.18) will help you determine what nutrients are lacking in your soil. Or take a close look at your shrubs. If they have pale or small leaves, few flowers and/or spindly growth, they could benefit from fertilization. Most shrubs planted in soils with average fertility will thrive with an application of liquid fertilizer or a light layer of well-rotted manure in the early spring and fall.

MULCH

Mulch your shrubs in all seasons to moderate soil temperature extremes and fluctuations and to conserve moisture. To keep the soil cool during the summer, apply 2"-3" of light mulch. Apply a heavier mulch in the fall, especially in areas with little snow cover and severe freeze/thaw cycles. The mulch will help protect your shrubs from the cold and reduce heaving, the result of the drastic temperature fluctuations during freeze/thaw cycles. For additional information, see "Mulch," p.36.

PRUNING

All shrubs have natural growth habits and structure, whether tall and leggy or short and round. Successful pruning works within these bounds to maintain shape, direct growth, increase fruit and flower production, as well as improve the health and longevity of both your evergreen and deciduous shrubs.

Pruning influences the growth and structure of the plant. Before you begin, carefully review the shrub, analyze what it can and can not do, then set a pruning goal. Maintain the natural character of the shrub while also improving its vigor. Use hand pruners, loppers, shears or pruning saws and make sure all pruning tools are sharp and clean to reduce the risk of disease in the open wounds.

HINT: Wear eye protection while pruning.

Be selective. With every cut, you are directing plant growth. All plant growth emanates from the buds located along the branches. The terminal bud, located in the branch's tip, dominates a branch's growth and determines its length. When it is removed, the plant's energy is redirected to the side buds (the buds growing along the stems), which then expand, making a branch bushy. Where you cut controls which buds will grow and ultimately determines the shape of the shrub.

Pruning Goals:
- To maintain health.
- To maintain or change shape.
- To direct plant growth, as in espaliers.
- To encourage flower and fruit production.
- To eliminate limbs damaged by storm, insects or disease.
- To create pathways and vistas.

Pruning Tools
When heading out to prune your shrubs be prepared to cut branches ranging from 1/4" twigs all the way to hefty main stems of 2" or more. Hand pruners are the perfect tool for getting the small twigs; loppers the branches up to 1" thick. If you are rejuvenating a shrub, such as a *Syringa* (lilac), a small saw may be necessary for removing thicker, old, nonproductive stems. When shaping a formal hedge, hedge shears with nice long blades will give you a clean, controlled cut. Use hand pruners for the selective pruning necessary to maintain an informal hedge.

Where To Cut
Always cut just above a bud, to avoid stubs and ensure that the cut will be obscured by new growth. Prune branches with opposite buds using a straight cut just above a pair of buds. Prune branches with alternate buds just above a bud at a 45° angle with the bottom of the cut opposite the base of the bud and the top of the cut just above the tip of the bud.

When removing branches, position the shears with the blade on top of the branch, the hook beneath it. To avoid leaving unattractive stubs, the blades should be as close as possible to the branch collar without cutting into it.

> *HINT: Prune to maintain the shape and density of a plant, not to control its size. A shrub growing in the right place should not require controlling.*

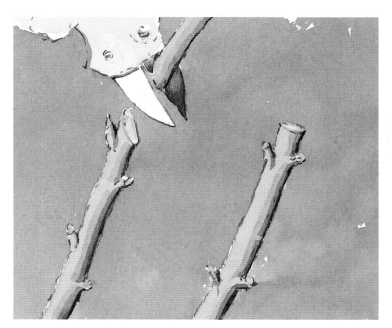

Prune shrubs with alternate buds (left) at a 45° angle just above the bud. Use a straight cut to prune shrubs with opposite buds (right).

Maintenance Pruning Of Deciduous Shrubs
For general maintenance, in late winter prune:
1. Crossing or crowded branches.
2. Diseased, dead or broken branches.
3. Weak branches.
4. Branches that detract from the shape of the bush.

Thinning Deciduous Shrubs
Thinning opens up the center of deciduous shrubs for better air circulation, allows sunlight to penetrate to the center, and reduces its size.

To thin a shrub, in late winter prune:

1. For maintenance. (See "Maintenance Pruning.")
2. Lateral branches back to main stems or by about one-third their length.

Pruning For Shape

Pruning for shape is an art. It takes careful consideration as well as muscle power. Before you shape a shrub, step back and look at its natural form and branching structure. Always think twice before removing major branches; imagine what the shrub will look like without them.

To shape a shrub, prune:

1. For maintenance. (See "Maintenance Pruning.")
2. Shoots that may interfere with the shape.
3. To encourage growth in a chosen direction.

> HINT: *When growing plants in masses, allow the plants to grow naturally together. Do not prune each plant individually, which could result in a "meatball" look.*

Pruning To Stimulate Flower Production

Pruning stimulates flower production by channeling the shrub's energy to selected buds. The most important consideration when pruning flowering shrubs is whether the shrub blooms on new growth or the previous year's growth. Spring and early summer flowering shrubs, such as *Deutzia, Magnolia stellata* (star magnolia) and *Syringa* (lilac) bloom so soon after breaking dormancy they don't have time to produce new buds before flowering. These early bloomers instead bloom on the previous year's growth. Prune them after they have bloomed or pick flowering branches to enjoy inside. Deciduous shrubs, which bloom during the summer, such as *Spiraea, Abelia,* and *Hibiscus syriascus* (rose-of-Sharon), flower on the current season's growth and should be pruned in early spring.

For summer- and fall-flowering shrubs that flower on the current year's wood, in early spring prune:

1. For maintenance. (See "Maintenance Pruning.")
2. Several main stems down to the base to maintain open form.
3. Back stems of previous year's growth to two to four buds to stimulate flowering.

For spring- and early summer-flowering shrubs that flower on the previous year's wood, after flowering prune:

1. For maintenance. (See "Maintenance Pruning.")
2. Shoots that have flowered.
3. Several main stems down to the base.

Pruning For Rejuvenation

A well-maintained shrub should not need the drastic pruning called for below. However, if you are moving into a new house with a garden that has been let go, rejuvenation pruning may be necessary.

To rejuvenate a deciduous shrub:

1. Cut back all main stems close to the ground during dormancy.
2. Fertilize, water and mulch well.

Be patient; the shrub should flourish in the second year. Then prune selectively to establish a new framework for the shrub.

Pruning For Color

As young shoots are the most colorful, it is necessary to regularly prune shrubs, such as *Cornus alba* 'Siberica' (red-twig dogwood) to encourage colorful new growth. There are two methods; the second is more drastic than the first. In the first, you remove one-third of the older branches each year by cutting them back to the ground. In the second method you cut all the branches back to about 6" every three years. For either, the best time to prune is late winter or early spring, which allows you to enjoy the colorful branches all winter.

Pruning Evergreen Shrubs

Needled, narrow- and broad-leafed evergreen shrubs have varying growth habits. The type and amount of pruning you will need to do responds directly to their natural growth and the use of the shrub in your landscape. A hedge can take shearing, while azaleas look best pruned with hand clippers. Keep the final shape of the shrub in mind at all times and always select the branches you remove with care. An elegantly branched shrub is a beautiful sight in the garden.

Needled evergreens, such as *Juniperus* (juniper), naturally grow in many shapes ranging from narrow columns to prostrate groundcovers. While columnar *Juniperus* will require little more than the removal of dead or broken branches; prostrate *Juniperus* may require the pruning of branch tips to keep them within bounds.

Most narrow- and broad-leafed evergreens with open growth habits, such as *Pieris japonica* (andromeda), will benefit from "thinning out" (see "Thinning Deciduous Shrubs"). Those with columnar habits, such as some *Ilex* (holly), need only their side stems pruned for shape.

Pruning Hedges

Shrubs used for hedges tolerate severe pruning. Give your hedge a good start by carefully training it during the first few years. When planting a new hedge, the fear is that the hedge will thin out at the bottom. With careful pruning from the outset, this can be avoided.

To shear new hedges:
1. Remove one-third of the top and side growth with pruning shears at the time of installation.
2. Shape them narrower at the top to allow more sunlight to the bottom branches.
3. Cut back half the new growth several times during the first growing season.
4. Trim off 3" to 4" three times during the second growing season.

To maintain a hedge:
1. Prune in spring and late summer.
2. For straight sides and flat tops, use a straight edge or a string stretched taught with a level on it as a guide.
3. For shaped hedges, use a wood template as a guide.

DEADHEADING

Deadhead by removing the spent blossoms after they have faded to direct the plant's energy from seed production to leaf production. Shrubs that benefit from deadheading include azaleas and *Syringa* (lilac).

FLOWER ARRANGEMENTS

Shrubs often produce lovely flowers, and with their fruit, foliage and bare branches, they can be impressive in flower arrangements. Use the foliage of shrubs, such as *Ilex* (holly) to form the structure of flower arrangements or the delicate foliage of *Santolina* as filler to offset flowers. Bare branches of *Cornus alba* 'Siberica' (red-twig dogwood) can make striking accents.

Forcing Branches

Get a head start on spring. Cut branches of *Forsythia*, *Hamamelis* (witch hazel) or *Magnolia* with lots of flower buds and force them to flower indoors by placing the branches in a vase of warm water on a sunny windowsill. They should bloom in two to four weeks. To speed up the process, some gardeners believe in first soaking the branches overnight in a tub (or bathtub) of warm water.

Picking Flowers

Remember that cutting flowers is like pruning a bush. Step back and take a good look. Only remove branches from areas that will not affect the overall shape. Ideally, the removal of a branch should enhance the bush's appearance!

To Prolong The Life Of Cut Flowers:

1. Use sharp clippers to make a clean cut.
2. Cut flowers before they are fully open.
3. Remove all foliage that will be below the water line.
4. Keep vase filled with water!
5. Change water daily to prevent buildup of bacteria.

Special Hints

FOR AZALEAS Burn the ends of the stems over a gas flame, then soak them in a solution of one tablespoon of alcohol per gallon of water. Or hammer the ends well and plunge in deep water.

FOR *COTONEASTER* OR *HAMAMELIS* (WITCH HAZEL) Hammer ends well and place in deep, cold water.

FOR *DAPHNE, HYDRANGEA, RHODODENDRON* Hammer the ends well or plunge them in 1" of boiling water, then soak in deep cold water.

FOR *VIBURNUM* Place stem tips of fragrant varieties in boiling water, then soak in deep, cold water.

WINTERIZING

Rake up all fallen leaves, add them to your compost pile, and renew the mulch in your shrub beds. Protect your tender shrubs from temperature extremes by applying a thicker layer of mulch, such as pine straw, composted leaves or other organic material (see "Mulch," p.36). On cold, windy sites, protect tender evergreens, such as *Rhododendron* and *Buxus* (boxwood), by surrounding them with burlap supported by wood or metal stakes.

SPRING CLEANUP

Remove excess mulch from your tender shrubs and add it to your compost pile. Prune any branches that may have been damaged during the winter.

AZALEAS AND RHODODENDRONS

The genus *Rhododendron* comprises an enormous number of species and varieties of azaleas and rhododendrons. But, while all azaleas are *Rhododendron*, not all rhododendrons are azaleas! Although azaleas are primarily deciduous, both rhododendrons and azaleas have evergreen and deciduous varieties. Available in a wide range of sizes and colors, azaleas and rhododendrons are justly famous for their spectacular show each spring. Most are hardy to Zones 6 and 7; a smaller selection to Zone 5. Both thrive in the Northwest, but are difficult to grow in many areas of the central states because they dislike alkaline soils. The hardier species do well along the Atlantic coast.

PLANNING Rhododendrons and azaleas are available in a brilliant range of colors from white to yellow, magenta and orange. When making your selection, coordinate the bloom sequence to prevent an unsettling clash of colors. Mass rhododendrons and azaleas together to create drifts of color in your garden.

SUN/SHADE Most rhododendrons and azaleas prefer part shade. Avoid dense shade as they may fail to bloom. Both do require some sunlight to set their buds. However, full sun can cause sunburn, brown patches on the leaves. Summer sunburn appears as brown spots along leaf edges and tips; winter sunburn as long brown patches adjacent to the midvein. Although not life-threatening themselves, sunburn spots do open the plant up to fungal infections, which can weaken your shrubs.

In Zone 5, exposure is just as important as the amount of light. Northern exposures are usually preferable. Avoid planting your rhododendrons in eastern exposures where they will receive early morning sun. In the winter, direct early morning sun can damage early-flowering hybrids by thawing the leaves and buds too quickly. Western and southern exposures are generally too hot for rhododendrons.

TEMPERATURE   Rhododendrons are sensitive to both the heat and cold. Many evergreen rhododendrons, for example, thrive in southern New England but expire in the extremely hot summers found further south.   If your summers are very hot, ask your local nurseryman for suggestions. 'Scintillation,' for example, is unusually heat-tolerant. And to combat the damage from alternating freeze/thaw cycles during mild winters, mulch your rhododendrons well.   Select only hardy rhododendrons in Zone 5.

FROST Late spring and early autumn frosts do the most damage to rhododendrons. Leaves may become misshapen and rough or be killed altogether.

WIND Rhododendrons are sensitive to wind, especially during the winter when the soil is frozen. If new growth has brown edges, your shrub may be suffering from windburn. Move it to a more protected spot in your garden or protect it with burlap.

SOIL *Rhododendron* thrive in moist, acid soils (pH 4.5 to 6.5) rich in organic matter. If you have dry or very alkaline soils, they may not be for you. Rhododendrons will be happiest if you add up to 50 percent leaf mold, peat moss or other well-rotted organic matter to your planting bed. The organic matter will improve the soil structure, retain moisture but allow for good drainage. Azaleas in particular are susceptible to root rot in poorly drained soils. Yellowing leaves, wilting or the total collapse of plants are indications of root rot.

PLANTING *Rhododendron* are shallow rooted and require excellent drainage. Plant them with the root ball slightly above ground level. Do not bury stems with soil.

CULTIVATING Never cultivate around rhododendrons or azaleas. They are surface rooters and cultivation could damage their roots.

FERTILIZING Fertilize with an acid fertilizer in the early spring when growth starts, just after they've bloomed, and monthly throughout the summer. If your plants are showing signs of weakness or yellowing leaves, give them a foliar feeding of an algae solution mixed with liquid fertilizer. Use organic fertilizers whenever possible as the salts from most synthetic fertilizers may damage the roots.

PRUNING All *Rhododendron* benefit from occasional pruning. *Rhododendron* bloom on the previous year's growth, so prune them after they have bloomed to thin and to remove broken, diseased or dead branches.

MULCH *Rhododendron* prefer cool roots. To moderate soil temperatures and retain moisture, apply a 2" to 3" layer of well-rotted oak leaves, pine needles, sawdust or other acid-rich mulch during the spring and replenish it in the fall.

DISEASE *Rhododendron* are generally trouble free when provided with the proper growing conditions. Although sucking insects may affect the leaves in hot weather, petal blight, a fungus that thrives in heat and high humidity, produces the most disappointment. It causes water-soaked spots on the petals that can spread like wildfire, destroying a garden full of blooms in short order. Petal blight is most likely to attack Indica azaleas. If you live in a humid area, good air circulation in the garden is your best defense.

Azaleas And Rhodendrons For Your Garden

Native Or Species Azaleas

Most are hardy to Zone 5 and fragrant, including:

R. austrinum (Florida azalea) (Zone 7)

R. arborescens (Sweet azalea)

R. atlanticum (Coast azalea)

R. calendulaceum (Flame azalea)

R. periclymenoides (Pinxterbloom azalea)

R. vaseyi (Pinkshell azalea)

R. viscosum (Swamp azalea)

Evergreen Azaleas

SOUTHERN INDICAS (Zone 7) are evergreen, grow better than most azaleas in full sun, and range in size from 6'-12'.

KURUME VARIETIES (Zones 6 tand 7) are evergreen, small-leaved, compact growing (2'-4'), with masses of small flowers, often in tiers. They prefer part shade and cannot tolerate hot, dry summer winds.

SATSUKI VARIETIES (Zone 7) are low-growing evergreens (2'-4'), including Gumpo and Macrantha hybrids, and have large flowers late in the season.

PERICAT VARIETIES (Zones 6 and 7) are similar to Kurumes with larger flowers.

GLEN DALE VARIETIES (Zones 5 to 8) vary in growth (generally 4'-6') and leaf size.

GABLE HYBRIDS (Zone 5) grow to about 3'-4'.

NORTH TISBURY HYBRIDS (Zones 6 and 7) are low-growing, spreading and can be used as groundcovers.

ROBIN HILL AND GARTRELL HYBRIDS (Zones 6 and 7) have the large Satsuki blossom, are low growing and hardy.

Deciduous Azaleas

EXBURY AND KNAP HILL HYBRIDS have the largest blossoms of all deciduous azaleas and grow up to 12'.

GHENT HYBRIDS are very hardy, upright shrubs that grow to 4'-6'.

NORTHERN LIGHTS HYBRIDS are very hardy and generally grow 4'-5'.

Native Rhododendrons

R. maximum, the hardiest.

R. catawbiense, the most common in the East.

Evergreen Rhododendrons

CATAWBIENSE HYBRIDS include: 'Catawbiense Album,' a vigorous, wide-spreading white and 'Roseum Elegans,' a very hardy lavender-pink with excellent heat tolerance.

DEXTER HYBRIDS have large leaves, generally grow to 6'-8' and include 'Scintillation,' a favorite luminous pink that grows to 8' and is heat-resistant.

CAUCASIAN HYBRIDS are early blooming and hardy, including 'Boule de Neige' (Zone 5), a dense, rounded low-growing rhododendron with white blossoms.

MEZITT HYBRIDS are small-leaved, very hardy, grow 3'-4' and include 'Olga Mezitt,' a clear pink with leaves turning bronze in winter.

PJM HYBRIDS have small leaves that turn a rich mahogany in winter, are very hardy and grow up to 6'.

Deciduous Rhododendrons

R. mucronulatum (Korean rhododendron) is the first to flower and grows to 6'.

CAMELLIAS

If you live in the less moderate climates of Zones 5 and 6, camellias are not for you. Camellias are subtropical evergreen shrubs that brighten the Zone 7 winter landscape along the Atlantic, Gulf and Pacific coasts. They thrive in mild, humid climates where they grow naturally in lightly shaded woods. Protect camellias from temperature extremes, intense sun and drying winds. And, if a freeze occurs, take special care to shield frozen buds and flowers from damaging morning sunlight.

PLANTING Plant camellias when they are dormant (when the new growth has hardened and there is no active growth), which is ironically during the blooming season. But plant your camellias early in their dormancy, so you can enjoy the bloom and allow the plant time to adjust to its new home prior to its growth period.

> HINT: Pine trees are good companions for camellias and azaleas. Their deep root systems don't interfere with the shrub plantings, they provide filtered light and their needles create an attractive acid mulch.

SOIL Like azaleas, camellias prefer a well-drained, humus-rich, moisture-retentive, slightly acid (pH 5 to 6) soil. Never plant camellias in clay as camellias require plentiful amounts of air in the soil, and clay particles are so tightly packed that the roots suffocate. Avoid planting camellias in low spots in the garden where drainage is poor. Their roots are susceptible to rot.

WATER Water your camellias regularly until they are established and don't forget the leaves. In hot, dry West Coast gardens, perk up your camellias with an overhead shower during the dog days of summer.

FERTILIZING Fertilize camellias with a balanced fertilizer in March, a month prior to the onset of growth in the spring, and again in May and June to ensure good bud production.

MULCH Camellias prefer cool roots, so mulch them well with a loose mulch, which allows air and water penetration.

PRUNING Many camellias will never need to be pruned. But if pruning is necessary, it should be done after the plants have finished blooming or in the summer and fall.

Shrubs

Best Bets For Your Garden

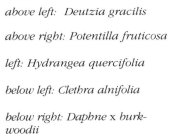

above left: Deutzia gracilis

above right: Potentilla fruticosa

left: Hydrangea quercifolia

below left: Clethra alnifolia

below right: Daphne x burk-woodii

Botanical Name / Common Name	Bloom Color	Height / Spacing	Sun/ Shade
DECIDUOUS SHRUBS			
SMALL (up to 4')			
Caryopteris x *clandonensis* 'Dark Knight'	Deep purple, blue	2' / 18-24"	○
Cotoneaster spp. Cotoneaster	Pinkish white	Varies	○ ◑
Daphne x *burkwoodii* Burkwood daphne	Pink	3' / 2-3'	○ ◑
Deutzia gracilis Slender deutzia	White	2-5' / 3-4'	○ ◑
Potentilla fruticosa Cinquefoil	Yellow, orange, red	3' / 3'	○
Rhododendron spp. Azalea	White, pink, red, coral, yellow, purple	Varies	○ ◑
MEDIUM (Up to 8')			
Berberis spp. Barberry	Red-tinged yellow	3-6' / 3-6'	○ ◑
Buddleia davidii Butterfly bush	Purple, pink, white, or purple-red	5-8' / 4-6'	○
Clethra alnifolia Sweet pepper bush	White	3-8' / 4-6'	○ ●
Cornus alba 'Siberica' Red-twig dogwood	Cream white	7' / 4-5'	○ ◑
Fothergilla spp. Fothergilla	White	Varies	○ ◑
Hydrangea macrophylla Big leaf hydrangea	Pink, white, blue (depending on pH)	3-5' / 3-5'	● ◑
Hydrangea quercifolia Oakleaf hydrangea	White	6-8' / 5-6'	○ ◑

Microclimate	Bloom Time	Comments
Hardy; seashore-tolerant	Summer	Borders; compact, rounded; dark green foliage; clusters of small flowers; light, well-drained soil; cut back nearly to ground in spring; attracts butterflies
Hardy; drought- and seashore-tolerant	Late spring - early summer	Banks, groundcover; glossy, dark green leaves, red in fall; small flower; red fruit; tolerates most soils but not waterlogged soils; deer-resistant; *Cotoneaster apiculatus* (cranberry cotoneaster) is excellent for Midwest
Hardy; little water	Late spring	Accent, borders; dense, rounded; light to medium green foliage; clusters of fragrant, star-shaped flowers; poisonous fruit; rich, well-drained soil; may be slow to establish; try 'Carol Mackie' and 'Somerset'
Hardy	Spring - early summer	Low hedges, mass plantings, borders; upright or spreading; bright green foliage; fertile, well-drained soil; 5-petaled flowers in clusters on arching stems; prune after flowering; pest-resistant
Hardy; drought- and heat-tolerant	Early summer - fall	Borders, mass plantings, low hedge; dense, bushy; grey-green foliage; small, saucer-shaped flowers; well-drained soil; tolerates alkaline and poor soil; cut out older stems annually; many cultivars
Hardy	Early: January-March Mid: March-April Late: April-May	Borders, mass plantings, foundation plantings; rounded to upright; small to large leathery leaves; some blooms fragrant; constantly rich, moist, well-drained, acid soil; intolerant of soil salts; surface roots benefit from acid-rich mulches such as pine needles and oak leaves; do not cultivate soil
Hardy; drought- and seashore-tolerant	Midspring	Hedges, barriers, borders; dense, arching; spiny branches; medium green foliage, brilliant orange-red in fall; small flowers; bright red fruit; tolerates all but waterlogged soil; many species and cultivars
Hardy; seashore-tolerant	Summer	Mixed borders; arching shrub; long, pointed, dull green leaves; fragrant plumes; attracts butterflies; deer-resistant
Hardy; seashore-tolerant	Summer	Mass plantings, hedges; vertical branching; dark green foliage; tiny, fragrant flowers in spires; moist, acid soil; tolerates wet soil
Hardy	Late spring - early summer	Mass plantings, borders; multistemmed, vase-shaped; current year's growth is coral-red in winter; dark green foliage; small flowers in flattened heads; round blue fruit; moist acid to neutral soil; cut out old stems to maintain good color
Hardy	Late spring	Borders, mass plantings, foundations; rounded; dark green to blue-green foliage, brilliant yellow, orange to red in fall; fragrant flowers in terminal spikes; acid, peaty, sandy, well-drained soil; many cultivars
Hardy to Zones 6 and 7	Mid - late summer	Accent, mixed borders; rounded; large, light green leaves; large, domed flower heads; flowers blue or purple in acid soils (pH of up to 5.5); pink in neutral or alkaline soil (pH over 5.5); white flowers not affected by pH; fertile, moist, well-drained soil
Hardy	Summer	Mass plantings, shrub and mixed borders; upright, little branching; older stems exfoliate; oaklike leaves; large, cone-shaped flower clusters; rich, moist, well-drained soil; pest-resistant

Shrubs

Best Bets For Your Garden

above left: Syringa vulgaris

above right: Hibiscus syriacus

left: Spiraea x arguta

below left: Ilex verticillata

below right: Euonymus alatus

Botanical Name / Common Name	Bloom Color	Height / Spacing	Sun/ Shade
Ilex verticillata / Winterberry	White	3-9' / 4-6'	○ ◑
Itea virginica / Virginia sweetspire	White	4-6' / 4-8'	○ ◑
Spiraea spp. / Spirea	White	5-7' / 4-6'	○ ●
Viburnum spp. / Viburnum	White	Varies	○ ◑
LARGE (Up to 15')			
Aesculus parviflora / Bottlebrush buckeye	White	8-12' / 4-6'	○ ◑
Euonymus alatus 'Compacta' / Burning bush	Inconspicuous	8-10' / 4-6'	○ ●
Exochorda racemosa / Pearlbush	White	10-12' / 4-6'	○ ◑
Forsythia x *intermedia* / Border forsythia	Yellow	8-10' / 4-5'	○
Hibiscus syriacus / Rose-of-Sharon	White, pink, rose, lavender	6-12' / 4-5'	○
Magnolia stellata / Star magnolia	White	10-12' / 10-15'	○
Myrica pensylvanica / Bayberry	Yellowish green	5-10' / 3-4'	○ ◑
Syringa vulgaris / Lilac	White, pink, rose, purple	8-15' / 5-6'	○
EVERGREEN SHRUBS			
SMALL (Up to 4')			
Arctostaphylos uva-ursi / Bearberry	White	2-3" / 3-4'	○

Microclimate	Bloom Time	Comments
Hardy	Spring	Borders, mass plantings; dark green foliage; small flowers; very showy red fruit especially on 'Red Sprite,' 'Sparkleberry' and 'Winter Red'; male needed for fruit; rich, moist, acid (pH 4.5 to 6.5) soil; tolerates light, heavy and wet soils
Hardy	Early summer	Specimen, mass plantings, borders; rounded, suckering; dark green foliage is orange to red or purple in fall; flowers in long clusters with light fragrance; moist, fertile soil; pest-resistant
Hardy; seashore-tolerant	Mid - late spring	Accent, borders; arching branches; green leaves turn rich red in fall; white flowers; easy to grow in most soils; many species and cultivars; try *S. prunifolia* 'Plena,' *S. vanhouttei*
Hardy to very hardy; seashore-tolerant	Spring - early summer	Borders, specimen, mass plantings; upright, rounded to broad rounded; medium to dark green, glossy to leathery foliage; showy flowers; often showy fruit; moist, well-drained soils; many species and cultivars; try *V. carlesii, V.* x *burkwoodii* for fragrant flowers and *Viburnum plicatum tomentosum* cultivars for showy bloom
Hardy	Summer	Mass plantings, shrub border; multistemmed with upright branches; bold, dark green leaves; yellow in fall; flowers in panicles; fertile, moist soil
Hardy	Late spring	Mass plantings, shrub border, hedges, screen; broad, spreading; dark green foliage, brilliant red in fall; well-drained soils; pH adaptable; water and mulch in dry areas; withstands heavy pruning
Hardy	Spring	Accent, shrub border; slender, open habit; deep blue-green foliage; showy clusters of flowers; moist, fertile, well-drained soil; resistant to oak root rot
Hardy; seashore-tolerant	Spring	Specimen, mass plantings, borders; upright with arching branches; dense foliage; blooms profusely; fertile, well-drained soil; thin out after flowering; deer-resistant
Hardy; seashore-tolerant	Midsummer - fall	Accent, mass plantings, shrub border; upright, yet bushy; dark green foliage; showy single or double flowers; tolerant of most moist, well-drained soils; no serious pests
Hardy	Spring	Specimen; rounded, tree-like habit; deep green foliage; many-petaled, star-shaped flowers before leaves; rich, moist, well-drained neutral to slightly acid soil; deer-resistant
Hardy to Zones 5 and 6; seashore-tolerant	Spring	Borders, mass plantings; semievergreen; upright, rounded; dark green, leathery foliage; gray fruit; poor, sandy soil as well as clay; lower-growing by coast; select plants grown in your region
Hardy	Spring	Specimen, borders; upright, open; dark green to blue-green foliage; fragrant clusters of flowers; rich, moist, neutral soil; deadhead after flowering; deer-resistant; many cultivars; select disease-resistant cultivars
Very hardy; drought- and seashore-tolerant	Summer	Groundcover, slopes; trailing; small, bright green foliage red in winter; small, urn-shaped flowers; bright red fruit; prefers acid soils; tolerant of poor soils and sand; may be difficult to grow in Midwest

Shrubs
Best Bets For Your Garden

above left: Buxus sempervirens

above right: Santolina chamae-cyparissus

left: Pinus mugo

below: Rhododendron hybrid

Botanical Name Common Name	Bloom Color	Height Spacing	Sun/ Shade
Buxus microphylla Littleleaf box	Inconspicuous	Varies	○
Buxus sempervirens 'Suffructicosa' True dwarf boxwood	Inconspicuous	2-3' *1-3'*	○
Chamaecyparis spp. False cypress	Inconspicuous	Varies	○
Juniperus spp. Juniper	Inconspicuous	Varies	○
Leucothoe axillaris Coastal leucothoe	White	3-4' *3-4'*	◑ ●
Pinus mugo Mugo pine	NA	Varies	○ ◑
Rhododendron spp. Rhododendron	White, pink, red, coral, yellow, purple	Varies	○ ◑
Rosemarinus officinalis Rosemary	Purple-blue	2-4' *4-5'*	○
Santolina chamaecyparissus Lavender cotton	Yellow	1-2' *1-3'*	○
Skimmia japonica Japanese skimmia	White	3-4' *2-3'*	◑ ●
Yucca filamentosa Adam's needle	White	1-2' *2-3'*	○
MEDIUM (Up to 8')			
Abelia grandiflora Glossy abelia	Pinkish white	4-6' *3-6'*	○ ●
Ilex spp. Evergreen, nonspiny-leafed	Inconspicuous	Varies	○ ●

Microclimate	Bloom Time	Comments
Hardy	Late spring	Low edging; slow-growing dwarf, dense; bright green leaves turn yellow-brown in winter; takes shearing well; tolerates all but waterlogged soils; deer-resistant. 'Koreana' (Wintergreen boxwood) is best for colder zones; 'Japonica' (Japanese littleleaf box) is tolerant of alkaline soil and nematode-resistant; many more varieties
Hardy to Zones 6 and 7; heat- and seashore-tolerant	Late spring	Excellent for low edging; slow-growing dwarf, dense; bright green leaves; can be clipped and maintained at as low as 6"; tolerates all but waterlogged soils; susceptible to nematodes; deer-resistant
Hardy	NA	Borders, foundation plantings, accents; upright to pyramidal or rounded; usually flattened, scale-like, green foliage; blue-green and yellow-green cultivars; moist, well-drained soil; protect from drying winds; deer-resistant
Very hardy; drought, heat- and seashore-tolerant	NA	Groundcovers, slopes, mass plantings; needles of varying colors; cones; tolerates all moist but not water-logged soils; tolerates some alkalinity; deer-resistant; many cultivars
Hardy	Late spring	Mass plantings; spreading, zigzag branching; glossy green foliage; drooping, bell-like flowers; moist, well-drained, acid soil; deer-resistant
Hardy	NA	Cultivars; borders, mass plantings, foundations; varies, prostrate or rounded; dark green, 2-needled; deep, moist soil; tolerant of lime soil; intolerant of desert heat; deer-resistant
Hardy	Early: January-March Mid: March-April Late: April-May	Borders, mass plantings, foundation plantings; rounded to upright; small to large leathery leaves; constantly rich, moist, well-drained, acid soil; intolerant of soil salts; surface roots benefit from acid-rich mulches such as pine needles and oak leaves; do not cultivate soil
Hardy to Zone 7; seashore-tolerant	Spring	Hedging, borders; dense, bushy; small, aromatic leaves; small flowers; well-drained soil; culinary herb; deer-resistant
Hardy to Zones 6 and 7	Mid to late summer	Borders, edging; rounded, dense; shoots covered with fuzzy, white growth; whitish grey, aromatic foliage; button-like flowers; well-drained soil
Hardy to Zone 7	Spring	Borders, foundation plantings; bushy, dense; mid- to dark green, glossy foliage; flowers in dense clusters; bright red fruits on female plants; must grow both male and female plants for bloom/fruit; rich, moist, acid soil
Hardy; drought-tolerant	Summer	Accent; architectural; stiff, sword-shaped, deep green leaves; bell-shaped flower; well-drained soil
Hardy to Zones 6 and 7; seashore-tolerant	Midsummer - fall	Hedges, borders; arching; glossy dark green foliage, bronze in winter; fragrant, small flowers; well-drained soil; attracts butterflies; pest-free
Hardy to Zone 7; heat- and drought-tolerant	Spring	Hedges, edging, borders; glossy, leathery leaves; bears fruit; moist, fertile soil; most take severe pruning; deer-resistant; many more varieties including *I. crenata* (Japanese holly); provide east or north exposure in desert for *I. cornuta*; *Ilex glabra* 'Nordic' (Inkberry) is hardier; *I. vomitoria* (Yaupon holly) is tolerant of dry and moist soils and somewhat tolerant of highly alkaline soil

Shrubs

Best Bets For Your Garden

above left: Picea glauca 'Conica'

above right: Thuja occidentalis

left: Mahonia aquifolium

below: Kalmia latifolia

Botanical Name / Common Name	Bloom Color	Height / Spacing	Sun/ Shade
Ilex spp. Evergreen, spiny-leafed holly	Inconspicuous	Varies	○ ◑
Kalmia latifolia Mountain laurel	White, pink, red	Varies	○ ●
Mahonia aquifolium Oregon grape holly	Yellow	3-6' 3-5'	●
Pieris japonica Japanese andromeda	White, pink	Varies	○ ◑
Taxus cuspidata Japanese yew	Inconspicuous	Varies	○ ●
LARGE (Up to 15')			
Camellia japonica Camellia	White, pink, rose, red	10-15' 6-8'	◑
Camellia sasanqua Sasanqua camellia	White, pink, rose, red	6'-10' 5-6'	◑
x Cupressocyparis leylandii Leyland cypress	NA	50-60'* Varies	○
Juniperus scopulorum Rocky Mountain juniper	NA	Varies	○
Ligustrum ovalifolium California privet	White	12' Varies	○ ◑
Picea glauca 'Conica' Dwarf Alberta spruce	NA	10-12' Varies	○ ◑
Thuja occidentalis 'Wintergreen' Wintergreen arborvitae	NA	20-30' Varies	○

Microclimate	Bloom Time	Comments
Hardy	Spring	Mass plantings, hedges, foundations, accent; upright; green spiny foliage; must have male and female for showy red fruit; moist, fertile, acid soil; takes pruning well. Protect *Ilex* x *meserveae* (Meserve hybrids) from drying winter winds; provide sun protection for *Ilex* x 'Nellie Stevens' (Nellie Stevens holly), in hot, dry areas; excellent in South
Hardy	Late spring - early summer	Borders, massing; dense, symmetrical, becoming loose and open; glossy dark green foliage; cup-shaped flowers in clusters; deadhead; cool, moist, acid, well-drained soil; many cultivars
Hardy	Spring	Specimen, borders, foundations; irregular, upright; sparsely branched; hollylike foliage opens reddish bronze turning glossy green; flowers in clusters; edible blue-black fruit; moist, well-drained, acid soils; protect from hot, drying winds; deer-resistant
Hardy	Spring	Specimen, borders, massing; neat, upright, spreading; bronze new growth turning glossy dark green; lily-of-the-valley-like flowers; rich, moist, acid, well-drained soil; protect from wind; many cultivars
Hardy	Spring	Foundations, hedges, screens, massing; erect, broad, narrow or spreading; glossy, dark green, leathery needles; red fruit; moist, sandy, well-drained soil; withstands heavy pruning; many cultivars
Semihardy to Zone 7	November - April	Borders, accents; densely pyramidal; glossy, dark green foliage; large flowers not fragrant and can turn brown in cold; rich, moist, acid, well-drained soil; intolerant of alkaline soil; shallow roots; prune after flowering
Semihardy to Zone 7	September - December	Borders, accents; densely pyramidal; glossy, dark green leaves smaller than japonica; smaller flowers not fragrant and can turn brown in cold; rich, moist, acid, well-drained soil; intolerant of alkaline soil; shallow roots; prune after flowering
Hardy to Zone 6; seashore-tolerant	NA	Screen, hedge, borders; pyramidal; upright branches; feathery, flattened, green foliage; small cones; tolerates most acid or alkaline soils; fast-growing; takes pruning well; *unpruned can grow to 60'
Very hardy; drought-tolerant; intolerant of humidity and warm southeastern summer nights	NA	Screens, hedges, background, foundation plantings; typically pyramidal, some globe-shaped; blue-green scale-like leaves; small, round cones; tolerant of most soils and adverse conditions; deer-resistant; many cultivars
Hardy to Zones 6 and 7; seashore-tolerant	Midsummer	Hedges, screen; bushy, dense; glossy, dark green foliage; panicles of small, unpleasantly fragrant, tubular flowers; prune in early summer to prevent bloom; takes pruning well; any well-drained soil
Very hardy; wind-, heat-, drought-tolerant	NA	Accent; densely pyramidal; slow-growing; light green, short needles; moist soil
Hardy	NA	Screen, hedge, accent; columnar pyramidal; scale-like leaves with good green winter color; single leader; moist, deep, well-drained soil; tolerant of alkaline soils; do not prune; deer-resistant

V
EDIBLE GARDENS

Vegetables
Herbs

VEGETABLES

Vegetables are among the most gratifying plants. They grow quickly, rewarding your hard work with delicious results. If you are a discriminating cook, try planting exotic and gourmet varieties that are hard to find at local supermarkets. Gardeners committed to an organic diet can control what they eat by using organic seeds, fertilizers and nontoxic pest controls. Plant enthusiasts can grow heirloom vegetables for their delicious flavor and to support genetic diversity. Everyone can enjoy vegetables for their beautiful shapes, texture and colors. But don't grow vegetables to save money. Once you've bought the plants, seeds, soil amendments, fertilizers and tools, and fenced and irrigated the garden, you may find that a head of home-grown lettuce costs more than the gas to go to the store. Grow them instead for their flavor, freshness and beauty and the sheer pleasure of watching them grow.

Grow Vegetables:

- For sustenance
- For freshness and flavor
- For exotic and gourmet varieties
- For genetic diversity
- To control your consumption of pesticides
- For their shape, color, texture and beauty
- To share with friends
- For pleasure

UNDERSTANDING VEGETABLES

Usually known by the edible part of the plant, vegetables include root crops, such as carrots and beets; leaf vegetables, such as lettuce, spinach, cabbage and Swiss chard; the flower heads of broccoli and cauliflower; the bulbs of onions and garlic; the enlarged stems of rhubarb, turnips and potatoes; the fruit of tomatoes, eggplants and peppers; and the seeds inside the fruit of corn and peas!

Annual Or Perennial?

Most vegetables are annuals and must be replanted each season. However, a few, such as asparagus, rhubarb and horseradish, are perennial and should have a special home in the garden where they will not be disturbed.

Vegetable Families

Vegetables, like flowers, trees and shrubs, are grouped together into families of plants with similar characteristics, including growing habits, temperature tolerance, soil preferences, and related pest problems. Understanding the nine major vegetable families will help you plan and rotate your garden, giving your plants what they need to excel.

AMARYLLIDACEAE OR LILIACEAE (The amaryllis or lily family) Includes onion-type vegetables and asparagus. Some, such as onions, are grown for their edible bulbs; others, such as chives, for their edible leaves and flowers. While most seeds require warmth to germinate, those in the lily family prefer a cool-weather start in rich, moist, well-drained soil. The longer the bulb grows, the larger it will be.

APIACEAE OR UMBELLIFERAE (Plants with umbel flowers) Includes many fragrant or flavorful plants, herbs such as parsley and dill, and vegetables such as carrots, parsnips, and celery. Prefer cool weather and deep, loose soils. All need light, moist soil to germinate.

ASTERACEAE OR COMPOSITAE (The sunflower family) Includes many ornamental plants, such as asters and daisies, and salad plants, including lettuce, endive, and chicory. Prefer cool weather.

BRASSICACEAE OR CRUCIFERAE (The cabbage or mustard family) Includes ornamentals, such as alyssum and candytufts as well as broccoli, Brussels sprouts, cauliflower, kale, collards, turnips, rutabaga, kohlrabi, watercress and radishes. Prefer cool weather and moist, rich soils. Susceptible to cutworms and cabbage worms.

CHENOPODIACEAE (The goosefoot family) Includes vegetables such as spinach, Swiss chard, beets as well as some herbs and shrubs. Among the most problem-free vegetables except spinach, which bolts in the heat. Prefer cool weather.

CUCURBITACEAE (The gourd or cucumber family) Includes cucumbers, squash, pumpkins, melons and gourds. Tendril vine-growing plants that prefer warm weather and rich, fertile soil. Susceptible to cucumber beetles.

FABACEAE OR LEGUMINOSAE (The legume or pea family, called legumes) Includes ornamentals, trees and vegetables such as peas, beans, peanuts, soybeans and clover. Cold tolerance varies. Nitrogen-fixing nodules on the roots of these plants convert nitrogen from the air into nitrogen in the soil.

This is extremely beneficial to the soil and a boon to plants rotated to their spot in the garden. Susceptible to diseases that are spread when the leaves are wet.

POACEAE OR GRAMINEAE (The grass family) Includes the most important grain crops, such as corn, oats, and wheat, as well as grasses, sugar cane, and bamboo. Many, such as corn, deplete the soil of nutrients and should be rotated annually.

SOLANACEAE (The tobacco or nightshade family) Includes tomatoes, peppers, potatoes and eggplants. Prefer warm weather and rich, moist soil. Crop rotation is important as plants are susceptible to disease. Some are used for medicinal purposes while others have toxic parts.

What's In A Name?

Like people, all plants are given names to differentiate them within their families. Only plants have two different types of names: a botanical name, which is in Latin and universally accepted, and a common name, which may differ from region to region. The Latin name consists of two words. The first is the genus; the second, the species. As a species is a subdivision of the genus, you'll find that all plants of a certain genus share common characteristics but differ in at least one habit. For instance, *Allium sativum* is a garlic and *Allium cepa* is an onion. However, while it is becoming an accepted practice to refer to many plants by their Latin names, edible plants are still most often referred to by their common names.

Varieties

Today there are thousands of varieties and cultivars (cultivated varieties) from which to choose. Although they retain most of the characteristics of the species, they may differ slightly in their drought or temperature tolerance, disease resistance, color or fruit size. Open-pollinated varieties reproduce by means of the wind or animals, such as birds and bees, so their fruits and flowers are never exactly alike. Seed companies simply select the best plants from the crop. Many of the heirloom vegetables are grown from open-pollinated seed. As hybrids are grown from seed that has been produced from deliberate cross-pollination, they have more consistent qualities. In the seed catalogs, open-pollinated and hybrid names are usually printed within single quotation marks. For instance 'Tall Telephone' (an heirloom pea) or 'Early Girl' (a tomato cultivar). Have fun choosing your plants. Experiment! There is bound to be one that's just right for your climate.

VEGETABLES IN YOUR CLIMATE

Vegetables require different amounts of sun and different temperatures to thrive. Begin by mapping out how much sun your vegetable garden receives each day, determine the expected summer temperatures, the length of the growing season and the first and last days of frost.

With your long growing season, and the hundreds of varieties from which to choose, you can plan a garden that is prolific all season long. Some vegetables like cool nights to germinate, while others are tender, preferring warm soil and air temperatures. Some ripen only in full sun all day, while others may bolt in the heat. Know what the plants need, what your climate can provide and plan your garden accordingly.

SUN/SHADE

Sun is the essential ingredient for an abundant crop of healthy vegetables. In your moderate climate, many vegetables grow best, and fastest, in full sun all day. However, some vegetables, such as leafy crops and tender young seedlings, may get too much sun in areas with excessively hot summers and may lose more water to transpiration than they can take up through their roots. Although happiest in early and late summer, given a little shade they too will thrive through the heat of the summer. If your garden doesn't receive light shade, you can easily construct a cover.

Few vegetables will produce abundant crops in the shade. If your garden receives less than six hours of sun, try the following vegetables:

- Arugula
- Cress
- Radishes
- Beets
- Endive
- Sorrel
- Broccoli
- Escarole
- Spinach
- Cabbage
- Leaf lettuce
- Swiss Chard
- Carrots
- Peas

Blanching

Some vegetables benefit from the denial of sunlight, referred to as "blanching." Blanching produces the colorless heads of cauliflower and makes other vegetables more tender and less bitter. To blanch cauliflower pull the leaves over the developing flower head and secure them with string.

Day Length

Vegetables are particularly responsive to day length — the number of daylight hours. The greater the number of daylight hours, the faster the growth; the fewer the daylight hours, the longer the time to ripen. For example, in northern areas with midnight sun, such as Alaska, vegetables grow very large, very fast.

Some plants are more sensitive than others to day length. Onions don't begin to form their bulbs until there are at least sixteen hours of daylight. On the other hand, the heads of cauliflower begin to develop as the days get shorter. Short days when combined with cool temperatures can be beneficial for "holding" leafy vegetables such as lettuce, cole crops such as broccoli and cabbage, and root crops such as carrots.

TEMPERATURE

Temperature controls the life cycle of vegetables. Seeds germinate and vegetables ripen in warm weather; cold weather usually signals the end of a vegetable's life cycle.

Annual Vegetables

Annual vegetables are extremely sensitive to climatic conditions and are categorized by their cold and heat tolerance. Be sure to keep your microclimate in mind when choosing plants. The different types of annual vegetables are:

HARDY VEGETABLES Can survive frost. Are successful when sown directly in the vegetable garden, even while cool temperatures prevail. Include broccoli, Brussels sprouts, cabbage, collard, kale, kohlrabi, leek, onion, and spinach.

HALF-HARDY VEGETABLES Will take some frost, but not as much as hardy vegetables. Include cauliflower, celery, chard, chicory, Chinese cabbage, endive and lettuce.

TENDER VEGETABLES Cannot tolerate frost. Many of these types need several weeks time in order to reach maturity, so they should be sown early indoors, in cold frames, or outdoors only after danger of frost has past. These can also be purchased as greenhouse-grown seedlings or rooted cuttings. Include cucumber, eggplant, muskmelon, pepper, pumpkin, squash, tomato and watermelon.

Consider the following when selecting vegetables:
- The lowest expected temperatures in the summer
- The highest expected temperatures in the summer
- The average last day of frost
- The average first day of frost
- The crop's germination temperature
- The crop's frost tolerance

Cool- and Warm-season Crops

A vegetable's hardiness influences whether it is a cool-season or warm-season crop. In Zones 5, 6 and 7, cool-season crops, such as peas, can be sown outdoors up to six weeks before the last spring frost and tolerate temperatures down to 25° Fahrenheit. They flourish in the spring and finish producing in time for warm-season crops to take over during the peak summer heat.

COOL-SEASON CROPS These hardy and some half-hardy vegetables can tolerate cool weather. Include beets, broccoli, Brussels sprouts, cabbage, cauliflower, greens and spinach, lettuce and salad greens, parsnips, peas and radishes.

WARM-SEASON CROPS These half-hardy or tender vegetables prefer warm temperatures and warm soil and may show no growth until the soil warms sufficiently. Include beans, corn, cucumber, eggplant, melons, peppers, potatoes, squash, sunflowers and tomatoes.

FULL-SEASON CROPS These vegetables can tolerate cool and warm weather. Include celery and onions.

HINT: Keep the soil warm. A plant with warm roots can better combat chilly air.

WATER

Water is essential; without it seeds won't germinate and plants won't grow. Many vegetables consist primarily of water, and consequently grow best when the soil is constantly moist. When you first sow your seeds it's particularly important to keep the soil moist to promote germination. Water the beds lightly early each morning and again during the day if the soil is dry. Water transplants regularly, keeping the soil wet for the first week. Water seedlings and transplants thoroughly but less often once they have begun to grow. Once plants are established, provide about 1" of water whenever the top 2" of soil is dry. The frequency will depend on your soil and microclimate. During hot, dry summers you will have to water more often than during rainy ones. If you live in a humid area water will evaporate more slowly.

Keep a close eye on the garden. Watch the soil to see how fast it dries; watch the plants for signs of stress. A well-watered plant will have turgid, glossy leaves; a dry plant, dull or wilting leaves. Try never to let plants wilt, but don't over-water either; wilting can also be a sign of overwatering or infestation by borers.

HINT: Water cucumbers evenly to avoid misshapen fruit.

PLANNING YOUR VEGETABLE GARDEN
Choosing The Site

The ideal site for a vegetable garden is healthy for both the plants and for you. For the plants, select a site that has full sun all day, good drainage, no competing roots from trees or shrubs and easy access to a water source. A gently sloping, south-facing site is ideal, but avoid low sites where water may collect. Be sure to check the history of the site for any secrets hidden in the soil. Were strong pesticides used nearby? Is it near a garage or driveway where oil or gas may have leaked into the soil? Has flaking lead paint or disintegrating asbestos from an old barn or house contaminated the soil?

What Should The Garden Look Like?

The location and purpose of the garden will help determine its style. If the garden is near the house, an ornamental vegetable garden is ideal. Make it a formal, geometric shape, with brick or stone paths, low borders or brick edging, or enclose it with espaliered fruit trees. Use poles, tepees, and tripods to add a vertical element to the garden, bringing vegetables up to eye level.

For an informal garden, design free-form beds and plant them with herbs, flowers and vegetables. When space is limited, intermingle herbs and vegetables with flowers in containers on your deck or terrace. But if you want a workhorse of a garden, or are very busy and won't have the time to keep the garden looking its best, choose a simple design, such as a rectangle, and locate it away from the house, perhaps behind a fence or hedge. But pay attention to the details. Each decision you make — the type of enclosure, the paths, the edging for the beds and the vertical plant supports — reinforces the style you have selected.

GARDEN DESIGN

There are so many delicious vegetables, it's very tempting to design a big garden. But start small. Select a few useful and easy-to-grow vegetables such as radishes, carrots, green beans, cabbage, leaf lettuce, summer squash and tomatoes. When making an ornamental vegetable garden, select vegetables for their appearance as well as their flavor. Think of vegetables the way you would perennials. Consider their growth habit, leaf size, color and texture: tall and narrow, short and bushy or vine-like; rosette-shaped heads like lettuce or feathery foliage like carrots and dill. Edge the garden with the beautiful shapes of lettuce or cabbage or intermingle them with herbs and flowers. Weave the fine tufts of carrots or dill through flowers such as dahlias or snapdragons for contrasting textures or add variegated sage or ruby basil for contrasting leaf color.

Plant vegetables with edible flowers. They are delicious in salads and beautiful as garnishes. Their flavors range from mild to peppery to sweet.

> HINT: Balance your sunlight by orienting your garden rows on a north-south axis. Place corn and tall plants toward the north end where they will block the wind but not the sunlight.

Edible Flowers

- *Alcea rosea* (hollyhock) — slightly sweet
- *Antirrhinum majus* (snapdragon) — mild flavor
- *Brassica hirta* (mustard) — warm, subtle mustard flavor
- *Calendula officinalis* (Calendula) — tangy flavor
- *Centaurea cyanus* (Bachelor's button) — mild flavor
- *Cucurbita* spp. (squash) — make excellent cups for fillings
- *Dianthus caryophyllus* — mild flavor
- *Fuschia* — tart lemon flavor
- *Hemerocallis* (daylily) — mild flavor
- *Hibiscus syriacus* (rose-of-Sharon) — sweet, mild flavor
- *Lavandula* (lavender) — lavender flavor
- *Lonicera* (honeysuckle) — sweet flavor
- *Monarda* (bee balm) — citrus flavor
- *Pelargonium* (scented geranium) — a variety of aromas from coconut to nutmeg
- *Petunia* x *hybrida* — mild, sweet flavor
- *Tagetes* spp. (marigold) — tarragon flavor
- *Tropaeolum majus* (nasturtium) — hot, peppery flavor
- *Rosa* — rose aroma
- *Viola* x *wittrockiana* (pansy) — mild flavor
- *Viola odorata* (violet) — sweet flavor

Only eat flowers you know are edible. Do not eat toxic flowers such as buttercups, *Delphinium*, common daisies, *Aconitum* (monkshood), *Narcissus* and *Nerium* (oleander).

Next select a shape for your garden: rectangular, square, round, triangular, crescent or free-form: the choices are as varied as your imagination. The easiest design is rectangular: 20' x 24' for a small garden; 40' x 60' for a large garden. Then decide whether you want to plant in rows or raised beds. Rows give you great design flexibility; raised beds are more permanent but are excellent when starting a garden in poor, shallow or poorly drained soil.

PLANTING PATTERNS

Now comes the fun part, known as the planting pattern, or how you arrange the vegetables within the beds. Planting patterns are integral to the overall design of the garden. Plant your vegetables in rows, blocks or beds.

Planting In Rows

Rows can be either single or several plants wide. Single rows are ideal for vegetables that are picked regularly; however, they take up a lot of valuable space in small gardens. Wide rows are more practical for vegetables that don't need as much attention, such as beets, radishes, carrots and greens.

Rows are easy to mulch and give you the opportunity to create contrasting patterns. Align the rows in different directions, including north-south, east-west and diagonally.

HINT: To prevent runoff and soil erosion, lay out your rows running across a slope, not up and down hill.

Planting In Beds And Blocks

Planting in beds and blocks saves space as paths are eliminated between the rows. Within the bed or block, plants are spaced equally in all directions, either in a grid pattern or staggered rows. When the plants are spaced so that they touch, few weeds will grow in their shade. If you like the look of mass planting, organize your plants in blocks or beds. Alternate blocks of different-colored lettuces to create a checkerboard effect.

EDGING

Edging clearly defines the planting beds, emphasizing the design of the garden. Brick or bluestone are beautiful but costly. 2 x 6 pressure-treated lumber makes a fine edge, is easy to install and is much less expensive.

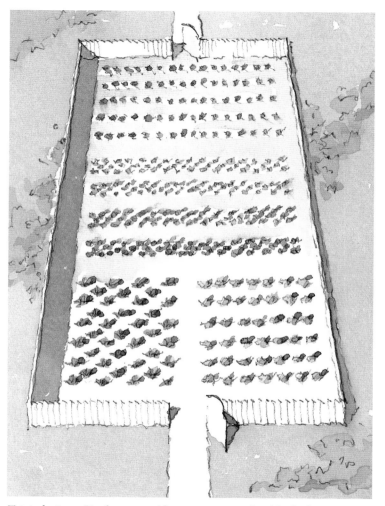

Top to bottom: Single rows, wide rows, staggered in blocks (bottom left), aligned in blocks (bottom right).

Build bottomless enclosures of pressure-treated 2 x 6 lumber and place them on top of the soil, leaving adequate space for paths between them. Dig topsoil out of the paths to fill the beds. Fill the paths with mulch, brick or stone to meet the original grade.

RAISED BEDS

Raised beds are also your best bet in areas with inadequate drainage, poor or shallow soils. By raising the soil level above the existing grade with amended soil, you will improve the soil while also increasing its depth and drainage. Use brick, bluestone, or 2 x 6 pressure-treated lumber edging to make raised beds. Corn, cucumbers, melons, potatoes, squash, tomatoes, peppers, pumpkins and eggplants grow better in the well-drained soil of raised beds, while lettuce, spinach, radishes, Swiss chard, carrots, and beets can be planted earlier in the warmth of raised beds. But raised beds are not for every garden. In dry climates they dry out more quickly, requiring additional watering.

HINT: When designing raised beds make them no wider than 4' to 6', allowing you to reach the vegetables in the center.

SPACING

Spacing depends on the growth habit of each plant and the planting pattern you have selected. Remember, seedlings are placed much closer together, because ultimately the weakest plants will be thinned out, leaving the sturdiest to mature. To plan your garden, see the spacing requirements in the Vegetable List, then lay out the rows or beds accordingly. In general, space plants as follows:

SINGLE ROWS Align single rows 3' to 4' apart; within the row, space small plants such as carrots 3" to 4" apart; large plants such as tomatoes 1' to 2' apart.

WIDE ROWS Align wide rows 3' to 4' apart; for vines, such as peas, make a single, 4" to 6" wide trench throughout which you can scatter the seeds; for lettuces, carrots, radishes and beets, make three or four parallel grooves, 4" to 6" apart in each row.

BLOCKS OR BEDS Space all plants equally in all directions according to the required spacing for the individual plant.

HINT: To shade soil and reduce water evaporation, space plants so that as they mature, their leaves will touch.

Spacing Guidelines

With a roll of string and a few stakes you can easily lay out your rows or divide your beds into equal spaces.

TO PLANT IN ROWS Insert a stake in the first corner of the prepared bed, then measure off the predetermined length of the row and place a second stake at the opposite end. Stretch a string between the two stakes. The string marks the center of the row. Sow your seeds or plant your seedlings in line with the string at the appropriate spacing.

TO PLANT IN A BLOCK OR BED For equal spacing, divide the prepared planting area into a grid of squares. First insert stakes at equal distances on all four sides of the bed (stakes should be directly opposite each other). Stretch string between opposite stakes. This will form a grid of squares. Position seeds or seedlings in the center of each square.

SUCCESSION PLANTING
Succession planting uses the garden space efficiently and provides you with a continuous flow of fresh vegetables. Consider your microclimate, the temperature preferences of your vegetables and their growing speed. For the best results use the following approaches:

- Plant different varieties of the same vegetable for early, midseason and late harvests.
- Stagger plantings of the same vegetable at two-week intervals for a continuous yield.
- Interplant vegetables that mature at successive intervals.

INTERPLANTING
Interplanting means growing two different vegetables in the same area. Interplanting makes efficient use of the space between slow-growing vegetables, such as corn, tomatoes and peppers, to grow fast-growing crops, such as lettuce, radishes and carrots. Interplant cool-season vegetables, such as lettuce, with tall-growing vegetables, such as corn and pole beans. The shade of the tall-growing plants will prevent the lettuce from bolting. But not all plants make good neighbors. Some vegetables attract 'destructive pests; others inhibit the neighboring vegetable's growth. Onions especially can be too much for other vegetables to handle. See the following chart for general interplanting guidelines:

VEGETABLE	COMPATIBLE WITH	INCOMPATIBLE WITH
Asparagus	Chard, basil, parsley	Onions, garlic
Bush beans	Marigolds, corn, beets	Onions, garlic
Carrots	Onions, leeks, savory herbs	Dill
Cucumbers	Corn, radishes	Potatoes, sage
Eggplant	Peas	Potatoes
Greens	Cabbages, potatoes	
Lettuce	Corn, tomatoes, broccoli, peppers	
Melons	Corn, cucumbers	Potatoes
Onions	Carrots, lettuce, radishes	Beans, peas
Peas	Carrots, radishes, turnips	Onions
Peppers	Carrots, eggplants, onions, tomatoes	
Radishes	Carrots, lettuce	
Squash	Beans, corn, radishes	
Tomatoes	Onions, parsley, carrots	Brassicas, corn
Turnips	Peas	

CROP ROTATION
When crops are rotated, their location in the garden changes from year to year. Rotate your crops to reduce the level of pests and disease in the garden and to maintain the soil's level of nutrition.

Different pests attack different plants. When you change the plants in a bed, the overwintering larvae will wake up in the late spring to plants that are not their vegetable of choice. Their appetites curbed, the less damage they will do, and the more slowly they will multiply.

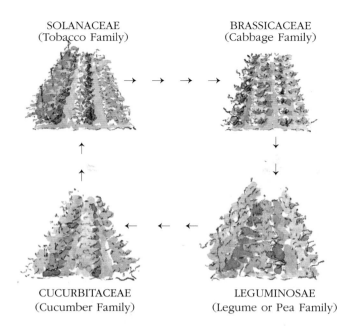

SOLANACEAE
(Tobacco Family)

BRASSICACEAE
(Cabbage Family)

CUCURBITACEAE
(Cucumber Family)

LEGUMINOSAE
(Legume or Pea Family)

Crop rotation is like musical chairs. Plants from the same family move from bed to bed each year.

Vegetables also have varying nutritional needs. Some, such as cabbage, are heavy feeders and deplete the soil of specific nutrients. Others in the legume family replenish the soil. By rotating your crops you ensure that no one nutrient is depleted.

The key to rotating your crops is to identify the plant family (see p.170). Plant vegetables from the same family, such as cabbage, broccoli and cauliflower, in the same bed the first year; grow them in another bed the following year. The vegetables that benefit most from rotation are the cucumber family, including squash, pumpkins and melons; the legumes, including peas and beans; the cabbage family, including broccoli and cauliflower; and the tobacco or nightshade family, including tomatoes, potatoes and eggplants. Although crop rotation may seem like a lot of work, it will mean less fertilizing, healthier plants and fewer pests.

> *HINT: Stay on the garden paths. Foot traffic can compact the soil and disturb the plants.*

GARDEN PATHS

Formal or informal, all vegetable gardens need paths for easy access to the plants. In small formal gardens use brick, stone, gravel or crushed oyster shells; in large gardens, grass is a less expensive alternative, but it needs to be edged and mowed. For an informal garden, lay down a thick layer of mulch such as ground wood chips, loose straw or salt hay. If you have the time to cultivate regularly to prevent weeds, let the paths compact naturally. Make paths at least 2' to 3' wide to accommodate wheelbarrows and baskets for weeding or harvesting.

FENCING

Good fences make for bountiful harvests; without them creatures other than you will be enjoying the benefits of your hard work. If you live in an area with deer, rabbits, woodchucks or other voracious eaters, good fences are essential. Make them formal, utilizing white pickets or ornamental metal, or informal, utilizing post-and-rail, split rail or wire. Tailor the fence to the critter. For instance, use wire with 1" openings for rabbits and skunks, aviary wire for gophers. If only a decorative wood fence with pickets spaced at 4" will do, add chicken wire on the inside to keep out the smaller animals. Be sure to make your fence high enough: go 3' to 4' feet for woodchucks and raccoons; 8' to 10' for deer. But don't stop there. Go underground too! Extend chicken wire 6" underground, then make an L, running it horizontally away from the garden for another 6". The garden gate is also a prime entry point. Add a width of chicken wire at the bottom, trying not to leave any gaps between the soil and bottom of the gate.

Extreme Measures

FOR RACCOONS If raccoons are making it over your 4' fence, add another 2' of chicken wire above it. Securely attach the bottom foot of wire to vertical posts, leaving the top foot of wire loose. When a raccoon tries to climb over, the loose wire will bend backward, tossing the masked intruder to the ground.

FOR DEER Because deer like to see where they are going, they rarely go over solid fences. But solid fences are expensive, so new designs are aimed at the deer's inability to jump long distances. Try erecting a double fence: two 4' high fences with a 3' wide space between them. If your vegetable garden is not in view of the house, try a 4' high fence to which a slanting wood-and-wire barrier has been added to the outside. To build the barrier, attach one end of an 8' long 2 x 4 to the top of each post, slant it down to the ground and secure it with a stake. Then run wire between the 2 x 4's, spacing it at 12" intervals. If all else fails, install an electric fence. For additional tips on keeping out uninvited guests, see "Pests And Intruders" on p.39.

PLANNING AT A GLANCE:
- Microclimate
- Length of growing season
- Soil
- Water
- Cool-season or warm-season
- Annual or perennial

- Time you have available to garden
- Time required for germination
- Time required from seeding to harvest
- Plant growth habit
- Height and width
- Leaf size, texture and color
- Vegetable family and crop rotation
- Spacing
- Harvest goals
- Time of harvest: one-time or continuous
- Garden style: formal, informal, ornamental
- Planting pattern: rows or beds
- Pest control

BED PREPARATION
To lay out the bed put stakes in the corners and stretch string between them. If the bed is in a lawn area, remove the sod (see "Removing Sod," p.33). Rototill to break up all chunks of soil and expose rocks and other buried surprises. Remove all weeds, with roots intact, and add them to your compost pile. Continue going through the soil until it is loose and free of all rocks and debris.

To get a head start in the fall, spread 3" to 4" of compost and manure over the bed, then work it into the top 8" to 12" of topsoil. Cover it completely with a continuous sheet of black plastic secured with heavy rocks. If this is applied early in the fall, any remaining weeds that try to come up will be frustrated by the darkness, leaving the bed practically weed-free for the spring.

If beginning in the spring, you won't have the benefit of the winter in which to kill weeds. If your new vegetable garden is located in an area where perennial grasses, weeds and/or shrubs were growing, finely rake the top 6" of soil to be sure you have removed all the grass rhizomes and weed roots. If you have a small garden use a riddle or piece of 1/2" screen to sieve out grubs, cocoons or cutworms as well. This will reduce future weeding and save your seedlings from hungry munchers. Add amendments as recommended by the soil test (see "Soil," p.18).

For small gardens, double digging (see "Double Digging" p.34) will improve the texture and nutrient content of even the most hard, compact garden soil. If you are making a garden near a newly constructed house, there may be little topsoil and the ground may have been compacted by heavy machinery. Double digging will be well worth the effort.

SOIL

Good soil preparation is essential for a bountiful vegetable garden. Consider your soil's composition, pH and fertility. The best garden soil is a deep loam with a neutral pH (6.0 to 6.8) and loose texture for good aeration. It should retain moisture yet have good drainage, be free of rocks and weeds, rich in nutrients, and teeming with microorganisms and earthworms. To check your soil, take a sample and send it to a local Agricultural Cooperative Extension Service to see which nutrients are lacking and whether or not you need to adjust your soil's pH level. Even if you are starting on a rocky, barren site, you can make good soil with a little elbow grease, time and lots of organic matter.

Amending The Soil

Vegetables grow best in a deep loam with a neutral pH (6.0 to 6.8). Add any soil amendments recommended by the results of the soil test. This may seem like a lot of work, but when your vegetables respond so enthusiastically, it will all seem worthwhile.

To raise the pH add ground limestone. A good rule of thumb is to add seventy pounds to raise the pH one point (from 5.5 to 6.5) over an area of one thousand square feet (a 20' x 50' bed). To lower the pH one point (from 7.5 to 6.5) over the same area, add twenty pounds of agricultural sulfur. Broadcast the limestone or sulfur over the bed, then thoroughly till it into the soil.

SEEDS OR PLANTS?

When it comes time to plant you have a choice between sowing or transplanting. Consider your climate, length of growing season and time required from sowing to harvest for the vegetables you've selected. You may want to get an early start in your garden by planting seedlings you have started indoors or purchased from a local nurseryman. However, with seeds you will find a much wider variety and a greater number of sources. If an organic garden is your goal, it may be difficult to buy organic seedlings. Whether you opt for seeds or plants, buy disease-resistant varieties whenever possible.

Buying Seeds

Vegetable seeds can be purchased from your local garden center or from a variety of mail-order sources (see "Sources"). You will find an enormous selection available through mail-order catalogs, including many improved and old-fashioned varieties, organic, gourmet and exotic seeds. They are available as loose seeds in seed packets or in a much more limited selection, as seed tapes and "Seed 'n Start" kits. Seed tapes are actually soluble tapes with seeds imbedded in them for perfect planting in rows! Seed 'n Start kits are cell packs filled with a lightweight starting mix and seeds, covered with clear tops to retain the moisture and enhance germination.

HINT: For the best germination rate, buy seeds bearing the current year's date.

Vegetables grow readily from seed especially in Zone 7 with its long growing season. Look for seed companies that specialize in seeds for your climate and will work well within your growing season. Experiment with different varieties.

Buying Plants

Buying vegetable plants is an easy way to start the season. Plants are usually available in flats, cell-packs and individual pots. See "Buying Plants" in "Annuals."

SOWING

Starting Indoors

Seeds need warmth, water, oxygen and light to germinate. Sow seeds in individual pots or plastic trays filled with a sterile, lightweight soil mix. Soilless mixes containing perlite, vermiculite and peat moss also provide excellent results. Follow the instructions for spacing and planting depths for each type of seed. Be sure not to plant them too deep as light must be able to reach the seeds. A good rule of thumb for determining planting depth is to plant seeds three times as deep as they are wide. See the Vegetable List on p.188 and read the back of the seed packets for more specific recommendations. Water the seeds in well and keep them moist, but do not overwater. Place them in a sunny spot where the temperature is between 60° and 70° Fahrenheit. If you don't have at least six hours of strong sun, a fluorescent light will speed up germination. Within two to three weeks true leaves should appear. This is the time to transplant the seedlings into divided trays or individual pots filled with slightly heavier potting soil.

Damping Off

Damping off is a soil-borne disease that attacks seedlings during germination, causing them to wilt. It spreads most easily in warm, moist conditions with poor air circulation. Prevention is the best defense against damping off.

To avoid damping off:
- Use clean pots or trays.
- Use sterilized potting soil.
- Keep seeds moist, but do not overwater.
- Do not crowd seeds; thin them out as necessary.
- Immediately remove infected seedlings from trays.

Timing

To ascertain when to start seeds indoors, determine the date of the last expected spring frost and subtract the number of weeks needed from sowing to transplanting size. The length of time varies with each plant as follows:

10 WEEKS Onions, leeks, peppers, early celery, eggplant, asparagus
9 WEEKS Parsley
8 WEEKS Early lettuce
6-8 WEEKS Tomatoes, basil
6-7 WEEKS Early cabbage, broccoli, Brussels sprouts, kale, early head lettuce
5-6 WEEKS Late cabbage, early leaf lettuce, cauliflower
4-5 WEEKS Cucumbers, melons, squash, pumpkins, gourds

Hardening Off

Before transplanting seedlings into the garden, they must be acclimated, or hardened off. Harden off seedlings by first moving them to a cold frame (a box with a light-permeable cover that can be opened and closed depending on the temperature) or a shady, protected spot outdoors. If unseasonably cold weather threatens, bring your seedlings back indoors. Water them regularly. After three days they should be prepared for their summer in the garden.

Sowing Outdoors

Sow seeds outdoors at the recommended depth and spacing for each specific vegetable. Avoid planting seeds too close; they won't grow as well. For small seeds, firm the soil at the appropriate depth and cover with a lightweight or soilless mix. Water seeds gently at the time of planting, keep the soil moist until the seedlings emerge, then water regularly.

HINT: Perennial vegetables, such as asparagus, do not have to be rotated.

SOWING IN FURROWS Furrows are shallow planting trenches, which can vary in depth depending on the size of the seed. Use furrows when you are planting in rows. After you have laid out the row using stakes and string (see "Spacing Guidelines" on p.176) form a trench directly beneath the string. Use the corner of a hoe to form deep furrows; the tip of a trowel for shallow furrows. Distribute the seeds evenly, then firm the soil over the furrow using the flat side of a rake. Some gardeners prefer covering seeds with a light, moisture-retentive soilless mix. Gently sprinkle the beds, taking care not to wash the seeds away.

SOWING IN RIDGES If planting time is cold and rainy in your area, it may be best to plant in ridges. Ridges will warm up faster and dry out more easily, preventing the seeds from rotting. Using a hoe, form ridges by hilling soil several inches high directly beneath the row guideline. Make a shallow furrow down the center for the seed.

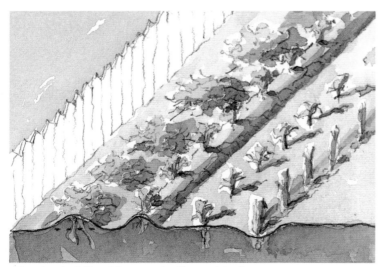

Planting in hills, ridges, on the flat and in furrows.

SOWING IN HILLS Plant seeds of vining plants that require warm, well-drained soil, such as cucumbers, pumpkins and squash, in hills. Use a hoe to form a mound 3" to 4" high and 12" to 18" across. Make a hole 2" to 3" deep in the center of the hill. Place a few seeds in the hole and gently firm the soil over them. Sprinkle the mound gently until it is completely saturated.

Thinning

When sowing, seeds are often so small it's difficult to space them just right. Several seeds may begin to develop right next to each other. To develop into a full, healthy plant, seedlings need enough space in which to grow. Look over your seedlings. Decide which are the most vigorous, then make room for them by thinning out, or pulling out, the less vigorous plants. To prevent disturbance to the remaining seedling, press down on the soil around it with your fingers, while simultaneously pulling out the other. Look at the seed packets for more specific directions.

TRANSPLANTING

Transplant home-grown or purchased plants into rows, ridges or hills. When transplanting, avoid damage to the stems as they are the plant's lifeline without which they cannot grow. If plants are growing in flats, carefully prick out the seedlings. If plants are in cell packs, push the root ball out from the bottom.

For most vegetables, dig a hole slightly bigger than the root ball. Holding the plant gently by the root ball or leaves, set it in the hole at the same level as it was growing in the container. Hold the seedlings gently by the leaves and carefully smooth the soil in around them. Softly tamp the soil to remove all air pockets, which enables the roots to make good contact with the soil. Water the seedlings in to further settle the soil.

Tomatoes are an exception. They actually benefit from

being planted slightly deeper. This encourages them to root along their stems where the additional roots provide greater support and improve moisture absorption.

When you remove a plant from a container, you inevitably injure a few roots, which may cause a slight setback in plant growth. Try these transplanting techniques to reduce stress:

- Plant seedlings immediately after removing them from their containers.
- Transplant on a cloudy day or in the early morning before the heat of the day.
- Water the seedlings before transplanting, gently spraying the leaves to reduce wilting.
- Water transplants thoroughly after planting.
- Shade plants if necessary.

FERTILIZING

Nutrient-rich soil produces a bountiful harvest. If your goal is to grow organic vegetables, organic materials such as manure, kelp, compost and/or bone meal can be added to the soil in the necessary amounts to satisfy your soil test. Just keep in mind the nutrient composition and pH of each material. For instance, bone meal is high in phosphorus (2-14-0), and cottonseed meal is very acidic. Making the calculations and spreading the amendments (you need twenty pounds of cow manure to equal the NPK content of one pound of 5-10-5 fertilizer) takes extra time and effort, but many gardeners feel the results are well worth it as the manure is more efficient at delivereing its nutrient load. Manure remains in the soil while synthetic fertilizers may evaporate or wash away. For additional organic amendments, refer to the chart on the next page.

You may opt to use a combination of organic materials and synthetic fertilizers. Synthetic fertilizers will efficiently provide the essential nutrients (NPK), while compost and manure will add the micronutrients and organic matter. Fertilizers are available in a variety of formulations, which benefit specific crops as follows:

5-10-5   For fruiting crops, such as squash and tomatoes
10-10-10   For leafy vegetables, such as lettuce, spinach and cabbage
5-10-10   For peppers and other crops requiring more potash

But as synthetic fertilizers are released more quickly than organic materials, you will have to apply them more often. If you are growing crops, such as melons, that take over one hundred days to mature, use a slow-release synthetic fertilizer. But keep in mind that fertilizers are potent. Use them with care. Do not let them come in direct contact with roots or stems and always water them in well. If you are experiencing a dry summer, fertilize with care and only if you can follow up with water.

FOLIAR FEEDING is often beneficial for watering in young transplants and to give sad-looking plants a midseason boost. Spray the liquid fertilizer directly on the leaves. Use a balanced 20-20-20 formula that comes in liquid and crystalline form or organic fertilizers such as seaweed extract and fish emulsion. Be sure to mix it well. For large areas use a hose attachment that automatically mixes the fertilizer at the correct rate. For young transplants use a weaker solution, particularly if you use manure tea (see p.185). This should be diluted 1:1.

SIDE-DRESSING is a good way to satisfy the special needs of specific vegetables in the garden. It is especially beneficial to vegetables that take more than sixty days to mature. You simply take a handful of the appropriate fertilizer and scratch it into the soil next to the plant several times during the growing season. Side-dress peppers after they have set their first fruits. Broccoli, side-dressed with 10-10-10 fertilizer after you have picked the primary head, will continue to produce. Bonemeal, blood meal, rock phosphate and cottonseed meal are good organic fertilizers for side-dressing.

Organic Amendment	N	P	K	Comments
Alfalfa Hay	2.5	0.5	2.1	Let rot as mulch first or use alfalfa meal instead. Fast-acting. Also contains trace minerals.
Blood Meal	12.0	1.5	0.6	Strong. Can burn plants. Use carefully as a side dressing. Medium- to fast-acting. Smelly. Repels deer.
Bone Meal (steamed)	1.0-4.0	10.0-34.0	0	Phosphorus available faster to plants than with rock or colloidal phosphate but still slow- to medium acting. Good for side-dressing. More expensive.
Canola Meal	6.0	2.0	1.0	Medium- to slow-acting.
Colloidal (soft) Phosphate	0.0	2.0	0	Phosphorus available faster to plants than rock phosphate. Best source of phosphorus for alkaline soil.
Compost (dry)	1.0	1.0	1.0	Good mulch; retains moisture. Slow-acting.
Compost (homemade)	1.5-3.5	0.5-1.0	1.0-2.0	Good mulch; retains moisture. Slow-acting.
Cow Manure (fresh)	0.3	0.2	0.1	May burn plants. Compost, let mellow for 3-4 weeks, or make manure tea. Medium-acting. If taken from manure pit, may be very gloppy. Smelly when wet.
Cornstalks (fresh)	0.3	0.1	0.3	Decomposes slowly. Shred well and compost first.
Cottonseed Meal	6.0	2.5	1.7	Acidic. Good for side-dressing. Slow- to medium-acting.
Fish Meal	10.0	4.0	0	Slow-acting. Smelly.
Grass Clippings (fresh)	1.2	0.3	2.0	Compost with dry material to avoid nutrient loss. Shred for quicker decomposition.
Granite Dust	0.0	0.0	4.0	Also contains silicas.
Greensand	0.0	0.0	5.0	Also contains silicas.
Guano (bat)	5.7	8.6	2.0	Medium-acting.
Guano (seabird)	13.0	11.0	3.0	Medium-acting.
Hoof and Horn Meal	12.0	0.5	0	Slow-acting. May take 4-6 weeks to be effective. Can be smelly.
Horse Manure (fresh)	0.3	0.15	0.5	May burn plants. Compost, let rot for 3-4 weeks, or make manure tea. Medium-acting. Best if horse is grain-fed and forages grasses not weeds.
Dried Kelp	.9	0.5	4.0-13.0	Apply lightly. Also contains natural growth hormones. Slow-acting.
Leaves (beech and maple)	0.7	0.1	0.7-0.8	Shred and mix with other amendments.
Leaves (oak)	0.7	0.1	0.5	Very acidic. Shred and mix with other amendments.
Pig Manure (fresh)	0.3	0.3	0.3	May burn plants. Compost, let rot for 3-4 weeks, or make manure tea. Medium-acting. If taken from manure pit, may be very gloppy. Smelly when wet.
Mushroom Compost	0.4-0.7	57.0-62.0	0.5-1.5	Slow-acting.
Peat	1.5-3.0	0.25-0.5	0.5-7.0	Acidic. Very slow-acting. Mix in well. Forms hard, impenetrable crust if not mixed in.

Organic Amendment	N	P	K	Comments
Pine Needles	0.5	0.1	0.0	Very acidic. Good mulch for acid-loving plants.
Poultry Manure (fresh)	1.5-6.0	1.0-4.0	0.5-3.0	Usually mixed with sawdust. Nutrient value is greater the lower the water content. May burn plants. Compost, let mellow for 3-4 weeks, or make manure tea. Smelly when wet.
Rabbit Manure (fresh)	2.4	1.4	0.6	May burn plants. Compost, let rot for 3-4 weeks, or make manure tea. Smelly.
Rock Phosphate	0.0	3.0	0.0	Slow-release. Long-lasting. Best source of phosphorus in acid soil. Good for side-dressing.
Salt Marsh Hay	1.1	0.3	0.8	Best when well rotted. Use as mulch first. Retains moisture.
Sawdust	4.0	2.0	4.0	Compost first with ammonium phosphate. Very slow-acting.
Sheep Manure (fresh)	0.7	0.3	0.9	May burn plants. Compost, let rot for 3-4 weeks, or make manure tea. Smelly.
Soybean Meal (dry)	6.7	1.6	2.3	Slow- to medium-acting.
Steer Manure (fresh)	0.3	0.2	0.1	May burn plants. Primarily processed grass. Medium-acting. Compost, let mellow for 3-4 weeks, or make manure tea. Widely available in West.
Straw	0.7	0.2	1.2	Best when well rotted. Use as mulch first. Retains moisture.
Wood Ash	0.0	1.5	3.0-7.0	Alkaline. Use with lime to raise pH. Do not apply more than once every 2-3 years. Fast-acting.

KEY: Nitrogen (N); Phosphorus (P); Potassium (K)

Manure Tea

Some manures, such as chicken manure, are too potent to use directly on the garden. Instead they are applied as a "manure tea." All you need to make manure tea is a large (fifty-five-gallon) barrel, a burlap bag or cheesecloth, water and manure. Fill the burlap bag with manure (about five gallons worth) and suspend it in a barrel of water. Wait two or three days and serve the nourishing tea to your vegetables. Dilute it further if it looks too strong. If you don't have a large barrel, mix the tea at a rate of two cups manure to one gallon of water.

If you want to use manure directly in the garden, be sure it is well rotted. Fresh manure is smelly and "hot" due to the high ammonia content. Well-rotted manure looks like rich soil, is odorless, and will not burn your plants. You can purchase it packaged from your local nursery or in bulk from a local farmer. Always ask for aged manure. If you have any doubts, let it age for a few weeks before applying it to plants.

HINT: Milorganite is a common organic amendment rich in nitrogen and iron, but as it is made up of sludge, which may contain high levels of metals, such as cadmium, it is not recommended for use on edibles.

WEEDING

Weeds compete with vegetables for water and nutrition. You'll be off to a good start if you remove as many weeds as possible when you prepare the bed and maintain a good layer of mulch to prevent weed seeds from germinating. Use a hoe to uproot weed seedlings. Pull larger weeds by hand to get all the roots without harming the vegetables. And remember, weeding isn't just for summer. Some weeds are cool-season performers and should be removed whenever you can work the soil. Add the weeds to your compost pile where they'll be able to do the garden some good!

CULTIVATING

Cultivate, or break up the soil, to remove weed seedlings and to increase air and moisture penetration. Soil should never be allowed to form a hard crust! Begin prior to mulching, once the seedlings are a few inches high. Cultivate often, if you do not mulch.

If your vegetables are planted in rows, cultivate them using a hoe to loosen the soil around the base of the plants, being careful not to break the stems or injure the roots. A three-pronged fork is excellent for hand cultivating small areas. Don't cultivate very deep; it will bring more weed seeds up to the surface.

MULCH

Once your seedlings are a sturdy height (3" or 4"), apply a fine-textured mulch, such as ground-up leaves, 2" to 3" thick or, if you prefer, a loose mulch of straw or spoiled hay 6" to 8" thick. Apply loose mulches in the fall to prevent the soil from freezing, allowing you to leave hardy root crops, such as carrots, in the ground later in the fall. When you're ready to eat them, simply pull aside the mulch, pick what you need, then replace the mulch.

STAKING AND TRAINING

Staking and training vining plants, such as tomatoes, beans and peas, is a wonderful way to save space in the garden, while providing excellent air circulation around the plants. Tomatoes that are staked are less likely to rot and will ripen faster and more evenly. Use stakes, tripods, trellises, netting, wire cages and even sturdy twigs for support. The climbing habit of the plant will determine the type of support required.

FOR INDIVIDUAL PLANTS, SUCH AS TOMATOES Use sturdy stakes or caging. Place the stake on the windward side to counter the force of the wind. Loosely tie the plant to the stake using green plastic tape or soft strips of cloth, such as old sheets or similar materials. Wire cages require less work as tomatoes grow freely without tying. Make a cage out of sturdy turkey wire supported by two or three stakes or buy a ready-made cage.

FOR CLIMBERS, SUCH AS POLE BEANS AND CUCUMBERS Use poles, tepees, netting, trellis or wire mesh. Attach the mesh to A-frames or 8' posts sunk 24" into the ground. When the seedlings are tall enough to reach the mesh, wrap them around the mesh to show them the way to grow.

HINT: Be sure to blunt the ends of all stakes and poles to prevent injury.

FOR TENDRIL CLIMBERS, SUCH AS PEAS Use the structures for climbers or use brush stakes. Stick a branch from a twiggy bush in the ground next to seedlings in the spring and let them grow up through it.

FOR LOW, RUNNING PLANTS SUCH AS MELONS Use a pole supported horizontally about 8" to 12" above the ground. The fruit or vegetables will be suspended until large and heavy enough to rest on the ground.

HINT: Many gardeners underestimate the strength they need from their supports. Plan ahead for the mature weight of tomatoes, pole beans, gourds and melons. They can get heavy!

PESTS AND COMPANION PLANTS

Prevention is the best practice when it comes to pests in the vegetable garden. Avoid pests and disease by rotating your crops, keeping a clean garden and enclosing your garden with a fence. Do not use pesticides on anything you are going to eat. See "Pests And Intruders," p.39.

EXTENDING THE SEASON

With a little help you can enjoy fresh vegetables earlier in the summer and later in the fall. For the most productive vegetable garden, your goal is to control the growing conditions and select vegetable varieties that work within your climate. To extend the season:

- Control the soil and air temperature with mulches and plant or row covers.
- Select vegetables that tolerate the cool weather in spring and fall.
- Select vegetables that thrive in the peak summer heat.
- Start seeds indoors, then move the seedlings outdoors to a cold frame until it's warm enough to transplant them into the garden.
- Use mulch and plant covers to add weeks at both ends of the growing season.
- Use plastic mulch to warm the soil in the spring. (See "Mulch," p.36.) Remove the black plastic when the weather is warm, but save it to reuse the following year.
- Use covers, like Wall-o-Water, for individual plants, such as tomatoes or eggplants, which take a long time to reach maturity. The Wall-o-Water will protect the plants from cold spring winds and release stored heat during the night.
- To extend cool-season crops, such as lettuce, into the summer, select heat-tolerant varieties, then keep them cool by providing shade using shade cloth or lath.
- Plant a second crop of cool-season vegetables, such as carrots, in the summer for harvest in the fall. To protect your tender plants from frost in the fall, cover them with sheets at night or make tunnels of plastic stretched over metal hoops. Be sure to remove the covers if it

becomes hot so your vegetables won't cook before you want them to.
- Water regularly and harvest often to keep your garden productive.

HARVESTING VEGETABLES

The harvest is your big payoff! After weeks of hard work, you are finally able to savor your bounty. Harvest vegetables as soon as they are ready. As with flowers that go to seed, if left too long, an unpicked vegetable will start to shut down, reducing the plant's productivity. Keep a close eye on lettuce, broccoli and other vegetables that may have to be picked daily. Regularly harvest plants that produce over a long period of time, such as peas and beans. Plan ahead for your harvest. If you are going to be away, select vegetables that ripen either before or after your trip and plant them at the appropriate time. Or let a favorite neighbor enjoy your bounty.

SEASONAL CLEANUP

Pull out all plants as soon as the crop is finished. Continue to weed so that weeds are removed before they set seed. Pull out all stakes and temporary structures, such as tomato cages, and clean them before storing them for the winter. Cultivate all beds except those planted with perennial vegetables. Apply mulch over the entire garden but especially to protect your perennial vegetables. This will prevent soil erosion and weed seed germination. If you have time, instead of mulching, you can plant a cover crop such as clover, oats or winter rye. In the Midwest where there is little snow cover, cover crops are especially beneficial. They not only prevent erosion, but, when they are turned under in the spring, also enrich the soil. Ask your local Agricultural Extension Service for the best cover crop for your soil and climate.

Vegetables... *For Your Garden*

Common Name Botanical Name	Key	Sun/Shade	Microclimate	Height	Depth	Spacing
Asparagus *Asparagus officinalis*	P	○	Hardy; cool-season	3-6'	Root crowns 6-8"	18-24"
Bean (pole snap) *Phaseolus vulgaris*	A	○	Tender; warm-season	6-10'	1 1/2-2"	6"
Bean (bush snap) *Phaseolus vulgaris* var. *humilis*	A	○	Tender; warm-season	10-24"	1"	sow 2" apart in rows; thin to 6"; space hills 1' apart
Beets *Beta vulgaris*	B/A	○	Hardy; cool-season	6-12"	1/4"	sow 2" apart; thin to 4-6"
Broccoli *Brassica oleracea* (Botrytis group)	B/A	○	Hardy; cool-season	18-36"	1/4 - 1/2"	18-24" apart
Cabbage *Brassica oleracea* (Capitata group)	A	○	Hardy; cool-season	12-15"	1/4-1/2"	10-24"
Carrot *Daucus carota* var. *sativus*	B/A	○	Hardy; cool-season	8-12"	1/4-1/2"	sow 1" apart; thin to 3-4"
Cauliflower *Brassica oleracea* (Botrytis group)	B/A	○	Hardy; cool-season	18-24"	1/4-1/2"	12-18"
Corn (sweet) *Zea mays* var. *rugosa*	A	○	Tender; warm-season	4-7'	1"	sow 3" apart; thin to 9-12"
Cucumber (slicing) *Cucumis sativus*	A	○	Tender; warm-season	4-6'	1/2"	sow 3" apart; thin to 6-9"
Eggplant *Solanum melongena* var. *esculentum*	P/A	○	Tender; warm-season	18-24"	1/4-1/2"	18-24"
Endive *Chicorium endiva*	A	○ ◐	Hardy; cool-season; heat-tolerant	8-14"	1/4-1/2"	8-15"
Garlic *Allium sativum*	B	○	Hardy; full-season	1-3'	1-2"	4-6"
Kale *Brassica oleracea* (Acephala group)	A	○ ◐	Hardy; cool-season	12-18"	1/2	sow 6" apart; thin to 2'

Key: Annual (A); Biennial (B); Biennial, grown as annual (B/A); Perennial (P); Perennial, grown as annual (P/A)

Row Spacing	Time to Harvest	Comments
4'	3rd year, then annually in spring	Rich, moist, well-drained soil; prepare bed as for perennial flowers; plant divisions in trenches or sow seeds after last frost; male and female root crowns; male plants produce more spears; mulch in fall
4'	55-75 days	Rich, well-drained, sandy soil; pH 6.0-7.0; sow seed successively outdoors 3 weeks after last frost; do not apply nitrogen fertilizer; provide support
2-3'	50-70 days	Rich, well-drained soil; pH 6.5-7.0; sow seed outdoors 2 weeks after last frost at 3-week intervals; plant in hills or rows; do not apply nitrogen fertilizer
2-3'	45-65 days	Rich, well-drained, sandy but rock-free soil; pH 6.0-6.8; rots in wet soils; amend clay soils with compost and gypsum; sow seeds outdoors 2-3 weeks before last frost in succession until hot weather; do not apply high nitrogen fertilizers
18-36"	70-95 days	Moist, loose, well-drained soil; pH 6.0-6.8; for fall harvest sow seeds outdoors 10 weeks before last frost; harvest center head first, to allow smaller heads to form
2-3 1/2'	65-125 days	Moist, well-drained soil; pH 6.0-6.8; transplant outdoors 2-4 weeks before last frost; sow outdoors 10-12 weeks before first frost for fall harvest; avoid midsummer heat; harvest before bolt in summer heat and before hard freeze in fall
12-15"	55-75 days	Well-drained, deep, sandy but rock-free soil; pH 6.0-6.8; sow seed outdoors 2-3 weeks before last frost; use raised beds for improved drainage; may become bitter in hot weather
2-3'	50-90 days	Moist, well-drained, neutral to alkaline soil; add lime as necessary; best as fall crop; transplant outdoors 2 weeks before last frost; for fall harvest, plant 8-10 weeks before first frost; blanch when heads are golf-ball-size.
2-3'	85-115 days	Well-drained, moist soil; pH 6.5-7.0; sow outdoors when soil reaches a minimum of 55°F or ideally 65°F; plant in blocks for best pollination
5-6'	50-70 days	Rich, loose, well-drained soil; pH 6.0-6.5; sow seed outdoors when soil is min. 65°F; water evenly for well-formed fruit; provide windbreaks in windy areas to allow for pollination; provide supports; harvest when flower falls off fruit
2-4'	60-85 days	Rich, moist, well-drained soil; pH 6.0-6.8; transplant outdoors when soil temperature is above 65°F and night temperatures are above 50°F; use black plastic mulch to raise soil temperature; harvest regularly; do not damage fruit
12-18"	60-85 days	Moist, well-drained soil; pH 6.5-6.8; sow seed outdoors from 2-4 weeks before last frost; transplant outdoors after last frost; blanch or buy self-blanching cultivars; better than lettuce in hot weather; flavor improves with light frost
12-15"	90-100 days	Moist, rich, well-drained soil; pH 6.0-6.8; plant sets (small bulbs) 4-6 weeks before first frost; pinch flowers in following summer; harvest in fall
2-4'	60-70 days	Rich, well-drained, evenly moist soil; pH 6.0-6.8; sow outdoors 3-4 weeks before last frost for late spring harvest; for fall harvest plant in late summer when evening temperatures drop

Vegetables... *For Your Garden*

Common Name / Botanical Name	Key	Sun/Shade	Microclimate	Height	Depth	Spacing
Lettuce / *Lactuca sativa*	A	○ ◐	Half-hardy; cool-season	6-12"	1/4-1/2	6-9"
Melons / *Cucumis melo*	A	○	Tender; warm-season	1-2'	1/2"	2-8'
Onion (bulb and globe) / (Cepa Group)	B/A	○	Half-hardy; full-season	1-4'	1/2" for seeds; 1" for sets	sow seeds 1/2" apart; thin to 3-8"
Pea (shelling) / *Pisum sativum* var. *sativum*	A	○ ◐	Hardy; cool-season	1 1/2-5' vines	1/2-1"	3-4"
Pepper (sweet or bell) / *Capsicum annuum* (Grossum group)	P/A	○	Tender; warm-season; intolerant of cool, wet climates	2-3'	1/4"	1-2'
Potato / *Solanum tuberosum*	P/A	○	Half-hardy; warm-season	12-30"	3-4"	10-12"
Pumpkin / *Cucurbita pepo* var. *pepo*	A	○	Tender; warm-season	12-18' vines	3/4-1"	18-24"
Radish / *Raphanus sativus*	B/A	○ ◐	Half-hardy; cool- to full-season	6-12"	1/2"	1-2"
Rhubarb / *Rheum rhabarbarum*	P	○ ◐	Hardy; cool-season	2-3'	2"	30-36"
Spinach / *Spinacia oleracea*	A	○ ◐	Hardy; cool-season	6-12"	1/2"	6-9"
Summer squash and zucchini / *Cucurbita pepo* var. *melopepo*	A	○	Tender; warm-season	1-4'	1/2-1"	2-2 1/2"
Sunflower / *Helianthus annus*	A	○	Tender; warm season	5-10'	3/4-1"	2-3'
Tomato / *Lycopersicon esculentum*	P/A	○	Tender; warm-season	4-10'	1/2"	2-3'
Tomato (cherry) / *Lycopersicon esculentum* var. *cerasiforme*	P/A	○	Tender; warm season	2-4'	1/2"	2-3'

Key: Annual (A); Biennial (B); Biennial, grown as annual (B/A); Perennial (P); Perennial, grown as annual (P/A)

Row Spacing	Time to Harvest	Comments
12-18"	50-80 days; 90-100 for crisphead	Moist, well-drained soil; pH 6.5-6.8; sow seed outdoors successively from early spring to warm weather; transplant outdoors after last frost; best flavor in good soil and temperatures between 60-65°F; harvest before bolts; shade from hot sun
5-7'	65-100 days	Rich, loose, well-drained soil; pH 6.0-6.5; sow seed outdoors in hills after last frost; provide extra water initially; reduce water as ripens to avoid watery fruit; harvest when achieve true color and are easily removed from stem
12-18"	75-120 days	Well-drained, sandy soil; pH 6.0-6.8; sow seed outdoors when soil reaches 45°F; plant sets (bulbs) outdoors 2 weeks before last frost; wait until tops yellow to harvest; look for long-day onions
2-3'	55-70 days	Deep, rich, moist, well-drained soil; pH 6.0-6.8; sow seed treated with a fungicide 6 weeks before the last frost for spring harvest; for fall harvest sow seeds 6 weeks before the first frost; provide support
2 1/2-3'	50-75 days	Well-drained soil; pH 6.0-6.8; sow seeds indoors 8-10 weeks before last frost; transplant outdoors 4 weeks after last frost; overhead watering may prevent pollination; provide supports, such as wire cages
2-3'	90-120 days	Rich, well-drained, sandy soil; pH 6.0-7.0; plant certified disease-free "seed potatoes" or "spud buds" with at least 2 eyes after last frost; hill loose soil around growing plants to provide sun protection for tubers
6-8'	90-115 days	Rich, well-drained soil; pH 6.0-7.0; water evenly; sow seed in hills outdoors after last frost
1'	27-35 days	Loose, moist, well-drained soil; pH 6.0-6.8; avoid heavy clay soil; sow seed successively outdoors in early spring for summer harvest; sow in late summer for fall harvest
3'	2nd year from spring - midsummer	Rich, well-drained, moist soil; plant root cuttings in spring; no fertilizing necessary
12-18"	45-55 days	Rich, well-drained soil; pH 6.0-6.8; sow successively outdoors from early-late spring; for fall harvest sow outdoors when evenings become cooler; more tender in cool weather
3-5'	50-55 days	Rich, loose, well-drained soil; pH 6.0-7.0; sow seed outdoors when soil reaches 60°F; transplant seedlings with true leaves outdoors after last frost; provide support for vines
6-8'	70-90 days	Average, loose, well-drained soil; sow seed outdoors in early spring
3-6'	55-95 days	Rich, well-drained soil; pH 6.0-7.0; water evenly to prevent cracks; transplant outdoors when soil reaches 70°F and night temperatures minimum 55°F; look for disease-resistant varieties; use cutworm collars; provide supports such as wire cages
2 1/2-3'	50-75 days	Rich, well-drained soil; pH 6.0-7.0; water evenly to prevent cracks; transplant outdoors when soil reaches 70°F and night temperatures minimum 55°F; look for disease-resistant varieties; use cutworm collars; provide supports such as wire cages

Peter G. Jones

HERBS

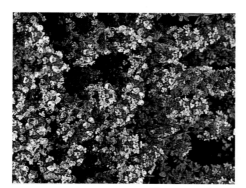

Thymus vulgaris

Grown for their flowers as well as their leaves, herbs are among the most useful plants in the garden. Powerful healers, herbs form the foundation of modern medicine. Let them soothe and satisfy the senses. Use them as ornamentals in the herbaceous border, to edge a flower bed or in pots on the terrace or deck where their foliage adds color, texture and fragrance. Plant herbs between the stones in a terrace or path where their fragrance will be released with each step. Topiaries of rosemary are elegant additions to any garden.

Grow herbs you use regularly in cooking near the kitchen door where you'll be able to step outside and quickly snip a few stems when preparing dinner. Use them to flavor food, make teas, infuse oils or flavor vinegars. Plant large blocks of annual herbs in the vegetable garden; freeze or dry your harvest to last you all winter long. Or interplant them with your vegetables to save space and repel pests. If you are just beginning, try easy-to-grow herbs such as basil, chives, dill, parsley, sage and thyme.

Grow Herbs:
- For cooking
- For healing
- For their fragrance
- For freshness and flavor
- For exotic and gourmet varieties
- To control your consumption of pesticides
- As ornamentals
- In terraces and paths
- For their shape, color and texture
- To share with friends
- For pleasure

SUN/SHADE

Most herbs prefer full sun. Some tolerate partial shade, including bee balm, bay, catmint, chamomile, lemon balm, lovage, parsley, mint, tarragon, thyme and violets.

TEMPERATURE

Some herbs, such as dill, basil, chervil and coriander, are annual; parsley is a biennial and tarragon, sage, chives, lavender, mint, oregano and thyme are all perennials. Like other plants their tolerance of heat and cold controls their life cycles. Warm weather encourages germination of most seeds and produces lush, leafy growth; cold weather usually signals the end of an annual herb's life cycle and the beginning of dormancy for perennial herbs.

Annual Herbs

Annual herbs are extremely sensitive to climatic conditions and are categorized by their cold and heat tolerance. The different types of annual herbs are:

HARDY HERBS Can survive frost. Are successful when sown directly in the garden, even while cool temperatures prevail. Include dill and chervil.

HALF-HARDY ANNUALS Will take some frost, but not as much as hardy herbs. Include anise.

TENDER HERBS Cannot tolerate frost. Many of these types need several weeks in order to reach maturity, and should be sown early indoors, in cold frames, or outdoors only after danger of frost has past. These can also be purchased as greenhouse grown seedlings or rooted cuttings. Include basil.

Perennial Herbs

Perennial herbs are also sensitive to both cold and warm temperatures. Look for plants that are cold hardy in your zone. But don't shy away from some of the best-loved herbs, such as rosemary and bay, which are tender perennials. Pot them up in the fall and bring them inside for the winter.

Consider the following when selecting herbs:
- The lowest expected temperatures in the summer
- The highest expected temperatures in the summer
- The average last day of frost
- The average first day of frost

HINT: *Basil and other Mediterranean herbs love the heat.*

SOIL

While many herbs, such as dill, rosemary and thyme, tolerate poor, dry soils, all herbs do better in well-drained, fertile soil with an average pH (5.5 to 7.0). If drainage is a problem, plant your herbs in raised beds. However, some will tolerate wet, but not water-logged, soils, including borage, horseradish, lovage and mint. Others, such as marjoram, oregano, rosemary, sage, santolina, tarragon, thyme and winter savory, tolerate dry soils that drain quickly. To increase the fertility, soil texture and water retention, amend the soil with organic matter. See "Soil," p.18.

WATER

Most herbs prefer moist, well-drained soil. The amount of rain you receive will affect the flavor of your herbs. During hot, dry summers, herbs left unwatered may become stunted and the flavor will become intensely concentrated. During rainy summers, the flavor may be diluted.

CHOOSING THE SITE

The ideal site for an herb garden has full sun all day, good drainage, no competition from the roots of trees or shrubs and easy access to a water source. A gently sloping, south-facing site is ideal, but avoid low sites where water may collect. As for all edible gardens, investigate the history of the site for contamination of the soil from pesticides, oil or gas, disintegrating asbestos and flaking lead paint.

DESIGNING THE HERB GARDEN

For a traditional, formal herb garden design a garden with geometric beds within the view of the house. Make the paths of brick or stone; clearly define the beds with decorative edging or a low hedge of boxwood or santolina. Add a focal point such as a bench, birdbath, sundial or sculpture. Ambitious gardeners may want to try making a traditional knot garden with low-growing herbs such as thyme and green and grey santolina grown in neatly trimmed, continuous bands or hedges that are interwoven in intricate patterns to define the edges of the beds. Fill the areas in between the bands with creeping herbs, flowers or colored stone.

Make an ornamental herb garden near the house, mixing flowers with the herbs and adding decorative pots, topiaries and arbors. For a cottage garden, design free-form beds filled with herbs, flowers, roses and shrubs.

> *HINT: Only plant herbs and flowers with the same cultural needs in the same beds.*

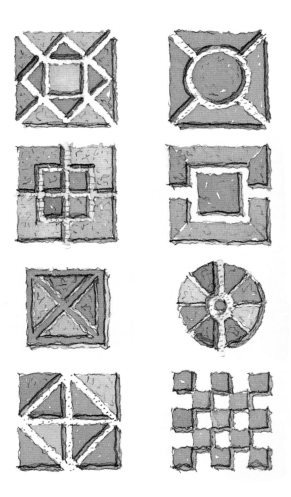

Geometric designs provide ideal frameworks in which to plant formal herb gardens. Use the individual beds to create blocks of contrasting colors and texture.

Planting Patterns

Planting patterns are integral to the overall design as they establish the planting order within the beds. Plant your herbs in rows, blocks or beds as in "Vegetables," p.175, or plan the bed as if you were planning a perennial border.

Spacing

The general rule of thumb for spacing annuals is to allow one half their mature height between plants. For perennial herbs allow at least 6" to 12" between plants. See the herb list for more specific spacing.

PLANNING AT A GLANCE:

- Microclimate
- Soil
- Water
- Annual or perennial
- Time you have available to garden
- Time required for germination
- Time required from seeding to harvest
- Plant growth habit
- Height and width
- Leaf size, texture and color
- Spacing
- Harvest goals
- Time of harvest: one-time or continuous
- Garden style: formal, informal, ornamental
- Planting pattern: rows or beds
- Pest control

HINT: All culinary herb flowers are edible and flavor food with a mild variation of the fragrance released by the leaf. Smaller blossoms make a pretty flower confetti sprinkled on salads and soups. Try basil, borage, chive and rosemary flowers.

SEEDS OR PLANTS?

When it comes time to plant you have a choice between sowing seeds directly or transplanting. Most annual herbs are grown from seed; perennials, from seed or transplants. Consider your climate, length of growing season and time required from sowing to harvest for the herbs you've selected. You may want to get a head start with seedlings you have started indoors or purchased from a local nurseryman. In Zone 5 you may wish to start off with larger transplants. Use small plants to cover areas quickly in stone paths, terraces and other places where there might be competition from weeds. If you are growing low herb hedges, buy the largest plants you can. For tips on selecting healthy plants, refer to "Buying Annuals" and "Buying Perennials" when purchasing your plants.

PLANTING AND MAINTAINING

For bed preparation, planting, weeding, cultivating and mulching see "Annuals" and "Perennials" in Chapter 3.

FERTILIZING

Most herbs are such enthusiastic growers, they won't need much encouragement at all. But all herbs benefit from a weak liquid fertilizer at planting time. Fertilize established perennial herbs in the spring, but do not fertilize them in the fall. Perennial herbs grown in cool climates need time to harden off before winter.

CONTROLLING RAMPANT HERBS

Perennial herbs can grow out of control. Mint is such a vigorous grower that without containment it will engulf its tame neighbors by midsummer. Plant vigorous growers in clearly defined beds, surrounded by lawns, embraced by stone or brick paths or edged with stone, brick or 2 x 6 pressure treated lumber. Impermeable mulches, such as 1" layers of newspaper covered with attractive mulches, will also help curb their spread. If all else fails, plant invasive herbs in sunken containers with holes drilled in the bottom for drainage.

PESTS

Although herbs are generally pest free, they aren't immune. In hot, humid areas, good air circulation will keep fungal diseases to a minimum. Remove pests by hand whenever possible, use insecticide soaps or only grow those varieties that are pest free in your area. Do not use pesticides on any herbs you plan to eat. See "Pests And Intruders" in Chapter 2.

HARVESTING HERBS

Allow your herbs to become well established before you begin to harvest them. Perennials, such as chives and tarragon, need a full year before you pick more than just a few leaves. Once they've begun growing vigorously, pick continuously without guilt or save your harvest until the late summer.

Although herbs picked early in the morning will last longer, there's nothing quite like herbs picked fresh just as you need them for cooking. Pick them as you would a flower, just above a node for branching herbs, such as rosemary or dill; at the base of the stem for single-stemmed herbs, such as parsley and chives. Always harvest the outside, or older, stems of parsley first to allow the inside stems to develop. Enjoy your basil before the leaves turn tough and bitter. Regularly cut annual herbs grown for their leaves to prevent them from going to seed; cut back perennials for a bushier plant. Pick annuals right up to the first frost, but stop picking perennial herbs three weeks prior to your first expected frost date.

PRESERVING HERBS

When harvesting herbs, your goal is to preserve the essential oils that provide the fragrance and flavor in their leaves and flowers. Wash herbs only if absolutely necessary, then dry them thoroughly. Avoid overdrying — the essential oils evaporate quickly. For the best flavor preserve herbs immediately after picking.

FOR FRESH HERBS Store them up to ten days between layers of paper towels in resealable plastic bags in the refrigerator. Make sure they are not wet as they will not last as long.

FOR DRIED HERBS Spread them in a single layer on screens or hang them upside down to air dry. If they are not dry in a week, dry them in an oven set at 100° Fahrenheit until they are crispy. Store them in airtight bottles.

TO FREEZE HERBS Place herbs in resealable plastic bags in the freezer. Pulverize herbs, such as basil, and freeze the mix in ice-cube trays. It is not necessary to add liquid to the puree.

FOR HERB SEEDS Pick the entire herb branches when the seeds are light brown or grey. Enclose the seed heads in plastic bags and hang them upside down to dry. When partially dry, shake the seeds loose and continue to dry them on screens. Separate the hulls by blowing on them or putting the seeds through a colander.

FOR HERB VINEGARS Place several stems of your favorite herbs in bottles. Warm the vinegar and pour it over the herbs. Set the bottles in a warm, sunny spot for two weeks to let the herbs steep.

HINT: If you plan to collect seed, keep a good distance between dill and fennel as they may cross-pollinate.

SEASONAL CLEANUP

Pull out all annuals as soon as the crop is finished. Continue to weed, making sure all weeds are removed before they set seed. Cultivate all beds except those planted with perennials. Apply mulch over the entire garden but especially to protect your perennial herbs. In areas of Zone 5 with little snow cover, perennial herbs will benefit from an additional covering of evergreen boughs. To block harsh winter winds especially in the Midwest, erect a windscreen of burlap stretched between wood stakes.

Herbs

Best Bets For Your Garden

Common Name Botanical Name	Key	Sun/ Shade	Microclimate	
Basil *Ocimum basilicum*	A	○	Tender; warm-season	
Chamomile *Chamaemelum nobile*	P	○ ◗	Hardy to Zone 6	
Chervil *Anthriscus cerefolium*	A	○ ◗	Hardy; cool-season	
Chives *Allium schoenoprasum*	P	○	Hardy to Zone 3	
Coriander (Cilantro) *Coriandrum sativum*	A	○ ◗	Hardy; cool-season	
Dill *Anethum graveolens*	A	○	Hardy; cool-season	
Fennel *Foenicumum vulgare*	P/A	○	Hardy to Zones 6 and 7; cool-season	
Marjoram *Origanum majorana*	P/A	○	Tender; heat-and drought- tolerant	
Mint *Mentha* spp.	P	○ ◗	Hardy	
Oregano *Origanum vulgare*	P	○ ◗	Hardy; drought-tolerant	
Parsley (curly) *Petroselinum crispum*	B/A	○ ◗	Hardy	
Rosemary *Rosmarinus officinalis*	P/A	○ ◗	Half-hardy shrub	
Sage *Salvia officinalis*	P	○ ◗	Hardy; heat- and drought- tolerant	
Santolina *Santolina chamaecyparissus*	P	○	Hardy to Zones 6 and 7; heat- and drought-tolerant	
Savory (summer) *Satureja hortensis*	A	○	Warm-season; heat- and drought-tolerant	
Savory (winter) *Satureja montana*	P	○	Hardy to Zones 6 and 7; drought-tolerant	
Tarragon *Artemisia dracunculus*	P	○ ◗	Hardy	
Thyme *Thymus vulgaris*	P	○ ◗	Hardy; drought-tolerant	

KEY: *Annual (A); Biennial grown as an annual (B/A); Perennial (P);*

Height	Seed Depth	Plant Spacing	Comments
10-36"	1/8"	Thin to 5-6"	Rich soil; pH 5.5-7.7; sow seed indoors in early spring or outdoors when soil is warm
6-9"	Transplants	Thin to 6"	Light, moist soil; pH 6.7-7.3; sow seed indoors or outdoors when soil warms above 55° Fahrenheit; transplant in spring
1-2'	1/8"	Thinning unnecessary	Rich, moist soil; pH 6.0-6.7; sow successively outdoors in early spring; goes to seed in extremely hot, dry weather
10"	Plant clumps 6" apart	Thin every 2 years when needed	Rich, well-drained soil; pH 6.0-7.0; sow seed indoors in late winter; transplant outdoors or divide in early spring; do not pick during first year
3'	1/2"	Thin to 4-5"	Rich, well-drained soil; pH 6.0-6.7; sow seed successively outdoors in spring; self-sows
3'	1/8"	Thin to 6-8" apart	Rich, well-drained soil; pH 6.0-6.7; sow seed successively outdoors in early spring; may not transplant well; self-sows; separate from fennel to prevent cross-pollination
18-24"	1/8"	8-10" apart	Average, well-drained soil; pH 6.0-6.7; sow seed outdoors in warm soil or transplant in late spring
1-2'	Transplants	8-10"	Light, well-drained soil; pH 6.7-7.0; sow seed indoors in early spring; transplant after last frost; grow well in containers that can be overwintered indoors
3-36"	Transplants	6-12"	Rich, moist, well-drained soil; pH 6.0-7.0; transplant spring or fall; keep flowers picked for best flavor; benefits from pruning; very invasive
12-30"	Transplants	8-10"	Average, well-drained soil; pH 6.0-7.0; sow seed early indoors or outdoors when soil warms above 45 degrees Fahrenheit; transplant in spring
8-12"	1/8"	1/8" 5-6"	Rich, moist soil; pH 5.5-6.7; sow seed successively outdoors from early spring to midsummer; transplant early spring; Italian parsley *var. neapolitanum* is more flavorful
2-3'	Transplants	1-2'	Light, well-drained soil; pH 6.0-6.7; sow seed indoors in early spring; transplant outdoors when soil warms; evergreen shrub; grows well in containers that can be overwintered indoors.
1-2'	Transplants	8-10"	Light, sandy, well-drained soil; pH 6.0-6.7; sow seed indoors in late winter or outdoors in late spring; transplant spring or fall
1-2'	Transplants	1-2'	Poor, well-drained soil; pH 7.0-8.0; evergreen sub-shrub; sow seed outdoors in late spring; transplant in late spring; insect-repellent
12-18"	1/8"	Thin to 3-4" apart	Best in Zones 6 and 7; light, well-drained soil; pH 6.5-7.0; sow seed outdoors when soil warms; may self-sow
1-2'	Transplants	6-8"	Poor, well-drained, sandy soil; pH 6.7-7.3; sow seed outdoors in late spring; transplant in spring or fall; attracts bees
18-24"	Transplants	8-12"	Average, well-drained soil; pH 6.0-7.3; sterile, so cannot be grown from seed; transplant outdoors in spring
6-15"	1/8"	6-10"	Sandy, well-drained soil; pH 6.0-6.7; good air circulation; evergreen sub-shrub; sow seed outdoors in spring; transplant in spring

Perennial grown as an annual (P/A)

Peter C. Jones

VI
SUREFIRE GARDENS

Annuals

Ageratum houstonianam (Ageratum)
Begonia x *semperflorens* (Wax begonia)
Calendula officinalis (Calendula)
Impatiens balsamina (Balsam)
Lobelia erinus (Lobelia)
Lobularia maritima (Sweet alyssum)
Matthiola incana (Stock)
Nicotiana alata (Flowering tobacco)
Pelargonium peltatum (Ivy geranium)
Pelargonium x *domesticum* (Fancy geranium)
Phlox drummondii (Annual phlox)
Portulaca cultivars (Purslane)
Salvia splendens (Salvia)
Scabiosa atropurpurea (Sweet scabious)
Tagetes spp. (Marigold)
Tithonia rotundifolia (Mexican sunflower)
Verbena x *hybrida* (Verbena)

Biennials

Dianthus barbatus (Sweet William)
Digitalis purpurea (Foxglove)

Perennials

Achillea spp. (Yarrow)
Ceratostigma plumbaginoides (False plumbago)
Chrysanthemum x *superbum* (Shasta daisy)
Coreopsis verticillata (Threadleaf coreopsis)
Echinacea purpurea (Purple coneflower)
Echinops humilis (Globe thistle)
Gaillardia x *grandiflora* (Blanket flower)
Gaura lindheimeri (Gaura)
Gypsophila paniculata (Baby's breath)
Heliopsis helianthoides (False sunflower)
Hemerocallis x *hybrida* (Daylily)
Heuchera x *brizoides* (Coralbells)
Hibiscus moscheutos (Rose mallow)
Iris spp. (Iris)
Limonium latifolium (Sea lavender)
Malva moschata (Musk mallow)
Nepeta x *faassenii* (Catmint)
Oenothera spp. (Evening primrose)
Perovskia hybrids (Russian sage)
Platycodon grandiflorus (Balloon flower)
Rudbeckia spp. (Black-eyed Susan)
Solidago hybrids (Goldenrod)
Veronica spicata (Speedwell)
Yucca filamentosa (Adam's needle)

Roses

Rosa rugosa (Rugosa rose)

Bulbs, Rhizomes And Tubers

Allium spp. (Ornamental onion)
Anemone blanda (Windflower)
Chionadoxa luciliae (Glory-of-the-snow)
Crocus spp. (Crocus)
Galanthus nivalis (Snowdrop)
Muscari armeniacum (Grape hyacinth)
Narcissus spp. (Daffodil)
Scilla siberica (Squill)
Tulipa spp. (Tulip)

Groundcovers

Cerastium tomentosum (Snow-in-summer)
Euonymus fortunei radicans (Wintercreeper)

Vines

Campis radicans (Trumpet vine);
  x *tagliabuana* 'Madame Galen'
Clematis x *jackmanii* (Large-flowered
  clematis, cultivars)
Clematis paniculata (Sweet autumn clematis)
Lathyrus latifolius (Everlasting sweet pea,
  beach pea)
Lonicera x *brownii* 'Dropmore Scarlet'
  (Honeysuckle Dropmore Scarlet)
Lonicera x *heckrotti* (Gold flame honeysuckle)
Parthenocissus quinquefolia (Virginia creeper)
Polygonum aubertii (Silver lace vine)
Wisteria sinensis (Chinese wisteria, many
  selections)

Ornamental Grasses

Chasmanthium latifolium (Inland sea oats)
Elymus arenarius 'Glaucus' (Blue lyme grass)
Panicum virgatum (Switch grass)

Shrubs

Abelia grandiflora (Glossy abelia)
Berberis julianae (Wintergreen barberry)
Berberis thunbergii 'Atropurpurea' (Crimson
  barberry)
Buddleia davidii (Butterfly bush)
Buxus sempervirens 'Suffructicosa' (True
  dwarf boxwood)

Caryopteris x *clandonensis* 'Dark Knight' (Bluebeard)
Clethra alnifolia (Sweet pepper bush)
Cotoneaster horizontalis (Rockspray cotoneaster)
Forsythia x *intermedia* (Border forsythia)
Hibiscus syriacus (Rose-of-Sharon)
Hypericum calycinum (Creeping Saint John's-wort)

Hypericum patulum (Saint John's-wort)
Ilex vomitoria 'Nana' (Dwarf yaupon holly)
Juniperis chinensis 'Pfitzerana' (Pfitzer Chinese juniper)
Juniperis conferta (Shore juniper)
Juniperus horizontalis (Creeping juniper, cultivars)
Ligustrum spp. (Privet)
Myrica pennsylvanica (Bayberry)

Rosmarinus officinalis (Rosemary)
Spiraea prunifolia 'Plena' (Bridalwreath spirea)
Spiraea x *vanhouttei* (Vanhoutte spirea)
Viburnum carlesii (Korean spice bush)

Plants on this list have moderate salt tolerance.

Asclepias tuberosa 'Gay Butterflies'

THE HEAVY CLAY SOIL GARDEN
Annuals
Gomphrena globosa (Globe amaranth)
Helianthus annuus (Sunflower)
Ipomea alba (Moonflower)
Ipomoea purpurea (Morning glory)

Biennials
Digitalis purpurea (Foxglove)

Perennials
Asclepias tuberosa (Butterfly weed)
Astilbe x *arendsii* (Astilbe)
Boltonia asteroides 'Snowbank' (Snowbank boltonia)
Centranthus ruber (Red valerian)
Chrysanthemum x *superbum* (Shasta daisy)
Echinacea purpurea (Purple coneflower)
Hemerocallis x *hybrida* (Daylily)

Hosta spp. (Hosta)
Monarda didyma (Bee balm)
Myosotis sylvatica (Forget-me-not)
Physostegia virginiana (Obedient plant)
Solidago spp. (Goldenrod)

Vines
Polygonum aubertii (Silver lace vine)
Campsis x *tagliabuana* 'Madame Galen' (Trumpet vine)

Shrubs
Aucuba japonica (Aucuba)
Berberis spp. (Barberry)
Chaenomeles (Flowering quince)
Clethra alnifolia (Sweet pepper bush)
Cotoneaster spp. (Cotoneaster)
Forsythia spp. (Forsythia)
Kalmia latifolia (Mountain Laurel)
Lonicera spp. (Honeysuckle)
Philadelphus coronarius (Mock orange)

THE POOR, SANDY SOIL GARDEN
Annuals
Calendula officinalis (Pot marigold)
Canna x *generalis* (Canna)
Centaurea cyanus (Batchelor's button, Cornflower)
Coreopsis tinctoria (Golden coreopsis)
Cosmos bipinnatus (Cosmos)
Eschscholzia californica (California poppy)
Helianthus annus (Sunflower)
Impatiens balsamina (Balsam)

Lobularia maritima (Alyssum)
Papaver rhoeas (Shirley poppy)
Portulaca grandiflora (Portulaca)
Tagetes spp. (Marigold)
Tithonia rotundifolia (Mexican sunflower)
Tropaeolum majus (Nasturtium)
Verbena x *hybrida* (Verbena)

Perennials
Achillea spp. (Yarrow)
Alchemilla mollis (Lady's mantle)
Asclepias tuberosa (Butterfly weed)
Baptisia australis (Wild blue indigo)
Centranthus ruber (Red valerian)
Echinops humilis (Globe thistle)
Gaillardia x *grandiflora* (Blanket flower)
Gaura lindheimeri (Gaura)
Helianthemum nummularium (Sun rose)
Hemerocallis x *hybrida* (Daylily)
Limonium latifolium (Sea lavender)
Nepata x *faassenii* (Catmint)
Rudbeckia hirta (Black-eyed Susan)
Salvia spp. (Sage)
Yucca filamentosa (Adam's needle)

Shrubs
Aucuba japonica (Aucuba)
Berberis spp. (Barberry)
Cotoneaster spp. (Cotoneaster)
Hypericum spp. (Saint John's-wort)
Juniperus spp. (Juniper)
Lavandula spp. (Lavender)

THE SPECIAL SOIL GARDEN

THE ALKALINE SOIL GARDEN

Annuals

Ageratum houstonianum (Ageratum)
Antirrhinum majus (Snapdragon)
Brassica oleracea (Ornamental cabbage)
Calendula officinalis (Pot marigold)
Callistephus chinensis (China aster)
Cosmos bipinnatus (Cosmos)
Eschscholzia californica (California poppy)
Gomphrena globosa (Globe amaranth)
Lobularia maritima (Alyssum)
Matthiola incana (Stock)
Phlox drummondii (Annual phlox)
Tagetes spp. (Marigold)
Tithonia rotundifolia (Mexican sunflower)
Zinnia elegans (Zinnia)

Perennials

Achillea spp. (Yarrow)
Anemone x *hybrida* (Japanese anemone)
Aquilegia canadensis (Native columbine)
Centranthus ruber (Red valerian)
Chrysanthemum x *superbum* (Shasta daisy)
Coreopsis lanceolata (Tickseed)
Dicentra spp. (Bleeding heart)
Dianthus spp. (Pink)
Echinacea purpurea (Purple coneflower)
Geranium spp. (Hardy geranium)
Gypsophila paniculata (Baby's breath)
Helenium autumnale (Sneezeweed)
Heuchera x *brizoides* (Coral bells)
Iberis sempervirens (Candytuft)
Paeonia lactiflora (Peony)
Rudbeckia hirta (Gloriosa daisy)

Salvia nemorosa (Salvia)
Scabiosa caucasica (Scabiosa)
Sidalcea malviflora (Prairie mallow)
Veronica spicata (Speedwell)

Bulbs

Lilium candidum (Madonna lily)
Lycoris radiata (Red spider lily)
Narcissus jonquilla hybrids (Jonquil)

Groundcovers

Adiantum pedatum (Maidenhair fern)
Ajuga reptans (Bugleweed)
Euonymus fortunei radicans (Wintercreeper)
Hedera helix (English ivy)
Hemerocallis x *hybrida* (Daylily)
Lamium maculatum (Dead nettle)
Pachysandra terminalis (Japanese pachysandra)
Vinca minor (Myrtle, Common periwinkle)

Vines

Actinidia kolomitka, Male (Arctic beauty kiwi)
Akebia quinata (Five-leaf akebia)
Campsis x *tagliabuana* 'Madame Galen' (Trumpet vine)
Euonymus fortunei radicans (Wintercreeper)
Hydrangea anomala petiolaris (Climbing hydrangea)
Wisteria sinensis (Chinese wisteria)

Shrubs

Aucuba japonica and cvs. (Aucuba)
Buddleia davidii and cvs. (Buddleia)

Buxus microphylla 'Japonica' (Japanese little-leaf box)
Buxus microphylla 'Koreana' (Wintergreen boxwood)
Buxus sempervirens 'Suffructicosa' (True dwarf boxwood)
Cotoneaster spp. (Cotoneaster)
x *Cupressocyparis leylandii* and cvs. (Leyland cypress)
Deutzia gracilis (Slender deutzia)
Euonymus alatus 'Compacta' (Burning bush)
Forsythia x *intermedia* (Border forsythia)
Forsythia ovata 'Northern Gold' (Northern gold forsythia)
Ilex vomitoria (Yaupon holly)
Ligustrum amurense (Amur privet)
Ligustrum ovalifolium (California privet)
Lonicera spp. (Honeysuckle)
Potentilla fruticosa varieties (Cinquefoil)
Rosa rugosa (Rugosa rose)
Rosmarinus officinalis (Rosemary)
Thuja occidentalis 'Wintergreen' (Wintergreen arborvitae)

THE ACID SOIL GARDEN

Shrubs

Arctostaphylos uva-ursi (Bearberry)
Clethra alnifolia (Sweet pepper bush)
Fothergilla spp. (Fothergilla)
Kalmia latifolia (Mountain laurel)
Leucothoe axillaris (Coastal leucothoe)
Pieris japonica (Japanese andromeda)
Rhododendron spp. (Rhododendron)

Annuals
Brassica oleracea (Ornamental cabbage)
Calendula officinalis (Pot marigold)
Callistephus chinensis (China aster)
Impatiens balsamina (Balsam)
Impatiens wallerana (Impatiens)
Matthiola incana (Stock)
Nicotiana alata (Flowering tobacco)
Phlox drummondii (Annual phlox)
Thunbergia alata (Black-eyed Susan vine)
Torenia fournieri (Wishbone flower)
Viola x *wittrockiana* (Pansy)

Biennials
Myosotis 'Blue Ball' (Forget-me-not)

Perennials
Aster novae-angliae (New England aster)
Aster novi-belgi (New York aster)
Astilbe spp. (Astilbe)
Hemerocallis x *hybrida* (Daylily)
Hibiscus moscheutos (Rose mallow)
Iris spp. (Iris)
Monarda didyma (Bee balm)
Myosotis sylvatica (Forget-me-not)

Bulbs
Crinum spp. (Crinum Lily)

Groundcovers
Euonymus fortunei 'Coloratus'
  (Wintercreeper)

Hosta spp. (Plantain lily)
Pachysandra terminalis (Japanese
  pachysandra)
Vinca minor (Myrtle, Common periwinkle)

Shrubs
Aesculus parviflora (Bottlebrush buckeye)
Calycanthus floridus (Carolina spicebush)
Chionanthus virginicus (Fringe tree)
Clethra alnifolia and cvs. (Sweet pepper
  bush)
Cornus alba and cvs. (Dogwood)

Deutzia spp. (Deutzia)
Forsythia spp. (Forsythia)
Hamamelis spp. (Witch hazel)
Ilex, deciduous types (Holly)
Kalmia latifolia (Mountain Laurel)
Ligustrum spp. (Privet)
Myrica pensylvanica (Bayberry)
Symphoricarpos x *chenaultii* 'Hancock'
  (Chenault coralberry)
Thuja occidentalis (Arborvitae)
Viburnum dentatum (Arrowwood)

Limonium latifolium (Sea lavender)

Annuals

Ageratum houstonianum (Ageratum)
Catharanthus roseus (Annual vinca)
Cleome hasslerana (Spiderflower)
Gaillardia pulchella (Blanket flower)
Gomphrena globosa (Globe amaranth)
Lavatera trimestris (Tree mallow)
Nierembergia hippomanica (Nierembergia)
Portulaca grandiflora (Portulaca)
Tithonia rotundifolia (Mexican sunflower)

Perennials

Achillea spp. (Yarrow)
Asclepias tuberosa (Butterfly weed)
Baileya multiradiata (Desert marigold)
Centranthus ruber (Red valerian)
Ceratostigma plumbaginoides (False plumbago)
Coreopsis verticillata (Threadleaf coreopsis)
Echinops humilis (Globe thistle)
Gaura lindheimeri (Gaura)

Heliopsis helianthoides (False sunflower)
Hemerocallis x *hybrida* (Daylily)
Liatris spicata (Gayfeather)
Limonium latifolium (Sea lavender)
Nepeta x *faassenii* (Catmint)
Perovskia hybrids (Russian sage)
Rudbeckia spp. (Black-eyed Susan)
Salvia spp. (Perennial salvia, sage)
Sedum spp. (Stonecrop)
Solidago hybrids (Goldenrod)
Stokesia laevis (Stokes' aster)

Roses

Rosa rugosa cultivars (Rugosa rose)
Rosa virginiana (Virginia rose)

Groundcovers

Cerastium tomentosum (Snow-in-summer)
Hedera helix (English ivy)
Hypericum calycinum (Creeping Saint-John's-wort)
Liriope muscari 'Silvery Sunproof' (Big blue lirope)
Liriope spicata (Lirope)
Ophiopogon japonicus (Mondo, Monkey grass)

Vines

Hedera helix (English ivy)
Polygonum aubertii (Silver lace vine)

Ornamental Grasses

Calamagrostis acutiflora 'Stricta' (Feather reed grass)

Carex morrowii 'Variegata' (Variegated Japanese sedge)
Elymus arenarius 'Glaucus' (Blue lyme grass)
Panicum virgatum 'Haense Herms' (Switch grass)
Sesleria autumnalis (Autumn moor grass)

Shrubs

Abelia x *grandiflora* (Glossy abelia)
Berberis thunbergii and cultivars (Barberry)
Cotoneaster spp. (Cotoneaster)
Ilex cornuta 'Burfordii Nana' (Dwarf burford holly)
Ilex cornuta 'Burfordii Needlepoint' (Needlepoint burford holly)
Ilex cornuta 'Carissa' (Carissa holly)
Ilex cornuta 'Rotunda' (Dwarf chinese holly)
Juniper spp. (Juniper)
Ligustrum spp. (Privet)
Myrica pensylvanica (Bayberry)
Potentilla spp. (Cinquefoil)
Yucca filamentosa (Adam's needle)

Herbs

Origanum majorana (Marjoram)
Origanum vulgare (Oregano)
Salvia officinalis (Sage)
Santolina chamaecyparissus (Santolina)
Satureja hortensis (Summer savory)
Satureja montana (Winter savory)

All drought-tolerant plants require water until they are established and most prefer regular water.

THE SHADE GARDEN

Annuals
Begonia x *semperflorens* (Wax begonia)
Coleus x *hybridus* (Coleus)
Impatiens balsamina (Balsam)
Impatiens wallerana (Impatiens)

Perennials
Dicentra spectabilis (Bleeding heart)
Hosta spp. (Plantain lily)
Iris ensata (Japanese iris)

Bulbs
Lilium hybrids (Lily hybrids)

Vines
Hydrangea anomola petiolaris (Climbing
   hydrangea)
Parthenocissus tricuspidata (Boston ivy)
Polygonum aubertii (Silver lace vine)

Groundcovers
Ajuga reptans (Bugleweed)
Asarum caudatum (British Columbia wild
   ginger)
Athyrium filix-femina (Lady fern)
Convallaria majalis (Lily-of-the-valley)
Dennstaedtia punctilobula (Hay-scented fern)
Epimedium spp. (Bishop's hats)
Euonymus fortunei and cvs. (Wintercreeper)
Galium odoratum (Sweet woodruff)
Hedera helix and cvs. (English)
Hosta spp. (Plantain lily)
Liriope muscari (Big blue lily turf)

Liriope spicata (Creeping lily turf)
Pachysandra terminalis and cvs. (Japanese
   pachysandra)
Vinca minor (Common periwinkle)

Shrubs
Aucuba japonica (Aucuba)
Calycanthus floridus (Sweetshrub)
Clethra alnifolia and cvs. (Sweet pepper
   bush)
Euonymus alatus compacta (Burning bush)

Ilex, many (Holly)
Kalmia latifolia and cvs. (Mountain laurel)
Leucothoe spp. (Leucothoe)
Mahonia aquifolium (Mahonia)
Pieris spp. (Japanese andromeda)
Rhododendron maximum (Rhododendron)
Skimmia japonica (Japanese skimmia)
Viburnum, most (Viburnum)

Plants on this list will thrive in full shade.

THE FRAGRANT GARDEN

Annuals
Ipomoea alba (Moonflower) — Evening fragrance
Lathyrus odoratus (Sweet pea)
Matthiola incana (Stock)
Nicotiana alata (Nicotiana) — Night fragrance
Verbena x *hybrida* (Verbena)

Biennials
Dianthus barbatus (Sweet William)

Perennials
Hesperis matronalis (Sweet rocket) — Night fragrance
Lavandula angustifolia (English lavender)
Oenothera spp. (Evening primrose) — Night fragrance
Paeonia spp. (Peony)
Phlox spp. (Phlox) — Night fragrance
Viola odorata (Sweet violet)

Bulbs And Tubers
Hyacinthus spp. (Hyacinth)
Lilium spp. (Lily)
Narcissus spp. (Narcissus)

Vines
Clematis paniculata (Sweet autumn clematis)
Wisteria floribunda (Wisteria)
Wisteria sinensis (Chinese wisteria, many varieties)

Groundcovers
Convallaria majalis (Lily-of-the-valley)

Shrubs
Clethra alnifolia (Sweet pepper bush)
Lonicera spp. (Honeysuckle)
Magnolia stellata (Star magnolia)
Rhododendron arborescens (Sweet azalea)
Rosa spp. (Rose)
Rosmarinus officinalis (Rosemary)
Viburnum x *burkwoodii* (Burkwood viburnum)
Viburnum carlesii (Korean spice bush)

THE CUTTING GARDEN

Annuals
Antirrhinum majus (Snapdragon)
Callistephus chinensis (China aster)
Centaurea cyanus (Bachelor's button)
Cleome hasslerana (Spiderflower)
Consolida spp. (Annual larkspur)
Cosmos bipinnatus (Mexican aster)
Helianthus annuus (Sunflower)
Lathyrus odoratus (Sweet pea)
Matthiola incana (Stock)
Papaver rhoeas (Shirley poppy)
Scabiosa atropurpurea (Sweet scabious)
Verbena x *hybrida* (Verbena)
Zinnia elegans (Zinnia)

Biennials
Campanula medium (Canterbury bells)
Dianthus barbatus (Sweet William)
Digitalis purpurea (Foxglove)
Papaver nudicaule (Iceland poppy)

Perennials
Achillea spp. (Yarrow)
Anemone x *hybrida* (Japanese anemone)
Aster novae-angliae (New England aster)
Aster novi-belgi (New York aster)
Campanula persicifolia (Bellflower)
Chrysanthemum x *superbum* (Shasta daisy)
Coreopsis verticillata (Threadleaf coreopsis)
Dahlia hybrids (Dahlia)
Delphinium elatum (Delphinium)
Echinacea purpurea (Purple coneflower)
Echinops humilis (Globe thistle)
Gaillardia x *grandiflora* (Blanket flower)
Gaura lindheimeri (Gaura)
Geum quellyon (Geum)
Gypsophila paniculata (Baby's breath)
Limonium latifolium (Sea lavender)
Perovskia hybrids (Russian sage)
Rudbeckia spp. (Black-eyed Susan)
Scabiosa caucasica (Scabiosa)
Solidago hybrids (Goldenrod)

Roses
Many Roses

Bulbs, Rhizomes And Tubers
Gladiolus spp. (Gladiolus)
Iris spp. (All irises)
Lilium spp. (All lilies)
Narcissus spp. (Daffodil, Narcissus, Jonquil)
Tulipa spp. (Tulip)

Annuals

Ageratum houstonianum (Ageratum)
Antirrhinum majus (Snapdragon)
Coreopsis tinctoria (Golden coreopsis)
Cosmos bipinnatus (Cosmos)
Gaillardia pulchella (Blanket flower)
Impatiens balsamina (Balsam)
Nicotiana alata (Nicotiana)*
Scabiosa atropurpurea (Sweet scabious)
Tagetes patula (French marigold)
Tithonia rotundifolia (Mexican sunflower)
Verbena x *hybrida* (Garden verbena)
Zinnia elegans (Zinnia)

Perennials

Achillea spp. (Yarrow)
Asclepias tuberosa (Butterfly weed)*
Aster spp. (Aster)
Centhranthus ruber (Red valerian)
Ceratostigma plumbaginoides (False plumbago)
Coreopsis verticillata (Threadleaf coreopsis)
Echinacea purpurea (Purple coneflower)
Echinops humilis (Globe thistle)
Helenium autumnale (Sneezeweed)
Hesperis matronalis (Dame's rocket)
Liatris spicata (Gayfeather)
Monarda didyma (Bee balm)*
Phlox spp. (Phlox)
Physostegia virginiana (Obedient plant)

Rudbeckia hirta (Black-eyed Susan)
Scabiosa caucasica (Scabiosa)
Sedum spectabile (Showy stonecrop)
Solidago spp. (Goldenrod)

Bulbs

Allium spp (Allium)
Lilium spp. (Lily)*

Shrubs

Abelia x *grandiflora* (Glossy abelia)
Buddleia davidii (Butterfly bush)*
Caryopteris x *clandonensis* (Bluebeard)
Clethra alnifolia (Sweet pepper bush)
Lavandula angustifolia (Lavender)

* *Attracts hummingbirds*

THE DEER-RESISTANT GARDEN

Annuals
Begonia x *semperflorens* (Wax begonia)
Calendula officinalis (Pot marigold)
Ipomea alba (Moonflower)
Ipomea purpurea (Morning glory)
Matthiola incana (Stock)
Salvia splendens (Salvia)
Tagetes spp. (Marigold)
Tithonia rotundifolia (Mexican sunflower)
Tropaeolum majus (Nasturtium)

Biennials
Digitalis purpurea (Foxglove)
Myosotis 'Blue Ball' (Forget-me-not)

Perennials
Alchemilla mollis (Lady's mantle)
Anemone x *hybrida* (Japanese anemone)
Aquilegia spp. (Columbine)
Asclepias tuberosa (Butterfly weed)
Aster novae-angliae (New England Aster)
Aster novi-belgi (New York aster)
Astilbe x *arendsii* (Astilbe)
Boltonia asteroides 'Snowbank' (Snowbank boltonia)
Centranthus ruber (Red valerian)
Chrysanthemum x *superbum* (Shasta daisy)
Coreopsis verticillata (Threadleaf coreopsis)
Echinacea purpurea (Purple coneflower)
Geranium spp. (Cranesbill)
Geum quellyon (Geum)
Helenium autumnale (Sneezeweed)
Iberis sempervirens (Candytuft)
Iris spp. (Iris)
Macleaya cordata (Plume poppy)
Monarda didyma (Bee balm)
Paeonia lactiflora (Peony)
Perovskia hybrids (Russian sage)
Rudbeckia spp. (Black-eyed Susan)
Salvia spp. (Perennial salvia)
Sedum spectabile (Showy sedum)
Solidago hybrids (Goldenrod)

Bulbs
Allium spp. (Flowering onion)
Chiondoxa luciliae (Glory-of-the-snow)
Crocus spp. (Crocus)
Galanthus nivalis (Snowdrop)
Muscari armeniacum (Grape hyacinth)
Narcissus spp. (Daffodil, Narcissus, Jonquil)
Scilla siberica (Siberian squill)

Vines
Akebia quinata (Five-leaf akebia)
Clematis spp. (Clematis)
Euonymus fortunei radicans (Wintercreeper)
Hedera helix (English ivy)
Lonicera spp. (Honeysuckle)
Parthenocissus quinquefolia (Virginia creeper)
Parthenocissus tricuspidata (Boston ivy)
Polygonum aubertii (Silver lace vine)
Wisteria spp. (Wisteria)

Groundcovers
Ajuga reptans (Bugleweed)
Arctostaphylos uva-ursi (Bearberry)
Ceratostigma plumbaginoides (Dwarf plumbago)
Cerastium tomentosum (Snow-in-summer)
Convallaria majalis (Lily-of-the-valley)
Epimedium spp. (Bishop's hats)
Galium odoratum (Sweet woodruff)
Lamium maculatum (Dead nettle)
Pachysandra terminalis (Japanese pachysandra)
Sedum spp. (Sedum)
Vinca minor (Myrtle, Common periwinkle)

Shrubs
Berberis spp. (Barberry)
Buddleia davidii (Butterfly bush)
Buxus spp. (Boxwood)
Chamaecyparis spp. (False cypress)
Cotoneaster spp. (Cotoneaster)
Forsythia spp. (Forsythia)
Ilex spp. (Holly)
Juniperus spp. (Juniper)
Mahonia aquifolium (Oregon holly grape)
Leucothoe axillaris (Coastal leucothoe)
Rosmarinus officinalis (Rosemary)
Syringa vulgaris (Lilac)
Thuja spp. (Arborvitae)

Deer will browse almost any plant if starving, but these plants are at the bottom of their wish list in most parts of the country.

Michael H. Dodge

VII

APPENDIX

G L O S S A R Y

ACID SOIL   Soil that has a pH below 7

ALKALINE SOIL   Soil that has a pH above 7

AMENDMENT   Material other than fertilizer that is added to improve the soil

ANNUAL PLANT   A plant that completes its life cycle within one growing season

BALLED-AND-BURLAPPED   Plants with their root balls wrapped in burlap for transplanting

BARE-ROOT   Plants transplanted during dormancy without soil around their roots

BIENNIAL PLANT   A plant that completes its life cycle within two growing seasons

BIODEGRADABLE   Made of materials that decompose naturally

BLUING   The turning blue of red and pink rose petals in intense heat and sunlight

BORDER   A narrow planting bed that edges a path, wall, fence or hedge

BROAD-LEAFED EVERGREEN   Evergreens that have broad, flat leaves, not needles, and do not bear cones

CALICHE   A concrete-like material under the soil's surface composed of calcium carbonate

CANDLE   New shoots at the tips of evergreen branches that send out new needles

CANE   On roses, major woody stems with pithy centers

CLAY SOIL   Soil with a greater percentage of clay particles than silt or sand

COMPOST   Decomposed organic matter, such as leaves and grass clippings, used to amend the soil

CONIFER   Cone-bearing shrubs and trees, which are usually evergreen with needled foliage

CONTAINER-GROWN   Plants grown in, not transplanted into, the containers they are sold in

CULTIVAR   A cultivated variety

CULTIVATION   The working of soil with tools, such as hoes, to break it up for improved aeration and weed control

DAMPING OFF   A fungal disease carried in the soil that kills seedlings

DEADHEAD   The removal of spent blossoms to encourage new blooms

DECIDUOUS   Plants that are not evergreen and lose their leaves at season's end

DIEBACK   The dying of woody plants in a downward direction

DIVISION   The dividing of plants that reproduce vegetatively, such as perennials, into two or more clumps

DOUBLE   Roses that have fifteen to thirty petals

DORMANCY   Period usually triggered by extreme heat or cold in which plant growth processes slow down

DRIPLINE   The outermost limits of a tree's canopy from which water drips

EVERGREEN   Plants that retain their foliage year-round

FAMILY   A category of plants sharing similar characteristics that is comprised of related *genera*

FERTILE   Capable of producing viable seed

FOLIAR FEEDING   The application of liquid fertilizer by spraying plant leaves

FREEZE-THAW CYCLE   Alternating hard freezes and rapid thaws that can cause severe damage to plants

FULLY DOUBLE   Roses that have more than thirty petals

GENUS   Class of related plants that comprise plant families

GERMINATION   The chemical and physical processes in which plants develop from seed

GLAUCOUS   Blue in color

GROUNDCOVER   Low-growing shrubs, roses, perennials, succulents or vines, which cover the ground quickly and thoroughly

HALF-HARDY   Plants that will take some frost, but not as much cold as hardy plants

G L O S S A R Y

HARDENING OFF   The acclimatization of seedlings raised under cover to outdoor conditions

HARDPAN   A hard, often densely compacted layer of soil, impermeable to water and air

HARDY   Plants that survive cold winter temperatures

HEELING IN   The temporary planting of bare-root plants

HERBACEOUS   Having soft, not woody, stems

HYBRID   A plant resulting from the crossing of two different species

INFLORESCENCE   The flower of an ornamental grass

INTEGRATED PEST MANAGEMENT (IPM)   Pest management by intelligent plant selection, biological and nontoxic controls with the use of pesticides only as a last resort

LIME   Calcium carbonate, a soil amendment for reducing acid levels

LOAM   Soil containing a good balance of sand, silt and clay

MASS PLANTINGS   Similar plants installed in large masses to form a bold, uncluttered statement in the landscape

MICROCLIMATE   A small area where growing conditions differ from the overall climate

MICRONUTRIENTS   Trace elements important for a plant's health, including boron, chlorine, copper, iron, manganese, molybdenum and zinc

MULCH   Organic or inorganic materials spread over the soil's surface to conserve moisture, moderate temperature and control weeds

NEMATODE   A threadlike worm living in the soil that feeds upon plant roots, bulbs and leaves

NEUTRAL SOIL   Soil with a pH of 7, neither acid nor alkaline

PERENNIAL   Plant that lives for more than two growing seasons

pH   The expression of a soil's relative acidity or alkalinity

PINCHING   The removal of a plant's growing tip to encour-age the growth of side branches

RESPIRATION   The chemical process in which a plant uses oxygen to break down carbohydrates to create energy, carbon dioxide and water

SALINE SOIL   Soil that contains a level of soluble salts damaging to plants

SEMIDOUBLE   Roses that have eight to fourteen petals

SEMIEVERGREEN   A plant that retains its leaves for most of the winter

SIDE-DRESSING   The application of fertilizer close to individual plants

SINGLE   Roses that have four to seven petals

SPECIES   A group of plants with similar characteristics, represented by the second word in a plant's botanical name

SPECIMEN PLANT   A plant with special characteristics in perfect condition that, like a sculpture, is placed to be viewed

SPIT   The depth of a spade's blade, a means of measuring a trench's depth when digging

TENDER   Plants that cannot tolerate frost

TOPIARY   The art of clipping and training plants into decorative shapes

USDA HARDINESS MAP   United States Department of Agriculture's map, which illustrates eleven different climate zones delineated by average minimum annual temperatures

VARIETIES   Plants that retain most of the characteristics of the species, but may differ slightly in their drought or temperature tolerance, disease resistance, color or fruit size

WATER TABLE   The upper limit of ground water

WINTER KILL   The dying back of plants due to severe winter conditions

XERISCAPE GARDENING   Water-efficient gardening, which incorporates plants compatible with the microclimate and the natural level of rainfall

AGRICULTURAL COOPERATIVE EXTENSION SERVICES

Alabama Cooperative Extension Service
Duncan Hall
Auburn University
Auburn, AL 36849-5612

Alaska Cooperative Extension
University of Alaska, Fairbanks
P.O. Box 756180
Fairbanks, AK 99775-6180

Cooperative Extension Service
College of Agriculture
University of Arizona
Forbes Building
Tucson, AZ 85721

Cooperative Extension Service
University of Arkansas
Little Rock, AR 72203

Cooperative Extension Service
Colorado State University
1 Administration Building
Fort Collins, CO 80523

Cooperative Extension System
College of Agriculture and Natural Systems
University of Connecticut
1376 Storrs Road
Storrs, CT 06269-4066

Cooperative Extension Service
University of Delaware
Newark, DE 19717-1303

Cooperative Extension Service
University of the District of Columbia
901 Newton St., N.E.
Washington, DC 20017

Cooperative Extension Service
College of Agricultural And
Environmental Sciences
The University of Georgia
Athens, GA 30602-7504

Cooperative Extension System
University of Idaho
Agricultural Science Building
Moscow, ID 83843

Cooperative Extension Service
University of Illinois
Mumford Hall
1301 West Gregory Drive
Urbana, IL 61801

Cooperative Extension Service
Purdue University
Agriculture Administration Building
West Lafayette, IN 47907

Cooperative Extension Service
Iowa State University
Beardshear Hall
Ames, IA 50011

Cooperative Extension Service
Kansas State University
Umberger Hall
Manhattan, KS 66506-3401

Cooperative Extension Service
University of Kentucky
Agricultural Science Building
Lexington, KY 40546-0091

Louisiana Cooperative Extension Service
Louisiana State University
P.O. Box 25100
Baton Rouge, LA 70894-5100

Cooperative Extension Service
University Of Maine
Libby Hall
Orono, ME 04469-5741

Cooperative Extension Service
University of Maryland at College Park
College Park, MD 20742

Cooperative Extension Service
University of Massachusetts
Stockbridge Hall
Amherst, MA 01003

Cooperative Extension Service
Michigan State University
Agriculture Hall
East Lansing, MI 48824

Cooperative Extension Service
Mississippi State University
Bost Extension Center
Mississippi State, MS 39762

AGRICULTURAL COOPERATIVE EXTENSION SERVICES

Cooperative Extension Service
University of Missouri
University Hall
Columbia, MO 65211

Cooperative Extension
University of Nebraska
Agriculture Hall
Lincoln, NE 68583-0703

Nevada Cooperative Extension
University of Nevada, Reno
Mail Stop 189
Reno, NV 89557-0106

University of New Hampshire
Cooperative Extension
Taylor Hall
59 College Rd.
Durham, NH 03834-3557

Rutgers Cooperative Extension
Cook College
New Brunswick, NJ 08903

Cooperative Extension Service
New Mexico State University
Box 3AE
Las Cruces, NM 88003

Cooperative Extension Service
Cornell University
Roberts Hall
Ithaca, NY 14853-4203

North Carolina Cooperative Extension
Service
North Carolina State University
Box 7602
Raleigh, NC 27695-7602

Ohio State University Extension
2120 Fyffe Road
Columbus, OH 43210

Cooperative Extension Service
Oklahoma State University
Agricultural Hall
Stillwater, OK 74078-0500

Cooperative Extension Service
Oregon State University
Ballard Extension Hall
Corvallis, OR 97331

Cooperative Extension Service
The Pennsylvania State University
Agriculture Administration Building
University Park, PA 16802-2600

Cooperative Extension Service
University of Rhode Island
Woodward Hall
Kingston, RI 02881

Cooperative Extension Service
Clemson University
Barre Hall
Clemson, SC 29634-0310

Tennessee Agricultural Extension Service
University of Tennessee
Box 1071
Knoxville, TN 37901-1071

Texas Cooperative Extension Service
Texas A & M University
System Administration Building
College Station, TX 77843

Cooperative Extension Service
Utah State University
Agricultural Science Building
Logan, UT 84322-4900

Cooperative Extension
Virginia Tech
Hutcheson Hall
Blacksburg, VA 24061-0402

Cooperative Extension Service
Washington State University
Hulbert Hall
Pullman, WA 99164-6242

Cooperative Extension Service
West Virginia University
P.O. Box 6031
Morgantown, WV 26506

SOURCES

PERENNIALS AND PLANTS

Companion Plants
7247 N. Coolville Ridge Road
Athens, OH 45701
(614) 592-4643
Herbs

Klehm Nursery
4210 N. Duncan Road
Champaign, IL 61821
(217) 359-2888 FAX 373-8403
Perennials

Kurt Bluemel, Inc.
2740 Greene Lane
Baldwin, MD 21013
(410) 557-7229 FAX 557-9785
Ornamental grasses

Plants of the Southwest
Route 6, Box 11A, Agua Fria
Santa Fe, NM 87501
(800) 788-7333
Perennials, grasses and natives

Wayside Gardens
P.O. Box 1
Hodges, SC 29695-0001
(800) 845-1124
Perennials, grasses, shrubs, roses and bulbs

White Flower Farm
Route 63
Litchfield, CT 06759-0050
(203) 496-9600 FAX 496-1418
Perennials, grasses, shrubs, roses, bulbs

ROSES

Jackson & Perkins Co.
One Rose Lane
Medford, OR 97501-0702
(800) 292-4769, 872-7673
FAX (800) 242-0329
Modern roses

Roses of Yesterday & Today
803 Brown's Valley Road
Watsonville, CA 95076-0398
(408) 724-3537 FAX 724-1408
Old, rare, unusual and modern roses

Royal River Roses / Forever
Green Farm
70 New Gloucester Road
North Yarmouth, ME 04097
(207) 829-5830 FAX 829-6512
Old-fashioned and hardy roses

The Roseraie at Bayfields
P.O. Box R
Waldoboro, ME 04572
(207) 832-6330
Old, modern and hardy roses

Vintage Gardens
3003 Pleasant Hill Road
Sebastopol, CA 95472
(707) 829-5342
Old and modern roses

BULBS

Dutch Gardens, Inc.
P.O. Box 200
Adelphia, NJ 07710
(908) 780-2713 FAX 780-7720

John Scheepers, Inc.
33 Tulip Drive
Bantam, CT 06750
(203) 567-0838 FAX 567-5323

SEEDS

The Cook's Garden
P.O. Box 535
Londonderry, VT 05148
(802) 824-3400 or 3406
FAX 824-3027
Vegetable, herb and flower seeds

Seeds of Change
P.O. Box 15700
Santa Fe, NM 87506-5700
(505) 438-8080 FAX 438-7052
Organically grown vegetable, herb and flower seeds

Thompson & Morgan
P.O. Box 1308
Jackson, NJ 08527-0308
(908) 363-2225, (800) 274-7333
FAX 363-9356
Flower and herb seeds

W. Atlee Burpee Company
300 Park Avenue
Warminster, PA 18974
(215) 674-4900, (800) 888-1447

SUPPLIES

Gardens Alive!
5100 Schenley Place
Lawrenceburg, IN 47025
(812) 537-8650 FAX 537-8660
Natural insect and disease control

The Natural Gardening
Company
217 San Anselmo Avenue
San Anselmo, CA 94960
(415) 456-5060 FAX 721-0642
Organic gardening supplies

Peaceful Valley Farm Supply
P.O. Box 2209
Grass Valley, CA 95945
(916) 272-4769 FAX 272-4794
Organic growing supplies, soil testing

TOOLS

Gardener's Eden
Box 7307
San Francisco, CA 94120-7307
(800) 822-9600
Tools, equipment and gadgets

Gardener's Supply Company
128 Intervale Road
Burlington, VT 05401
(802) 660-3500 FAX 660-3501
Tools and equipment

Smith & Hawken
117 East Strawberry Drive
Mill Valley, CA 94941
(800) 776-3336
Tools, equipment, ornaments

INDEX

Better Homes and Gardens.

indoor gardening

WILEY

John Wiley & Sons, Inc.

Better Homes and Gardens® Indoor Gardening

Contributing Writer: Kate Carter Frederick
Contributing Designers: Lori Gould, Sundie Ruppert, Cathy Brett
Editor, Garden Books: Denny Schrock
Editorial Assistant: Heather Knowles
Contributing Copy Editor: Fern Marshall Bradley
Contributing Proofreaders: Susan Lang, Kelly Roberson
Contributing Indexer: Ellen Sherron
Contributing Photographers: Marty Baldwin, Pete Krumhardt,
    Dean Schoeppner, Denny Schrock

Meredith® Books
Editorial Director: Gregory H. Kayko
Editor in Chief, Garden: Doug Jimerson
Art Director: Tim Alexander
Managing Editor: Doug Kouma
Business Director: Janice Croat

John Wiley & Sons, Inc.
Publisher: Natalie Chapman
Associate Publisher: Jessica Goodman
Executive Editor: Anne Ficklen
Assistant Editor: Heather Dabah
Senior Production Editor: Jacqueline Beach
Production Director: Diana Cisek
Manufacturing Manager: Tom Hyland

This book is printed on acid-free paper.

Published by John Wiley & Sons, Inc., Hoboken, NJ
Published simultaneously in Canada

Note to Reader: Due to differing conditions, tools, and individual skills, Meredith Corporation assumes no responsibility for any damages, injuries suffered, or losses incurred as a result of following the information published in this book. Before beginning any project, review the instructions carefully and, if any doubts or questions remain, consult local experts or authorities. Because codes and regulations vary greatly, you should always check with authorities to ensure that your project complies with all applicable local codes and regulations. Always read and observe all the safety precautions provided by manufacturers of any tools, equipment, or supplies, and follow all accepted safety procedures.

Better Homes and Gardens Magazine
Editor in Chief: Gayle Goodson Butler

Meredith National Media Group
President: Tom Harty
Executive Vice President: Doug Olson

Meredith Corporation
Chairman of the Board: William T. Kerr
President and Chief Executive Officer: Stephen M. Lacy

In Memoriam: E. T. Meredith III (1933–2003)

For general information on our other products and services or for technical support, please contact our Customer Care Department within the United States at (800) 762-2974, outside the United States at (317) 572-3993 or fax (317) 572-4002.

Wiley also publishes its books in a variety of electronic formats. Some content that appears in print may not be available in electronic books. For more information about Wiley products, visit our web site at www.wiley.com.

Library of Congress Cataloging-in-Publication Data

Better homes and gardens indoor gardening.
    p. cm.
  Indoor gardening
  Includes index.
  ISBN 978-1-118-18238-3 (pbk.)
  1. Indoor gardening. I. Better homes and gardens. II. Title: Indoor gardening.
  SB419.B46 2012
  635.9'65--dc23
                                          2012028935

Printed in the United States of America

10 9 8 7 6 5 4 3 2 1

table of contents

the joys of gardening indoors

Discovering creative and practical uses for plants in your home is one of the great pleasures of life.

p.**6**
BRINGING NATURE INDOORS
Plants breathe life into a room, connecting people with the natural world in refreshing, fascinating ways.

p.**8**
YEAR-ROUND GARDENING
A house with plants in it becomes a home. Plants enhance lifestyles and add to holiday celebrations in every season.

p.**10**
HOUSEPLANTS & HEALTH
Interacting and living with plants has measurable benefits. But some plants have a dark side too.

Bringing nature indoors

Sunshine, lush greenery, fresh flowers, aromatic soil—

these elements are what lure people into gardening indoors. The soul-soothing process of coaxing plants to grow in a sunny window keeps people close to nature, especially when winter wind rattles the glass and snow piles up outside the sill. Plants bring nature indoors. Adding life, producing fresh air, and reducing indoor air pollution—plants make homes more livable. When you watch seeds sprout and bulbs grow overnight, you feel the pride, joy, and astonishment that only nature inspires.

Plants showcase a multitude of fascinating talents indoors, where they can be appreciated up close daily in the form of multicolored leaves, twining stems, trimmable shapes, and edible parts. Their weather-defying feats prove marvelous, as forced branches bloom while the garden still sleeps outdoors and seeds and bulbs begin growing long before the gardener can till the soil outdoors.

Indoor havens

With nothing more than potted plants, you can create a fragrant, blooming indoor haven that is every bit as pleasurable as any conventional garden. Gardening indoors isn't the same as digging in a yard. But it enables you to garden if your home has no yard or when the climate forces you indoors. No rain falls indoors. But after you water plants, the plants produce humidity, and you all benefit. It may not seem natural, but within the haven of a home's four walls and behind glass, plants flourish.

Fortunately for the home gardener, plants have no idea whether they are growing in a guest room or a greenhouse. All they need is a smattering of sun, a dependable supply of water, reasonably benevolent temperatures, adequate

nutrients, and a whiff of fresh air now and then. Each generation of indoor gardeners discovers that the key to successful growing hinges on ingenuity coupled with an abiding love and respect for growing things.

For centuries, people have matched their wits against the elements in order to grow living plants nearby. Ancient Romans kept their dwellings brimming with fragrant and edible plants. Victorians who first dared to put palms in their parlors and ferns on pedestals also added heated conservatories to their homes so they could grow even more plants indoors.

A world of plants

It's possible to grow a range of indoor plants, from groundcovers to vines, shrubs, and trees, and from disposable holiday gift plants to long-lived heirlooms. Although indoor gardening trends come and go—from macramé plant hangers to the latest craze over air plants— passion for tropical plants persists.

Tried-and-true houseplants remain. What's more, new generations of houseplants with tropical origins have become easier to grow, requiring less light and little maintenance. Sturdy flamingo flower and indestructible snake plant join adaptable zeezee plant in the easy-growing category. New color patterns of Chinese evergreen and dracaena turn houseplants into home decor accessories.

A trip to the grocery or building supply store can expand your indoor gardening horizon when you bring home an unexpected orchid or other blooming treasure. Plants once hard to find are now common and affordable. Today, gardeners have a world of plants within reach via a computer.

Above left: **An antique terrarium becomes a stage for a miniature woodland garden, with** *Streptocarpus,* **ferns, and variegated ivy.**

Above middle: **Plants delineate a transitional space between outdoors and indoors.**

Above right: **Long-lasting succulents need little care and make themselves at home in a large shell.**

Opposite: **A mini tabletop garden heralds spring with pink cyclamen, yellow and purple violas, blue grape hyacinths, and bright yellow daffodils. Reindeer moss conceals soil and holds in moisture.**

Year-round gardening

Anyone with an instinct for gardening or a yearning for spring knows that growing plants indoors is an act of faith and hope. The benefits are a great motivation to poke seeds and roots into containers in every season. Plants help sustain people, providing tangible rewards (beautiful flowers, luscious fruits) as well as loftier ones (raising spirits, relieving stress).

No matter how many or which types of plants you grow, the experience of gardening indoors will enrich your life. This fact alone explains why people garden. Regardless where you live, you can have fresh herbs and other edibles indoors year-round, with natural or supplemental light or both.

Bromeliads create the festive ambience for a party—and a spark for table talk. Longer lasting than any cut flowers, colorful plants combine to make unique centerpieces.

Time for gardening

If you're willing to spend as little as a few minutes per week, you can easily manage a few plants indoors. Whether you opt for tough foliage plants that can live for decades with little more than occasional watering and fertilizing, or blooming plants that need more specific and attentive care, indoor gardening easily fits most lifestyles. As you master the mechanics of growing plants indoors, you can explore a wider variety of intriguing plants and creative arrangements. Instead of limiting yourself to a few easy-care houseplants, you can explore, learn, and grow with this book as your guide.

For the veteran grower, winter is neither the end of the gardening season nor the only time for indoor gardening, but simply the start of another cycle. Everyone has a reason for gardening, whether it's a passion for plants, solace, entertainment, inspiration for art, personal satisfaction, religion, way of life, or something else. Sheltering walls and sunny windows make gardening possible—no matter the weather.

Some newbie plant handlers might be skeptical about growing things indoors. After all, plants come from the great outdoors where there is plenty of sun, rain, and soil. But all outdoor gardens are at the mercy of seasons and weather, even in the mildest climates. Indoors, a gardener can control the climate. An indoor garden brings spring to the frozen North and creates jungles in the desert. Gardening indoors is just the right antidote to cabin fever when winter keeps people housebound. Wishing for spring won't make it come any faster, but displaying flowering plants around the house is encouraging.

Seasons and holidays

Plants provide long-lasting, cheerful gifts—to or from gardeners—instead of a predictable bouquet or bottle of wine. Beyond their beauty and fragrance, seasonal plants bring symbolic connections to holidays and form an integral part of traditions. As a holiday cactus cherished by generations of a family reblooms annually, it reminds them of those who have passed along plants and shared their penchant for gardening with heirloom cuttings. Poinsettias and tabletop evergreen trees add to winter celebrations with their festive charms. Easter lilies trumpet spring; chrysanthemums complete autumn gatherings. Flowering bulbs create a season-to-season parade, from winter amaryllis to spring daffodils, summer lilies, and autumn crocuses. Plants enhance home interiors, from the entryway to the hearth, and from the kitchen windowsill to the dinner table. They add color, fragrance, and timeless appeal to some of life's most memorable moments.

Below left: **In late winter or early spring when the surroundings outdoors are typically dreary, a colorful tabletop garden sings a lovely song of spring. Cheerful pansies, violas, and crocuses join hyacinths, daffodils, and pussy willow branches.**

Below right: **Cans that held imported tomatoes boast colorful labels and get extended use in housing a kitchen-window herb garden.**

Healthful houseplants

Plants improve the quality of people's lives.

At home and in public spaces, plants enhance mental, physical, and social health. As people spend less time outdoors breathing fresh air, indoor plants counteract the negative effects of the pattern by boosting oxygen and moderating humidity to more natural levels. People who work with or near plants and flowers have lower blood pressure, less stress, and an increased sense of well-being. Scientific research bears out these and other benefits of sharing indoor spaces with plants, from bolstering serenity to reducing depression, soothing the senses, and evoking happy memories.

Natural air cleaners

In our increasingly energy-efficient houses and office buildings, there exists an unhealthy lack of fresh air and a preponderance of pollutants. The Environmental Protection Agency ranks indoor air pollution as one of the top threats to indoor health. Synthetic furnishings and building materials that release toxic chemicals add to the problem. Hundreds of volatile

Air-cleaning plants add more than a welcoming touch of greenery to a home. These include (clockwise from left) Chinese evergreen, peace lily, and snake plant.

organic compounds (VOCs) that form toxic vapors at room temperature are commonly found in plastics, cleaning products, and other household chemicals.

Research by NASA has proved that an array of houseplants significantly reduces indoor pollutants by filtering them and also particulate matter from the air. The NASA study suggests that as few as 15 houseplants can reduce the pollutants in an average home. All it takes is one potted plant per 100 square feet to clean the air in an average-size house or office.

Toxic houseplants

Most plants are harmless but some are poisonous and should be grown with caution, especially if your household includes young children and pets. Be careful when growing plants with spines or thorns, such as cactus, pygmy date palm, and sago palm. Other plants are harmful if chewed or swallowed. The good news is that most must be consumed in large quantities to cause damage. Poisonous plants include Chinese evergreen, croton, flamingo flower, peace lily, pothos, schefflera, and splitleaf philodendron.

If you suspect that a child or pet has been poisoned by eating or touching a houseplant, call the 24-hour National Capital Poison Center at 800/222-1222, call your doctor or veterinarian, or go to an emergency room. It helps to have a plant sample or photo with you to correctly identify the problematic plant.

Nature's air filters These houseplants reduce common indoor air pollutants. Gerbera daisies and mums top the list of flowering plants most effective as air cleaners.

BOSTON FERN
Nephrolepsis exaltata is especially efficient at removing formaldehyde (found in carpet, fiberboard, and foam insulation) and adding humidity to the indoor environment.

CHINESE EVERGREEN
Research has shown that *Aglaonema* is particularly effective in filtering benzene (found in glue, spot remover, paint, varnish, and paint stripper).

DRACAENA
D. deremenis 'Janet Craig' and 'Warneckii', *D. fragrans* (corn plant, shown), and Madagascar dragon tree (*D. marginata*) filter trichloroethylene from paint, varnish, and adhesive.

ENGLISH IVY
Hedera helix also has proved effective at absorbing benzene (sources include cigarette smoke and car exhaust) and formaldehyde (commonly found in building materials).

PALM
Effective at removing most indoor air pollutants, choice plants include areca palm (*Dypsis lutescens*), bamboo palm (*Chamaedorea erumpens*), and lady palm (*Rhapis excelsa*).

PEACE LILY
Spathiphyllum wallisii is effective at absorbing benzene and trichloroethylene toxins commonly contributed by paints, lacquers, and adhesives.

POTHOS
Epipremnum aureum ranks high for removing formaldehyde, often found in insulation, paper products, household cleaners, and cigarette smoke.

SNAKE PLANT
Sansevieria trifasciata 'Laurentii' is one of the best plant filters of benzene, formaldehyde, trichloroethylene, xylene, and toluene.

SPIDER PLANT
A single *Chlorophytum* in an enclosed chamber filled with formaldehyde removed 85 percent of the pollutant in a day in the NASA study.

WEEPING FIG
Ficus benjamina works especially well at absorbing formaldehyde, toluene, and ammonia from indoor air.

decorating with plants

See how to use potted plants to improve your home's appeal, making it more pleasing and inviting.

p.**14**
DESIGN BASICS
As part of indoor decor, plants add the delights of living colors, textures, forms, and fragrances.

p.**18**
EXPRESSING YOUR STYLE
Choose plants and containers that reflect your personality and suit your home's character.

p.**20**
ROOM FOR PLANTS
Add just a few plants, and a windowsill, floor, or table becomes a superb indoor gardening space.

p.**22**
STRATEGIC PLACEMENT
Situate plants where they will provide the most impact whether on their own or in attractive groupings.

Design basics

Plants add personality to a home or office,

dressing it up with all the decorative qualities possible where design matters. You'll find diverse plant possibilities to brighten the dullest corners with living forms, textures, and colors. For the most effective, and long-lived appeal, vary the shapes and sizes of leaves and flowers. Blending plants with interiors and existing furnishings need not be complicated. But awareness of design details ensures that plants fit into and enhance a room.

Form

A plant's outline or overall shape creates a strong initial impression. Combining a vertical (snake plant or pothos climbing a moss pole) with a mounded form (peperomia) creates a bit of drama and excitement. Plants may be arching, trailing, creeping, or rosette shape, and bushy, dense, wiry, or frilly. Leaf shapes, which range from feathery to swordlike, heart shape, grassy, or serrated

Grouping plants with different forms as well as contrasting leaf shapes, textures, and colors creates a pleasing effect.

can be contrasted or harmonized to increase interest. When selecting a plant for your indoor garden, consider its form and how it will work in the room and with other plants.

Texture

Leaves and flowers create visual interest with their endlessly fascinating textures. Highly textured begonias or aralias contrast with smooth-leaf peace lilies or cast-iron plants, creating a sense of depth and an energetic dynamic. Planting ruffly primroses at the base of spring flower bulbs adds texture to the display as well as movement and intrigue.

Color

Of course you can match plant colors to interior decor schemes. Also use color to create a more welcoming and comforting home, playing with warm, exciting reds or cool, calming blues. Purple grabs attention; yellow and pink convey optimism. Colors clearly have emotional value. Fortunately, soul-soothing green is the primary color of indoor plants and you'll find hues of green as well as seemingly endless variegations (green marked with a pattern of white, gray, silver, yellow, red, pink, or purple). Picking colors is part of the fun of gardening indoors. Your color preferences will likely change with the seasons, shifting from winter's white and icy blue to spring's bright pinks, purples, and yellows. Bold colors make beautiful, energized statements in summer's stronger light, but most gardeners enjoy the transition to autumn's muted, earthy hues and a comparably quieter ambience.

Nature provides a mind-boggling array of leaf and flower colors and combinations. Pale or brightly colored foliage and flowers brighten dim areas; dark leaves and flowers stand out against a lighter background. When combining plants in a display, concentrate on the interplay between two or three colors, such as chartreuse, white, and pink. If you choose plants and containers that you like, focusing on your favorite colors, the result is often more a work of art than an act of nature.

TEST GARDEN TIP

Leaf color

Many foliage plants with colorful leaves need bright light to bring out the richness of their leaves. When given insufficient light, some revert to all green.

Playing with color
The power of color extends to pots and accessories. You don't have to live with leprechaun-green plants in dull terra-cotta pots. Paint pots to suit your style or use cachepots (decorative vessels) to hide utilitarian pots and set the tone for your decor.

BOOST COLOR
Foliage plants in low-light areas can display splashes of color. Gold bands on snake plant and red leaf margins on Chinese evergreen amp up the color.

CATCH LIGHT
Gather bottles old and new; blue and green are soothing. Add water and cuttings of coleus or other favorite plants.

ADD SHEEN
White and silver blend well with other colors and lighten plantings, such as cyclamen, star of Bethlehem (*Ornithagalum umbellatum*), and kalanchoe.

REPEAT EFFECTS
Bold colors of matching containers create the pattern of a wall display. The leaf textures and shapes of the plants (Swedish ivy, baby's tears, snake plant) stand out.

Plantings by design

Single plants—showy caladium and water lettuce—come together in minutes as a desktop garden.

Indoor gardening presents continuous planting choices.

A vast palette of versatile plants offers foliage and flowers to fit any design. Foliage plants may form the backbone of an indoor garden, with variegated leaves adding splashes of color, but flowering plants make an indoor garden spectacular. Combine foliage and flowering plants to make an impact.

All kinds of plants

Various plants have qualities that make them desirable for an indoor garden as well as effective in beautifying a home. Trailing and climbing plants can form verdant curtains, room dividers, or a living wall. Tropicals grace indoor rooms with their architectural forms and do the same in outdoor rooms in summer. Low-maintenance succulents and cacti have amazing textures and forms. Like bonsai, they provide living art.

Adding plants

When acquiring a plant, look beyond aesthetics and think about where you will place the plant and how it might work with other plants in your home. One plant displayed by itself in an outstanding pot makes a stellar focal point. Repeating the same plant in multiple containers creates a rhythmic pattern that's sure to draw attention and liven up a room.

Grouping plants

It takes some experimentation to combine plants with different sizes, shapes, and textures in an artistic display. Most indoor gardens evolve over time with periodic changes. There are at least two ways to group plants: as single plants in individual containers or as a mixed planting in an accommodating container. When combining plants in one container, choose only varieties that need the same cultural care. Select one plant—usually a larger one—to anchor the group. Let smaller and trailing plants reside at the perimeter of a grouping. Decide how to arrange a group of plants depending on how it will be viewed, from one or more sides.

When designing a foliage-only display, focus on one shared quality of the plants—such as their heart-shape leaves—to simplify the process and achieve a successful combination. Grouping very different plants in same-color pots or otherwise similar containers also achieves effective results, and these potted plants can easily be regrouped or displayed on their own. Using similar containers for all of your plantings unifies the decor.

As another option, massing multiples of one plant variety in one container also works well, especially for plants that appear skimpy on their own (such as geranium, Norfolk Island pine, or dracaena). Whether grouping a few small plants in a terrarium or multiple plants in a large container, leave space between the plants to allow air circulation as well as growing room. Grouped plants benefit from the increased humidity among them.

TEST GARDEN TIP
Preview plants

When shopping for plants at a nursery or garden center, see how combinations of plants work by placing them together in a shopping basket or cart.

Group arrangements
A grouping of plants does not automatically add up to a pleasing indoor garden. Choose and arrange your plants according to simple design principles that take advantage of your personal style, your home's decor, and the plants' natural aesthetic qualities.

SHARED SHAPE
Heart-shape leaves unite this group, which includes a flamingo flower, arrowhead plant, begonia, and satin pothos.

COLORFUL ACCENTS
Grouping plants such as orchids gives them a stronger presence. Small pots fit on gravel-filled trays. A mirror reflects the colorful display.

TABLETOP GARDEN
Make a long-lasting centerpiece in minutes using small potted succulents and tumbled stones— unconventional but attractive.

MIXING SINGLES
Herbs and tulips, potted singly in vintage cream-colored containers for cohesion, form a pretty windowsill garden.

Expressing your style

Nothing brings a room to life the way plants do.

Their added color, texture, and vibrancy change the ambience of an interior space. Just think of plants as living decorative accessories, and use them to complement the design style of the setting as well as the furniture. Although the decorating scheme of any home is unique and a personal expression, your plant selections can work as finishing touches that make a stylistic statement. Minimalist, retro, eclectic—whatever your style, plants make a home more comfortable.

Architectural accents
Use plants in any room to enhance the architecture. If you have a large open room with a vaulted ceiling, place a 5-foot-tall palm on a pedestal to give the illusion of a large plant that won't overwhelm the space. Other architectural features that call for plants include an alcove, ledge, fireplace mantel, built-in bookcases, and windows of all kinds. Wherever you display one plant or many, attention will be drawn there.

Container choices
Continue expressing your style with the selection of pots. Use building materials, wall colors, and fabrics as a guide, or go with neutral containers that will work in any setting. Paint terra-cotta pots any color, or use only metallic cachepots.

Plants add their lively charms to any home. Succulents in diverse containers create artful accents rich in texture.

MINIMALIST

This contemporary style simplifies with zenlike focus: less clutter and more essential beauty, elegance, and calm. Low maintenance is a bonus.

PLANT POSSIBILITIES
Aloe
Sedum
Snake plant

CASUAL

Call it cottage, country, or garden style, a plant collection helps combine comfortable-yet-chic decorating with other natural elements.

PLANT POSSIBILITIES
Bromeliad
Moss
Orchid

MODERN

A spare architectural setting with sleek lines uses single plants as living sculpture for striking effects.

PLANT POSSIBILITIES
Agave
Kentia palm
Schefflera

TRADITIONAL

Composed with attention to bold and graceful lines, this style balances formal embellishment with livability.

PLANT POSSIBILITIES
Fern
Peace lily
Topiary

REGIONAL

Desert surroundings offer a cue for decorating with native plants, a fitting color palette and local stone and wood.

PLANT POSSIBILITIES
Citrus
Ornamental chile pepper
Prickly pear cactus

URBAN

Loft or condo living calls for the personal flair of bold colors, strong patterns, and lush greenery.

PLANT POSSIBILITIES
Croton
Dracaena
Zeezee plant

Room for plants

Improving the appearance of a room

by incorporating plants can be thought of as interior landscaping or plantscaping. Each room in a home has a different function, and its practical use combined with the growing conditions determines which plants could do well there. The growing conditions usually vary in different parts of a room, depending on the location of windows, doors, and air vents.

Secrets to success

Be aware of the common pitfalls in various rooms and take steps to help plants overcome the challenges of their location. Areas near doorways are subject to blasts of cold air that can devastate some plants. In entryways and hallways, choose hardy plants that fit the space. Plants should not obstruct stairs or doorways. Wherever you place plants, ensure they can be easily watered, and place an impermeable barrier under any container to protect surfaces from moisture and scratches. In living rooms where families gather and people often entertain, plants should enhance the setting rather than add clutter. Lack of humidity and low light are the main obstacles to growing plants in a living room. Overlooked rooms—master bedroom, guest room—are often ideal places for plants.

If an entryway has a window, there will be enough light to keep herbs going for a few months. Trading them for seasonal bloomers keeps the display fresh.

ENTRYWAY

Colorful, pretty plants create a positive first impression and help people feel at home. A window enhances what is often dim light.

PLANT POSSIBILITIES

Chinese evergreen
Ivy
Ti plant

LIVING ROOM

The light level is typically medium, and there is room to group plants with ornamental objects and furniture.

PLANT POSSIBILITIES

African violet
Cyclamen
Pothos

KITCHEN

Typically a good place for plants, a kitchen offers easy access to water and higher humidity than other rooms. If there's a window, you're in luck.

PLANT POSSIBILITIES

Culinary herbs
Lettuce
Succulents

DINING ROOM

Living centerpieces and floor plants are ideal. Choose short tabletop plants to allow uninterrupted eye contact. Heavily scented plants compete with food aromas.

PLANT POSSIBILITIES

Begonia
Oxalis
Peperomia

BATHROOM

Take advantage of the higher humidity near a sink, tub, or shower and add a plant where space allows.

PLANT POSSIBILITIES

Bromeliad
Fern
Orchid

WORKSPACE

In a home office or other spare room where there are multiple windows and ample light, most plants will be content.

PLANT POSSIBILITIES

Orchid
Scented geranium
Swedish ivy

Strategic siting

Displaying herbs, ivy, wheatgrass, and forced bulbs at different levels makes a room more inviting and interesting. Potted plants work best when set away from foot traffic.

Once you have determined how much space for plants your home allows, it's time to select specific plant-friendly locations. If you have an area you want to accentuate, or a bare and boring place, start there to decorate with plants. On a windowsill or coffee table, shelf or pedestal, plants create privacy, decorate for a party, mark an entry, keep produce handy, or add flowery fragrance. Strategically placed plants can camouflage less-than-desirable views or separate a large room into inviting areas for different uses. If a room has an unused area that's too small to accommodate a functional piece of furniture, or too large to be ignored, put plants to work there.

Location, location

Windowsills are among the most natural perches for indoor plants due to the optimal light conditions. Choose small potted plants that will stand steadily on a sill, or mount a deeper shelf on a window frame to hold bigger pots. Vining and trailing plants work well in hanging planters. Suspend them to screen or frame the view outdoors.

Any plant that is low growing and interesting when viewed from above makes a good tabletop plant. Group a few small plants for an intriguing tabletop display, or start with a single spectacular plant. When a plant outgrows a tabletop, move it to a bookcase or other shelf where it might cascade or best show off its maturing form.

Architectural plants

Most furniture is not designed to fit into a corner, but a plant or a group of plants bring an empty corner to life. Large plants with interesting forms (weeping fig, palm) or large leaves (alocasia, philodendron) command a place of prominence. Place an architectural plant where its silhouette will stand out against a wall.

Lily-of-the-valley and other fragrant plants merit a place of honor where their pleasant scent will waft across a room.

Places for plants
Feature a prized plant—or a grouping of plants—prominently where it will create a stir and everyone can enjoy its presence.

FLOOR PLANT
A plant (aloe) too large for a tabletop or grouping can be placed on the floor and produce drama from its size alone.

PLANT STAND
Raising plants on a tiered stand gives the grouping greater impact. The plants ('Song of India' and 'Janet Craig' dracaenas and Red Flame *Vriesia*) create a more effective display.

WALL ART
Staging a *Phalaenopsis* orchid on a wall sconce gives it the spotlight it deserves. The ribbon and ornament add a holiday note.

Special effects
from plants

Fiddleleaf fig *(Ficus lyrata)* is one of many trees that will live happily indoors for years and have a bold presence. Other tree-size plants include Norfolk Island pine and African milk tree *(Euphorbia trigona)*.

When deciding where and how to situate plants in your home,

the amount of available space may be the determining factor. If you want to have the drama of an extra-large potted tree, the ceiling height of a room will make it possible—or not. The scale or proportion of rooms are also important considerations. Make a bold statement with a 9-foot-tall weeping fig tree in your living room only if the plant and its container fit together and in the room proportionately. They will not overwhelm the space or each other.

Big and little plants

Both large and small plants create attractive focal points. It pays to take advantage of a plant's size in relation to the scale of the setting. Big or tall plants have the most distinctive effect when placed on the floor away from other plants and furniture. Regard them as furniture or sculpture that adds style, beauty, and even function in your home rather than just taking up space. Small plants draw attention to their diminutive stature. Group a few small potted plants on a tray or in a dish, terrarium, or other eye-catching container for starters, then situate them in a place where they're certain to get a closer look. Lining up a few ivies in silver pots on a mantel or gathering several orchids in a flat basket on a side table will have more impact than scattering single potted plants around a room.

If space is limited, locate plants where they will add color and character without competing for room. Several well-placed, 2- to 3-foot-tall plants can freshen a room's decor instantly. A selection of seasonal beauties—kalancho, begonia, cyclamen—brightens clusters of plants, whether added individually or massed.

Balance

Ultimately the selection and placement of plants depends on what appeals to you and makes a positive impact. Any arrangement that includes plants and other objects should be balanced either formally or informally. Using two single potted plants to flank a feature, such as a fireplace or doorway, has a formal effect. Topiaries, tree-form plants, and upright cacti work well in formal schemes. Informal designs are asymmetrical and freely contrast the forms, colors, and other design qualities of an odd number of plants.

Pots of blooming kalancho form a contrasting skirt at the base of a tall cactuslike African milk tree. Holiday cactus or small poinsettias would also work well.

Special arrangements

Displaying plants attractively may take several attempts to find just the right plant or combination for the location.

FOLIAGE FOUNTAIN
Although this stone fountain no longer pumps water, it provides a creative framework for air plants (*Tillandsia* spp.).

SEASON'S SENSATION
A trio of braided-stem azaleas forms an outstanding formal centerpiece on a dining room table.

LIVING TREASURE
Tiny air plants (*Tillandsia caput-medusae*) deserve to be showcased where they will receive notice—as in this card deck-size box.

Ideal
environment

Sheer curtains diffuse
the bright light directly in
front of a south-facing
window, making it ideal for
African violets, begonias
and maidenhair ferns.

The best place for any plant is where it will receive the light it needs to survive and

thrive. Placing plants where they contribute to the decor is only part of a gardener's task in making a successful indoor garden. If you have any doubt about a spot's suitability for a particular plant, it's okay to experiment. Just be aware that the plant may not grow well or remain alive for a long time. A more dependable approach starts with knowledge about each plant's environmental needs for light, humidity, temperature, and air circulation.

Habitats for plants

Understanding a bit about a plant's place of origin will help you map out areas of your home that can offer conditions conducive to its well-being. In their natural habitats, plants have evolved and adapted to specific climatic and soil conditions. As a gardener, you can match plants to comparable conditions in your home and adjust the level of heat, humidity, or air movement as needed.

Microclimates

Just as plants' needs for light and water change with the seasons, the conditions in your home will vary from month to month, room to room, and within some rooms. Your home has microclimates where windows, vents, and other features affect the environment, making it warmer or cooler; more or less humid. You can use these microclimates to benefit plants. For instance, north windows keep a room cool during the winter and make a perfect place for plants that rest between late fall and early spring. Plants native to arid climates like living near a heat vent; plants that hail from the tropics appreciate the high humidity of a bathroom or kitchen. Placing a plant on a mantel or other spot near a fireplace may appear pleasing to the eye, but the plant should be moved away from the area if a fire is started; this avoids the risk of the plant being scorched.

Warmth and bright light are crucial for the success of herbs including rosemary, sage, thyme, parsley, and chives.

Light conditions The amount of light available to a plant indoors is critical to its health. The classifications of low, medium, and bright natural light provide guidelines for placing plants.

BRIGHT LIGHT

Plants receive four or more hours of high or bright light in an unobstructed window that faces south or southwest.

PLANT POSSIBILITIES

Cactus	Jade plant (shown)
Citrus	Orchids
Croton	Peperomia Purple
Flowering maple	passion plant
Hibiscus	Succulents

MEDIUM LIGHT

In an east or west window, this site receives a few hours daily of early-morning or late-afternoon sun.

PLANT POSSIBILITIES

African violet	Fig
Begonia	Nerve plant (shown)
Dracaena	Peperomia
English ivy	Schefflera
Ferns	Spider plant

LOW LIGHT

In a place well away from a north-, east-, or northeast-facing window, plants get some light but not direct sun.

PLANT POSSIBILITIES

Cast-iron plant	Parlor palm
Chinese evergreen	Peace lily
Dieffenbachia	Philodendron
Dracaena	Satin pothos (shown)
Lady palm	Snake plant

caring for plants

The fundamentals of growing healthy plants indoors include tried-and-true techniques as well as updates that will further your know-how.

p.**30**
THE RIGHT ENVIRONMENT
Learn how to provide adequate light, water, humidity, and other factors key to your plants' success.

p.**36**
PLANTS & POTS
Get the most suitable plants and containers for your home and then use them to create marvelous displays.

p.**46**
PLANT CARE
Attention to a few details keeps plants looking their best and prevents problems.

p.**52**
PESTS & DISEASES
Routinely checking plants helps minimize maladies. Learn to distinguish between healthy and plagued plants.

The right light

Light is vital to plants. Their ability to grow, maintain health, and produce flowers depends on light. More specifically, plants need light for photosynthesis—which produces the food and energy necessary to keep them alive—as well as for hormone production, to induce flowering. Ideal light levels vary by plant species and sometimes cultivar.

If a plant is sited in more or less light than it needs for optimum growth, it will be stressed and more prone to problems, such as weak growth, minimal flowering, disease, and pests. A plant will usually show a sign of light imbalance. Symptoms of insufficient light include stretching or leaning toward a light source, growing sparsely or becoming spindly, losing foliage color or variegation, and producing smaller leaves. Symptoms of too much light include whitish scorch marks on foliage, wilted and shriveled leaves, or bleached leaves.

Light levels

Before you place a plant indoors, identify the amount of light it will need and the location where that light is available. You may need to experiment until you discover where the light in your home best suits a plant. For more details about increasing light, see page 81.

The plant tag usually tells you what level of light a plant needs: low, medium, or bright (see page 27). Some plants thrive in a range of light levels. Low light may be enough to keep a plant alive, but not enough to promote flowering. Several hours of bright light in a west window sustains herbs and succulents, but they'll grow better in the full strength of midday sun in a south window. Bright, indirect light can often be found within three feet of a sunny window. You can use a light meter to gauge the amount of available light. Or look for shadows: the brighter the light, the stronger the shadows.

Some plants are more forgiving of light levels, including the intensity, quality, and duration of sunlight, which changes with the seasons. Winter light is less intense than summer light, but it extends farther into a room because the sun is lower in the sky.

Most homes, even the smallest apartments, offer a variety of light conditions. Each setting is an opportunity for different plants. Foliage plants usually need less light than flowering ones.

Intensity: The closer a plant is placed to a window, the more intense the light. Bright, direct light in a south- or west-facing window suits succulents and seedlings, but it could toast African violets and bromeliads. Sheer curtains diffuse bright light and help prevent sunburn (yellow to brown scorched leaves). This indirect light is usually better for indoor plants that require low to medium light. Moving plants away from a window reduces the light they receive. A plant that needs moderate or medium light will thrive in an east-facing window but should be set a few feet away from the more intense light of a west window.

The intensity of direct light coming through a window also varies with seasonal changes. In summer, when the sun is high in the sky, an overhanging roof can block its rays. The winter sun is lower in the sky, but its light is less intense. Outdoor elements, such as trees and neighboring buildings, can reduce light coming indoors; reflective surfaces, such as light-colored walls and mirrors, increase it. Relocate plants periodically to maintain their health by ensuring they're getting the amount of light they need.

Quality: Sunlight is the best source of full-spectrum light for plants. Supplement natural light with artificial light to provide plants with the amount and quality of light (wavelengths in the red-blue spectrum) they need to thrive.

Duration: Most indoor plants need from 8 to 16 hours of light daily. Too many hours of light slow plant growth. Too few hours cause elongated shoots and thin, easily damaged leaves. Many plants' blooms are triggered by length of day and night cycles.

Supplemental light: When natural light is inadequate, provide supplementary light to help plants fare well, especially during winter. Seedlings and flowering houseplants, such as African violets and begonias, benefit from an added light source. Most plants respond best to normal cycles of 12 to 16 hours of light and 8 to 12 hours of darkness when given supplemental light. Place the light within 4 to 6 inches of plant tops. Fluorescent lights are available in various shapes and sizes, and as cool- or warm-white tubes, at hardware stores. They're economical and remain cool to the touch, allowing plants to grow close to the tubes without damage. Costlier fluorescent grow-lights mimic full-spectrum light. Other more intense and expensive options for avid gardeners include metal halide lights and high-pressure sodium bulbs.

TEST GARDEN TIP

Effective light

Replace fluorescent bulbs periodically. When the ends of a bulb darken, it is an indicator that the tube is working less effectively and should be replaced.

Supplemental lighting
To ensure plants' survival, it is sometimes necessary to provide artificial light for them. As an indoor gardener, you have options, whether you live in a place where winter days are short and often gray, or where window light is limited.

SHOP LIGHT
A fluorescent light fixture holds one cool-white tube and one warm-white tube that produce sufficient light for seedlings indoors. An electrical timer turns the light on and off, providing a consistent and convenient light source for a sufficient time.

LITTLE LIGHT
Where natural light is lacking, a supplemental LED (light-emitting diode) light stick casts a refined spectral wavelength to meet an individual plant's needs. This efficient light source uses little power, produces little heat, and lasts longer than most bulbs.

EASY FIXTURE
A clamp-on fixture outfitted with a grow bulb provides an attractive means of shining full-spectrum light onto plants in an otherwise dark corner. Adding a grow bulb to a small table lamp works too.

Watering

Water can be a cure-all or a killer for a plant, depending on when and how it is applied. No single rule applies for watering, because there are many variables. A plant's needs change with the seasons. Plants absorb more water when the light is bright, temperature is high, or humidity is low.

The thirstiest plants include those with flowers, large leaves, tropical or marshy origins, or large root balls in a confined space. Plants in unglazed terra-cotta pots, baskets, and wooden vessels need more frequent watering than those in plastic, metal, or glazed clay pots. A

When watering, pour water on the soil, not on the plant. Wetting leaves promotes water spots and disease. Pouring water onto the crown (center) of some plants can cause them to rot.

lightweight soilless potting mix dries out faster than heavy potting soil. Fast-growing plants (ferns, dracaena, palms) need more water than slower-growing ones (succulents, snake plant). Small pots dry out faster than large ones.

When to water

Check potted plants' soil twice a week to learn about their water needs. Feel the soil before watering, or use a moisture meter. Using your finger as a dipstick, poke it into the soil 1 inch (to the first knuckle) to determine if the soil has begun to dry; 2 inches (to the second knuckle) to feel for moisture. A plant's need for water is individual. You will learn to feel the difference in soil that is dry, damp, moist, or wet, and when water should be added to maintain a particular level of moisture or dryness.

Underwatering and overwatering can result in the same symptoms: wilting, pale, lackluster foliage. Without enough water, a plant becomes stunted; leaves turn yellow or brown. If you water before a plant wilts and suffers permanent damage, it may recover. With too much water, roots can't function normally due to lack of oxygen in the root zone, and the plant suffocates.

Over time, you will discover which plants get by with weekly watering and which plants need more- or less-frequent hydrating. Plants usually need water more often in spring and summer, when they're actively growing, than in winter.

Water in the morning, if possible. This gives wet foliage a chance to dry out during the day and minimizes disease. It also gives you a chance to see if excess water has pooled in a saucer and needs to be poured off.

The best way

When watering a potted plant, pour water over the entire soil surface and let it soak into the soil. Add more water until it starts to seep out of the bottom of the container. This practice thoroughly moistens soil and leaches excess salts from the soil. Allow the soil to soak up any excess water, then pour off the remainder to avoid letting a plant stand in water, which can damage the roots. Self-watering pots (with a water reservoir) and capillary mats work the same way as bottom watering (see How to water, below), wicking moisture into the soil. They work well for plants that need to stay evenly moist and during times when you will be away; for more details about vacation watering, see page 51.

Types of water

Tap water suffices for plants, unless they are sensitive to hard (alkaline) or soft water (which contains salts). Rainwater agrees with plants, unless air pollution in the region causes acid rain. Use slightly warm or tepid water for plants to avoid shock and possible root damage from extreme temperatures.

TEST GARDEN TIP
Water meter

For plants that are finicky about watering, use a moisture meter to measure the soil's water content. Meters are inexpensive and help take the guesswork out of watering.

How to water
You'll find more than one way to water plants indoors. The best methods saturate soil adequately without spilling or leaking water on furniture, floors, and other surfaces.

WATERING CAN
Use a watering can with a long, slender spout to easily guide water to all sides of a pot and avoid spills. Watering cans come in a range of sizes. A small can serves one or two plants; a larger can saves trips to the sink when watering multiple plants.

WATERING BULBS
These decorative devices provide a slow-but-steady supply of water to a plant, directing moisture to the roots, where it is most needed, and keeping soil evenly moist. Various forms are available. The bulbs shown are blown glass.

BOTTOMS UP
Water African violets and other plants with sensitive leaves from the bottom, filling a saucer or reservoir with water and allowing the soil to wick it up through the pot's bottom until the soil surface is damp. This method prevents water marks on leaves.

REHYDRATE SOIL
If dry soil has pulled away from the pot so water runs down the sides without wetting the soil, immerse the entire pot in a bucket or sink of tepid water. Let the pot soak for 20 minutes, then drain.

Success factors

The conditions indoors affect plants' well-being and survival.

Indoor conditions can be tough on plants, especially when soil dries out quickly during winter (thanks to low humidity) and summer (due to excessive heat). If these conditions prevail where you live, help your houseplants succeed by starting with varieties that can survive periods of drought. Also keep in mind that small pots dry out faster.

Humidity

Moisture in the air is just as important to a plant as moisture in the soil. Warm air holds more water, so humidity tends to be higher in the summer, although air conditioning dramatically lowers humidity. In the winter, indoor humidity tends to be lowest when a heating system dries the air. Generally, the colder the air outside, the drier the air indoors. The humidity in most homes varies from 20 percent in winter up to 65 percent in summer, and from room to room. A hygrometer is a device that measures humidity. Devices that measure humidity and temperature are widely available.

More often than not, you will need to increase humidity for plants in your home. Low-humidity problems are intensified if the soil has dried, or if the plant sits in a draft or is flooded with unfiltered light. Methods for boosting humidity include running a humidifier, setting individual pots or groups of plants on a pebble tray, and

A pebble tray is one of the easiest ways to boost humidity. Add pebbles to the saucer of a single potted plant or fill a larger communal tray. Cover the gravel with water, but avoid letting pots and plant roots stand in water, which promotes rot.

planting in a terrarium. Group plants—their leaves release moisture (transpire) and raise humidity among them. Double-pot plants, setting a terra-cotta potted plant inside a larger pot and filling the space between the pots with damp sphagnum moss; keep the moss damp by watering it. Misting plants rinses the leaves and promotes disease of some plants, but it does not effectively raise humidity. The higher humidity of rooms with running water (kitchen, bathroom, laundry room) suits peace lily, African violet, ferns, and other plants from the humid tropics, as long as they get enough light too.

Temperature

The year-round temperature between 60 and 75°F (and cooler at night) in typical homes suits most plants just fine. Interior temperatures vary from season to season, room to room, and within a room. Take advantage of these differences by matching plants to the conditions and moving them as needed. You'll know within a week or so whether a change has improved a plant's health. Most plants are sensitive to a sudden drop in temperature. An extreme change can cause leaf damage or drop, or even plant death. Buds and flowers especially need warmth.

Microclimates exist within a room. A sunny, unheated porch or place close to a window in winter provides a cool microclimate that suits cyclamen, azaleas, and some orchids. A chilling draft near a window, door, or entryway can injure some plants enough to cause leaves to droop, turn black, or drop off, but a spider plant or schefflera will appreciate a cool location. Cacti and succulents are among the few plants that are happy in a home's warmest places: near a heat vent and on sunny windowsills in summer. Warm air rises, making a toasty place on top of a bookcase; cool air sinks, so the air near the floor is cooler.

Air circulation

Movement of air benefits plants by evaporating moisture from leaves and preventing disease; promoting denser, sturdier growth; and keeping some insect populations in check. Open a window during mild weather to increase air movement. Keep air moving in winter with a ceiling fan or a small fan placed near plants.

Plant signals **Plants have ways of demonstrating when the conditions are not suitable. They show symptoms of stress that give you clues if a change is needed in their environment or care.**

HUMIDITY

TOO LITTLE: Leaf tips brown and shrivel as on this peacock plant; leaf edges turn yellow. Buds fall off and blossoms wither.

TOO MUCH: Plants are more susceptible to rot, mold, and mildew.

TEMPERATURE

TOO COLD: Leaves curl, turn black or brown (shown), wilt, and fall off; buds drop when conditions are too chilly. Plant tissues, including roots, can succumb to cold.

TOO WARM: Lower leaves wilt and turn brown. Flowers die quickly. The plant produces small leaves or weak, leggy growth in good light.

AIR CIRCULATION

TOO LITTLE: Fungal disease (powdery mildew, shown on rosemary) or insect problems (whiteflies) may proliferate.

TOO MUCH: Wind shreds leaves, dries soil, and shakes off buds or flowers.

Selecting healty plants

Choose new plants carefully. Be aware of a plant's potential size and needs, or you may find that cute little plant you couldn't resist quickly grows into a plant too large for the space, or its needs prove difficult to fulfill.

Acquiring indoor plants entails as much thoughtful selection and careful shopping as other purchases that will last for years. When you buy plants, find reputable local greenhouses or garden centers, or order by mail from a specialty catalog or website. You might find an irresistible plant at a grocery store, botanical center, plant society sale, or another opportunity. Shipping plants is risky. A dependable source will ship when conditions are right and will guarantee to replace damaged plants.

Selecting a healthy plant

Examine plants before buying and pick the healthiest plants you can find. They will be lush, colorful, dense, and full. New growth is a good sign; recent heavy pruning is not. Be wary if some plants in a display look good and others do not, especially if some are wilted. Closely inspect plants for indications of pests (webs, sticky residue, cottony masses) or disease (mushy, discolored, or distorted parts). A yellow leaf or two is not cause for concern, but lots of fallen leaves or extremely dry soil indicate stress and could signal inadequate care. Look at the undersides of leaves and poke into the soil for clues. Avoid plants that have weak or spindly growth, crawling or flying insects, or sour- or rotten-smelling soil. A discounted plant is not a bargain if it is sick.

Be certain of your purchase. If the plant does not have a tag that tells you its name and growing requirements, ask someone on staff to give you this information. Ensure that the plant suits the conditions you have to offer it at home, especially in terms of light and space needs. Young, small plants cost less than large ones; they travel and acclimate with less stress too.

Transitioning plants

When you acquire a new plant, remember that it will be vulnerable to changes in its surroundings, whether you transport the plant or it endures shipping. Do what you can to give the plant extra-tender care in the process. Make sure it is well-packaged for travel and wrapped to protect it, especially from cold temperatures, between the point of purchase and your home. When transporting plants, avoid letting them sit in a hot car for an extended period: in winter, preheat the car and place plants near the heater, not in the trunk. Once new plants—including mail-order purchases—arrive at your home, unwrap them right away. Set a new plant in the sink and water it thoroughly.

Isolate a new plant for a few weeks in a room away from other plants, if possible, allowing the plant to recuperate from the stress of environmental change. At the same time, ease the plant through its adjustment to your home. Place it in high light for a week or so, and then gradually move it to locations with less light if its intended place has medium or low light. Take care to avoid overwatering during this stage.

TEST GARDEN TIP

Change averse

Some plants (croton, weeping fig) are so sensitive to change that it's best to place new residents in their permanent spots and acclimate them there. Tougher plants (dracaena, philodendron) can be acclimated gradually and moved to different locations around your house in the process.

New plants' success **Here are a few more tips to help you with the best plant selection and to ensure that your plants adjust well to their new digs.**

LASTING BLOOMS
When choosing a flowering plant, buy the one with lots of buds—it will reward you with longer-lasting blooms. A plant in full bloom will soon fade and may or may not bloom again.

KEEPING TRACK
It's easy to forget pertinent information about a plant: its name, source, and date of purchase. Use a journal or file to store the details, and save the receipt to help track your plant's success, or obtain a refund.

WELCOME HOME
Help acclimate a new plant by nurturing it in highly humid conditions for two weeks. Set the plant in indirect, bright light and tent it with a plastic bag. Poke a hole or two in the bag every few days.

Choosing containers

As the home for plants, containers provide adequate space for roots to develop and plants to grow and flourish. They come in an array of colors and styles, which makes choosing a container almost as much fun as selecting a plant. It is a matter of personal preference whether to coordinate plants and pots with your home's style for decorative results. If you acquire quality containers that can withstand rough handling and outdoor conditions, then they—and the plants they hold—can be moved outside for the summer.

Choosing containers

Consider a container's size, weight, and shape in relation to the plant. The container should be no taller than one third of the plant/pot combination to appear balanced. Selecting a pot 2 inches wider than the plant's root ball gives the plant growing room—but not too much. An oversize pot not only appears disproportionate, but holds more moisture than the plant needs. Besides, many plants need cozy quarters to grow well. Small containers can become a source of frustration if plants outgrow them, and they will require watering more often. Heavier containers stabilize their contents, preventing toppling of top-heavy plants. The weight of large pots filled with soil, plants, and water limits their portability. Lighter-weight pots are more easily portable. Balance an upright plant in a tall pot, a mounding plant in a square pot, and a trailing

Containers accent the color and style of a home, whether new or old and even whether they hold plants or not.

plant in a V-shape pot. Experiment with combinations of plants and shapely pots that appeal to you.

Drainage

Good drainage is crucial. A potted plant's survival depends on a drainage hole or other means of releasing excess water. Without adequate drainage, the plant's roots can suffocate and rot. If a container does not come with at least one drainage hole, drill one.

Cachepots

In lieu of drilling into a container, use it as a decorative cachepot instead, hiding the nursery pot inside it. When watering a plant in a cachepot, pour off any excess water that is not absorbed into the potting mix and drains from the nursery pot. When using an ornamental cachepot that is made of wood, wicker, metal, or another material that could be damaged by

moisture, set a plastic saucer under the nursery pot to protect the cachepot from damage. When hiding an ordinary nursery pot inside a cachepot, conceal the rim of the plastic pot under a thin layer of preserved green moss, long-fiber sphagnum moss, or Spanish moss.

Material matters

Key to a plant's success is the container's ability to hold soil and moisture, which depends on its construction material. Porous materials, such as terra-cotta and wood, dry out faster and are good for plants that prefer soil on the dry side. Nonporous materials, including plastic and glazed ceramic, hold moisture more evenly and longer. Well-made containers stand up to watering and weather. Unless treated with a waterproof sealant, wet wood rots and metal corrodes. Find more information about containers in Chapter 6.

Types of containers
Containers are available in an enormous range of styles and materials. Each type has benefits and drawbacks for you to consider.

TERRA-COTTA
Affordable terra-cotta is weighty and porous, washable and breakable. High-fired terra-cotta is most durable; hand-thrown and Mexican pots are more fragile.

GLAZED CERAMIC
Choose from an array of colors and patterns that can tie into a room's decor. Handle pots carefully to avoid chipping. Ceramic pots are weighty.

BASKET
Sturdy and attractive options include an array of woven materials. Natural materials require more protection from moisture damage. Plastic and metal prove durable.

WOOD
Line wooden containers with plastic before planting or use them to hold pots. Choose rot-resistant cedar or wood that has been painted, stained, or sealed.

REPURPOSED
Turn all sorts of objects into planters, from old coffee cans with rusty patina to desk drawers, beach buckets, and wastebaskets. Drill a drainage hole.

PLASTIC
Plastic is lightweight, relatively unbreakable, and easy to clean and store. Prices vary widely with finish and quality; plastics can be long lasting or not.

VINTAGE
Planters from another era have charm and collectability. Pots with chips, peeling finishes, or other imperfections may be available at a discount. Use them only indoors.

RECYCLED
A new generation of eco-friendly containers are made from recycled plastic, paper, rubber, or other materials, saving the resources from being consigned to landfills.

METAL
Galvanized metal, copper, and zinc offer versatile style and long life. Shiny metal surfaces fade into subtle patinas, unless they're powder-coated, painted, or polished.

SELF-WATERING
A built-in reservoir allows plants to draw moisture from it as needed. This is a valuable service for plants that like evenly moist soil.

Displaying pots

Plant stands give legs to a container, protecting the floor from water damage and using vertical space to display plants.

Little else will dampen your enjoyment

of an indoor garden more than a leaky container and moisture damage to surfaces. Few surfaces are waterproof, and it doesn't take long for water to stain or ruin your carpet, wood flooring, furniture, windowsill, or countertop. Take a preventative approach to moisture damage. Avoid placing plants on precious furniture, such as a piano or an antique item.

Saucers and trays

Always use a saucer or tray under a pot to catch excess water that drains from the container. The saucer or tray should be at least as wide as the pot's widest diameter—and then some—so water can drain into the saucer or tray and not overflow.

Also protect the surface under the saucer or tray from any moisture that sweats, seeps, or spills and collects enough to do damage. Use a large ceramic tile, cork coaster, or trivet that will raise the saucer or tray off the surface and allow air to help keep the surface dry. Even a cachepot, ceramic pot, or other container that you think will hold water should have a saucer. Clear plastic saucers are widely available and inexpensive for use inside a cachepot or basket, or as a liner for a terra-cotta or glazed saucer.

Other options for raising pots above surfaces and preventing damage include pot feet or risers.

Instead of a saucer or tray, you can repurpose vintage plates, cross sections or slabs of wood, or remnants of a stone countertop. You can also have glass cut to fit a tabletop, windowsill, or other surface and protect it from potential water damage and scratches. Have the edges of the glass ground so you can safely handle it.

Use felt to make coasters for potted plants with saucers. Cut a piece of felt the same size as the bottom of the saucer and tack it in place using white glue. The coaster will prevent the saucer and potted plant from scratching the surface of furniture when you set them on it.

Plant stands

Instead of placing potted plants on furniture or windowsills, set them on a plant stand. Some plant stands have feet, others have legs, and all raise a potted plant—or multiple pots—above surface level. Consider using a plant stand with multiple shelves and a tiered design as a means of displaying a container garden at varying heights and putting plants within easy reach. Whether made of metal or wood, the ideal plant stand moves outdoors with your plants for the summer and weathers the elements. Just beware of setting large and heavy containers on the top shelf of a tiered stand, making it top-heavy. A tall or tiered plant stand or baker's rack may need to be secured to a wall.

Ways to hold pots
Give your indoor garden a lift, using a pot holder of any kind to literally raise containers off a floor, table, or other surface.

STANDING PLANTER
A collection of ferns stands out in a wicker planter. The grouping of two maidenhair ferns and a rabbit's foot fern in 6-inch pots fills the painted wicker with lush greenery.

SAUCERS GALORE
A wide variety of saucers, drip trays, and coasters are available in different styles and materials, from terra-cotta to plastic, ceramic, copper, stone, and cork.

PLANT CADDY
Setting a large, heavy potted plant on a caddy with casters makes it easy to move it around the house or outdoors. Some caddies feature a built-in saucer.

STEPPED-UP DISPLAY
A small, painted step stool makes an effective holder for small pots on a table. The flowering garden includes calla lily, hydrangea, lily, and kalanchoe.

Potting and repotting

This Chinese evergreen completely fills its container with a mass of roots and stems. The plant has become so large for the pot, it tips over easily. Time for repotting!

Any young plant growing in a small pot

will need to be repotted before long. Surprisingly, many mature plants seldom need repotting. Some plants bloom and perform better when their roots are snugly enclosed or even crowded in a pot. When the roots have filled a pot so tightly that they begin circling the root ball or the pot's bottom, the plant has become pot-bound or root-bound and needs more growing room in a larger pot.

Time to repot

Plants give you lots of clues to help determine when it is time to repot them. Lift the pot and see if roots have begun growing out of the drainage holes. The roots may be so densely packed that little soil is left and water runs through the pot. Check this by tipping the pot on its side, gently dislodging the plant, and sliding it out of the pot to examine the root ball.

A few plants grow less vigorously and won't bloom if they become pot-bound. After blooming for two years in the same pot, holiday cactus, wax plant, clivia, and spider plant benefit from repotting just after a bloom period. Ferns, palms, amaryllis, and some other plants that don't like to be disturbed by repotting or do best in close quarters will benefit from fresh soil each year. Carefully scrape off the top inch of soil and replace it with new soil.

Other signs that a plant needs repotting include: The plant has become too top-heavy for its container and topples easily; wilts soon after watering; develops new leaves with decreasing size; displays yellowing lower leaves; or has become infested with insects.

Microclimates

Your attention to details when potting or repotting helps ensure a strong, healthy plant. A day or two prior to repotting, thoroughly water the plant to prepare it for transplanting. To repot a plant, tip the container on its side and carefully slide out the plant. If it doesn't come out easily, run a table knife around the inside of the pot. If the soil is depleted or infested with insects, take the plant outside and rinse the root ball with a garden hose. Examine the roots for any problems, prune out damaged or diseased areas, and repot the plant.

When potting, set a plant at the same soil level as its previous planting. Burying any portion of a plant too deeply can cause rot. When grouping plants in a pot, first arrange them in their nursery pots. When you are satisfied with the grouping, remove the plants from their nursery pots, setting the largest plant in place first and the smallest plant last. Add soil to fill in between plants, leaving 1 to 2 inches of watering space between the soil surface and the pot's rim.

ASK THE GARDEN DOCTOR

How can I tell if a plant is root-bound?

ANSWER: Slide the plant out of its pot. If the roots are tightly massed and circling the root ball, the plant is root-bound and needs to be repotted. Gently loosen the roots before repotting.

How to repot a plant

Repot a plant outdoors, cover the work surface with newspaper, or repot on a waterproof countertop. When adding new soil to the planting, do not pack it into place—roots need air space for water and growth.

1 LARGER POT
Choose a new pot 1 to 2 inches larger in diameter than the plant's root ball, giving the plant room for root growth to the sides and bottom of the pot, as well as space for watering above the soil line.

2 LOOSEN ROOTS
If the plant won't budge from its old pot, gently squeeze the root ball to loosen the roots. If the roots are tightly bound, push a finger up into the mass and tease loose the roots.

3 WATER WELL
Fill one third to one half of the new pot with fresh potting soil. Add time-release plant food. Set the plant in place and fill around it with fresh soil. Water thoroughly.

Soil mixes

Get the most from your indoor garden by cultivating healthy growing habits and promoting successful plants. Potting mix or soil helps provide plants with the water, nutrients, and air they need to thrive. It also anchors a plant in its container.

The ideal soil will not come from your yard—garden soil is too heavy, compacts easily, drains poorly in pots, and may harbor insects or diseases.

Potting mixes

The term "potting soil" is generic in the marketplace. Unless a package indicates the ingredients, it is difficult to know what you are buying. Potting soil varies considerably, but it is often little more than sterilized topsoil, which by itself is too heavy for potted plants.

For most container gardens, choose a potting mix. Packaged ready-made mixes usually contain peat moss, coir (coconut husk), or decomposed bark and vermiculite or perlite—no soil—in various proportions. If you need a potting mix with other ingredients, a wide range of packaged mixes adequate for most plants is available, or you can blend your own mix.

Soilless mixes drain well and dry out quickly. Sometimes they contain only peat moss or coir and perlite and are too lightweight to adequately anchor a plant, especially a large or top-heavy plant. Soilless mixes also contain few if any nutrients and need to be fertilized. A soil-based mix made with sterilized soil or compost is heavier and holds moisture and

Soilless potting mixes work for all kinds of plants and containers and can be customized according to the pot as well as the plant.

nutrients longer. Experiment with both types of mixes and see which works best for your plants.

Custom mixes

You can customize a growing mix according to individual plant needs and save some money by adding ingredients to a standard potting mix. Potting mixes for flowering plants typically contain more organic materials that retain moisture, such as leaf mold (decomposed leaves) or compost. A moisture-holding mix usually includes water-retentive polymer crystals and suits plants that prefer damp soil. Cacti and succulents need a mix that contains sand and drains extremely well.

The ingredients in a potting mix should also complement your choice of containers. Vermiculite works well in porous pots such as terra-cotta. Perlite works well in plastic, glazed, and metal pots.

A premium mix that contains slow-release fertilizer helps sustain long-term plantings and won't require added plant food for the first growing season.

Specialty blends
Choose a potting mix based on the plants you intend to grow in it. The soil mix you select should be blended to provide the water, air, and nutrients the plants need.

FLOWERING PLANTS
Mix equal parts sand, peat moss, sterilized topsoil, and leaf mold. Sometimes a comparable blend is sold as African violet mix.

EPIPHYTES, ORCHIDS & BROMELIADS
Mix equal parts sphagnum moss, coarse bark, and coarse perlite. Add 1 tablespoon dolomitic lime and 1 cup horticultural charcoal to 3 quarts mix.

CACTI AND SUCCULENTS
A desert-like potting mix that contains equal parts sand, perlite, and potting soil provides porous, fast-draining conditions.

FERNS
Blend 3 parts soilless potting mix with 3 parts leaf mold and 1 part compost. Then add 1 cup horticultural charcoal to 2 quarts of this mixture.

ALL-PURPOSE MIX
Combine 3 parts peat moss or coir, 2 parts compost, 2 parts perlite or vermiculite, and 1 part coarse sand. Add slow-release fertilizer and water-holding granules, as desired.

Individual ingredients
Components of potting mixes vary and affect the way the mix works, in terms of holding water, draining excess moisture, and more.

PERLITE
These heat-expanded granules of volcanic ash do not absorb water, but they help potting mix drain and resist compaction.

VERMICULITE
Flakes of mica (a mineral) expanded by heat absorb water, release it slowly, and make potting mix more porous.

PEAT MOSS
This partially decomposed plant material soaks up water and nutrients like a sponge. Coir substitutes for this limited resource.

COARSE SAND
Its tiny rock particles can help open up soil and allow air to penetrate it. Choose washed or sterilized sand.

CHARCOAL
Horticultural-grade charcoal absorbs salts and byproducts (including odors) from plant decay.

Fertilizing plants

High-performance plants need nutrients

to produce vigorous foliage and bright blooms. Regular fertilizing during the growing season is important to keep potted plants healthy, because frequent watering flushes important nutrients out of the soil. More frequent fertilizing is needed by some plants, including vigorous growers, flowering plants, and those growing in a soilless mix. Less frequent feeding is required by other plants, including many foliage-type houseplants, citrus, cacti and succulents, and plants that rest or go dormant over winter.

The numbers

Although fertilizer is also called plant food, plants make their own food via photosynthesis. Fertilizer amends the soil with the nutrients plants need most. Fertilizer labels indicate

When using dry fertilizer granules or pellets, carefully scratch them into the soil. Water after adding dry plant food to the soil.

the percentage of the three key nutrients as a series of numbers, such as 15-30-15, ideal for flowering plants, which means that 15 percent of the product's weight is nitrogen; 30 percent is phosphorus; and 15 percent is potassium. Nitrogen is needed for stem growth and green leaves; phosphorus fuels strong roots and flowering; potassium enhances stem strength, disease resistance, and formation of flowers and fruit. An all-purpose, 20-20-20 blend suits most plants.

For good health, plants need other minerals (sulfur, calcium, magnesium) and micronutrients (copper, zinc, and others) available in balanced products and noted on their labels. If plants are nutrient-deficient they may show symptoms, such as yellowish or reddish foliage and stunted growth. If you suspect a deficiency, apply a soluble fertilizer rich in micronutrients.

Types of fertilizer

Plant foods come in various forms that are applied in specific ways. What matters most is that fertilizer must be dissolved to be of use to plants; soil moisture dissolves nutrients so they can be absorbed by plant roots. Water-soluble crystalline, granular, and liquid fertilizers are convenient to use by diluting with water. A solution reduces the potential for burning caused when excess fertilizer damages roots and leaves.

Dry plant foods include granules, powdery crystals, slow-release pellets, and spikes. You can make multiple applications of a soluble fertilizer that is taken up relatively quickly by plants and used up within about a month; or make fewer applications of a less-soluble fertilizer. Slow-release formulas are made for a single application each growing season and last for six to nine months under average conditions. Organic fertilizers include compost, fish emulsion, worm castings, and kelp products. Edible plants and long-term plantings benefit from organic plant foods that enrich soil and improve its structure.

Applying plant food

Follow package directions when using fertilizer. Fertilizing is not advised when the plants are wilted, sickly, or lacking light. Under most circumstances, you'll need to fertilize plants regularly during spring and summer, when they're actively growing. Skipping or missing a dose of plant food does not have the same deleterious effects as forgetting to water. Overfertilizing hurts plants more than it helps them and shows up as burned leaf edges, poorly shaped leaves, and white crust on the soil surface or inside the pot's rim. Occasionally leaching or rinsing soil helps minimize salts that build up from fertilizer and water. If a plant is sensitive to the mineral salts in fertilizer or the fluoride in water, replace its soil periodically.

TEST GARDEN TIP

Fertilizer and clay pots

Clay containers dry out faster and need more frequent watering. This leaches fertilizer out of the soil. The plants in them may need to be fertilized more often than those in plastic pots.

Mulching indoor plants

Mulch is a layer of loose material that covers the surface of the potting mix in a container and works primarily to conserve soil moisture. It also prevents soil from splashing on foliage and washing out of a pot when you water. If you move plants outdoors in summer, mulch helps insulate soil and plant roots, keeping them cooler during the hottest days. Mulch can deter cats and squirrels from scratching in potted plants. It's a colorful and pretty embellishment. Apply a 1-inch layer of mulch—polished stones, glass beads, crushed recycled glass, marbles, shells, rinsed gravel, or moss—evenly over the soil.

Grooming plants

Each plant has particular preferences for moisture and heat, depending on its origin. But most plants adjust to indoor conditions, especially with the gardener's awareness of their needs and assistance in fine-tuning the environmental variables. As the conditions change seasonally, be aware of how your indoor plants will be affected.

From tidying to pruning

The first step in grooming is to remove old and dead leaves as well as faded flowers. Some withered leaves fall off on their own and should be tidied up to eliminate harbors for pests and disease. Yellow or brown leaves won't turn green again. Pluck or snip them off to make the plant more attractive. If the leaves are large and have brown tips or edges, trim the brown section using sharp scissors and let the remainder of the leaf recover. Flowers

Bromeliads thrive with regular misting as their source of water. Although misting does little to boost humidity, it can rinse dust off leaves. Dusty leaves absorb less light.

that aren't destined to become fruit, such as those on African violets or hibiscus, should also be plucked when spent. Removing dead flowers often makes way for new ones.

Pinching back and pruning improves a plant's shape and promotes healthy new growth. Pinch or snip off the growing ends of fast-growing or untidy plants that show signs of unruliness or unattractive bare stems. Cut or pinch just above a node where new leaves or branches can develop. Although some plants may never need pruning, others require it to encourage and direct growth; remove damaged, diseased, or dead branches; or adjust a plant's height or width. Keep the natural shape of the plant in mind when pruning. If you're afraid to cut off a branch, cover it with your hand before you make the cut, and picture how the plant will look without the branch.

Using your fingertips to pinch out the stem tip and its topmost leaves promotes side branching and bushier growth. Coleus, nerve plant, and peperomia are among many plants that benefit from frequent pinching. Trailing plants, such as Swedish ivy and pothos, also respond positively to periodic pinching.

Dusting plants

Use a household duster or soft cloth to remove dust from leaves at least once a month. The particles block light and clog the leaf pores, interfering with transpiration. Hold one hand under a leaf, supporting it as you dust with your other hand.

Another way to remove dust is to bathe a plant. Place small potted plants in a sink and spray them with tepid water, using a spray nozzle. Place large plants in the shower. To prevent soil from washing out of the pot, slip the container inside a plastic bag, pull the top of the bag up over the soil, and cinch it around the plant's stem. Secure the cinched bag by tying it with twist ties or twine.

How to groom plants
Regularly clean up any litter—fallen leaves, flowers, or twigs—that collects on soil and between potted plants. Also, when watering plants, rotate pots one-quarter turn clockwise to promote even growth. Other practices that bolster plant health include repotting, adding fresh soil to pots, fertilizing, and mulching.

DUSTING
Use a soft, damp cloth to wipe dust off large, glossy, or waxy leaves. As you work, frequently rinse the cloth in clean, warm water.

BRUSHING
Dust plants that have fuzzy leaves (African violet, purple passion plant, some begonias) with a soft bristle brush, such as a cosmetic brush or paintbrush.

PINCHING
Pinch or cut stem tips of plants such as aluminum plant that have soft stems. Pinching prompts the plant to send out new shoots, making the plant full and lush.

PRUNING
Always use clean, sharp pruners to trim plants. It's best to prune during spring or summer, when a plant will grow quickly to cover the pruning wound.

Plants on vacation

Many indoor plants enjoy a summer respite outdoors in mild weather as much as gardeners do, especially after a long, dark winter. Think of it as giving your plants a summer vacation. They can serve you in the process by adding their tropical appeal to your outdoor living areas.

Outdoors, the plants will thrive with filtered light, increased air circulation, and refreshing rain showers. Their health and appearance improves as their energy recharges, so you might notice lusher foliage, more saturated color, vigorous growth, and profuse flowering. Natural insect predators can also go to work for you and rid plants of pesky mites and scale.

Outside for the summer

Take outdoors only the toughest plants—those that can handle periodic wind, hard rain, and unexpected chill. Wait until early summer, when warmer weather patterns have settled in, then move plants outside gradually. Help them adjust to the change in environment by setting them outside for a couple of hours one day, and a few hours the next, and increasing their time outside more each day. Place them in a protected place with afternoon shade to prevent damage from wind, hail, and sun. Some houseplants such as cacti tolerate full sun outdoors once they are acclimated to their summer environment.

Pothos, philodendron, spider plant, and others happily move outdoors to spend the summer in a shaded spot. They create a pretty display outdoors too.

Keep low-light plants under trees, shrubs, or a structure in full shade. Monitor soil moisture carefully—potted plants dry out much faster outdoors, especially when the weather is warm and breezy.

Moving back indoors

Bring plants back indoors in late summer, before temperatures drop at night. If you wait until early fall to make the transition, your plants will have to adjust to changes in temperature and humidity in addition to a lower light level, which is stressful. Ease plants through the adjustment again by moving them to a shadier place outdoors for a couple of weeks before moving them indoors. Inspect and groom all plants to minimize any chance of bringing pests and diseases indoors with them. Consider repotting any plants that have grown substantially over the summer—completing this task outdoors leaves the mess outside. If many of your plants have vacationed outdoors, bring in a few at a time, giving each one careful attention. Leaving a big move to the last minute when frost threatens can stress gardeners and plants.

While you're away

Plants should fare well for a week if you leave them well-watered. Move them out of direct, bright light to prevent overheating and sunburn damage. If you plan to be away two or three weeks, consider these options: A thorough watering, followed by tenting each plant in a spacious plastic bag, keeps most plants supplied with adequate moisture for several weeks. Leave some openings for air circulation, and insert stakes into the pot to prevent the plastic from touching the leaves. Alternatively, use a wick-watering system. Place a large container of water next to the plant and extend narrow tubing or an absorbent shoelace from the water into the soil. As the soil dries, water wicks into it via capillary action. Just let the lower end of the tubing or shoelace reach down to the bottom of the water container.

TEST GARDEN TIP
Pretty combos

Keep plants in their usual pots when you move them outdoors or combine ones with similar light needs in spacious containers such as self-watering buckets.

Left: **Before moving a plant indoors after a summer vacation on the patio, give it a strong shower, using a garden hose to blast off any hitchhiking insects. Rinse the tops and bottoms of leaves.**

Below: **A two-wheeled dolly makes it much easier to lift and haul large potted plants indoors and out. Large pots can also become mobile when set on caddies with casters.**

Watch for pests

Aphids

ander (life size).

...are curling, discolored,
...e leaves. A shiny or sticky
...st-off insect skins. Leaves may
...ed, green, soft.
...buds, young stems,
...s are occasionally
...festation.

Citrus mealybugs on coleus (2x life si...

Problem: White cottony or waxy insec...
Particularly in crotches or where leaves are at...
a cottony appearance. Cottony masses that co...
A sticky substance may cover the leaves or drip o...
can result from the sticky substance. Infested plant...
die if severely infested.

Analysis: Mealybugs are among the more serious problem...

Before you take steps to remedy a pest or disease, identify it correctly. A magnifying glass helps a lot. Here, the problem appears to be a mealybug.

An ounce of prevention truly pays off when it comes to plant pests,

and it is doubly important within the confines of an indoor garden. Healthy plants are amazingly able to resist problems. But rascal insects can ride in on a new plant or their eggs can hide in potting soil. If you neglect your plants, forgetting to water and feed them, the resulting stress will make them more susceptible to insect infestations and diseases.

Minimizing pest problems

Make it part of your routine to check for signs of problems whenever you water plants. You can correct a problem much more easily if you catch it early. Look for obvious signs (insects, eggs, sticky sap, webs) and subtle clues (weak, pale, or distorted growth; yellow or dropped leaves; stippling or tiny yellow dots on leaves).

When you notice a change—the Boston fern is shedding more leaves than usual, the hibiscus has more than a couple of yellow leaves, one or two fungus gnat sightings a month have turned into daily appearances—take a closer look. Problems such as these need to be tended before they spiral beyond control.

Identify the problem

If you notice wilted leaves on a plant, consider the possibilities: Does the soil feel dry? Is the plant getting too much sun? Has it outgrown its pot? Are there any signs that indicate disease?

Distinguishing between a cultural problem and a pest or disease is half the solution.

Resolving problems

In time you'll recognize the difference between a healthy plant and one that needs help. If you spot signs of an insect or disease problem, move the affected plant away from others while you take steps to solve the problem. Choose the mildest remedies first: Pick off insects or affected leaves, then rinse the plant with a solution of soapy water (using Fels Naptha or castile soap; most dish soaps are too harsh for plants). If the problem persists, apply horticultural oil or insecticidal soap. Repot the plant if it has a root disease or soil pests. If the problem continues, prune the affected parts. If you use an insect- or disease-control chemical formulated for indoor use, check the label to determine if it is also formulated to treat the specific problem affecting your plant, and then follow the directions. The last resort: Discard the plant.

After dealing with the problem, evaluate the plant's growing conditions again and adjust the light, water, humidity, temperature, soil, or fertilizer accordingly. Have patience—the least toxic methods of pest control may take some weeks to resolve the situation. In the meantime, focus on bolstering the plant's health to aid its recovery.

TEST GARDEN TIP

Sticky trap

Cut a 6×8-inch piece of yellow cardstock. Brush petroleum jelly or Tanglefoot (from a hardware store or garden center) on both sides of the card. Hang it near plants to trap insects.

Common indoor insect pests

Damage to indoor plants is common because natural predators rarely reside indoors. Become familiar with the most common pests and employ simple methods to eliminate them.

MEALYBUGS
These cottony insects suck plant sap from leaves and stems. The plant weakens and new growth is deformed. Wash the plant with soapy water; apply rubbing alcohol to the mealybugs. Use neem or horticultural oil.

SCALE
Crusty brown or reddish-gray bumps or cottony white masses appear on stems and leaves. Leaves turn yellow, drop, or collect sticky residue. Repeated applications of horticultural oil smother adult insects.

FUNGUS GNATS
Dark fungus gnats fly around plants and crawl on soil, leaves, and nearby windows. They lay eggs in soil; larvae feed on roots and kill seedlings. Use a yellow sticky trap to snag adults; Bt (*Bacillus thurengiensis,* a naturally occurring bacterium) to kill larvae.

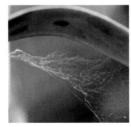

SPIDER MITES
These troublesome pests thrive in heat and low humidity. Look for stippling on leaves; webbing in extreme cases. Adjust conditions; bathe the plant. Use horticultural oil if necessary.

WHITEFLIES
Feeding mainly on the undersides of leaves, the tiny insects create a sticky residue. Use yellow sticky traps. Resort to insecticidal soap for extreme cases. Air circulation is vital for prevention.

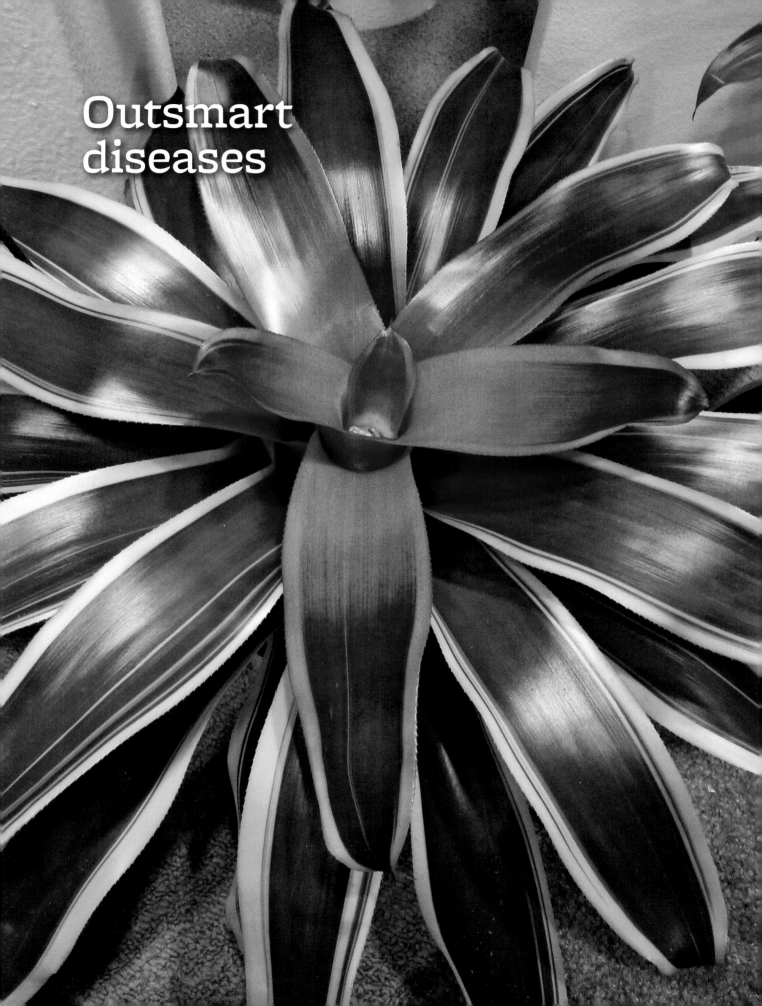

Outsmart
diseases

Disease is seldom found on a thriving plant.

Ensuring that plants get what they need in terms of soil, light, water, and food is key to their success. Sometimes problems occur due to an issue with one of these elements—too much or too little, whatever the case may be. A weak, damaged, or stressed plant is more prone to disease.

Bacterial diseases, although uncommon, proliferate by rapidly reproducing and damaging plant tissue. A fungal disease takes hold when a spore contacts a leaf, becomes a parasite, and destroys plant tissue. A virus, often present in certain plants but dormant, infects a stressed plant and weakens it. Viruses are carried from plant to plant by insects or people, or on infected tools.

Disease prevention

Regular grooming prevents many problems. Immediately getting rid of leaves or stems that show signs of trouble is a good practice, regardless of the cause. Allowing fallen dead leaves to remain on the soil can exacerbate a problem. If one of those leaves has a disease, even in the early stages, it will be nurtured and spread via the damp soil. It's easy enough to pick up the leaves and put them in the garbage—problem prevented or minimized.

The presence of disease usually indicates an issue with the plant's culture or conditions.

Powdery mildew, a fungus that appears as white powder on leaves, tells you to improve air circulation, lower humidity and temperature, decrease watering, and prune out diseased leaves. By correcting these cultural issues, you'll fend off other, more serious diseases.

Typically more harmful and difficult to control than pests, diseases develop in the greenhouse or at home. Look for signs of problems before you buy a plant, especially viruses, which kill the plant they attack and spread easily to other plants. Isolate any new plants for a week or two after you bring them home to make sure they are free of diseases and insects. Understand your plants' needs and give them the proper care they need to reduce stress and prevent problems.

Problems and solutions

When plants show signs of trouble, a single symptom can have different causes. Yellow spots on leaves may indicate one or more problems, including a bacterial infection, a viral infection, or sunburn, depending on the size, shape, and prevalence of the spots. Learning to identify diseases can be tricky. Sending a photo or plant sample of your plant to a nearby university extension plant clinic will be helpful.

Opposite: **A healthy plant has a natural vigor and shine. Bromeliads such as this *Neoregelia carolinae* 'Franca' tend to be free of disease, but unfavorable growing conditions can cause problems.**

Common indoor plant diseases

Once you have identified a plant's problem, you can choose appropriate solutions. The top line of defense should be to learn about and provide the best conditions for the plant.

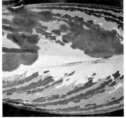

BACTERIAL BLIGHT
Soft, sunken areas with water-soaked margins appear on leaves or stems. Leaves may turn yellow and severely wilt. Inner stem tissue turns brownish. Take a healthy cutting or two and discard the plant. The condition is not curable.

LEAF SPOT
Caused by bacteria or other pathogens, the disease is seen on leaves as circular reddish-brown spots with yellow halos that may join to form blotches. Snip off badly spotted leaves. Water carefully to keep leaves dry.

POWDERY MILDEW
White or gray powdery fungal patches form on leaves, stems, and flowers. Remove infected parts. Give plants adequate light and air circulation. Use potassium bicarbonate to prevent infection.

ROT
Excessively wet soil stresses a plant. Fungi proliferate and affect the leaves, stems, crown, or roots. The affected part appears dull and turns brown or black and mushy. Let the soil dry between waterings. Remove and destroy damaged parts.

VIRUS
The plant grows slowly, without vigor. Leaves are mottled or streaked with yellow and distorted. No cure exists. Infected plants should be discarded. When pruning, dip tools in a disinfectant (diluted bleach or rubbing alcohol) between plants.

room
to grow

Explore the range of places designed especially for indoor gardens, from a glasshouse fantasy to the easiest do-it-yourself options.

p.**58**
GREENHOUSE GARDENING
Is there a greenhouse in your future? What kind of greenhouse fits into your scheme of things? First, look at the big picture and then consider the practicalities.

p.**60**
CONSERVATORIES & OTHER HAVENS
If not a greenhouse, then what? Imagine the possibilities appropriate for your home and the type of indoor garden room that suits your lifestyle.

p.**62**
POTTING PLACES
Discover the most budget-friendly ways to make your indoor gardening endeavors more convenient, organized, and enjoyable.

p.**64**
PLANT SHELVES
See how shelving helps you conserve space and display plants to their best advantage.

Greenhouse basics

Open the door to a greenhouse

on a dull winter's day and escape into a gardener's dream where plants grow beautifully no matter the weather, amid earthy aromas and a peaceful hush. The warm, humid, light-filled place supports a wider range of plants than typically grown inside a home. Flowers bloom every month of the year, exotic fruits thrive, fresh vegetables turn ripe for picking, seedlings sprout, and tender plants sail

through winter. It is the ideal place to keep tropical plants that would ordinarily head to the compost heap at summer's end.

A greenhouse also supports happy gardeners. Picture yourself puttering away inside a climate-controlled haven tending plants or relaxing with a book—while rain or snow falls outside. As a garden room or an extension of your home, a greenhouse provides cozy living space. It can

This greenhouse built with cedar lumber and polycarbonate (strong plastic) siding has a bench built at counter height, drainable brick flooring, and a convenient centrally located door.

create a seamless transition between inside and out; it can be used for work or entertaining as well as a personal retreat.

Practical considerations

Greenhouses come in a vast range of styles, sizes, and materials, but all are designed to capture light and heat by way of transparent roof and wall panels. Plan carefully to get a greenhouse that suits your needs whether you buy a ready-made structure, assemble one from a kit, or build a glasshouse using salvaged windows.

Site To get the most winter sunlight, a greenhouse should face south. Choose a site that receives at least six hours of sun daily. A heat-absorbing brick or paver floor can help keep the greenhouse warm at night.

Style Depending on how permanent you want a greenhouse to be, you can choose a freestanding or lean-to structure. For visual continuity, select a style that matches or complements the architecture of your house and outbuildings. Styles include A-frame, Gothic arch, gambrel roof, and dome. Some are raised on stone or concrete foundations. Northern dwellers will want a structure that shrugs off snow and ice; windows should be mounted on low walls, which increase the ability of the greenhouse to retain heat.

Size The climate of a larger greenhouse is easier to maintain than that of a small one because a large space is less prone to rapid temperature changes. An 8×10- or 10×12-foot greenhouse is usually adequate.

Construction Research building plans and check out local codes for permit requirements. Temperature extremes in your region will determine the right materials for your structure. Glass is the traditional choice for its superior light transmission and longevity. It's scratch-resistant and easy to clean. Double-glazed glass offers better heat retention, but may require shade in summer. Plastic is strong, easier to install, less prone to breakage, and energy-efficient for year-round gardening. It must be cleaned carefully to avoid scratching. Plastic diffuses light.

Greenhouse maintenance

Monitoring the conditions in your greenhouse will help make the most of it and ensure your plants' success. Maintain a healthy environment by keeping the house clean and quarantining new plants. Watch closely for signs of pests and diseases, and remedy a situation promptly.

TEST GARDEN TIP
Building material

The ideal greenhouse covering lets in the maximum amount of light while allowing the least amount of heat to escape. Also consider the material's longevity and upkeep.

Greenhouse options
When planning the ultimate indoor gardening setting, consider your purpose in having a greenhouse. Be realistic about the time and expense involved in maintaining a specialized plant-care structure.

GARDEN VIEW
Designed as a new room, an attached greenhouse enhances the home. French doors link the structures and allow climate control of temperature and humidity.

LEAN-TO
A greenhouse attached to an exterior wall of the house is convenient and eliminates having to build one wall. It also passively collects solar heat for your home.

LIVING SPACE
Comfortable and practical furnishings give a greenhouse multiple uses and withstand extremes of humidity and heat. A mesh or bamboo shade helps deflect the sun's hot summer rays.

Conservatories & other havens

A conservatory or sunroom provides a climate-controlled space where the growing season continues nonstop. In this oasis, time slows to the pace of plant life.

By definition, a greenhouse is a structure specifically designed to have as much transparent surface as possible oriented toward the sun. A conservatory is a greenhouse, but each is used in different ways. A greenhouse usually shelters and nurtures plants, while a conservatory serves primarily as a retreat. It offers a place to grow plants indoors as well as a place for people to hang out and soak up warmth, relax, or entertain. A sunroom, sun porch, and greenhouse window are among other options that provide some of the benefits of a greenhouse.

Garden rooms

Call it a conservatory, solarium, or sunroom—in any case it is most likely a room attached to the house. Insulated glass windows make it a four-season room. The design should suit the architecture of the house. It may be sleekly contemporary or fanciful with old-world charm. Some rooms have angled rooflines, others have curved eaves. The framing varies too, from wood to steel or aluminum.

Designed to cater to the comfort of people, a conservatory or sunroom is typically cooler and less humid than a greenhouse. The best location for a warm, sunny room is a southern or western exposure, but shades of some sort are needed, especially in summer. A room with eastern or northern exposure is cooler, shadier, and best suited to plants that need medium or low light.

Select furnishings for a solarium that enhance the setting and make it more livable. Comfort and durability are key. Select fabrics designed for outdoor use that can withstand exposure to sunlight and will resist water, stains, and mildew.

Window greenhouses

A deep window works like a greenhouse, creating a warm and sun-drenched environment for plants. It may include glass shelves as well as a vent or circulating fan to allow for climate control. Use a greenhouse window to start seeds or root cuttings, raise herbs for snipping all winter, or pamper African violets. If a greenhouse doesn't fit your budget, perhaps a bump-out window will.

ASK THE GARDEN DOCTOR

What is the best flooring material for a greenhouse or conservatory?

ANSWER: A gravel floor allows quick drainage. Brick set in sand can be hosed or swept and also drains easily. Concrete footings may be needed in deep-freeze climates.

Indoor gardening spaces
Homeowners have discovered the pleasures that come with adding a sun-filled garden living area to their home. These additions are designed for year-round enjoyment, but they accommodate plants too.

CONSERVATORY
A European-style structure brings elegant and classic style to a home. The glass roof and walls allow unobstructed views of the outdoors.

SUN PORCH
Retrofitted with high-efficiency insulated windows, a once-drafty porch becomes an energy-saving addition to an updated home.

SUNROOM
French doors transform a back entry or mudroom into a winter haven for plants that thrive in a cool, sunny place.

WINDOW
A greenhouse window fits most budgets and can be a weekend project. Tile forms a resilient surface that is easy to clean.

Potting places

Start with a plain potting bench and jazz it up to make it more attractive and serviceable. Stain it black, then add drawer pulls, a curtain rod, curtains, and a grill grate.

Gardeners have a way of accumulating tools, pots, watering cans, potting mixes, plant supports, and all sorts of necessities. Of course, it would be lovely to have a roomy shed or greenhouse where you could organize all this gardening accoutrement and have work space too. Storage space helps you keep gardening gear within easy reach; it saves time when tending plants and searching for tools. But for most people, the reality of a potting area is less than ideal and most often a kitchen counter or a corner of the garage.

Happy work

Designating a small portion of your home as a work area makes indoor gardening more convenient and enjoyable. If it isn't practical to set aside a room or a section of one for your horticultural activities, a corner, potting bench, or table will suffice. Set up a place for tending plants indoors that is well-arranged and outfitted to provide you with years of growing success. When determining a potting place, consider how you will access water and electricity to make the spot as convenient as possible.

Whether you design a potting place from scratch or adapt an existing area, include conveniences as much as possible. Make it a priority to have a water source nearby to avoid countless trips to the kitchen sink. You'll need water for hydrating plants, transplants, and newly sown seeds, as well as for washing hands, pots, and tools. You will also want a work area with easy-to-clean surfaces—tabletop and floor—where you can sweep up soil swiftly.

Locate your potting place near a sunny window. Your plants and seedlings will benefit from the light, and so will you. Even if a window isn't an option, plan on good lighting so you can see clearly, whether you're sowing seeds or reading a plant catalog.

Garden central

It doesn't take much to set up an indoor gardener's workstation. Whether you start with a potting bench or a repurposed tabletop, allow several feet of work surface for your activities. Check the height—you'll want to work comfortably, whether standing or sitting.

Top tools

Scaled-down tools designed for indoor gardening make tasks easier and less messy. Tools made for cutting, cultivating, and scooping fit into pots and among plants.

Indoor gardener's workstation **You need an organized and efficient work space where you can keep all the important tools and supplies, whether you plan to transplant seedlings or repot large plants.**

SHELVING
A salvaged bookcase hung high on a wall puts containers at the gardener's fingertips. An old dresser becomes a potting bench when the top is wrapped with sheet metal.

CORNER
Furnish your garage or basement with a gardening corner, using a length of countertop, pegboard, and kitchen cabinets. These economical items came from a building materials reuse center.

BENCH
Make a potting table complete with storage in minutes. Lay a piece of painted medium-density fiberboard across repurposed kitchen cupboards. Add a slatted-wood pot rack on the wall.

Plant shelves

Consolidating your plant collection on a shelf, rack, or

other supportive structure makes it easier to tend the plants. Setting them closer to eye level means you can inspect them readily too. Spacing the plants on shelves or some sort of tiered rack or stand creates an attractive display. A vertical display conserves space and gets potted plants off your floors and tables.

Shelving possibilities

Depending on your living situation and plant collection, your indoor garden setting can be large or small, portable or built-in. Build a framework custom fit to your situation or buy a commercial plant stand. Shelves of all types make good supports for plants as do tall, slim étagères.

Don't despair if strong, natural light is limited in your home or if you've run out of plant places close to windows. With grow-lights easy to install on many types of shelving, you can garden in almost any room. When placing plants on shelves, use saucers, trays, or some other type of moistureproofing to keep water off the shelving, floor, and other plants.

Custom shelving

A floor-to-ceiling place for plants turns one wall of a room into a vertical garden. This type of

plant shelf can be constructed of pine lumber, using 2×4 uprights and 1×10 shelves to form a ceiling-high set of shelves in front of a window plus tiered risers in front of the shelves. The shelving can be designed to come apart easily for moving or rearranging.

If you don't have the tools, time, or inclination to construct shelving, look around—you might be surprised to find all sorts of ready-made options. Or customize a new or used shelf, changing out wooden shelves with glass ones to maximize available light, or adding casters to make the structure portable for scooting it across a floor or sliding it into summer storage.

Make it safe

Ensure the strength and stability of a plant stand or shelf by starting with a well-made, secure structure. Keep in mind that pots filled with plants and wet soil become quite heavy. Avoid overloading a shelf, and place the heaviest pots at the bottom of a vertical structure, not at the top. If you have small children who might try to scale a shelving unit or plant stand, remove any casters. A base made broader than the bottom of the shelf can add support and help keep plants away from the reach of young children and pets, so plan accordingly.

Opposite: **A bookshelf transformed into a customized plant stand features casters, a broad base, and colorful paint. Glass shelves and rimmed wood shelves combine for a multipurpose structure.**

Indoor garden central **Create a place that will accommodate a small collection of plants and still have room to start seeds and store a few tools. Here are a few ideas to help you get started.**

SEED-STARTING STATION
An inexpensive steel-wire shelving unit becomes a seedling haven with the addition of a fluorescent shop light. Chains and S hooks hold the light in place.

WALL UNIT
Securely mounting a plant shelf on a wall requires anchoring it into studs using long screws. The decorative face board at the top of the shelf conceals a plant light.

A-FRAME STAND
A multitiered, A-frame or ladder-style plant stand can be built or bought. Start with a used ladder or a small amount of lumber and a simple plan for this economical option.

making more plants

Various propagation techniques enable you to get the most out of your indoor plants by creating new ones.

p.**68**
CUTTING TECHNIQUES
Follow our step-by-step guide to this dependable means of multiplying favorite plants.

p.**70**
DIVIDING PLANTS
This tried-and-true technique transforms a single plant into many and results in other benefits too.

p.**72**
PLANTLETS & OFFSETS
These are among the most common and easiest ways to propagate some plants.

p.**74**
LAYERING TECHNIQUES
Learn two ways to accomplish layering and some of the plants that depend on it.

p.**76**
STARTING FROM SEEDS
Bringing to life a new generation of plants fulfills one of gardening's greatest promises.

Cutting techniques

Add to your plant collection without subtracting from your bank account by learning to take cuttings. Growing houseplants from cuttings is the most popular form of vegetative propagation because it is so easy and rewarding. An array of plants, from annuals to perennials and shrubs, will grow well from cuttings and be ready to transplant within a month or two. Just be sure not to take cuttings of trademarked or patent-protected plants that say "propagation prohibited by law" on the tag.

Cutting methods

The most common propagation methods include taking cuttings of young, green (softwood) stems from late spring until midsummer when plants are growing strong; or partially mature, current-season (semiripe) stems from June through August. Depending on the plant, you can take cuttings from stems as well as leaves or roots.

Cuttings will root in various media: soilless potting mix, vermiculite, commercial rooting gel, or water. Although it doesn't work for every plant,

Cuttings of plants that root well in water include tradescantia, scented geranium, coleus, begonia, and ivy.

rooting begonia, Swedish ivy, and purple passion plant in water is super easy. Just cut a 3- to 4-inch-long stem tip, snip off the lowest leaves, and tuck the cutting in a jar of water set in bright, indirect light. Change the water weekly to keep it fresh and to minimize growth of bacteria. When roots develop, transplant the cuttings into a container filled with potting mix. The roots that form in water are coarser and more fragile than roots formed in soil, so keep the potting mix evenly damp for the first couple of weeks to help the plant adjust and develop terrestrial roots.

Leaf cuttings

Take leaf cuttings of plants with thick leaves or leaf stems, such as African violet, begonia, peperomia, and succulents of all kinds. Remove the leaf as close to the parent plant as possible. Dip the cut end in powdered rooting hormone and tuck it into damp rooting medium, following the directions for stem cuttings. After a few weeks, roots will start to form; within a few months, a new shoot with leaves will emerge.

Root cuttings

To make a new plant from a root cutting, cut a 2-inch-long section of thick root and place it horizontally in rooting medium. When a new plant develops, transplant it as you would other cuttings that have rooted. Plants suitable for root cuttings include ti plant and arrowhead plant.

TEST GARDEN TIP
Rooting mix

Make a propagating medium that works well for cuttings of leaves (above), stems, or roots: Mix equal parts sterilized coarse sand, perlite, peat moss, and vermiculite.

How to make stem cuttings
Prepare nursery containers by filling small pots or cell packs with premoistened soilless potting medium. Many potting soils hold too much moisture.

1 CUT
Use a clean, sharp knife to cut a 3- to 4-inch-long nonflowering stem. Cut off the bottom leaves.

2 DIP
To encourage root growth, dip the cut end into rooting hormone powder.

3 PLANT
Poke a planting hole in the damp medium, using a chopstick or pencil. Insert the cutting.

4 HUMIDIFY
Place the pot in a plastic bag held shut with a twist tie, creating a humid, greenhouselike environment.

5 TRANSPLANT
Set cuttings in bright, indirect light. Water as needed to keep the medium damp. When roots develop, transplant into a larger pot.

Dividing plants

When dividing a plant into new clumps, you can sometimes tease apart the roots by hand and at other times cut them with a sharp knife or pruning saw.

The immediate result of division is two or more plants

of respectable size. When dividing a plant, you're pulling apart clumps that have multiple stems arising from the soil surface and separating underground roots for each clump. Then you pot each new section or plant division in its own pot.

Candidates for division

Division is an excellent way to rejuvenate a plant that has outgrown its pot and its setting—the plant appears top-heavy or roots have filled the pot. This is an ideal opportunity for sharing one of your favorite plants with a gardening friend, rather than repotting the plant into a larger pot. Spring is the ideal time to divide plants, when they are on the verge of the growing season.

Plants commonly propagated by division include Chinese evergreen, pothos, snake plant, (how-to shown *below*), Boston fern, asparagus fern, peperomia, and cast-iron plant.

Dividing tubers and rhizomes

Caladium and tuberous begonia are among the plants that produce plump underground growths called tubers. As long as roots and growing points are present on the tubers, they can be separated and established as new plants. Alocasia and zeezee plant are among the plants that grow from tuberous rhizomes, underground stems of sorts that produce shoots above and roots below.

Divide tubers and rhizomes in fall, when the plant is not flowering and is starting a period of rest or slower growth. To divide a rhizome, cut it into pieces, making sure that each piece has a growing point. Then plant each piece individually. Over time, tubers often develop two or more distinct growing points. At planting time, just before potting them, you can cut carefully between two growing points to yield two separate tubers.

TEST GARDEN TIP
Divide a tuber

Carefully cut between two growing points. Set the sections aside to let them dry and heal for a week, then plant each section.

How to divide a plant

Division enables you to easily propagate one plant into two or more. The process consists merely of separating the plant into sections, then potting each of those pieces individually.

1 DIVIDE
Remove the plant from its pot. Separate the leaves into clumps and pull or cut apart the root ball into corresponding clumps. You may need to use a pruning saw or large serrated knife to saw some plants apart, but others break apart by hand.

2 SECTION
Make sure each division includes some of the main root and stem system. Position the division in the center of the container, giving its roots room to expand.

3 REFRESH
Set up a new pot with fresh potting mix for each division. Plant each clump in its new pot, with the base of the plant at the same level as the original planting.

4 WATER
Add potting mix around and covering the roots. Water the new planting, thoroughly moistening the potting mix and settling the new planting into it. Add more mix as needed.

Plantlets & offsets

Spider plant, also called airplane plant, reproduces itself by sending out miniature plants on runners or long stems.

Two common methods of propagating plants are especially easy because the parent plant does most of the work for you by producing plantlets or offsets. In both cases, the parent plant forms miniature replicas of itself.

What are plantlets?

A plantlet develops at the end of a long stem or runner—a lifeline—or on a mature leaf. A plantlet develops roots while it is still tethered to the parent plant. The long, flexible stems of spider plant and strawberry begonia that connect the older and younger plants can be bent enough for the plantlet to be nestled into soil in the pot of the parent plant or in its own small pot. Within a few weeks, the young plant has enough strong roots to survive on its own. Cut the tether and the baby becomes a fully independent plant. Species that produce plantlets on their leaves include piggyback plant and a few kalanchoes. The plantlets of piggyback plant can be snuggled into damp soil and secured with a hairpin or U-shape wire. The plantlet will soon root and become a full-fledged plant.

The plantlets of some houseplants, such as spider plant and tradescantia, start to develop roots before they contact soil. Encouraged to root more in damp soil or water, the plantlets quickly comply and can soon be separated from the parent plant.

What are offsets?

Offsets form at the base of a parent plant and remain attached to it. When an offset is big enough to survive on its own and—ideally—has its own roots, it may be separated from the parent plant and planted in its own pot. Common plants that propagate themselves with offsets include many bromeliads, cacti, and succulents.

Piggyback plant (Tolmeia menziesii) makes new plantlets at the base of its leaves. These plantlets root easily when placed in soilless potting mix.

How to perpetuate plantlets and offsets
Growing new plants is easy when you imitate nature and follow the plants' lead. These smaller replicas of the parent plant—plantlets and offsets—root easily.

PLANTLETS
Strawberry begonia produces plenty of identical offspring, or plantlets, ready for rooting in a nearby pot. Secure a plantlet in damp potting mix, using a hairpin or bent wire. When the plant roots, sever the connection to the parent plant.

OFFSETS
Peanut cactus (Echinopsis chamaecereus) forms offsets at the base of the parent plant. Snap off or cut away each offset, with or without roots. Snuggle it into damp potting mix, keeping it damp until roots form. It should grow on easily.

Layering techniques

This ti plant presents multiple opportunities for using the air-layering technique to propagate several lush new plants from a gangly mature one.

In many cases where cuttings will not work, layering can be used to make new plants. It is also a good way to rejuvenate a plant that has become overly leggy or lost its lower leaves and become too top-heavy. The technique of layering is similar to rooting cuttings, except that the part of the plant (usually a branch or stem) to be rooted remains attached to the parent plant while rooting is in progress.

The advantage of layering is that the parent plant supplies the new plant with water and nutrients while its roots form. Daily maintenance is unnecessary. For slow-to-root plants this is a distinct advantage. At the same time, there is a disadvantage: New plants formed by layering develop roots more slowly than from cuttings. The process takes a few weeks to several months before the new plant is ready for separation from the parent plant and potting in its own container.

Propagation techniques

There are two ways to accomplish layering: in soil and in air. Creeping and trailing plants, such as pothos and philodendron, are ideal subjects for layering in soil. Air layering proves most suitable for plants with woody or thick stems, such as diffenbachia, croton, dracaena, rubber tree (*Ficus elastica*), fiddleleaf fig (*Ficus lyrata*), and ti plant.

Soil layering

A suitable plant for soil layering has one or more stems low enough to enable you to bend it down and ensure that it touches soil. Some plants self-layer, developing roots where their stems touch soil. In this case, you can snip off a newly rooted plant and transplant it into a new pot. Otherwise, facilitate layering by setting a pot full of damp potting mix next to the parent plant, anchoring a trailing stem in the soil mix but leaving the growing tip free. You can layer more than one stem from the parent plant in this pot, as long as each stem contacts the soil mix. When the layered stems have rooted, cut them free from the parent plant.

TEST GARDEN TIP
Protect your hands

When handling sphagnum moss, wear waterproof gloves to avoid potential skin irritation. Soak the moss in warm water for an hour before using it for air layering.

How to air-layer a new plant
A ti plant is one of the houseplants that benefits from air layering. As the plant matures, it develops tall stems with no lower leaves. The new plant will be shorter and lusher in appearance.

1 NOTCH
Holding the stem securely, make a slanting cut upward, no more than halfway into the stem. Cut again to remove a sliver of the stem. Continue holding the upper stem so it won't fall over and snap off.

2 WRAP
Wrap a handful of premoistened sphagnum moss around the layering site. Encase the moss with plastic wrap. Secure the top and bottom edges of the wrap with electrical tape or twist ties.

3 ROOT
Allow roots to fully develop and begin filling the encasement—this often takes several months. Open the top of the wrap weekly to add water to the sphagnum moss, keeping it moist.

4 DETACH
After the roots are well-developed, remove the tape and plastic. Cut the stem below the roots. Transplant the new plant into a pot of fresh potting mix. Water thoroughly.

Starting from seeds

Most houseplants are propagated from cuttings or divisions, but some can be grown from seed or spores. For example, you can decide what color and variety of geranium or flowering maple you want to grow. Seed starting provides the most economical route to raising a wide variety of annuals and edibles. Ferns and bromeliads have many more family members than the market offers widely, but with patience, you can grow the rare ones from seeds or spores.

Growing plants from seeds

Seed starting is a wonderful late-winter and early-spring activity for indoor gardeners. Before the outdoor gardening season gets into full swing, you can coax seeds into seedlings within weeks. Gather up a large bag of soilless seed-starting mix, plastic flats with inserts (or any kind of clear plastic container), plant labels, and a waterproof marker. Your winter greenhouse

Make as many free seed-starting pots as you can use, rolling 4-inch-wide strips of newsprint around a 2-inch-diameter glass. Fold under the bottom edges to shape a biodegradable pot.

can be as simple as an arrangement of shelves with a fluorescent shop light hung from each or a roomy table with a shop light propped up above a flat or two.

Most seeds are sold in seed packets that include detailed information about sowing them and raising the plants, from how deep to plant the seeds to how many weeks the seedlings need to grow before they're ready for transplanting.

Raising seedlings

Seeds have varying requirements for germination (sprouting). Some seeds need warmth; others need a chilling period in order to germinate. Some seeds require light and should not be covered with seed-starting mix. Others need to be covered. Push them into the soilless medium with a pencil eraser. See how to start plants from seeds, *below*.

When seedlings emerge, remove the cover from the germination container, and set the tray under a fluorescent shop light equipped with one cool- and one warm-spectrum fluorescent bulb. Keep the soilless mix damp by watering from the bottom of the container. By the time seedlings are big enough for transplanting—with at least two sets of leaves and roots that have begun to fill their cell pack—they're also ready for a dose of half-strength fertilizer.

How to start plants from seeds To sprout seeds, you need only a few supplies. Then become acquainted with seeds' basic needs and forge ahead.

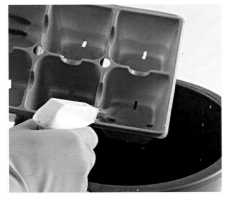

1 CLEAN
Start with clean seed-starting containers that allow excess moisture to drain away.

2 MOISTEN
Moisten soilless seed-starting mix with warm water and fill the cell pack or other container with this mix.

3 SOW
Sow one or two large seeds per cell; sprinkle three or more smaller seeds into a cell.

4 COVER
Follow seed packet instructions regarding how deep to sow the seeds, and cover them accordingly.

5 WATER
Sprinkle the plantings with water and cover the container with clear plastic to hold in moisture.

6 WARM
Warming the soilless medium using an electric heating mat can speed seed germination.

creative planting projects

Gather ideas, inspiration, and tips
to fashion all sorts of indoor gardens
any time of the year.

**p.80
WINDOWSILL &
TABLETOP GARDENS**
Use these stylish garden
ideas to bring colorful,
interesting plants to prime
surfaces around your
house where you will
enjoy them most.

**p.92
SEASONAL
CENTERPIECES**
Add pleasing color and
interest to a tabletop from
season to season.

**p.96
SHAPING PLANTS**
Learn how to trim, twine,
sculpt, and take advantage
of some plants' innate
acrobatic talents.

**p.104
BLOOMS OUT OF
SEASON**
Start with bulbs or branches
to create flowering visions of
spring indoors.

Windowsill gardens

A few cheery plants on a sunny windowsill

bring life to any home and add a touch of warmth on drab days, especially in areas where winters are cold. If you have only one sunny window in your home, there are plenty of ways to garden there, whether you arrange small pots on rows of shelves across the window or extend the sill by bumping a tabletop up to it. Use a window to frame your plant display, making it more artful. And use plants as living curtains, obscuring the view into your home.

Light requirements

Providing plants with enough light indoors is crucial to their success. How much light is enough? That depends on each plant and the conditions in your home. You can find plants to suit almost any indoor environment. Most plants will do fine with slightly more or less light than is optimal, especially for a limited time.

Widely varying levels of light are needed for plants to grow, and the levels of light in any home's windows vary too. One type of plant may

Succulent kalanchoe blooms for weeks on a sunny windowsill. Removable glass shelves span the window and let plenty of bright light reach the plants.

simply survive while another fares well with low light. In some cases, the plant may grow well, but won't bloom in the low-light conditions. Flowering plants typically need high light in a south- or west-facing window. If there is enough sunlight in a room to read or do handiwork without turning on a light, it will be a suitable place for plants—such as a range of houseplants that need low to medium light. Given enough bright light, traditional outdoor plants, such as culinary herbs or salad greens, can grow indoors.

Increasing light levels

Most indoor settings are actually darker than they seem to the human eye. If it is difficult to read a newspaper in your home at midday, supplemental light is needed. Similarly, unless plants needing bright light are situated directly in front of windows, the plants will need added light. Plants show signs of inadequate light: They fail to grow well, have lighter green or smaller leaves than normal, or become spindly and stretch toward a window or other light source.

Some strategies for increasing the light plants receive include keeping windows clean, removing screens when they're not needed, hanging mirrors strategically to reflect light, painting walls flat white or light colors to reflect light, periodically washing or wiping foliage, and replacing small windows with larger ones.

TEST
GARDEN
TIP
Can-do shelving

Choose from an array of stylish-yet-sturdy shelf brackets made to hold glass shelves. Easily mount each bracket on a window frame using a couple of screws. Get cut-to-fit shelves in a desired width and thickness from a glass, mirror, or windshield supplier. Save money by comparing prices before ordering.

Left: **The direct, bright light of a south-facing window sustains a collection of cacti and succulents. The individually potted plants live contentedly in a drywaller's pan. Gravel hides the pots.**

Below: **A metal shelf mounted on a window frame keeps herbs within easy reach for cooking. Herbs and other edibles do best in the sunniest south- or east-facing windows.**

Dish gardens

A dish garden presents an opportunity to grow a group of plants

in a single container on a tabletop or a windowsill. The requirements are few: A shallow container and a grouping of shallow-rooted plants, such as cacti, succulents, or small houseplants, comprise a dish garden. A small, low-growing design for a tabletop proves engaging and won't interfere with across-the-table conversations. A large dish garden can be quite dramatic and colorful.

Making a dish garden

As you decide on a container for your dish garden, consider the conventional—a deep terra-cotta saucer or a shallow ceramic bowl—or be more creative. Transform a cup and saucer, vintage roasting pan, or hubcap into a dish garden. If the container has a drainage hole, your dish garden will need less maintenance. A container without built-in drainage must be watered very carefully to avoid waterlogging plant roots, unless the dish garden is made with water-loving plants, such as dwarf papyrus (Cyperus) and fiber optic grass (Isolepis).

Prepare the container for planting by covering the bottom of it with a thin layer of horticultural charcoal. The charcoal helps prevent the soil from turning funky when it holds too much moisture and not enough air. Add a 2-inch layer or more of potting mix.

Group plants with similar soil, moisture, and light needs. A classic dish garden featuring succulents in well-draining soil by a warm sunny window can go a couple of weeks without watering—it's one of the lowest-maintenance indoor container gardens. A leafy plant grouping benefits from the higher-humidity microclimate that results from their proximity. Massing several of the same begonia or similar plants with showy foliage intensifies their effect too. Choosing slow-growing plants helps prevent overcrowding.

Planting arrangements

Before you plant a dish garden, keep plants in their pots and play around with planting schemes. Try the tallest plant in the center of the arrangement with the shortest plants at the container's perimeter. Or try an asymmetrical grouping, with the tallest plant off-center and a cluster of smaller plants balancing the display. Leave growing room between the plants. If they are not overcrowded, it will be easier to remove an ailing plant without disrupting the roots of other plants. Trimming plants periodically can also help prevent overcrowding.

Some dish gardens benefit from the addition of an accent or focal point. Naturally fitting objects include driftwood, stones, or seashells pocketed on vacation. A decorative figurine may be the best way to give a dish garden your signature touch. Covering the soil surface with gravel can be a nice finishing detail.

Above left: **A deep terra-cotta saucer provides a good home for succulent kalanchoe as long as it also contains ample pea gravel and sand for drainage.**

Above middle: **Colored gravel or tumbled glass adds contrast to a group of succulents and cacti in a contemporary dish garden.**

Above right: **A variety of small succulents contribute to an interesting dish garden that works as a centerpiece and a topic of conversation.**

Opposite: **This hot combo of houseplants includes 'Red Hot' flamingo flower, a rex begonia with silver streaks, and purple passion plant in a cool blue bowl.**

Little landscapes

A miniature garden, typically contained within

a box, tray, or dish, takes you into another realm of gardening. Making a teeny-tiny plantscape complete with wee furnishings, itty-bitty plants, and plenty of hide-and-seek mystique inspires a playful sort of garden design. The closer you approach to view it, the more beautiful and complex the garden appears. What's more, this could be a small-scale version of your dream garden.

Tiny gardens with big appeal

Your little landscape may be even more charming than a full-size counterpart. Imagine a garden that requires few materials, novice planting skills, and little upkeep. Once planted, a miniature garden can be long-lived, moving outdoors to a partly shaded spot over summer and back indoors to a sunny windowsill during winter.

Miniature gardening proves so engaging and entertaining that it has become a popular hobby for both adults and children. Creating a garden fit for a fairy is an ideal opportunity to get kids to dig into gardening and stretch their imaginations. By calling it a fairy garden, you can play up its whimsical nature and escape to a place where mythical fairies dwell. But you

Miniature tuteurs, tiny bricks, and pea gravel create the basis for this small-scale formal garden. Asparagus "trees" frame a pergola seating area that overlooks hens-and-chicks *(Sempervivum)* and air plant *(Tillandsia).*

don't have to believe in pixies to be enchanted by these little gardens.

Making a mini garden

A well-crafted miniature garden begins with a plan. Establish a theme, such as a pint-size patio or formal knot garden. As you proceed, keep everything to scale for best results.

Design your little landscape to live indoors and outdoors, if you like. It's a good project for a rainy day indoors that can bring a lot of pleasure for months to come. During the gardening season, move the container outdoors and give it a special hideaway where it will provide the most surprise and delight for anyone who discovers it.

Container: Be creative or settle on a rough-and-ready holder that will weather indoor-outdoor life. It should give roots room to grow and allow proper drainage to prevent soggy roots. Set the container on a tray to protect the surface where you display it.

Plants: Choose dwarf (slow-growing) varieties that have similar needs for light and water. Plants of diminutive size with small flowers and leaves work best. Dwarf conifers and herbs that thrive in sun with once-a-week watering minimize maintenance. Faster-growing plants require frequent trimming and eventual replacement. Tiny standards or tree-form plants, such as myrtle (*Myrtus*) or euonymus topiaries, make trees that are in scale in a miniature setting. Young herbs, such as rosemary or thyme, serve as itty-bitty shrubs that can be trimmed easily into neat forms.

Accessories: Collect objects related to your garden's theme, from tiny furniture to fences, pots, and tools. You'll start to notice potential of objects around your house and yard: a marble becomes a gazing ball; a birdhouse provides a garden shed. These are the details that will make your miniature garden more fascinating.

TEST GARDEN TIP
Easier planting

Using a wooden skewer or comparable tool works better than fingers to plant tiny root balls and position other elements in the confines of a teeny garden.

Tiny tabletop gardens
It's so easy and fun to create a miniature garden, chances are you'll make more than one. Start with a container and a theme, add a focal point, then tuck in plants, and finish with details.

VINTAGE CONTAINER
A metal picnic box adds to the whimsical quality of a fairy garden. Working with a container that lacks drainage means you'll need to provide a way for excess water to drain away from the plants' roots. Cover the container's bottom with a 1-inch layer of gravel before adding potting mix or, better yet, drill drainage holes in the bottom of the container first.

SCALED DOWN
Using a glass tray or similar container for a mini garden helps keep a simplified scheme. This tidy, formal design includes only one plant, Scotch moss (*Sagina subulata*). Pea gravel forms pathways, and preserved moss creates beds of green. Different colors of moss and gravel can be useful in any mini garden.

JUNK DRAWER
This pint-size plot demonstrates the thrifty side of miniature gardening. Starting with a repurposed drawer, the design uses bits of broken terra-cotta pots to shape a patio. Garden suppliers offer an array of tiny accessories, such as wire chairs and picket fencing. To find more details about planting a wooden container, see pages 86–87.

IN THE ROUND
Make a miniature knot garden in a standard pot and achieve a design that can be viewed from any angle. Based on historical garden designs with patterned plantings, the hedges of this display are made with grass and moss. The dwarf conifer and urn can be replaced with a little sundial or figurine if desired.

Wooden planters

A wooden planter with a footed bottom and miniature wire fencing provides a rustic touch to this living room.

Containers made of wood, from stylish boxes to sturdy crates,

often provide a desirable home for an indoor garden. Wooden containers may be just right for your plans for various reasons: They're easy to find and usually economical. Wooden containers typically have simple lines and suit a range of decorating styles, from raw and rustic to sleek and modern. Part of the beauty of wood is that you can change its appearance to suit your home's style by adding a coat of paint, stain, or another finish.

Protect your investment

When choosing a wooden container for a garden, consider its potential for disintegrating when exposed to wet soil. Some woods, such as cedar and teak, withstand challenging conditions better than others. What's more, you'll want a container that's weather-resistant if you plan to expose it to outdoor life. To help preserve the integrity of a wooden container, apply several coats of exterior waterproofing sealant to its interior. Seal the exterior too, or protect it with two coats of exterior-grade paint or stain.

Ready for planting

Start with an inexpensive wooden container from a crafts store for the project shown and transform it with paint. Combine a graceful weeping pussy willow (*Salix*) with a selection of small spring-flowering bulbs and velvety moss for a delightful tabletop garden that lasts for weeks. After the little tree finishes blooming, it can be transplanted into the garden where it can grow on and rebloom for years to come, reaching a height of 6 to 7 feet with a spread of 5 to 6 feet in full sun. You can transplant the forced bulbs and hope they'll rebloom next year or add them to the compost pile. Either way, the container is reusable if it is well-protected before planting.

TEST GARDEN TIP

Adaptable wood

The wooden container shown in the tabletop garden project is deep enough (7 inches) to hold the little willow tree and can be painted any color. It's easy to drill a drainage hole in a wooden container.

Make an easy tabletop garden as a cure for cabin fever.

Use this miniature landscape as a centerpiece that brings hints of spring indoors with fragrant flowers and a little greenery. Setting it in a spot away from bright light and heat will help it last longer.

1 PROTECT
Line the bottom of a wooden container with a sheet of plastic or set the planter on a tray to protect the tabletop from potential moisture damage.

2 LINE
Cut cotton batting (available at a fabric store) and press it into place. This liner holds moisture as well as the soil, so water sparingly when the soil feels dry.

3 PLANT
Add potting mix to the container and then position the willow. Add more mix to about 2 inches below the rim of the container then snuggle other plants into place.

4 FINISH
Make a pleasing arrangement of plants and fill in between them with potting mix and bits of preserved moss.

Basket gardens

This grouping of prayer plant, arrowhead plant, dracaena, cyclamen, palm, and pothos combines foliage and flowering plants in a way comparable to a floral arrangement.

Any plant lover can make room indoors for a basket of blooms or greens any time of the year. As a temporary home for plants, a basket works beautifully. Baskets blend well with all kinds of decorating styles. Better yet, they're drainable, lightweight, and portable. They can even be hung to highlight a vining or trailing plant. For your planting needs, you can easily find a range of basket options, whether small or tall, round or shapely, spacious or compact, rustic or refined.

Baskets abound

You may already have a collection of baskets in your basement or garage—ready for planting. If not, some of the most economical options can be found at yard sales and thrift stores. Once you decide where you'd like to display a basket garden, choose an appropriate container for the setting. Place a large basket on the floor as an accent to an entryway, but keep the plants away from cold drafts. Place smaller baskets on tabletops, counters, or windowsills where they'll add interest.

Wicker baskets contrast naturally with their contents, whether green or flowering plants. Of course, not all baskets are woven with willow, jute, reed, wood, or other natural materials. You might find a basket made of metal, plastic, or concrete. Each material has its charms. It just depends on what appeals to you and suits your home. It's easy to change a basket's character or update it with a coat of paint or stain.

Waterproofing a basket

Most baskets do not provide a watertight container for plants. Protect the basket and extend its utility by using it as a decorative cachepot, lining it with sheet plastic or a saucer before planting. Most baskets deteriorate over time when exposed to moisture. Minimize water damage by brushing the basket with several coats of exterior-type polyurethane, allowing the sealer to dry completely each time before adding the next coat.

Planting a basket

Create a tabletop garden in minutes, combining common houseplants, annual flowers, or seasonal bloomers. Keep to a simple color scheme, group green plants with very different textures, or change out seasonal plants. Be bold and daring. Because basket gardens are temporary, you can easily change out various elements of the combination to come up with a different look.

Combine plants with similar light requirements. When using a basket as a cachepot for a combination of potted plants, your plant selection may include ones with differing water needs. If you plant directly in a basket, first line it with sheet plastic, landscape fabric, sheet moss, or cotton batting to hold the soil, and then water only enough to moisten the soil.

Design a basket garden by gathering potted plants and trying different groupings until you have a pleasing arrangement. Group odd numbers—three, five, or seven plants—for an effective display that can be viewed from all angles. When you're happy with the design, either leave the plants in their pots or remove the pots and sprinkle potting mix in between the root balls. Variety and lushness are important, but leave growing room between the plants. For the easiest garden of all, fit a single plant such as a lush fern into a basket.

TEST GARDEN TIP

Instant garden

Small baskets hold nursery pots of Siberian squill (*Scilla siberica* 'Alba'), daffodils, and small fritillaria in a spring tabletop garden that blooms for weeks. Sprinkle grass seed onto the soil between the potted bulbs to sprout a fresh green fringe within days.

Bloomin' basket **Fill a sturdy wire basket with enough fragrantly blooming plants to give visitors a colorful welcome that will leave a lasting impression. Set the basket on a saucer or tray to protect the surface beneath it or hang it at eye level for all to enjoy.**

1 LINE
Use preserved sheet moss from a crafts store to line your basket and hold soil. Cover the interior—bottom and sides—of the basket, overlapping the pieces of moss.

2 PLANT
Remove plants from their nursery pots and position them in the basket. This display features colorful primroses and aromatic hyacinths. Fill in between plants with potting mix.

3 ENJOY
Park your spring-in-a-basket display next to a doorway where it can be appreciated most. Water the plants lightly to sustain them during their flowery show.

Creative containers

One way to add to the fun of gardening indoors comes with finding and using unusual containers. The best containers are functional: They provide space for roots to develop and plants to grow and flourish. A drainage hole or other means of releasing excess water is crucial to potted plants' survival. Containers can be small enough to hold only one plant apiece, or large enough to accommodate a junglelike display of foliage and flowers.

Finding special containers

Indoor gardens benefit from a vast selection of potential containers and exotic plants to put in them. Even traditional houseplants such as scheffleras appear more exotic when planted in effective containers. Any container garden makes a style statement, so use your planting schemes to express the colors, shapes, and textures that fit your home. As you match plants with planters, also consider how they will look in their setting. Colorful containers bring energy to green plantings, for instance; earth-tone planters meld with most settings. When choosing unusual containers for indoor gardens—whether long-term plantings or temporary projects—be wary of amassing too many eclectic plant holders, which can result in a hodgepodge. Simple planters let plants dominate. But improvisation encourages experimentation.

The strong stem cuttings of a dracaena known as lucky bamboo resemble a tropical grove rising from a sea of black polished stones in a copper wok. The stem cuttings will develop more leaves and a lush, tropical appearance.

Treasure hunting

As seasons come and go, gardening interests and decorating styles go with them. The lacquered pots chosen for last winter's holiday plants may have lost your favor after a year or two in storage. New plants and different planting ideas call for fresh containers. You'll find potential planters in many places, aside from the usual garden centers and nurseries. Whether you're on the hunt for a vintage birdcage or you need a home for the new geranium varieties you acquired at a plant sale, look for container possibilities at thrift stores, rummage sales, auctions, and flea markets. Sometimes the funkiest junk—a rusty bedspring or bait bucket—makes the coolest planter.

Special containers

In addition to traditional pots and planters, you'll find other ways to house plants that are less obvious but widely available. Self-watering pots, wall pots, and strawberry jars are some of the special containers that work well for plants. Sometimes the buckets, baskets, and planting pockets sold for outdoor gardening are easily adapted to indoor use and they'll usually last longer too.

A strawberry jar demonstrates the adaptability of a classic garden container. A glazed or unglazed strawberry jar has plantable pockets that enable you to grow multiple plants in a single pot. Planted indoors, lily-of-the-valley rootstock (rhizomes called pips) can be brought into sweetly fragrant bloom weeks ahead of the gardening season.

TEST GARDEN TIP

Pick a pocket

When planting a strawberry jar, fill it creatively with a medley of herbs, sedum, ivy, or scented geraniums. Start with younger plants from packs or flats. They'll fit into the pockets easily, have more room for rooting, and result in healthier plants.

Use a strawberry jar creatively. Plant mail-order prechilled lily-of-the-valley pips (rootstocks) indoors and savor their prespring show of perfumed blooms in three to four weeks.

1 PREPARE
Soak the pips in warm water for two hours before planting. Meanwhile prepare the jar by adding a layer of sand and then adding potting mix up to the first pocket.

2 PLANT
Carefully plant several pips in each pocket, aiming the pointed shoots up. Cover the pips' roots in each pocket with sphagnum moss. Cover the moss with potting mix.

3 DRAIN
Stand a section of drainage material in the center of the pot. Add potting mix to the pot's top opening or next level of pockets.

4 FINISH
Plant any remaining pockets and the top opening of the pot. Cover the roots with sphagnum moss and potting mix. Water slowly and thoroughly.

5 MAINTAIN
Set the pot in a cool (60°F) location with indirect light from a north or east window. Water only to keep the potting mix damp.

Seasonal centerpieces

Many gardeners take pleasure and find inspiration in anticipating the seasons and planting as a celebration of each dynamic and distinctive time of year. In many households and families, seasonal celebrations are a way of life. A dining table offers a platform for a regularly changing display of plants and accents as evocative decorations, whether festive or casual.

Follow nature's lead

Instead of adhering to rules, find inspiration in the world around you, and then arrange elements that appeal to you. When your orchid blooms, start with that as a centerpiece. If you're planning a party, let the small potted plants from your tablescape become take-home gifts.

If you prefer to create seasonal displays somewhere other than the middle of your dining table, consider a mantel, entryway table, or shelf instead. Let ordinary cut flowers and evergreen boughs give way to potted spring-flowering plants and dwarf evergreen trees in a series of colors, textures, and scents.

Make it tidy

Keep the display fresh and clean. A view of exposed soil is tolerable, albeit not so appetizing, but crumbs of soil won't be welcome in or near food. Tabletop arrangements should allow room for serving pieces and other dishes for meals as well as unobstructed eye contact.

Inspired by nature's rhythms, a tabletop garden that changes with the seasons creates interest as well as a tradition laced with happy memories.

JANUARY: Starting over Indoor bulbs and fresh blooms chase away winter's dreariness, bringing cheer to short, dark days. Welcome the new year with ethereal paperwhite narcissus, bright pansies, and young dwarf myrtle (*Myrtus communis*). Candlelight adds a warm glow.

FEBRUARY: Romantic expressions Fill the indoors with the anticipation and excitement of the sweet-scented season. Mini roses and white cyclamens make lovely valentines; fresh-cut pussy willows warm hearts and encourage hopes for spring—and maybe a little romance.

MARCH: Spring returns Pots of posies, including primroses and crocuses, herald the arrival of the annual gardening season. Count on a local garden center, nursery, or florist to have a seasonal selection of small, economical potted plants that are perfect for tablescapes.

JUNE: Casual gatherings Long days, strong light, and heat send gardeners into the cool shade. Find inspiration from under leafy green trees where you can sit back, enjoy the plants, and just breathe. Take time to relax and sip icy tea among verdant ferns and other green plants.

AUGUST: Summer's end Make a place where you will unwind and eat fresh fruit at the end of a high-energy day. As summer gives way to fall, embrace simplicity during the season of plenty with a simple still life. Select a few garden treasures for their sculptural qualities.

DECEMBER: Winter warmth The indoor garden keeps gardeners happy and welcomes visitors with all the warmth and spirit of a cheerful home. Gather tiny evergreeen trees, sparkling baubles, and plenty of candles to make merry.

Topiary towers

JULIUS SHULM...
MODERNISM
REDISCOVERED

A pair of double-ball
eugenia *(Syzygium)*
topiaries enhance the
setting with their
sculptural forms. Similar
ready-made topiaries are
widely available and may
be made with euonymous,
lavender, or rosemary.

Experiment with the ancient art of shaping plants

that elevates pruning to an art form. Topiary conjures a feeling of elegance and tradition, but requires little more attention than a typical houseplant. Indoors, a topiary provides a neat and portable focal point. Grouped topiaries of different plants, shapes, and sizes make a fascinating garden.

Plants for topiary

Start with a ready-made topiary and maintain its shape with periodic trimming, or sculpt a plant into a sphere, cone, spiral, animal shape, or other form. Either way, the easiest topiaries are those with simple geometric lines. Depending on your choice of plants, a preformed topiary frame can make shaping easy.

Moss-stuffed wire forms covered with small-leaf plants, such as ivy or creeping fig, are fun to make. The plants root into the moss and need to be kept damp and clipped regularly. Make two-dimensional topiaries by winding trailing or vining stems around a wire frame (see the ivy spiral topiary how-to project on page 165).

When selecting a plant for topiary, choose from herbs and evergreens with dense, compact foliage that respond well to pruning, including rosemary, lavender, santolina, scented geranium, myrtle, cypress, and boxwood. It can take a year or two to transform a healthy plant into a double-ball form.

Shaping topiary

To maintain a ready-made topiary, clip the tips of new growth, removing up to 2 inches to encourage branching. When training a new topiary, select a plant with a strong central leader or stem, and then decide what shape and ultimate size you want. Use floral scissors or pruners to trim plants. For a ball shape atop a main stem, start by pruning the lower branches to reveal the stem. The type of plant and the shape you want will determine how often you trim. Compact myrtle needs clipping every six to eight weeks; boxwood can be kept in shape with trimming three times a year.

Let topiaries rest in winter; lay off clipping and feeding for two or three months. Otherwise, fertilize a topiary monthly during the growing season. Take topiaries outdoors for the summer, and move them back indoors to a sunny windowsill for the winter.

TEST GARDEN TIP

Water carefully

Topiaries usually start out small—in equally small pots in which soil dries quickly. Keep an eye on the moisture level in small pots like these, especially in the dry heated air of a sunny room in winter. Give topiaries ample water when the soil surface begins to feel dry.

Rosemary topiary
Rosemary is an ideal plant for making into a standard or tree-form topiary. Its woody stem and needlelike leaves develop into a nifty little tree, and you can use the aromatic trimmings in cooking.

1 TRANSPLANT
Remove the plant from its nursery pot and give it fresh potting mix in a slightly larger pot of suitable scale.

2 STAKE
Cut a stake; push it into the soil next to the plant. Tie the stem loosely but securely to the stake using raffia or twine.

3 SNIP
Every few weeks during the growing season, snip stem ends to promote bushy side shoots.

Plants on support systems

Some plants need support to look their best. Make or buy pot-size trellises or tepees to hold up vining and climbing plants. Vines may twine or cling to a support on their own with little encouragement. Other climbing plants require training to get them started on a support and keep them growing. Use long bamboo poles, string, or monofilament to connect a windowsill planter to the top of a window frame and guide the stems to grow into a living curtain.

Creative staking

There are plenty of opportunities to use plant supports creatively rather than merely pushing a stake into soil and tying a plant to it. You might train a vine to an arching trellis or a topiary form, coax plants to climb into a

When needed by a plant for support, a trellis or stakes can hide among the foliage or add to the decorative nature of the display.

living wall, or sculpt plants using an imaginative trellis. Sometimes staking provides a temporary solution, upholding a tall, large, or sprawling plant while it overcomes lopsided growth; later the stake can be removed.

Staking: When and how

Start staking or training plants when they're young and pliable. Prune the plant to cover its support as it grows. Training a plant onto a form takes extra maintenance time. Be prepared to allow two years or more to develop an attractive topiary.

Choose a support that is at least as thick as the stem you want it to uphold. Thin stakes break and flimsy tepees crumple, especially as the plant becomes heavier with growth. Stakes and other supports made of bamboo, bentwood, or metal—especially green or brown—blend in among foliage. If you want the support to add visible structure, make it white or a contrasting color.

If a plant cannot entwine or cling to a support on its own, tie it to the stake or trellis using a soft material, such as jute, raffia, or fabric ribbon. Wire and twist ties can injure plant stems. Tie loosely, giving the plant room to move and grow. As a plant grows, check the ties occasionally; remove and retie them if need be.

Make a moss pole

Philodendron, Swiss cheese plant, and pothos are among the plants with aerial rootlets that prefer to grow on a damp medium such as a moss-filled post. Made by rolling a length of chicken wire into a 2- to 3-inch-diameter cylinder and filling it with sphagnum moss, the post can be anchored in a pot at planting time and become a permanent part of the plant/pot combination. Use hairpin-shape wires to train the plant stems to attach themselves to the pole. Water the moss well at planting time and keep it damp with weekly misting.

TEST GARDEN TIP

Supporting orchids

Use a clip and a stake to keep slender orchid stems upright and sturdy. Stake a bloom spike when buds form, using a support that's about the same height as the flowering stem.

Scented topiary ring

Scented geranium varieties with small leaves and a trailing habit, such as nutmeg and lavender, work well to make a lovely, fragrant topiary ring. Start with an 8-inch pot, two scented geraniums, and an 8- to 10-inch-diameter ring bent from heavy-duty wire or a clothes hanger.

1 PLANT
At planting time, set the plants at an angle to follow the ring—one right, the other left.

2 TIE
Use fine twine to tie the geraniums to the ring here and there. Add ties as the plants grow.

3 TUCK
Gently tuck in new growth or errant stems. Keep the plants in bright light.

Bonsai

An aralia branch—
barely covered with
soil—has sprouted
and formed what
appear to be
miniature trees. For
bonsai, choose plants
with naturally small
leaves, flowers,
fruits, and branches.

Combining art with gardening, bonsai also mixes in a bit of magic to transform trees and shrubs into diminutive potted treasures. Bonsai— pronounced *bone-sigh*—originated in China more than two thousand years ago, before being popularized in Japan. Although some bonsai specimens live for centuries and become heirlooms, it is possible to create a basic bonsai within a few years.

Beginning bonsai

Like many gardening endeavors, passion often propels an interest in bonsai to grow into a collector's hobby. The small plants are artistically trimmed and trained to appear ravaged by time, windswept, cascading, or draping a rock. Cultivating the miniaturized forms may seem intimidating at first. But some fundamentals will help you take up this garden art.

Plants: Choose a tree or shrub that suits your climate and lifestyle. Some plants need more maintenance than others. Cultivate trees such as evergreens, oaks, and elms outdoors. They need cold-winter dormancy to maintain their vigor, but must be protected from weather extremes. Some tropical and subtropical shrubs work well for bonsai and can be kept indoors year-round.

Start with an already formed bonsai, if you prefer, and practice annual root pruning in spring and regular branch tip pinching.

Pots: Bonsai live in shallow pots, usually at least three times as wide as the height. The container is part of a harmonious composition, and it suits the plant's size and style. The pot must have at least one drainage hole.

Culture: Depending on the plant and the climate where you live, some bonsai need intense light; others adapt to bright or moderate light. If a plant does not get enough light indoors or its location changes, it may drop its leaves.

An ideal potting mix for bonsai is porous, containing equal parts sifted bark and ground lava rock. Frequent watering—daily during hot weather—is necessary. Water when the soil feels slightly dry. Fertilize every other week throughout the growing season with diluted all-purpose plant food.

Repotting: Repot bonsai with fresh potting mix every two to four years, depending on the plant's needs.

Training and pruning: You can guide the plant to grow into a graceful form by shaping the branches using copper wire and pruning the roots, branches, and leaves. Shaping requires time and patience. You can create your bonsai with one of many different styles including formal upright, slanting, cascade, or forest (multiple plants).

TEST GARDEN TIP

Good candidates

Some houseplants are suitable for bonsai growing indoors. Fig does well if kept in very bright light. Other options include schefflera, Japanese serissa (*Serissa japonica*), and dwarf pomegranate.

Create a bonsai. **Potting a bonsai begins with preparing a young tree or shrub for its new home. Keep an indoor planting away from heat vents, fireplaces, and drafty windows and doors.**

1 POT Prepare the shallow pot for planting. Anchoring wires will help hold the plant in the pot.

2 COMB To promote root growth, use a metal hook to comb out roots and loose soil.

3 CUT Prune away excess roots, making the root ball compact enough to fit the shallow container.

4 WIRE Keep the top-heavy tree from tipping out of the pot by wiring it in place.

Hanging planters

TEST GARDEN TIP

Watering hanging plants

Exposed to warmer, drier air nearer the ceiling, hanging planters may need more frequent watering than floor-level plants. Find a watering system that allows you to leave the plant in place instead of hauling it to a sink. Consider ease of watering when you set the height of the hanging container.

Take your indoor garden to the next level, literally,

by raising plantings to eye height or higher. The plants will be easier to see and appreciate when separated from the cluster on a tabletop. Hanging planters take advantage of vertical space that is usually overlooked, suspended from a window frame, ceiling, or wall. This is an opportunity to create more beautiful displays of plants, adding instant interest, enlivening a stark corner, or putting plants to their best use. Also use hanging plants to highlight architectural details or camouflage unattractive ones.

Ideal plants

A range of plants are especially adaptable to hanging. Candidates include those that trail or cascade (string of pearls, burro's-tail, grape ivy, creeping fig, ivy) and those that climb (jasmine, Madagascar jasmine, heartleaf philodendron). Naturally arching plants—holiday cactus, spider plant, and staghorn fern—also strut their best in a raised display. Choose a plant that will

make a good impression as a focal point with its outstanding form, color, or fragrance.

Containers

Hanging planters also can present a challenge: water drainage. You won't want water dripping on your floor or furniture, so choose a container that will catch any drips. Some pots come with an attached saucer. Water carefully and empty the saucer to avoid overflow. Alternatively, place a potted plant inside a plastic-lined basket or a decorative cachepot without a drainage hole. Use lightweight containers suitable for hanging.

Hardware

Explore your options for hanging plants from a window frame, ceiling, or wall, and take extra steps to secure suspended containers. Plenty of sturdy hooks, brackets, and other supports are available to help you handle the job. Install hangers and shelving by anchoring them into wall studs and ceiling joists, not into drywall or plaster. Choose hangers that have built-in swivels so you can easily rotate all sides of the planter toward the sun.

A container garden can become quite heavy with wet soil and plants. Only use supporting materials that can handle the weight. Fill planters with a lightweight potting mix instead of heavy potting soil.

Above left: **Plastic-lined window box-style baskets hide the lightweight nursery pots of these peace lilies.**

Above right: **Small ceramic hanging pots hold rosemary and sage within easy reach.**

Opposite: **Fast-growing tradescantia forms curtains of living color. The 6-inch-diameter pots are not too heavy to hang from a sturdy curtain rod.**

Forcing bulbs

You can fool Mother Nature, and flowering bulbs grown indoors prove it. Why wait until spring to enjoy the beautiful blooms of daffodils, tulips, and other bulbs when they can be tricked into flowering indoors weeks ahead of their usual schedule? The process known as forcing enables you to make spring bulbs bloom as if by magic during the quiet months of winter. There's more than one way to force bulbs, and once you've tried it, you'll know that forcing isn't complicated.

You can even force a series of bulbs and savor a nonstop show with spectacular blooms, fragrance, and color.

Mark the calendar
Plan ahead to force bulbs in a three-stage process that is easily managed over months. First purchase bulbs in fall and, instead of planting them in the garden as you would for spring blooms, plant the bulbs in pots of soil and

Spring-flowering bulbs, including daffodils, hyacinths, and tulips, bring a blissful antidote to winter's shorter, darker days, when forced into bloom indoors.

chill them. Most types of hardy bulbs require chilling at 35°F to 48°F for at least 12 weeks in a refrigerator or unheated garage or shed.

When prechilling bulbs in the refrigerator, store them away from fruit. The bulbs will not develop and flower if exposed to ethylene gas released by some ripening fruits. Label each bulb variety with the date when chilling will be complete. Identify the bulb's required chill time, which varies from 12 to 14 weeks for hyacinths and squill; up to 15 weeks for daffodils, fritillaria, and grape hyacinth; and 14 to 20 weeks for tulips.

Planting and forcing

Plant bulbs for forcing in 4- to 6-inch-deep pots full of all-purpose potting mix. Each container should have a drainage hole and a saucer. The pot size depends on the type and quantity of bulbs you are forcing. One large daffodil bulb or five crocus bulbs will fill a 4-inch pot; six hyacinth bulbs need an 8-inch pot. Plant the bulbs with their points up and poking through the surface of the potting mix. Avoid pressing on the bulbs and the soil to help the roots grow more easily. Water thoroughly to moisten the mix. Keep the plantings evenly damp, watering throughout the forcing process when the soil begins to feel dry. If the potting mix is too wet, the bulbs may rot or fail to grow well.

When the chilling period is complete, move the potted bulbs to a cool room and set them away from direct light. Keep them there for several more weeks, while roots develop. When the bulbs' tips reach 1 to 2 inches tall, move the pots to a warmer room with more light. Within a few more weeks, your bulbs will begin flowering. Keep them out of direct sun to extend their blooms.

After bloom

Forced bulbs cannot be forced into bloom again. But bulbs that have been forced indoors can be transplanted into the garden and may resume flowering after a year or two of recuperating. It's worth a try. After the forced blooms fade, cut the flower stalks (but keep the leaves), and continue to provide water and sunlight. In spring, transplant the bulbs into the garden, allowing the foliage to wither naturally and help feed the bulbs' future blooms.

Easiest bulbs

Get a quick fix by purchasing pots of chilled, just-sprouting bulbs from a garden center or nursery and turning them into a delightful indoor garden. Just bring home potted bulbs, tuck them into pretty containers (left in or removed from their nursery pots), and watch them grow.

Varieties of paperwhite narcissus require neither soil nor prechilling for forcing. Using a container that holds water, such as a shallow bowl or wide vase, plant paperwhites in a potting medium of pebbles, glass marbles, or soil. For more details, see directions *below*.

TEST GARDEN TIP

Chilling requirements

Prior to chilling bulbs for forcing, identify the bulb's required chill time.

Don't wait for spring. Paperwhite narcissus bloom within a month of planting. Plant them every few weeks for an ongoing display of intensely scented flowers.

1 PLANT
Place a 2- to 3-inch layer of pea gravel or other medium in the container. Set bulbs shoulder to shoulder.

2 COVER
Add water just to the bottoms of the bulbs. Cover the bulbs up to their necks with pebbles.

3 ENJOY
For best blooms, keep the bulbs in a cool (60°F) room. Add only enough water to moisten the roots.

Forcing hyacinths

The marvelous, sweet scent of hyacinths triggers visions of spring. Like many bulbs, hyacinths can be grown in soil or gravel when they're being forced. But it's easiest to force hyacinth bulbs in water.

Traditional forcing

Hyacinth bulbs have been popular for forcing since the Victorian era. People still use the traditional hourglass-shape forcing vases ideally suited to the task, with a narrow neck that holds the bulb just above the water's surface. Various common household containers make excellent forcing vessels too, as long as they hold water. A glass container—clear or tinted—is particularly desirable for displaying forced hyacinths because it allows you to see the water level easily and the entire bulb as it develops. Hyacinth varieties bloom in hues of pink and purple to blue, apricot, yellow, and white.

Bringing richly scented hyacinth bulbs into bloom in simple containers of water is a fun winter ritual. Plan ahead by purchasing bulbs in the fall. Find a wide variety of bulbs on the Internet from mail-order sources.

Hyacinths—as well as crocuses and daffodils, such as tazetta and poetaz types—force well in the refrigerator. Chill hyacinth bulbs for 12 to 14 weeks. After chilling, you have the option of planting the bulbs in a pot of soil with their tips poking out of the soil.

To force the bulbs in water, set an individual bulb in a forcing glass. Alternatively place a 3-inch layer of pebbles in a roomy vase or other watertight container and add water until it barely reaches the surface of the stones. Add a handful of horticultural charcoal chips to keep the water fresher longer. Set the hyacinth bulbs on the pebbles with their bottoms at the surface of the water. Place the forcing glass or vase in a cool room out of direct sunlight.

After several weeks, the bulbs will show signs of growth as little green tips sprout. Add water to the container only as needed to reach the developing roots. Move the container into a warmer room with more light. Within a few more weeks, your bulbs will be ready to bloom. Gently transplant them into pretty arrangements, if you like. To use potted bulbs in arrangements, unpot them, gently tug their roots apart, and rinse the soil off their roots. The flowers last longest when displayed away from bright light and sources of heat.

Slender canning jars work as forcing glasses. Combined with a tepee of forced forsythia branches, top-heavy flowering hyacinth is less likely to topple.

Above: **A vintage glass punch bowl makes a lovely centerpiece when brimming with hyacinths. The bulbs snuggle in a bed of clear recycled glass and white garden rock that mimic ice and snow. Move the centerpiece off the table during meals to prevent olfactory competition between fragrant hyacinths and aromatic food.**

Top: **Place several inches of colorful marbles in the bottom of a glass pillar, add water to barely cover the marbles, then add hyacinth bulbs, and— voilà!—you've made a perfect home for hyacinths in minutes.**

Above: **A classic forcing vase holds a single hyacinth bulb. The bulb blooms about eight weeks after chilling begins.**

Forcing branches

Forsythia is one of the earliest-blooming shrubs, and it forces easily. Cut branches as early as mid-January and bring them into bloom indoors within a few weeks.

Just when a colorful pick-me-up is most welcome

in a winter-weary home, it's time to bring in branches of flowering shrubs and trees and coax them to blossom ahead of the season. In the process of gathering branches for indoor arrangements, you'll get the additional benefit of accomplishing some winter pruning. Forcing works well for many spring-bloomers, from apple to quince and serviceberry.

Forcing is easy

Late January through March is the usual window of opportunity to gather branches. Depending on where you live, begin snipping branches after plants have had their winter rest, or dormancy, for at least eight weeks of temperatures below 40°F. The later in winter you cut the branches, the shorter the forcing time becomes.

Select healthy, young branches with lots of flower buds (flower buds are typically larger and plumper than leaf buds). Choose branches from crowded sections of the plant where it will benefit from pruning, keeping in mind that you are removing some of the plant's spring display.

For a handsome display, start with cuttings that are 1 to 3 feet long. Shorter snippets less than a foot long can also be forced and used to create beautiful, smaller arrangements.

Depending on the variety of tree or shrub you cut, the buds will open in two to four weeks. Branches that can be forced to bloom in as little as two to three weeks include Eastern redbud, forsythia, honeysuckle, and pussy willow. Branches that need more time for forcing include magnolia, mock orange (*Philadelphus*), and rhododendron.

Quick arrangements

Choose a sturdy vase for forced branches that include cherry, almond, and plum in a range of bright white to pastel blooms. Use a heavy vase for 2- to 3-foot-long branches—large displays can be top-heavy and prone to tipping over. Compose the essence of spring in a vase by combining flowering branches with pussy willow stems and cut tulips. The pussy willow branches need no forcing. Just cut them for indoor arrangements before the fuzzy buds are past their prime. Keep the branches out of water to arrest the buds' development.

TEST GARDEN TIP

Pussy willow branches

Common varieties of pussy willow, such as the small tree *Salix discolor* and large shrub *S. caprea,* are among the first signs of spring, and no forcing is required.

Forcing branches

Forcing spring-flowering branches means bringing well-budded prunings indoors and tricking them into flowering as if spring has sprung. Follow these steps, then wait for the buds to swell and show color. That's when it is time to move the branches into a warmer room and enjoy the blooms that will soon appear.

1 CUT
Use pruning shears to cut pencil-thick branches at least 12 inches long. Strip the lowest buds from the branches.

2 HAMMER
Use a hammer to crush the branches' cut ends and prepare them to absorb water.

3 SOAK
Gather and wrap the branches in newspaper. Submerge the bundle in warm water for 12 hours to help the shoots wake from dormancy.

4 WAIT
Stand the branches in a bucket of water and set the container in a cool room. Change the water twice a week.

OAK SPRING FLORA   OAK SPRING GARDEN LIBRARY

MARTIN &
CLINEFF

gardens under glass

Inside a shelter of sparkling glass, plants get the boost they need to thrive indoors, and you get a bird's-eye view of the action.

p.**112**
MOSS GARDENS
Green tufts of moss are marvels of nature and as lovely as the treasures in a jewel box when planted in containers.

p.**114**
TERRARIUMS
Small plants find happy homes inside self-contained gardens where moisture is always recycled and ample.

p.**122**
GLASS BUBBLES
These delicate orbs appear to float while helping sustain the simplest of plantings.

p.**124**
CLOCHES
A clear dome creates a nurturing environment, making plants more manageable and likely to thrive.

Moss gardens

Moss—and little more than that—makes a marvelously simple miniature garden with Zen appeal. Combined with a few stones and tiny pinecones or well-placed handfuls of fine gravel, a moss garden is more minimalist than elaborate. Making a moss garden can be a contemplative process with a serene effect.

Mosses are primitive evergreen plants that form emerald carpets in the landscape. Hundreds of species can be found in North America, growing in creeping or mounding colonies. You can use a single species of moss in a dish garden or combine mosses in a brocade of soft and nubby textures, depending on what's available. Lush green moss can be used to add its jewel tones to many types of container gardens. An all-moss garden is best displayed near eye level where it may be appreciated most.

Growing moss indoors

When growing moss in an indoor garden, start with potted plants from a nursery or collect and transplant moss from your yard. Gathering moss from areas such as a park, public land, or protected area is illegal. If you prefer, purchase fresh sheet moss from a florist or floral supplier and soak it in water for an hour before placing it in a container garden. Dyed and preserved mosses present more options that need no special treatment. They're available at craft stores and garden centers. Online sources offer live and preserved mosses.

Container-grown moss will thrive for several months indoors given conditions similar to those where it is found in nature: moist, acidic soil and high humidity. After planting, press down on the moss to establish good contact between it and the soil. Keep moss damp, but not soggy. Place a live moss garden in indirect light.

Opposite: **Composed inside a clear glass vase, a miniature garden includes tufts of green moss and gray lichen. The girl looking down on the garden is a faded photo secured to the outside of the glass.**

ASK THE GARDEN DOCTOR

How does moss grow?

ANSWER: Moss does not have flowers or roots—it grows and spreads via spores. Moss gets its nutrients from the air and usually continues producing spores as long as there is adequate moisture. Moss prefers poor soil with low nutrient levels.

Up on a pedestal **Convert a pedestal cake plate with a domed glass cover into a little moss garden. Enjoy the verdant scene any time of year, whether you use living or preserved moss.**

1 PLANT
Place pieces of moss on the plate, mounding them over soil in places to mimic the contours of a natural woodland terrain.

2 EMBELLISH
Add a few rocks, twigs, pinecones, or pieces of bark to enhance the scene. Include a tiny violet or other plant, if desired.

3 SPRITZ
Spray the arrangement with water, and then cover it with the glass dome. Mist the moss weekly or when it appears dry.

4 AIR
If the dome fogs over, lift off the cover for an hour or two to adjust the humidity level.

Tabletop conservatories

Miniature conservatories, also known as Wardian cases,

have been favorites of cold-climate gardeners since Victorian times. The fanciful glass enclosures are downsize versions of the elegant greenhouses and conservatories often pictured in English gardens. The full-size glass and metal or wood structures remain fantasies for most gardeners. But miniature conservatories offer a reasonable alternative for those with smaller budgets. All it takes to make one of these gardens under glass is a conservatory and a few humidity-loving plants, such as ferns, dracaena, and nerve plant.

The Wardian case

These charming enclosures for indoor gardens were developed in the early 1800s by a London doctor, Nathaniel Ward, who wanted to watch a sphinx moth chrysalis develop in a closed jar. Ward was so enthralled with his project's success, he began growing plants of all sorts in glass enclosures. Before long, the plant hunters of that time, roaming the planet in search of exotic new plants, depended on Wardian cases as a way to transport their finds with minimal watering and attention.

Today, miniature conservatories have staged a comeback with the resurgence of indoor gardening and the renewed popularity of terrariums. A stylish conservatory becomes a beautiful tabletop garden when filled with small, seasonally blooming annuals or bulbs. It's also an ideal nursery for young plants, especially ferns and others that thrive in the humid environment created by the structure.

Many miniature conservatories are so architecturally captivating, they're used as a handsome backdrop for a few plants or other decorative objects. Some conservatories come with a built-in tray. You can plant in a deep-enough tray or set potted plants on it.

Planting in a conservatory

If your conservatory doesn't have a built-in tray, set it on one of an appropriate size and cover the bottom of the tray with a 1-inch layer of pea gravel for drainage. Sprinkle horticultural charcoal over the gravel. Or, if the tray is at least 3 inches deep, you can finish filling it with potting mix for direct planting. Set the conservatory in diffuse light to prevent it from overheating and scorching plants.

Maintain plants in a little conservatory by checking them periodically and watering as needed. Remove the container's top to ventilate the plants every few days and to prevent fungal or mold problems in the humid conditions.

A long list of plants thrives in the moist conditions of a conservatory, terrarium, or similar garden under glass. These plants will need watering less often than they would in outdoor conditions or when grown ordinarily as houseplants. Favorite foliage plants include dwarf sweet flag (*Acorus*), baby's tears, papyrus (*Cyperus*), ferns, fig, nerve plant, and Scotch moss (*Sagina*); and flowering plants, such as begonia, impatiens, orchid, and primrose.

Above left: **A miniature conservatory gives plants a decorative showplace and a draft-free, moist environment. Add visual interest to the display by including colorful pebbles or flowering plants.**

Above middle: **Given room to grow on its own, a brake fern thrives under glass. When a plant outgrows its glass enclosure, it's time to swap it out, cut it back, or trim and divide it.**

Above right: **A tall Wardian case with a built-in tray has room for several plants: maidenhair fern, arrowhead plant, artillery plant, and prayer plant. Vents in the top supply fresh air to the container.**

Opposite: **Individually potted orchids thrive inside a Victorian-style Wardian case on a four-legged stand. Set on a pebble-filled tray in bright, indirect light, the flowering beauties hit their stride.**

Terrariums

Nerve plant, lady slipper orchid, and fern cohabit in a reproduction apothecary jar. A butterfly made of feathers completes the scene and withstands the damp environment.

A terrarium defies many of the typical challenges of gardening.

Crafted in minutes, the miniature garden encased in glass rarely sprouts a weed. The need for supplemental watering is reduced by condensation forming and water droplets dribbling back down to the soil, recycling moisture in the self-contained environment. The portable container allows you to move the garden into bright-but-indirect light in different rooms.

Magic under glass

A terrarium can be full of surprises, holding exquisite orchids, lichen-covered branches, or a collection of small, compatible plants that like low light and high humidity. Children are drawn to terrariums as miniature landscapes where they can learn about gardening. All it takes is a few plants and an old aquarium or goldfish bowl. Easy-care terrariums can hold potted plants, making it a breeze to change the display whenever you want.

The container you choose helps give the terrarium its appeal, from the sparkle of a giant clear-glass globe to the shapely charm of a lidded apothecary jar. A terrarium that's open at the top allows air to flow freely; an enclosed terrarium needs little watering, but regular opening to allow ventilation. Scour crafts stores, flea markets, and garage sales for containers, whether you prefer an oversize brandy snifter or an old pickle jar. Choose a vessel that you can fit your hand into to ease planting and maintenance. Always start with a clean container.

Planting a terrarium

Your terrarium might include a few usually hard-to-grow carnivorous plants or tried-and-true dwarf and slow-growing houseplants that will appreciate the low light and high humidity inside it. Plants with bold-color foliage are easiest to see inside the glass and contrast with other plants. Start with various-size plants for a grouping. Succulents, cacti, and other plants that like dry conditions rot rapidly in a closed or moist terrarium. But you can plant them in an open glass container in sterile sand layered with pebbles.

Make an ideal potting mix for a terrarium by blending two parts peat-based potting mix, one part sterile sand, and one part perlite or vermiculite. After planting, top the soil mix with moss, more gravel, or sand for a decorative effect.

Keep it growing

Lightly dampen the soil after planting, sprinkling water until it drips into the pebbles. Water an open terrarium when the soil appears dry—every 10 days or so. A closed terrarium may need watering every two weeks or more. Remove yellowed leaves and spent flowers when they appear. Periodically wipe the glass inside and out with a clean cloth.

TEST GARDEN TIP

Open air

If condensation clouds the glass of your terrarium, open the lid or remove the stopper to allow ventilation. Opening a closed terrarium for an hour or two every so often works well.

Make a terrarium

Prepare the best home possible for plants by covering the bottom of the terrarium with a layer of drainage material (glass beads, pebbles, or aquarium gravel) and sprinkle in a handful of horticultural charcoal chips.

1 DRAIN
Place glass beads about 1 to 2 inches deep in the bottom of a clear glass container.

2 ADD SOIL
Layer potting mix 2 to 4 inches deep, depending on the size of your container.

3 PLANT
Gently place each plant, tucking the root ball into the soil mix and covering it.

4 FINESSE
Use a makeshift long-handle tool to reach into a narrow-neck jar.

Bottles & jars

Everyday containers, such as bottles and jars,

are among the array of potential vessels for terrarium gardening. The difference is when you plant a cider jug, juice bottle, or other vessel with a small opening or neck, the process typically entails some dexterity and customized tools to meet the challenge. But a bottle garden can be one of the most successful terrariums possible, giving plants an ideal home in which they can thrive for years with little upkeep.

Bottle gardens were made popular during the era of bell-bottom blue jeans and macramé plant hangers in the 1960s and 70s. Today, they join other forms of terrariums in the latest lust for decorative indoor gardens that require minimal outlay and fuss. What better way to display a few plants than in a beautiful glass vessel that can make even the most ordinary plants stellar? As with other terrariums, look for attractive glass containers of any size or shape you like. Choose clear over colored glass, which filters out some wavelengths of light needed by plants to be healthy. The smaller the opening and neck a container has, the trickier it will be to plant and maintain.

Planting a bottle garden

As with any terrarium, you will fill the bottom of the bottle or jar with a sterile, inert drainage material: pebbles, sand, or glass. Roll a sheet of stiff paper into a cone shape and use it as a funnel to add those materials to the bottle. Add horticultural charcoal chips to absorb soil impurities. The rest of the planting process is different than planting other terrariums.

Add a 3- to 5-inch layer of premoistened soilless potting mix. Most of these mixes are made with peat moss, fine sand, vermiculite or perlite, and added nutrients. As long as the mix is premoistened at planting time and kept damp, the bottle garden should do well. If you let the mix dry out completely, it can be difficult to remoisten.

Round up a few small, moisture-loving plants that will fit inside the bottle or jar. Now fashion a planting tool from an 18-inch length of bamboo stake by attaching a small plastic teaspoon to the end of it. A length of stiff wire with a spiral or small loop twisted at one end can also be useful.

Carefully coax each plant through the opening of the container and use the planting tool to nestle their root balls into the soilless mix and cover the roots. Work slowly and patiently to arrange and settle the plants.

A key to success

Overwatering is the most common problem that occurs with bottle gardens and other terrariums because excess moisture does not drain out of the container. The soil should feel damp, not soaked. It's better for your terrarium to be a bit dry than too wet. Experiment until you get a feel for how much supplemental water is enough for your plants and how often it is needed. Of course, you may not be able to touch the soil inside a bottle or jar. Learning to distinguish the appearance of wet or dry soil mix is key to the plants' well-being. Too little moisture, and plants will suffer or die; too much moisture fogs the bottle and plants can rot.

When the soil mix appears dry or there are no moisture droplets inside the container, add a tablespoon of water. If the soil still appears dry the next day, add another spoonful of water.

Above left: **Add color to your terrarium using recycled glass for drainage. Place a bottle garden in bright, indirect light and occasionally turn it slightly to help plants grow evenly.**

Above right: **A crystal decanter or vase would work as well as a small pitcher to hold a mini potted rose. Green moss disguises the pot and adds to the charm of this display.**

Opposite: **Spacious containers, such as carafes, vases, and jars, house long-lasting gardens. These showcase (from *left*) a mini guzmania bromeliad; maidenhair fern and club mosses; and club moss, button fern, and variegated false aralia.**

Living treasure troves

A child's nature-inspired terrarium teaches basic gardening lessons. Pint-size plants along with treasures from the backyard take up residence in a cookie jar-turned-terrarium.

Mini biospheres, complete with plants and added finds from nature,

give intrepid gardeners the big rewards of a small world. Making a little biosphere is a quick and easy project. Tucking in a few treasures gathered from the yard or a nearby natural setting adds another layer of interest as well as an outdoor adventure. Prizes might include seed pods, bark, or lichen-covered twigs picked up from the ground. Just avoid digging plants from the wild, gather seed pods only if several others are found nearby, and leave abandoned bird nests alone.

Making a terrarium

Even young hands can plant and manage a simple terrarium. Make the terrarium in any lidded glass or plastic container with an opening wide enough for easy access. Canning jars, lemonade jugs, and canisters are among easy-to-locate prospects. If the container has no lid, top it with a small clear-glass plate or plastic wrap.

When placed in the right location with bright indirect light, an encased ecosystem can survive on autopilot with an occasional peek. Condensation from moisture in the soil collects on the glass and dribbles down, keeping the potting medium moist in a continuous cycle. A bit of added moisture may be needed once in a while, especially if the lid is left off.

Terrarium troubleshooting

Follow these tips to keep your terrarium plants in top condition:

If leaves turn yellow or leaf tips turn brown, allow the terrarium to dry out a bit by taking off the lid for a few hours each day for a week or two.

If plants are stretching to reach light and becoming spindly, place the terrarium closer to brighter light.

If leaves are touching the glass or falling off the plants, trim plants that have grown to reach the glass and remove spent leaves and flowers.

Wonders of nature

When adding natural treasures to a terrarium, select dried objects (such as pinecones, twigs, and bark) that are less likely to lead to fungal growth.

Size matters.
Start with small plants that won't quickly outgrow the terrarium. Check plant tags or consult an expert when selecting nursery plants, if you're unsure of their potential size.

TRAILING CLUBMOSS
(Selaginella kraussiana)

The cultivar 'Aurea' is a spreading tropical groundcover with chartreuse mossy foliage. It needs high humidity to grow well.

GUPPY PLANT
(Nematanthus gregarius)

It's fitting for a fishbowl: a guppy with orange flowers and shining foliage. Pinch the plant tips to prompt branching.

BEGONIA
'Bethlehem Star'

Miniature rhizomatous begonias with colorful leaves thrive in the moist conditions of a terrarium.

EARTH STAR
(Cryptanthus bivittatus)

A striking bromeliad that makes an ideal companion for carnivorous plants, earth star requires little care.

STRAWBERRY BEGONIA
(Saxifraga stolonifera)

This beauty has silvery patterned foliage like a begonia and plantlets like a strawberry.

Glass bubbles

Contemporary globe
terrariums hold fuss-free
tillandsias or air plants.
These epiphytes need no
soil, only bright light and
occasional misting or a
weekly plunging into water.

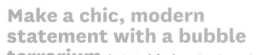

Keep it up

Air plants displayed in glass holders prefer bright but filtered light—in an east- or west-facing window, or a few feet back from a south-facing window. Take the plant out of the bubble for a weekly splash in a water-filled bowl, and then return it to its place.

Make a chic, modern statement with a bubble terrarium designed for hanging in a window or setting on a table or shelf. You'll find various shapes for hanging, from oval to teardrop and round, as well as different sizes of clear glass globes to accommodate the plants you want to display. Use a bubble-shape bowl or spherical terrarium for tabletop displays.

Hang 'em high

Glass bubbles made for hanging have a hanger built into their tops. When suspended from the top of a window frame using a strand of invisible monofilament, a bubble-glass garden catches light and attention. Hang them at eye level where they can be viewed easily up close without getting bumped. A grouping of bubbles, whether the same or different sizes and shapes, has artful appeal and suits a small space.

Tillandsias, sculptural bromeliads also known as air plants, live happily in glass bubbles and add their exotic forms to a creative display. The hanging type of a glass bubble also works well for young plants or treasured varieties that benefit from the extra warmth and moisture in this sheltered environment.

These small (3- to 8-inch) glass globes, teardrops, and other hanging vessels usually have one or more openings in their sides for planting. Handle plants carefully to avoid damaging them when planting. If you want a carefree-but-effective display, make a little bed of moss in a glass bubble and tuck in a couple of earthy treasures gleaned from your yard. Try adding an acorn, skeletonized leaf, sprig of berries—whatever works together and brings nature indoors for all to see.

Tabletop versions

Various styles of spherical containers work beautifully to make tabletop terrariums. They can also be displayed on a shelf and sustained with supplemental lighting. A goldfish bowl, bubble vase, and large sphere with a side opening are among the container options widely available from craft stores, florist suppliers, and online sources.

Stretch your imagination when making a little garden in a glass bubble. Take advantage of the container's clean lines to plant a miniature floating garden using a single water plant such as water hyacinth. Or create a miniature landscape with a few tiny plants, a bit of moss, and a structural accent (a doll-size chair, wheelbarrow, or animal figurine).

Above left: **A teardrop-shape bubble and a glass corsage bowl pair to create a mini naturescape.**

Above right: **This 18-inch-diameter bubble can be viewed from any angle. It holds false aralia, dracaena, 'Sinbad' begonia, polka-dot plant, 'Ripple' peperomia, and rex begonia.**

Cloches

A 16-inch-tall glass cloche sits on a bed of bark chips and sphagnum moss, housing a pretty (and hungry) group of insectivorous plants: 'Scarlet Belle' pitcher plant, Mexican butterwort, and Venus flytrap. Insects can enter the raised dome on their own or be fed to the plants.

Some plants deserve special treatment, if not to be placed on a pedestal.

Using a glass dome or cloche and a pedestal to display plants takes them to a stellar level and also provides a nurturing environment. In addition to the aesthetic appeal of this type of glass-enclosed planting, a cloche works as a mini greenhouse for a plant that prefers warmth and humidity when kept in a home where winter heating and summer air-conditioning systems can challenge the hardiest of plants.

Put a cloche to work

Better yet, a glass cloche can serve you in the garden outdoors too. Also known as bell jars, cloches have been practical garden ornaments for centuries. Antique bell jars from Old English, French, or Early American gardens are rare treasures. But any contemporary reproduction brings the graceful character of traditional cloches to gardens today, sheltering seedlings from frost. Indoors, the glass dome can provide housing for cuttings and seedlings, complete with the extra warmth and moisture that prompts their growth.

Prop up the cloche by placing a wooden block or similar object under the bottom edge to allow air into it and heat and moisture out. A cloche makes a mostly airtight seal, so if you forget to prop it open or remove it daily or weekly, depending on its contents, the plants may perish.

Seedlings thrive under glass cloches when placed away from bright light to avoid baking the tender young plants. Raise the jar on blocks or wood pieces to allow airflow.

Top: **This glass act features jewel orchid, arrowleaf fern, and 'Chocolate Stars' earth star on a Victorian-style cake stand. Moss stabilizes and hides the soil and plants' roots.**

Above: **Kept temporarily under bell jars, young scented geranium standards—or tree forms in training—benefit from the moist setting placed away from direct light.**

edibles indoors

A surprising array of delicious and nutritious plants can make themselves at home indoors with you. Simple methods make it happen.

p.**128**
HERBS
Lush, aromatic plants grace a sunny windowsill and reward you through the winter.

p.**130**
PLANTS FROM PRODUCE
You might rescue the beginnings of exotic plants from your compost bucket.

p.**132**
CITRUS
No matter where you live, some citrus plants will grow well indoors in containers.

p.**134**
MUSHROOMS
Have an adventure in gourmet gardening. Growing flavorful treasures is easy.

p.**136**
SPROUTS
Fresh and delicious, sprouts are one of the quickest, easiest crops you can grow.

p.**138**
MICROGREENS
Raise all sorts of colorful seedlings on a windowsill and enjoy tasty harvests.

p.**140**
WHEATGRASS
This nutrient-rich green grows easily and provides decorative possibilities too.

Herbs

When grown in containers, herbs bring indoors all the benefits of garden plantings—beauty, fragrance, flavor, well-being—plus convenience. Among the traditional outdoor plants that fare well indoors, some herbs excel in a sunny window yielding incomparable fresh flavors for cooking and serving as delightfully aromatic houseplants. Herbs and other edible plants provide surprising beauty as well as bounty indoors, and it's simply fun to see how many ways you can use and enjoy them.

Some culinary herbs grow especially well indoors on a sunny windowsill. Good options include basil, oregano, parsley, and thyme.

Growing herbs indoors

The culinary herbs that you would use in cooking are ideal for a kitchen or dining room with a super-sunny window that faces south or west and provides direct, bright light. Most herbs need at least six hours of sunlight daily; supplemental light can help.

You'll have good results starting with young plants. Grow them in a window box or individual pots on a sill; or group them in a hanging basket. Annual herbs, such as basil, cilantro, and dill, will be challenged to survive a long, cold winter where the light is not always bright, but they may last for a couple of months. Plants started from seeds will grow nicely indoors throughout the winter. If you want to bring herbs indoors from your garden, the best candidates are tender perennials, such as rosemary, bay, and lemon verbena—especially plants that have spent the summer growing in containers.

One of the best things you can do to help keep herbs growing indoors is to pinch the stem tips often. The plants' growth slows naturally during the winter, but progresses and quickens in spring. Popular uses of herbs in the kitchen include snipping the fresh leaves into a salad, omelette, or spreadable cheese. Their aromas and flavors enhance any tea or fruit drink. Harvest no more than one third of a stem's length to keep the plant growing productively.

Herbs around the house

Think of other ways to use herbs around the house. Group small potted plants on a dining table for an aromatic centerpiece. Let shapely herb topiaries accent a tabletop with their elegant charms. Flowering lavender plants serve as delightful albeit temporary pleasures indoors. Deck your house with large pots of rosemary and bay laurel as cheerful winter decor. Embellish the plants with sprigs of evergreens and bright baubles. To get the most benefit and pleasure from growing herbs indoors, make them part of your everyday life, rather than something saved only for special occasions. Try gently squeezing a few basil leaves to release their fragrance momentarily or tucking a sprig of rosemary into a hand-penned note: The simple pleasures can be the sweetest.

TEST GARDEN TIP

Rosemary's survival

To succeed indoors over winter, rosemary needs somewhat different care than most herbs. Keep the plant in a sunny but cool spot. Water consistently to keep the soil damp, but not soggy.

Growing herbs on the sill
Create a snippable indoor herb garden in a sunny location in your home. Culinary herbs provide extra-special pleasures with their flavors and fragrances.

1 GATHER
Start with young plants, terra-cotta pots and saucers, and potting mix. Transplanting takes less than an hour.

2 TRANSPLANT
Remove plants from their nursery pots and slip them into the terra-cotta pots, adding fresh potting mix.

3 FINISH
Water well after transplanting. Avoid overwatering herbs by allowing the soil to begin drying between waterings.

Plants from produce

You may find treasure—and some gardening fun and adventure

—in your kitchen trash or compost bucket. The beginnings of easy plants are contained in the seeds, pits, roots, and other seemingly useless parts of edibles. Instead of tossing them, consider growing the plants shown opposite, as well as many others that grow readily from a seed, tuber or rhizome. Date, ginger, fig, strawberry guava, loquat, and others with less-familiar names have potential for a windowsill garden. Citrus of all kinds sprout easily from seed—read more about some good options beginning on page 132.

Almost any unprocessed vegetable or fruit has potential as a fascinating houseplant, whether it grows as an annual, perennial, shrub, tree, or vine. The goal isn't an orchard, but a few houseplants to provide greenery and maybe some produce.

Plants once considered exotic—papaya, mango, kiwi—are now available year-round in supermarkets and furnish some of the most satisfying gardening adventures. Fair game includes any exotic fruit that you bring into your kitchen that has not been cooked, pickled, or

Even inexperienced gardeners can pluck a seed from fruit, poke it into soil, and enjoy the seed-starting magic that ensues. Next time you go grocery shopping, consider sweet potato, lime, passion fruit, or papaya for its garden potential.

irradiated (rendered sterile and won't grow). But you don't need tropical conditions or great skill to succeed. Some of the nation's most experienced produce-sprouters belong to the Rare Pit and Plant Council (aka "the Pits") and hail from the Big Apple. (Where else?) They meet in the members' high-rise apartments where their garden experiments grow. Sometimes the plants require patience as you wait for them to sprout—some seeds take up to 12 weeks to germinate—but kids of all ages can enjoy the process and keep the plants going from year to year.

Growing exotic plants

Start new plants from roots, bulbs, tubers, cuttings, or seeds. Most of the plants shown *below* grew from a seed or pit. Ginger grows from a knobby rhizome. A pineapple plant starts with a fresh-looking leaf rosette from the top of a ripe pineapple. Many seeds sprout within one to eight weeks when taken from ripe fruit. Remove the seeds or pit from the fruit and rinse well to remove any flesh. Soak the large seed of a mango in water for two or three days, then pry open the softened outer husk and remove the inner seed for planting.

Start seeds in damp potting mix or soilless mix. Cover the container and set it on a heating pad to help prompt germination. As the seedlings begin to develop leaves, uncover them. Place the seedlings under a grow-light or in a warm sunny window and keep the potting mix damp. When seedlings' roots outgrow their original container, transplant them into a slightly larger pot using a compost-enriched potting mix.

Keep plants in bright light, such as a south-facing window or sunroom, or use supplemental lighting to keep them growing strong. The plants will need a warm (65°F–90°F) location. Move tropical plants outdoors for the summer, where they will thrive in the sun and fresh air—rainfall and humidity will be bonuses.

Bring the tropics home
Start a collection of homegrown tropical plants and raise these exotic wonders in containers on a warm, sun-drenched windowsill.

AVOCADO
Peel the papery skin of an avocado (*Persea americana*) before planting. A tree grown from a pit rarely fruits; purchase a grafted clone to produce fruit.

GINGER
Zingiber officinale reaches 3 to 4 feet tall and will bloom in summer, if you're lucky. The plant drops its leaves and rests from late fall through winter.

PAPAYA
The maplelike leaves of *Carica papaya* make it a handsome tree. The plant grows quickly but most likely will not bear fruit indoors.

PASSION FRUIT
Passiflora edulis vines are self-fertile and reach fruiting size one year from sprouting seeds. Passion fruit produces exquisite blossoms in bright light.

PINEAPPLE
Twist the leafy crown off the fruit and pull off the bottom leaves before planting your *Ananus comosus*. Watch for fruit after two years.

POMEGRANATE
Slow-growing *Punica granatum* may not fruit indoors but it makes a lovely plant. Pinch the stem tips of a young plant to prompt branching.

STARFRUIT
The feathery leaflets of *Averrhoa carambola* fold at night. The tree grows about a foot a year.

SWEET POTATO
Long a favorite of indoor gardeners, the tubers of *Ipomoea batatas* sprout in water or soil and produce quick-growing vines.

Citrus

Potted citrus trees bring a touch of the tropics to a sunny room, especially during the winter. Among the best choices for container growing indoors are the calamondin, dwarf orange, and 'Meyer' lemon.

Yes, you can grow citrus trees indoors,

and dwarf varieties are particularly well-suited to pot culture. Worthy candidates for homegrown citrus include calamondin, kumquat, Clementine tangerine, Mexican (key) lime, 'Meyer' lemon, and myrtleleaf orange. Citrus plants offer something for all seasons: glossy dark green foliage, sweet-scented blossoms, and colorful, long-lasting fruits (depending on the maturity of the fruit). The flowers will fill a room with their fragrance. Many citrus plants are available in striking variegated forms, which bloom and fruit as readily as all-green ones.

Where to begin

Start with dwarf-variety plants that will grow 3 to 6 feet tall indoors. Varieties other than these would grow to 25 feet outdoors, reach up to 10 feet indoors, and require regular pruning. Set plants outside to summer on the deck or patio or in the garden.

It's possible to grow most citrus from seeds salvaged from fresh, ripe, store-bought fruit. But most supermarket fruits are produced by hybrid trees, and plants grown from their seeds will not likely fruit. Or the tree may flower after many years, but the fruit may not be the same as the seed source. Nonetheless, citrus trees are lovely houseplants, whether they produce edible fruit or not. Sometimes the fruit of indoor-grown trees is sour or bitter when eaten fresh, but it can be used to make luscious marmalade or candied fruit.

What citrus need

Adequate light is essential to success when growing citrus indoors. The trees will grow well in a sunroom or conservatory. Otherwise, situate them near a bright, south-facing window where temperatures range between 60°F and 85°F. Gradually acclimate a tree to more or less light when moving it outdoors in late spring and back indoors in early fall. Once outdoors, progressively move a tree into more and more light for about three weeks. Reverse the process in fall to help a tree adjust to less light indoors. Citrus are sensitive to cold and should be protected from frost. Also protect trees from harsh winds outdoors.

Pot a tree in a high-quality potting mix enriched with pine bark, sphagnum moss, and gradual-release plant food. Water consistently to keep the soil damp, when the top inch has dried. Fertilize throughout the growing season. Give the plant a regular shower to clean dusty leaves. Prune citrus after flowering to shape the tree, and remove any dead or damaged wood as needed.

TEST GARDEN TIP

You be the bee

Citrus trees rely on bees for pollination. Ensure fruiting indoors by aiding the process. Use a fine paintbrush to transfer pollen grains from the stamens of a flower to the pistils in other flowers.

Repotting a large plant
Citrus trees grow well in containers when their roots are constricted. If the plant wilts between waterings and needs watering more than once a week, it's time to repot. Otherwise, repot annually.

1 GET SET
Start with a pot 15 inches wide and deep for a young tree. When repotting, increase the pot size by no more than 25 percent.

2 UNPOT
Gently tip over the plant and slide off the old pot. Handle the tree by its root ball or, if you must, grasp it at the base of the trunk.

3 RELEASE
Loosen the root ball with your fingertips if the roots have become packed or tightly wound. Dislodge old loose potting mix.

4 REFRESH
Fill the bottom of the new pot with fresh potting mix. Set the tree in the pot and fill in around the root ball with the mix. Water thoroughly.

Mushrooms

The convex brown crowns of

One word—yum!—best describes this foray in gourmet gardening.

If you like mushrooms, a ready-to-grow kit makes it simple and downright entertaining to raise impressive crops of delectable mushrooms indoors. The process is reminiscent of a school science experiment and requires neither special tools nor soil. A tabletop mushroom garden can produce the exotically flavored goodies that may be hard to find or prohibitively costly at local food stores.

Start with a kit

A mushroom-growing kit from a mail-order source enables you to grow mushrooms indoors anytime. An array of varieties are available, from delicate-tasting pearl oyster to traditional Italian pioppino with a sweet, mellow flavor. The cost of the kit varies depending on the variety, and it may not translate into budget savings for your household, but it makes an excellent gift.

When the kit arrives, you'll see that it consists of a block of compressed sawdust or straw (sizewise, picture a 5-pound bag of sugar) wrapped in plastic. The instructions for a kit lead you through the process: Mist the block daily with water—nonchlorinated and nondistilled—and keep it tented with plastic to maximize humid conditions.

Cultivating gourmet mushrooms

Mushroom culture comes with a language and science of its own. The block, called a mushroom patch or substrate, has been inoculated with the spawn or mycelium of the desired variety. It is similar to the mushroom-spawning technique used by some commercial growers but on a much smaller scale.

As fungi, mushrooms reproduce by spores, not seeds, which germinate into threadlike mycelium. When conditions are right, mushrooms—the stems and caps called fruiting bodies—develop. Mushrooms grow best in a moist medium in indirect light, high humidity, and temperature of 50°F–70°F.

Every day you mist the block and wait. Mist and wait. After a few days, frosty white growth and brown bumps appear here and there. Within a week, teeny clusters of mushrooms form. These develop into robust bouquets with plump caps in another week or two. Some crops take longer than others, and the kit won't produce indefinitely, but you can harvest two or three flushes of mushrooms over a couple of months or more.

When a kit stops producing mushrooms, it's time to break up the block and toss it into the compost pile. Mushrooms might naturalize there, especially if the location is usually damp, warm, and partially shaded.

TEST GARDEN TIP

Drying Mushrooms

Shiitake and other varieties dry readily for later use. Lay the mushrooms on a rack or screen and set them in a warm airy place until they're brittle-dry. Store dried mushrooms in an airtight container for up to one year.

Harvesting and using mushrooms

When your mushrooms have developed to their full size, harvest them with a few quick strokes of a sharp knife. Wise cooks employ mushrooms for their unique flavors, from the oaky shiitake to other varieties that taste sweet, woodsy, smoky, or fruity. Mushrooms add texture and aroma to food. What's more, they pack considerable nutritional punch—protein, amino acids, vitamin D, niacin, potassium, and selenium—with few calories and no fat.

Sprouts

Germinated seeds or sprouts are one of the quickest, easiest, and most delicious crops for indoor gardeners. The most commonly grown sprouts, including alfalfa, radish, lentil, azuki bean, mung bean, red clover, beet, buckwheat, and broccoli, are widely available from supermarkets, food co-ops, and health food stores. But they often come with a premium price, and, by comparison, it's so inexpensive to grow them on your kitchen counter. There is neither soil nor windowsill involved. You can start with a packet of organic seeds or buy bulk seeds from an online source for the most economical approach.

Even if you haven't eaten sprouts, perhaps you recognize them as a healthy food. Sprouted seeds pack a lot of nutritional wallop, typically high in protein, vitamins, and minerals but low in fat and calories. Sprouts add their tasty fresh crunch to salads and sandwiches. They can also be cooked in soups, stir-fries, breads, muffins, and more.

Just-sprouted alfalfa seeds have barely developed leaves but loads of nutrients. To green up sprouts, leave them without a cover for a few hours in bright but indirect sunlight.

How to grow sprouts

The most common method of sprouting seeds requires a pint or quart jar, moisture, and plenty of air circulation. It takes less than a week to grow most sprouts. You can easily keep successive crops going. Use a slightly different gardening technique to grow just-leafing microgreens, shown on pages 138 and 139. Taste sprouted seeds as they develop and use them when you best like the flavor. When sprouts are 1 to 2 inches long, depending on the variety, rinse them thoroughly before eating. Drain unused sprouts and refrigerate in a covered container for up to one week.

Avoid salmonella poisoning from raw sprouts by starting with certified pathogen-free seed and following these guidelines:

Treat seeds before sprouting. Heat to 140°F a solution of 97 parts water and 3 parts hydrogen peroxide. Immerse the seeds in the heated solution for five minutes.

Place seeds in a container, and add water to cover them plus 1 inch. Skim off floating seeds and other debris.

Sprout seeds using a clean jar and a new screw-top canning band washed with soap, rinsed, and sterilized with boiling water. After sprouting, wash the jar and lid, then disinfect them using 3 tablespoons bleach per gallon of water. Use new, clean mesh for each batch of sprouts.

Grow your own sprouts.

Growing fresh sprouts at home requires no fancy equipment. Take a couple of minutes to tend the seeds each day, and you'll be munching nutritious, flavorful sprouts in four to six days.

1 START
Place 1 to 4 tablespoons of prepared seeds in a clean, sterilized wide-mouth jar.

2 COVER
Top the jar with fiberglass mesh and screw on the metal canning-jar band.

3 RINSE
Use lukewarm water to rinse the seeds. Swirl and drain.

4 SOAK
Add about 1 cup of lukewarm water. Soak the seeds for 12 to 24 hours.

5 DRAIN
Pour off the water. Rinse and drain seeds twice a day, pouring off all excess water.

6 GROW
Keep the jar at room temperature. Rinse and drain twice daily as sprouts develop.

Microgreens

Microgreens are very young seedlings

Microgreens are very young seedlings with their first pair of true leaves. Grown for harvest at this teeny stage, microgreens are tasty and nutritious enough to elevate salads, appetizers, and other dishes to gourmet fare with a snip and a sprinkle. Chefs have bolstered the itty-bitty greens to the hippest status among food trends. Home gardeners have caught on, as the freshest of produce is one of the easiest windowsill crops.

Microgreens are not sprouts (germinated seeds, eaten root and all). If left to grow, microgreens become seedlings and then full-fledged plants. Many vegetable and herb seeds produce delicious young leaves and stems that are ready for harvesting as microgreens by snipping the stems after two or three weeks. Unlike sprouts, these plants need soil and bright light to grow. Microgreens have more developed flavors than sprouts, and they're often grown for their different colors, leaf shapes, and textures too.

Superb variety

If you sow a different type or two of microgreens every other week, you can enjoy an ongoing supply of microgreens. Yet even after a year, you would have sampled only a fraction of the realm of possibilities. Among lettuces and salad greens alone there are dozens of mild and tangy options, from arugula to spinach. Each variety of microgreen has a different flavor and appearance—just as the full-size plants do. Choose your crops of microfennel, microcabbage, or anything else with thoughts of how you might use them: as gorgeous garnishes or distinct flavor ingredients. Consider sowing seeds of purple basil, red amaranth, and 'Bull's Blood' beet just for their colors. You can also customize a blend of microgreens, sowing a mix of seeds with similar rates of germination.

Growing microgreens

Sow seeds in a container with a 2- to 3-inch-deep layer of premoistened soilless seed-starting mix or potting mix. Sprinkle the seeds evenly, leaving up to ¼ inch of space between them—even microsize plants need room to grow. Cover the seeds with ¼ inch of vermiculite. Water gently. Cover the container with clear plastic until the seeds germinate. Remove the cover and set the container in bright light. A south-facing window is best; supplement with full-spectrum lights if need be. Keep the planting medium damp by watering from the bottom.

Most seeds will germinate within 4 to 14 days, and will be ready for harvest in another week or two. Winglike cotyledons form first, followed by a pair of true leaves: harvesttime. Use the microgreens soon after harvesting. They'll keep for up to three days, refrigerated in a plastic food storage bag. If allowed to grow on, the microgreens will develop into seedlings of transplantable size. Some cut-and-come-again lettuce varieties will regrow; otherwise the crop is finished once cut. Reuse the seed-starting medium several more times and then replace it.

Above left: **Use sharp scissors to snip the stems a bit above soil level. Cut as much as you want; harvest the rest later.**

Above middle: **Mix several types of microgreens together for a colorful, flavorful treat.**

Above right: **A simple appetizer such as a stuffed mushroom becomes gourmet fare with a sprinkling of microgreens and edible flower petals.**

Opposite: **Many types of vegetable and herb seeds produce crops of colorful microgreens, perfect for winter salads. The seedlings, such as those of beet, radish, basil, and kale, have mild flavors compared to their full-size counterparts.**

Wheatgrass

Indoor gardeners know that anything green and growing provides a sure cure for cabin fever. Sowing a tray or smaller pots of fresh wheatgrass brings an early dose of spring within days. Wheatgrass has several popular uses: It forms a sophisticated-but-minimal tabletop garden. Cut it and process it in a juicer to make a health drink. Cats enjoy munching on wheatgrass during the winter. It gives them an indoor lawn of sorts—felines will lie on wheatgrass as well as nibble it.

How to grow wheatgrass

Use these directions to plant a 10×20-inch flat of wheatgrass—enough to make fresh juice every day for a couple of weeks or a generous-size centerpiece. Presoak fewer seeds and plant them in small individual pots or other containers, if you prefer.

To prepare the wheatgrass seeds: Place 1½ cups of hard red winter wheat (*Triticum aestivum*) in a large jar. Fill the jar with water and soak the seeds for 12 hours or overnight. Use a fine-mesh colander to strain the seeds, and then rinse them thoroughly under a faucet.

To plant: Prepare a seed-starting flat by adding a 2-inch layer of potting mix. Completely moisten the mix with warm water. Sprinkle the presoaked seeds over the potting mix, distributing them as evenly as possible. Sprinkle with warm water to help the seeds and potting mix make good contact. Allow excess water to drain. Set the flat on a tray or in another flat that does not have drainage holes. Cover the seeds with a single-sheet layer of damp paper towels.

Set the flat in a warm place with indirect light for a day or two. Mist the paper towels with water daily to keep them damp. When the seeds germinate and sprout, remove the paper towels. Continue misting with water daily to keep the potting mix damp.

Harvest your wheatgrass in about 7 to 10 days when it has reached 4 to 6 inches tall. Use sharp scissors to cut the grass. Harvest only what you will use fresh to make juice, cutting close to the soil. Or trim all of the grass evenly to a desired height, if you are using it decoratively. Either way, the grass will grow out again and eventually deteriorate.

Opposite: **It's easy to keep up a steady supply of fresh wheatgrass. It germinates quickly and can be used to make nutritious juice.**

TEST GARDEN TIP

Juicing wheatgrass

Bright green wheatgrass juice is a perennial favorite at juice bars and health food stores. You can make it at home most effectively using a juicer that will strain the plant material properly.

Decorating with wheatgrass
Large trays and small pots of wheatgrass have decorative appeal. It grows easily and quickly enough to make a large quantity of tabletop gardens for a wedding or other special event. Small pots work well as name-card holders. Line a mantel or windowsill with small pots. Plant Easter baskets with wheatgrass (line the basket with landscape fabric before adding soil). Use a tray or a large, low-profile container of wheatgrass as a centerpiece. Tuck in glass votive holders, cut flowers, or other embellishments to suit a theme or your decorating style. A wheatgrass centerpiece never fails as a conversation starter. After 7 to 10 days, snip the grass evenly to keep it lush; cut it a couple more times over several weeks before replacing it with new wheatgrass.

favorite plants

For gardeners of all skill levels, these beauties offer plenty of options for celebrating every season in style.

p.144
SEASONAL SELECTIONS
The prettiest of traditional plants outlast the holidays and highlight the seasons.

p.152
AFRICAN VIOLET
The treasures of collectors, these bloomers offer diversity and longevity.

p.154
BEGONIA
Individuality excels in this large group of plants with outstanding qualities.

p.156
BROMELIAD
Exotic and sculptural, the plants in this family have unusual lifestyles.

p.158
CACTUS
If any plants thrive on neglect, cacti do. Collect them from thousands of varieties.

p.160
COLEUS
There's more to the enduring appeal of the colorful plants than their fast-growing foliage.

p.162
FERN
Simple, arching fronds mark the irresistible allure of these elegant plants.

p.164
IVY
Varieties climb, twine, or trail and provide candidates for topiary and other creative projects.

p.166
JASMINE
Known for their seductive fragrances, the plants need little pampering to prosper.

p.168
ORCHID
Plenty of varieties are surprisingly undemanding and enjoyable houseplants.

p.170
SCENTED GERANIUM
The delicious fragrances and textural leaves of these distinctive plants explain their popularity.

p.172
SUCCULENT
Easy-growing beauties weave textural effects in indoor gardens, planted solo or in combinations.

Fall into winter

No matter what the time of year, seasonal flowering

and foliage plants make lovely gifts. Some specialty plants last only a few weeks; others live on for months or even years.

Whether the recipient is a gardener or not, a plant is intended as a token that lasts longer than cut flowers. A large, potted amaryllis bulb is a sure-to-please gift for anyone. It will bloom dependably and sometimes perform with successive blooms of spectacular flowers—and it needs little more than occasional watering. Gardeners love to receive gift plants and sometimes gift themselves with irresistible finds of the season. And any plant, from the smallest herb to the largest poinsettia, helps extend the gardening year.

Seasonal splendor

Gift plants bring nature indoors and contribute to celebrations of the seasons and holidays. From fall through spring and beyond, gift plants capture attention and reinforce cherished traditions. A potted chrysanthemum summons the essence of autumn to the kitchen counter or the home office and enlivens the room with its bold color and sharp fragrance. Just as the busiest holiday season begins, fall and winter plant offerings of showy cyclamen, ornamental peppers, and more appear at garden centers and supermarkets, in time for purchasing as host or hostess gifts.

The four most common kinds of gift plants are annuals, perennials, flowering bulbs, and shrubs. Varieties grown as gift plants may be different from those grown in the garden. Most often, the plants have been raised in the ideal conditions of a greenhouse and forced into bloom at a time not in sync with their natural growth and life cycle.

The blooms of amaryllis bulbs create stunning cut-flower bouquets that last for weeks. Handle the stems and buds carefully because they bruise easily.

AMARYLLIS (*Hippeastrum* hybrids) Pot the large bulb or groups of them any time from fall into winter. Mix varieties with different bloom times for a long-running show. The bulbs like to be potted snugly and kept in a warm place. Amaryllis will bloom again given a rest and proper care.

CHRYSANTHEMUM (*Chrysanthemum* hybrids) Known as florist mums, these gift plants are most widely available in fall but can be found in any season. Greenhouse grown, they're not as hardy as garden mums. Choose plants that have more buds than open flowers and keep them in a cool room and direct light for longest enjoyment (four to six weeks).

CYCLAMEN (*Cyclamen persicum*) With its heart-shape leaves and butterflylike blooms, cyclamen grows easily in a cool room with the bright light of a south- or west-facing window. The plant will bloom for several months. Water consistently to keep the soil damp. After a summer rest, the plant may rebloom.

HOLIDAY CACTUS (*Schlumbergera* hybrids) These popular flowering plants grow easily indoors year-round and are worth keeping from year to year as they grow larger. Cultivars are available for an annual bloom time around Thanksgiving, Christmas, or Easter. The season prior to your plant's annual bloom (late summer for a Thanksgiving bloomer; autumn for a Christmas bloomer), cut back on watering and light to prompt budding.

Winter into spring

In the midst of winter, lively gift plants bring hints of spring indoors along with welcome color and cheer. Although most of these plants are intended as temporary residents, it is possible to keep them growing long after the holidays have passed.

Long-term strategies

Some plants can take up extended residence in a well-lit spot: The Norfolk Island pine that served as a tabletop Christmas tree makes an easy transition to a long-lived houseplant. Some gardeners are happy to accept a small flowering shrub (azalea, mini rose, or hydrangea) but cannot bear to consign it to compost when the flowers fade. Others are content to keep the plant alive as long as possible and leave it at that.

A gift plant's long-term potential depends on the variety of plant, how and where it has grown, and the climate where you live. Because of these variables, even when you give a plant the best care possible, it may live only for a season or two.

Some gift plants, such as holiday cactus and amaryllis, need a rest period after blooming. Every plant has preferences for conditions and individual care that will enable the plant to live on and bloom again. Research a plant's needs before you decide how much you are willing to fuss with it.

Florist azaleas put on a spectacular display in late winter to spring, but are difficult to force into bloom again indoors. The shrubs may live outdoors in a mild climate.

AZALEA (*Rhododendron* selections) In a cool room with bright, indirect light, the gorgeous blooms of a potted azalea may last for months. Keep the plant going from season to season by moving it outdoors in spring and fertilizing it regularly during the growing season. Bring the plant back indoors in fall and give it another chance to bloom.

NORFOLK ISLAND PINE (*Araucaria heterophylla*) This long-lasting tropical conifer—not a true pine—likes medium light and damp soil. Kept indoors, it typically grows slowly; moved outdoors for the summer, the tree's growth is stimulated. Growers often plant several seedlings in a pot, although over time one or two of the plants will dominate the grouping.

KALANCHOE (*Kalanchoe blossfeldiana*) These succulents are grown for their clusters of brightly colored flowers that last for weeks. Place the plant in bright light and allow the soil to dry between waterings. Snip off the spent flowers. This plant with thick, waxy dark green leaves will live outdoors in frost-free areas.

MINIATURE ROSE (*Rosa* hybrids) The diminutive plants add their charm and color to a tabletop display. They need bright light and cool air with good circulation to stay healthy throughout the winter indoors. Roses grow best outdoors in full sun, and the plants can be transplanted into the garden in late spring. Remove yellow leaves and spent flowers.

Winter into spring

Enjoy it while it lasts. This is the easiest and least guilt-inducing strategy when adopting a gift plant. The plant may come with limited instructions, but basic care usually ensures that it will live until the blooms fade or seasons change.

Survival tips

Many gift plants come packaged in a colorful wrap. Remove the wrapping as soon as the plant arrives at home and replace it with a saucer. A wrap left on the pot can trap excess water, preventing it from draining away. This can damage the plant's roots. Camouflage the plastic nursery pot by setting it in a basket with a liner or pot saucer, or inside a handsome cachepot.

Gift plants most commonly come into homes and offices during the months when light levels are lower and heated air means drier conditions. In order to thrive at least temporarily, most gift plants need bright, indirect light and cool (60°F–65°F) temperatures. If your home or office lacks sunny windows, find the brightest spot possible for the plant and bolster its health with a grow light.

In order to live, the plant will also need water. Soaking the soil once a week will usually suffice. When the plant reaches a point of having seen better days, let it go. Toss it onto the compost pile with thanks for the memories. The plant fulfilled its purpose.

Two different types of *Euphorbia*—the ever-appealing poinsettia and the frilly newcomer, 'Diamond Frost' euphorbia—combine with fresh-cut evergreens in a wrought-iron basket to create a long-lasting holiday display.

ORNAMENTAL PEPPER (*Capsicum annuum*) Deck your halls with chile peppers and see why the once-popular Victorian tradition is being revived with the advent of new varieties. The compact plants have small, upright, edible fruits that often pack tangy heat. Some varieties show holiday-specific colors, turning from yellow to orange for Thanksgiving, or red to white for Valentine's Day.

POINSETTIA (*Euphorbia pulcherrima*) Thanks to busy plant breeders, indoor gardeners have more color options than ever, from reds to whites, pinks, and variegated beauties. The colorful leaves called bracts are not flowers. To keep a poinsettia looking great for weeks, place it in bright, indirect light and away from hot or cold drafts. Water when the soil begins to feel dry.

PRIMROSE (*Primula* spp.) Pots of primroses in vivid colors tell us that spring is just around the corner. These florist plants are not long-term houseplants, but if you select healthy-looking primroses with lots of buds and only a few open flowers, you'll get maximum blooms while the plants last. The plants fare best with bright light and damp soil in a cool room.

OXALIS (*Oxalis* spp.) Also known as shamrock plant, flowering oxalis species come in different colors—green, dark purple, orange—and leaf shapes. Plant bulbs in the fall; plants develop in six to eight weeks. Set the plant in medium to bright, indirect light through the winter. Keep the soil damp, but avoid overwatering.

Spring into summer

You will find florist hydrangeas with pink, blue, purple, or white blooms. Most will be a mophead type (large, round flower heads). Ask the supplier if the plant is cold-hardy enough to be transplanted into your garden.

Gift plants that are grown from spring

into summer can live indoors or outdoors. A plant that begins the season indoors needs some care to make a smooth transition to brighter light levels and windier conditions outdoors. Start by setting the plant outdoors in a sheltered spot for a limited time, then leave it outside a little longer each day. After a couple of weeks, it should be ready for a place in a container garden or a garden bed, as long as all threats of frost have passed. Plants kept in containers can spend the summer outdoors in a partly shaded location and then transition back indoors in late summer.

Saving gift plants
Some potted gift plants, including miniature roses and hydrangea, will fare better outdoors than they do indoors. In spring, acclimate the plant outdoors and transplant it into the garden if it is hardy in the climate where you live.

Potted bulbs and tubers, such as Easter lily and caladiums, can move into a garden to live on in regions where they are hardy. When the plant is finished blooming, leave the foliage to wither naturally. Then transplant the bulb into the garden. Dig nonhardy bulbs in fall and take them indoors. Store them in vermiculite or peat moss over winter in a cool, humid location.

CALADIUM (*Caladium* hybrids) Grown for their dramatic, paper-thin leaves, the varieties display different patterns and colors. Ordinarily, plant the tubers in late winter indoors, then move the sprouted caladiums outdoors for the summer, where they'll thrive in shade. Protect the tubers from freezing by bringing them back indoors to rest over the winter.

CALLA LILY (*Zantedeschia* hybrids) This elegant bloomer can grow indoors in bright light during fall and winter, and medium light during spring and summer. Plant the rhizomes in late fall. Keep the soil moist and feed the plant every two or three weeks. Then enjoy the long-lasting flowers.

EASTER LILY (*Lilium longiflorum*) Prolong the bloom period by starting with a budded lily and placing it in a cool, bright room. Keep the soil evenly damp. After the blooms fade, let the plant dry down naturally. Plant the bulb in a sunny part of your garden where it will likely rebloom next year.

HYDRANGEA (*Hydrangea* hybrids) Although greenhouse-grown hydrangeas are gorgeous, they have been raised for a spectacular one-time show. Keep the plant well-watered and extend its life by transplanting it into an outdoor container, protected from afternoon sun. The plant may adapt to growing in the garden in Zone 6 or warmer.

African violet

Modern African violets impress with their showy characteristics. 'Kaylih Marie' boasts variegated leaves. 'Ultra Violet Saturn' has white-and-magenta flowers.

Once thought of as a favorite houseplant of grandmothers, African violet (*Saintpaulia ionantha*) offers an ideal experience for any indoor gardener. Few plants match African violet's ability to thrive and bloom indoors for months on end. Rosettes of fuzzy foliage and velvety leaves give violets a cuddly quality that has attracted admirers since the plants were discovered in eastern Africa in the late 1800s and introduced commercially. The plants are not true violets but members of the Gesneriacae family and cousins of gloxinias.

Good growing

This diversity has sparked the popularity of African violets as collectible flowering houseplants. But violets are more than a seasonal pick-me-up. With proper care, the plants can bloom continuously and live for decades. Plenty of bright, indirect light is essential for an abundance of blooms. If natural light is too strong, the foliage can burn and grow extremely compact and brittle. If light is too weak, the new growth will be spindly and no flowers will appear. Violets need a warm room (65°F–80°F) and ample humidity. Many African violet enthusiasts attest that 12 hours of fluorescent light daily is key to more vivid color and larger blooms.

Overwatering commonly spells the end of African violets. Water from the top or bottom, but only when the soil feels dry. Use room temperature water and avoid dripping water on the leaves, which can cause spots. When using a saucer, self-watering pot, or other bottom-watering method, do not let the plant sit in water for more than 20 minutes.

Potting and other pointers

Hold off on repotting a new plant after you bring it home. Let the plant adjust to new surroundings. Repot only once or twice a year. African violet likes to be potbound, which allows the plant to put its energy into blooming. Choose a pot that's one third the diameter of the plant, whether it's a standard variety that can reach 10 to 12 inches in diameter or a miniature that grows less than 6 inches in diameter. Plastic pots work well because they help keep soil evenly moist. Use a lightweight potting mix of equal parts sphagnum moss, vermiculite, and perlite. A plastic pot lends itself to pretty display options because it can be set inside a decorative container.

A dilute dose of water-soluble fertilizer (a 15-30-15 formula at the rate of ¼ teaspoon per gallon) when watering will boost the plant's health and keep it blooming. Remove spent flowers and leaves. Remove dust or debris from the plant using a soft-bristle brush.

TEST GARDEN TIP
Cheers for *Chirita*

As an alternative to African violet, try growing its Asian cousin. Chirita (*Chirita sinensis*) is distinguished by its trumpetlike blooms, but its needs are similar to those of African violet.

Secrets to success **African violets thrive in a stable environment, especially given a warm setting with morning sun and no chilly drafts. Try these tips for making plants happy, producing more blooms, and starting new plants.**

WATER
A long-spout watering can and a pebble tray make it easier to give African violets the water and humidity they prefer.

REPOT
Use fresh, well-balanced potting mix when repotting plants. Make the mix yourself or use a commercial mix formulated for African violets.

PROPAGATE
It's a snap to start new plants from leaf cuttings. Start with a healthy leaf cut at the base of a stem. Keep cuttings warm and damp.

Begonia

Iron cross begonia has distinctive
puckering and a dark cross-shape
pattern on its apple-green leaves.
It prefers to grow indoors and can
be finicky about its care.

Diverse begonias bring their tropical flair to any setting,

whether grown for their distinctive flowers, showy foliage, or both. Their growth habits range from tall and upright to bushy, creeping, climbing, tuberous, or trailing. Most of the plants can grow and bloom year-round in a conducive climate, although others must have a period of rest or dormancy during the winter; some bloom intermittently. None tolerates cold.

Meet the begonias

Explore this plant family by starting with a type of begonia that appeals to you. Begonias are differentiated into three main groups. Rhizomatous begonias have creeping stems that root as they grow, and include rex begonia (*B. rex-cultorum* hybrids) and iron cross begonia (*B. masoniana*). Another group, which grows from a fleshy, bulblike stem base or tuber, includes tuberous and semituberous begonias. The fibrous-rooted group includes the hardiest cane-stemmed begonias (*B.* selections), shrublike begonias (*B.* selections), and wax begonias (*B.* × *semperflorens-cultorum*).

Growing begonias indoors

It's easy to find a begonia for a warm (65°F–70°F) room with bright, indirect light—usually in an east or west window. Varieties with red leaves do better in higher light levels. Plants stretching toward a window need more light; plants with scorched leaves should be moved into less direct light. Begonias in terrariums can adapt to a north window; others fare well under fluorescent lighting 14 hours a day.

Repot a begonia when its roots fill the pot. Use a peat-based potting mix. Let the surface of the soil mix dry between waterings. Set the pot on a pebble-filled saucer to help prevent the plant's roots from sitting in water and rotting. Water plants less often during the winter. From spring through fall, feed plants weekly when watering, using a quarter-strength fertilizer.

Start new plants from pieces of rhizome, leaf, or stem cuttings. Pinch stem tips during the growing season to promote bushier growth, but avoid removing flower buds. Allow potted tubers to rest over winter, storing them indoors in a cool, dark place and watering only occasionally.

TEST GARDEN TIP
Planting tubers

Collecting and growing all kinds of begonias is fun, but plants can be pricey. Save by planting rhizomes of rex begonias and other tuberous types. Plant either rhizomes or tubers in a damp soilless mix with the top at soil level.

Begoniaceae family **As representatives of the huge begonia family, which includes more than a thousand species, these are among the most common:**

TUBEROUS
Start the tubers indoors, but grow the plants of *B.* × *tuberhybrida* outdoors and enjoy spectacular flowers in a variety of shapes and colors (such as 'Nonstop Mocha Yellow').

ANGEL WING
The leaf shape gives angel wing begonia (*B. coccinea*) its name. With dangling flower clusters, varieties such as 'Lana' (shown) can grow to 4 feet and become shrubby.

REX
Fancy-leaf begonias (*B. rex cultorum* hybrids) such as 'Houston Fiesta' are grown for their colorful and patterned markings. They like high humidity.

RIEGER
A type of elatior begonia, rieger begonia (*B.* × *hiemalis*) grows low and bushy with green or bronze leaves and brightly colored camellialike flowers.

CANE-STEMMED
Tough, easy-to-grow plants include 'Dragon Wing'. It blooms intermittently throughout the year, given enough bright light.

Bromeliad

This trio of tillandsias includes (clockwise from left) *T. tricolor melanocrater*, *T. stricta*, and *T. caput-medusae*. Display them in a glass or shell, or on a chandelier.

Among the most architectural of houseplants,

bromeliads make dramatic statements with their exotic, sculptural forms and spiky textures. Some have colorful bracts or specialized leaves that resemble flowers. Bromeliads bloom, usually when the plant is three to five years old, and then decline slowly. But before it dies, the plant produces offsets or pups—the next generation of plants. When buying a plant, choose one that has yet to bloom.

Unusual lifestyles

Bromeliads' adaptability, resilience, and comparatively easy care have bolstered their popularity in modern homes and offices. You can move the plants outdoors over the summer. They'll appreciate the fresh air and humidity, but need some shelter from sun.

Bromeliads prefer small, shallow pots. They can become top-heavy and topple easily, so set a small pot inside a larger one to prevent this. A bromeliad planted in a too-large pot can rot easily.

In the rainforests of South America, high deserts of Mexico, and their other native lands, bromeliads grow on trees and rocks, as well as other plants, and in the ground. The plants are not parasitic, regardless where they grow. You will find these plants in three groups:

Terrestrial bromeliads have roots, which enable them to grow in soil. This group includes the best-known bromeliad, pineapple (*Ananas*), as well as earth star (*Cryptanthus*), and dyckia. These plants are not efficient at absorbing water and nutrients by way of their leaves. Plant them in an appropriate potting mix and water as needed. The plants' light needs vary.

Tank bromeliads are mostly epiphytic, living on tree branches and trunks in the wild, gathering moisture from rainfall and dew, and nutrients from particles in the air and falling debris. Plants in this group collect and store nourishment in a cup-shape rosette of leaves called a "tank." Grown on bark slabs or driftwood, tank bromeliads develop enough roots to anchor the plant for support but the roots absorb little water. Those grown in pots develop a more extensive root system that does absorb water. Refill the tanks of these bromeliads regularly with fresh water and moisten their potting mix when it feels dry. Provide high humidity to mimic their native conditions. This group includes silver vase plant (*Aechmea fasciata*), guzmania, and blushing bromeliad (*Neoregelia carolinae*). Some tank bromeliads need bright light; others prefer medium light.

Epiphytic bromeliads, or air plants, are often natives to climates where intense evaporation and scarce water challenged their evolution. Some developed scale-covered leaves that absorb moisture; other have cup or vase shapes that hold water. A quick plunge into warm water twice a week keeps air plants hydrated, and a mist of fertilizer solution once a month provides nutrients. *Tillandsia* is the largest and most varied group of epiphytes. They do not grow well in soil or potting mix. Tillandsias need bright, indirect light.

TEST GARDEN TIP

Prompting blooms

Easy-to-grow silver vase plant needs bright light to produce flowers. You can help stimulate flowering by placing the plant in a large, clear plastic bag with an apple for a couple of weeks.

Growing bromeliads
Half the fun of growing bromeliads is figuring out imaginative ways to display them. Just remember, your bromeliads will need sufficient light, moisture, and air circulation in order to thrive.

TILLANDSIA
Tack air plants onto a wire wreath form using dabs of hot glue. Take the wreath down for a twice weekly bath in the sink.

SILVER VASE PLANT
A tank bromeliad prefers to be filled with rainwater or distilled water. Hard water can stain the leaves.

EARTH STAR
Grow this terrestrial bromeliad in a pot or dish garden for its rosette of colorful, wavy leaves.

Cactus

A wooden frame holds a collection of small desert cacti. A large screw, inserted through the wood, protrudes and reaches into the drainage hole of each pot, holding the pot in place.

Cacti are any busy gardener's dream plants.

They thrive in the warm, dry air of many homes and offices. There's no big secret to success with cacti. Their basic requirements are simple: lots of sun, sandy soil, and occasional soakings. It's often said that cacti thrive on neglect.

Desert cacti

Most members of the cactus family are succulents, but not all succulents are cacti. Although cacti and succulents have similar cultural needs, please read more about succulents on page 172. To simplify matters, this discussion will focus on the best-known desert cacti. These plants store water in their stems, and most have spines. There are also leafy cacti that include the holiday cactus varieties mentioned on page 145.

For the majority of desert cacti, their natural conditions consist of cool to cold (40°F-50°F) winters, warm and wet springs, and hot summers. Mimicking these conditions is key to the plants' success in home gardens. Smaller desert cacti tend to bloom well indoors as long as they have a distinct dormant period with little or no water and cool or cold conditions. Larger desert cacti will usually bloom only when mature (20 years old or more), but they are prized for their statuesque and spiky forms.

A collection of cacti will help you appreciate their diversity, and there are thousands of species from which to choose. You'll find an array of desert cacti, from squat and round to thin and trailing to flat and candelabra-shape. Some varietes are widely available. Slow-growing barrel cactus (*Echinocactus grusonii*) is round with prominent ribs and works well in a dish garden or an individual pot. Rattail cactus (*Aporocactus flagelliformis*) has long (up to 6 feet) stems covered with delicate spines and is best displayed in a hanging basket. Bunny ears or prickly pear (*Opuntia microdasys*) has broad, flat pads covered with bristly tufts; it stands out in grouped containers.

Caring for cacti

Plant cacti in a porous, freely draining mix of sand, perlite, and potting soil. The ideal container is a clay pot, slightly larger than the plant. It must have a drainage hole.

Indoors, cacti like as much sun as possible. Grow them in high light—a south-facing window is best; an unobstructed western exposure is second choice. Give cacti a summer vacation outdoors, setting them in a spot where they'll get some shade.

Water cacti thoroughly but infrequently. Overwatering will rot the roots, so let the soil dry between waterings. In the winter, when plants are resting, let an extra week go by between waterings and water just enough to keep the plants from shriveling. Use an all-purpose, water-soluble fertilizer every second or third watering during the growing season.

TEST GARDEN TIP

Grouping cacti

A dish garden provides a pleasing way to display a small collection of desert cacti. It includes plants of varying forms, from low and wide to tall and slender. Spread gravel mulch for a neat, natural effect.

Handling cacti

Although cacti are easy to maintain, they merit special handling. Use these tips to avoid a painful poke from the sharp spines that cover most cacti.

Display cacti where they won't easily make contact with skin or eyes, and keep them away from kids and pets who may not be aware of the need to avoid their spines.

Repotting is necessary every few years when a plant pushes out of the pot or the stems reach the edges of the pot. When transplanting cacti, wear heavy gloves and wrap a folded sheet of newspaper around a small cactus; a length of thick fabric around a large one.

If cactus spines stick in your skin, press very sticky tape on the area and then pull it off to remove them.

Coleus

Showy coleus standards (tree forms) happily overwinter indoors given plenty of light. Most varieties of coleus respond well to training as a standard.

As one of the most colorful indoor plants,

coleus has had several waves of popularity. When it debuted in Europe as a cultivated plant two centuries ago, the native of Java flaunted its colorful foliage and easy-growing nature. Victorians treasured coleus as a showy bedding plant that overwintered readily as a houseplant grown from cuttings.

The next coleus wave crested in the 1970s when the seed-grown varieties that had changed little since Victorian times moved indoors again as ubiquitous houseplants. These old-school varieties required frequent pinching to remove the negligible flower stalks and keep the plants growing dense and compact. The ease of coleus propagation from cuttings that originally boosted their popularity, as well as desirable qualities garnered from rediscovered heirlooms, has prompted a recent breeding heyday. Because of the ease of perpetuating coleus and its quick growth, coleus has been known as the rabbit of the indoor gardening realm.

Coleus culture

As part of its modern makeover, coleus has been reclassified botanically as *Solenostemon scutellarioides*. The range of plants varies in leaf colors, patterns, sizes, and shapes. Newer varieties bask in bright light or the less sunny conditions preferred by older coleus selections. Many varieties display their richest colors when grown in bright enough light; colors fade in less-than-ideal light. If your coleus starts becoming spindly or bending toward light, move the plant to a spot where it will get more sun. Pinching off the growing tips, especially when flowers start forming, helps keep a plant bushier.

Coleus do best in temperatures between 60°F and 68°F indoors, with ample humidity. If the air is too dry, you may notice leaves shriveling and falling. Water regularly, when the soil surface begins to feel dry, and prevent the plants from wilting.

Keep coleus going

As a tropical plant, coleus thrives in long, hot summers—better than many gardeners. When moving plants outdoors for the summer, place them in a partly shaded spot and water generously. The plants grow quickly in these conducive conditions and they'll need repotting. Protect them from cold. Take cuttings or prune plants to half their size before taking them indoors in late summer.

To start new plants, snip 4- to 6-inch stem cuttings in late summer. Root the cuttings in a glass of water or in cell packs filled with soilless medium. After roots develop, transplant the young coleus plants into small pots of potting soil, and keep them growing on a sunny windowsill until late spring.

TEST GARDEN TIP

Coleus varieties

All sorts of coleus varieties including 'Freckles', provide attractive plant material for indoor gardens, whether you train them into a standard form or not. Some reach 4 to 5 feet tall, others grow 2 to 3 feet.

Train a coleus standard

With regular pinching, coleus grows dense with increased branching, and plants can be trained into an impressive standard or lollipop-shape tree within a year or so. Start with a strong, single-stem plant; choose a variety that would ordinarily reach about 3 feet. Transplant into a weighty 6- or 8-inch pot to help prevent the plant from becoming top-heavy. Stake the plant to reinforce the main stem. Snip off any side stems from the bottom two thirds of the main stem, leaving the top third to grow bushier. Pinch off the tips of the remaining stems monthly to encourage branching.

Fern

The arching fronds of ferns

bring their simple beauty to indoor settings. Grown in a pot or urn, smaller ferns add elegance to a dinner table. A large fern in a hanging basket creates a lush, tropical effect. Some species, such as staghorn and tree ferns, form sculptural accents—they truly are living works of natural art.

Helping ferns thrive

The lineage of these primitive plants reaches back more than 300 million years. Earth was wetter then than it is now, but many of the ferns we grow today have changed little from their ancient ancestors. The natural habitats of the thousands of fern species vary widely. Delicate feathery ferns (maidenhair, rabbit's foot) favor continually warm and humid tropical conditions; the more leathery-leaf varieties (brake, Japanese holly, bird's nest) tolerate cooler, less humid environments.

Humidity is essential to a fern's well-being. Some varieties need high (60 percent or greater) relative humidity that is difficult to provide in a heated home during winter. Raise the humidity around your plants by setting pots on pebble-filled saucers or trays, or double-pot the ferns, placing the potted fern inside a larger container and filling the space between with pea gravel or sphagnum moss.

When watering ferns, do not let them stand in excess water. Most varieties prefer moist soil. The plants will drop their leaflets if watered too much or too little. Mulching plants with leaf mold, chopped leaves, or chipped bark preserves soil moisture and adds nutrients to soil. Ferns need only half-strength fertilizer every other week during the growing season.

Differing needs

Light requirements vary too, from medium to bright, indirect light, but no ferns prefer full sun. If a plant grows weakly, move it into brighter light. The light from a north or east window typically sustains a fern. Most of the plants benefit from being moved to a shady spot on the patio for the summer, but don't be surprised if they drop leaflets when you move them back indoors. Although ferns generally prefer indoor temperatures between 60°F and 70°F, they'll be less stressed by cooler temperatures than they will be affected by heat—especially dry heat. These plants can also be sensitive to pesticides, tobacco smoke, and leaf-shine products.

Opposite: **The delicate or leathery foliage of ferns makes them popular houseplants, and their diversity provides many plants to know and love. Varieties combine well in containers with other plants that also like moist conditions.**

Ferns for indoor gardens

When choosing a fern for indoors, see what appeals to you at the garden center, but match the plant's needs to the environment in your home.

BOSTON FERN
Tolerant of indoor conditions, *Nephrolepis exaltata* develops a large mass of long, arching fronds.

CROCODILE FERN
An easy-growing fern, *Microsorum musifolium* 'Crocodyllus' has an interesting texture.

RABBIT'S FOOT FERN
Known for its furry rhizomes, *Phlebodium aureum* requires consistent moisture.

MAIDENHAIR FERN
Adiantum pedatum demands humid conditions such as those found in a bathroom.

BIRD'S NEST FERN
Asplenium nidus needs evenly moist soil and high humidity.

LEMON BUTTON FERN
A small fern with a lemon scent, *Nephrolepis cordifolia* grows easily in a terrarium.

STAGHORN FERN
Grow *Platycerium bifurcatum* on a bark slab in a humid setting.

BRAKE FERN
Also known as table fern, pteris has different frond styles, some variegated.

ASPARAGUS FERN
High humidity is needed by *Asparagus densiflorus*, a member of the lily family.

JAPANESE HOLLY FERN
Slow-growing *Cyrtomium falcatum* tolerates dry, cold air. Try it in an entryway.

Ivy

Ivy arrived in America in the form of cuttings that colonists carried with them across the ocean. The plant has proved itself adaptable by thriving in various conditions, outdoors and indoors.

Ivy grows so easily indoors, some people think of it only as a houseplant. It is among the most popular houseplants, with its evergreen foliage on wiry, trailing tendrils. Indoors, ivy is most often displayed in a hanging basket. The plants also can be trained to climb a topiary form, trellis, moss pole, or window frame. Ivy even scrambles up a rough surface such as a brick wall because it has aboveground (aerial) roots that help it cling.

Make an elegant and festive centerpiece in minutes starting with English ivy and a classic urn. Garden centers often have hanging baskets of ivy with long, trailing stems.

Types of ivy

Hedera is a small genus with only about a dozen species. The two species commonly grown indoors—*H. helix* (English ivy) and *H. canariensis* (Algerian ivy)—originated in Europe and North Africa, respectively. English ivy is more common as a houseplant. It is available in hundreds of varieties with differing shapes and leaf colors.

Collectors describe ivy leaves by their shape: heart, fan, bird's foot, and curly. The basic ivy leaf has three to five lobes in a pleasing hue of glossy green. Leaves range from the largest Algerian ivies to miniature English ivies, including 'Duckfoot', 'Pixie', and 'Lilliput'. Older cultivars produce long stems with widely spaced leaves. Pinching the tips of English ivy encourages branching and a fuller appearance. Many modern cultivars are self-branching and grow more densely on their own.

Green is never monotonous when you invest in ivy. Foliage hues range from yellow-green to eerie blackish green. Some ivies show off a silvery, yellowish, or reddish sheen or contrasting veins; others an array of marbled green, gray, gold, and ivory.

Indoor ivy care

Ivies need medium to bright, indirect light and will become spindly in poor light. The plants do best in cool temperatures (60°F–65°F) and like cooler (to 50°F) conditions during the winter. Water regularly, allowing the top inch of soil to dry between waterings. Ivy loves a warm shower or bath, especially when dusty, and gleams afterward. When plants take a winter rest, water sparingly but avoid letting the soil dry out completely. During the growing season, feed plants monthly with a high-nitrogen fertilizer. Multiply your ivy collection by taking 4-inch cuttings from the branch tips and rooting them in a soilless medium. Beware: Susceptible individuals can develop a skin rash from handling English ivy.

ASK THE GARDEN DOCTOR

Why are the leaves of my ivy turning yellow and falling off?

ANSWER: Overwatering is most often the culprit, especially during the winter. Lighten up on the watering regimen, allowing the top inch of soil to dry between waterings. Watch for tiny webs and reddish spider mites. Rinse them off with a forceful spray of water, or use insecticidal soap to kill them.

Make an ivy topiary

If you love the appearance of topiary but don't have the time or patience for the repeated trimming required by herbs and dwarf evergreens, train an ivy to climb and fill a frame instead.

1 START
Gather materials, including a 10- to 12-inch pot, a 10×24-inch spiral topiary frame, four or five small ivy plants, cloth-covered florist wire, moss, and potting mix. A hefty pot works best to anchor a top-heavy design such as this.

2 SET UP
Press the legs of the topiary frame into the pot full of potting mix. Secure the frame with an added stake.

3 TRANSPLANT
Select plants with long trailers to get a finished effect more quickly. Space the plants evenly, giving them room to grow.

4 TRAIN
Start twining the longest trailers on the topiary form, using short twists of cloth-covered wire to hold the ivy in place. As the plant grows, continue training it to the spiral form.

5 FINISH
Water the topiary after planting, and thereafter whenever the soil feels dry. Covering the soil surface with decorative moss helps maintain soil moisture.

Jasmine

Little boosts spirits more than fragrant flowers blooming indoors, especially during the winter months. Jasmine (*Jasminum*) is a favorite aromatic flower. Its scent is smooth, sensuous, and intoxicating, whether the plant is just coming into bud or blossom, or is fully flowering and showering the floor with small, starry-white flowers. When jasmine is placed on a sunny windowsill, the sun's warmth intensifies the perfume, which is neither assertive like a hyacinth nor strident like a paperwhite narcissus.

Choose a jasmine

Not all species of jasmine smell the same; some have no fragrance. They are shrubs or climbing plants that grow well indoors, often blooming in winter, and are even happier when moved outdoors for the summer. Vining and twining jasmines require staking and regular pinching to enhance their growth and form. Even the shrubby varieties have long branches that lean on nearby plants for support.

For vigorous growth and ease of culture, grow J. *polyanthum*, winter or Chinese jasmine. It needs a sunny, cool (40°F–60°F) place indoors throughout fall and into winter for optimum growth and budding. Arabian jasmine (*J. sambac*), such as the leathery-leaved 'Maid of Orleans' and double-flowering 'Belle of India', is shrubbier than most and blooms heavily in summer. Poet's jasmine (*J. grandiflorum*) blooms from spring through fall in temperate regions; it provides an everblooming vine in the South. Other jasmine varieties will pique the fancy of collectors. No matter how many plants you have, make the most of jasmine flowers: Toss a handful into a warm bath or float a single blossom in a cup of tea, and inhale the fragrance.

What jasmines need

The plants need bright light for abundant flowering. When summering your jasmine outdoors, set it in half-day sun. Weekly watering gives jasmine the moisture it needs without overwatering. Use a half-strength fertilizer monthly throughout the summer. A cool room is key to keeping the plant healthy indoors in winter. Vining plants can reach 6 feet and need annual spring pruning after flowering. Shrubby plants benefit from regular pruning too. Snip the brown or broken stems as well as overly lengthy ones to keep a plant bushy and dense. Prune shrubby plants after flowering, being careful not to remove flower buds. Propagate your jasmine by taking stem tip cuttings in early summer.

Opposite: **Winter jasmine dazzles with its marvelously fragrant flowers and vines on a trellis or other support. It is a member of the olive family (Oleaceae), which includes about 200 species.**

Other fragrant flowering vines
Vining plants cascading from a hanging basket or clinging to a trellis deliver a soothing sweep of greenery. The fragrance of some flowering vines provides another dimension of beauty as well.

PASSIONFLOWER
Passiflora spp. is another proven indoor performer with fragrant flowers. The vigorous vine will bloom all year given enough light in a south- or west-facing window or under grow-lights.

MADAGASCAR JASMINE
Stephanotis floribunda makes a fine indoor plant with extraordinarily fragrant flowers in summer. The climbing shrubby vine needs a sturdy support.

WAX PLANT
Hoya spp. are easy-growing vines with beautiful clusters of fragrant star-shape flowers. The older the plant, the more spectacular the blooms.

Orchid

Grouping orchids on a pebble tray creates a pocket of humid air around them. This group features good options for novice gardeners: cattleya, nun's orchid (*Phaius*), slipper orchid (*Paphiopedilum*), and moth orchid (*Phalaenopsis*).

Do you think you need a greenhouse or other special conditions to pamper these plants with a prima donna reputation? Definitely not. Bring home an orchid and see how undemanding it can be. If you select one of the easy-to-grow orchid varieties, you'll find they require less care than some common houseplants and will succeed in the environment most home settings provide. Situated near a sunny window, an orchid will surely prove alluring and enjoyable.

Today's orchids

Modern propagation techniques have significantly increased the availability of orchids and lowered the cost of many cultivars. As one of the largest and most sophisticated plant families in the world, orchids astound with their tongue-twisting names. But undemanding *Phalaenopsis* and *Paphiopedilum*—moth and slipper orchids—are among those widely sold at florists, nurseries, grocery stores, and home centers.

When buying an orchid, choose one with grassy green leaves and stems with buds and flowers just starting to open. That way, you can witness the blooming process, which will last a month or longer. With proper care, orchids will grow and rebloom, rewarding you with their breathtaking beauty.

Growing orchids indoors

Most orchids grown as houseplants are epiphytes, which are plants that grow naturally on tree branches and have thick aerial roots. Planting an orchid in a pot with lots of side holes and a light, aerated potting medium allows the roots to absorb plenty of air, which is essential to the plant's survival. Chopped bark, available commercially, is the standard potting medium because it is difficult to overwater. Most orchids' roots will suffocate in soil or soilless potting mix. Sphagnum moss works as a potting medium but proves tricky.

As an extremely varied group of plants, orchids' other cultural needs differ considerably. They require medium to bright light. Generally, the larger an orchid's leaves, the less light it needs. But if your orchid does not flower, chances are the light level is too low. Average indoor temperatures of 65°F–85°F suit *Phalaenopsis*, *Dendrobium*, and *Oncidium*. Many orchids need a temperature change of 10 to 20 degrees between night and day for several weeks to prompt flowering. Keep plants on the windowsill in a cool room and turn down the thermostat at night to help promote flowering.

Orchids' water needs also vary. But overwatering is the most common way to kill them. Weekly watering works for many commonly grown orchids. But your watering schedule will depend on the conditions of your home and the type of pot—water evaporates faster in a dry climate, in a sunny location, and in a clay pot.

TEST GARDEN TIP

Decorate with orchids

Orchids make delightful and unexpected holiday decorations. 'Yu Pin Lady' and 'Dong Beauty Queen' *Phalaenopsis* orchids team up in a 6-inch pot staged in a cast-iron tree stand.

Tips for orchid success
Each type of orchid has differing needs. Many orchids come with care instructions, but you can find detailed advice for various types at the American Orchid Society's Website: *aos.org.*

WATER
Take the pot to a sink and run warm water through the bark medium for a couple of minutes. Let the pot drain, then return it to its usual place. If an orchid is left standing in water, the roots will rot.

REPOT
Every year or two, transfer your orchid to a slightly larger pot when its roots outgrow the old one. Replace the potting medium with fresh bark. Covering the bark with a bit of green moss helps hold moisture.

REFRESH
When repotting an orchid, snip off roots that are dead, shriveled, or broken. Feed moth orchids year-round; other orchids every other week from spring through fall, using a half-strength formula.

HUMIDIFY
Although some orchids can survive low indoor humidity, setting pots on a bed of wet pebbles boosts the air's moisture content. Plants also benefit from grouping, which humidifies the air around them.

Scented geranium

Herb gardeners and collectors have long favored
charming plants that invite interaction. The textured leaves—fuzzy, velvety, or crinkly—release delicious fragrances of spices, flowers, and fruits when jostled. Their names reflect the varieties' scents, ranging from lemon to apple, mint, rose, cinnamon, chocolate, and more. These are the scratch-and-sniff plants of the gardening realm. What's more, they're good enough to eat.

Distinctive geraniums
The genus *Pelargonium* includes the flowery darlings grown widely as annuals. Many of these have fancy leaves too and some, such as varieties known as zonals and regals or Martha Washingtons, grow well indoors. Their scented-leaf cousins grow happily in a sunny garden, but are tender perennials that must be potted up and moved indoors over the winter for protection from freezing temperatures.

Scented geraniums, such as lacy-leaf variegated mint rose and upright lavender varieties, exhibit diverse characteristics. These plants that invite touching are fun to have around, although their distinctive scents may be left to the nose of their beholder.

You can grow scented geraniums easily in pots year-round in bright light. Although some varieties have pretty little flowers, the leaves are the plants' most notable feature. The dozens of scented geraniums come in a range of leaf shapes and hues, from ruffled to serrated, gray-green to white-variegated. The leaf sizes vary too. Small-leaf varieties such as lemon 'Crispum' work especially well for topiaries.

Indoor gardening advice

Grow scented geraniums in a south- or west-facing window that offers bright light. If you give lower light for the plants to overwinter in a semidormant mode, provide cooler temperatures between 50°F and 60°F.

Pinch or snip stem tips regularly to keep the plants growing strong and bushy. You can generate new geraniums easily from 4-inch-long stem cuttings. Fall is a good time to take cuttings. Overwinter them on a sunny windowsill and you'll have substantial new plants ready to move into larger pots in late spring. Let them grow outdoors for the summer, if you like. They'll likely need repotting and cutting back by a third by the time fall arrives.

Water scented geraniums thoroughly, then let the soil begin to dry before watering again. Soil that is too wet causes root rot. Keep plants healthy by watering with a half-strength all-purpose fertilizer solution throughout the summer. Lay off feeding during the winter.

Using scented geraniums

The dried leaves add distinctive scents to potpourris and sachets. The citrus, spice, and rose fragrances blend especially well with rose petals and lavender flowers.

Cut fresh stems and tuck them into bouquets—they'll provide long-lasting scent. Enjoy the leaves' refreshing flavors by using them in iced tea and baked goods.

Scented geranium varieties
Scented geraniums are distinguished by their fragrance. The sizes of the plants and their leaves vary, as do other leaf characteristics.

CHOCOLATE MINT
P. tomentosum has a dark variegation at the center of the leaves and a minty (but chocolaty) fragrance.

ATTAR OF ROSES
A reliable rose-scented variety, *P. capitatum* may bear lavender-pink flowers if conditions are bright enough.

OLD SPICE
With its spicy fragrance and compact habit, *P. × fragrans* is a good choice for topiary.

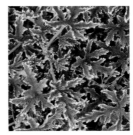

FROSTED
Only a few scented geraniums have variegated leaves. *P. citrosum* 'Frosted' has white tips.

SPANISH LAVENDER
One of the larger species, *P. cuculatum* reaches 2 to 3 feet tall and has velvety, almost-cupped leaves.

LEMON
An excellent culinary variety, *P. crispum* has small crinkled leaves with a strong lemon flavor.

COCONUT
A round-leaf variety, *P. grossularioides* has a sweet, light fragrance. It is lovely in bouquets.

PINE
With its deeply cut leaves, *P. denticulatum* has a pungent scent of pine.

PEPPERMINT
A refreshingly pungent variety, *P. tomentosum* has large velvety leaves. Its trailing habit suits hanging baskets.

CITROSA
Sold as a mosquito-repelling "citronella plant," lemon-scented geranium is unproven as an insect deterrent.

Succulent

Fleshy, water-storing leaves, stems, and roots earn these plants the catchall classification "succulents." Especially well-adapted to arid climates, succulents hail from worldwide locales, ranging from the sunny and dry to the damp and cloudy. Many succulents form simple rosettes. Some sprawl along the soil's surface, and some grow upright. Others tumble over pot edges, their leaf-studded stems cascading stiffly. Leaf colors vary widely, from chartreuse to gray-green hues, reds, and almost black. Sometimes flowers appear in spring or summer, depending on the variety, and especially when the plants are growing outside in full sun. Planted solo or in artful combinations, these jewels weave textural tapestries indoors as well as outdoors, and they look good year-round.

Succulent culture

Succulents' laid-back personalities make them generally easy to grow and a good option for gardeners of any skill level. They're naturals for containers. It's fun to choose from the array of plant varieties and then display the succulent in a complementary pot that highlights the plant's form and color. Keep the display simple and geometric, or combine plants in a texture-rich dish garden.

Many succulents' diminutive size, from 2 to 6 inches, is another reason for their popularity in indoor gardens. Small pots of them fit as readily on a windowsill as in a wall planter. Tuck their shallow roots into the pockets of a strawberry jar or into a wooden box. Clay and other porous containers make it easier to control the moisture level of the potting medium because they allow more evaporation. (Plastic, glazed ceramic, and glass containers hold moisture longer.) Repot plants every few years. Succulents prefer to be crowded in a container, so wait until the roots have no more growing room before repotting.

Excellent drainage and bright light are essential to succulents' well-being. Their roots do not like standing in water, and plants will become thin, elongated, or pale without adequate light. Add sand, pea gravel, or perlite to a potting mix for a quick-draining blend. Place succulents in the brightest light available indoors during the winter months.

The surest path to premature death of succulents is not through frosty nights on a windowsill but rather by overwatering. Water plants sparingly through the winter—just enough to keep roots alive and prevent plants from dehydrating and shriveling. In summer, water more often, especially if you move plants outdoors. Feed plants only during the growing season, using a quarter-strength solution.

Opposite: **Small, flower-shape succulents (*Echeveria*, *Sedum*, *Pachyveria* and silver squill) reach elevated heights in mercury glass vases. Bits of reindeer moss complete the decorative effect.**

Succulent planting ideas
Many succulents are stiff and bulky; others are looser and flexible. Whatever their form, the plants have a sculptural presence and provide textural materials for decorative displays.

AEONIUM
Tall containers hold top-heavy 'Sunburst' aeonium, burro's-tail (*Sedum morganianum*), and echeveria.

AGAVE
Stone mulch and a neutral-color pot help showcase an agave or other subtle-hued succulent.

ALOE
In a sunny kitchen window, *Aloe vera* is pretty and practical. Gel inside the leaves provides first aid for burns.

BURRO'S-TAIL
A vintage beverage bottle crate becomes a vertical garden planted with burro's-tail and ghost plant (*Graptopetalum*).

JADE PLANT
For interesting results, put a vintage treasure to work when displaying a jade plant (*Crassula ovata*).

SEDUM
Creeping and low-growing sedums create artistic mosaics in hanging wall planters.

ECHEVERIA
Wrap the root balls of echeveria with sphagnum moss before wiring them to an evergreen wreath with a heavy-duty wire base.

SEMPERVIVUM
When planting a repurposed container, improve drainage by poking a hole in the bottom of each planting pocket.

STRING OF PEARLS
Senecio rowleyanus provides the jewelry for a mixed planting of variegated aeonium and sticks on fire (*Euphorbia tirucalli*).

KALANCHOE
This panda plant (*Kalanchoe tomentosa*) lives in a copper pot. Embellishments include princess pine, variegated boxwood, and eucalyptus.

houseplant encyclopedia

The possibilities for indoor gardens are better than ever, from the traditional plants to the newest varieties. Start here to find the options best suited to your home.

IDEAL CONDITIONS

Knowing how much light, humidity, and heat each plant needs will help you match plants with settings and ensure success.

GARDENING ADVICE

Take the guesswork out of watering, fertilizing, repotting, and propagating. Your plants will thrive as you cultivate confidence.

PREVENTIVE CARE

Many plants have special needs or idiosyncracies. Get the inside scoop and minimize surprises as well as potential problems.

Alocasia
(*Alocasia* hybrids)

The striking foliage of this tropical inspired its other common name, elephant's ears. Only a few of the dozens of species and hybrids are sold as houseplants. The green, blackish-green, or silver-green foliage usually has contrasting veins and lobed or wavy margins. The plants reach 2 to 6 feet tall.

YOU SHOULD KNOW
Some alocasia varieties with enormous leaves are especially popular in outdoor container gardens. The tubers must be stored in a cool, dry, frost-free location over winter.

Best site

This showy houseplant does best with bright to medium light in winter; indirect, medium light in summer—never direct sun. Alocasia depends on warm (65°F–70°F) temperatures and high humidity. A pebble tray is effective in raising humidity around a plant. Avoid exposing the plant to temperatures below 50°F, cold drafts, and extreme temperature changes. The plant benefits from living outdoors in a mostly shaded spot during the summer, especially if the area where you live is warm and humid.

Growing

Use a well-draining, moisture-control potting mix. A 2-inch layer of bark mulch helps keep the potting mix evenly moist. Water as needed to maintain soil moisture, but avoid creating soggy soil. Allow the soil to become a bit drier during the winter. Alocasia is sensitive to the chemicals in municipal water, so use room-temperature rainwater whenever possible to hydrate your plant. Feed the plant monthly during the growing season, using a standard liquid fertilizer for foliage plants; do not feed in winter. Bathe the plant or wipe its satiny leaves with a damp cloth occasionally to remove dust and grime. Propagate alocasia by carefully removing side shoots with roots attached; or by lifting the plant from the pot, removing a rhizome or tuber, and cutting it into pieces for rooting. This plant is generally pest-free, but you may notice spider mites, mealybugs, or scale on a stressed plant.

Special notes

Alocasia can be temperamental about its growing conditions—if not warm and humid enough, the plant tends to drop leaves. Too much moisture causes the plant to rot. Leave the top of the rhizome or tuber exposed when repotting to help prevent rot. The plant may drop all but a couple of leaves, but if you correct the growing conditions, it will send out new growth.

varieties:

1 **'MOROCCO'** is a fast grower with pretty pink stems and glossy dark green leaves with bright greenish white veins and burgundy undersides.

2 **'POLLY'**, a dwarf cultivar, grows to 2 feet tall and has greenish-white veins.

3 **'STINGRAY'** leaves resemble a sea creature with a long, pointed tail. Plants grow 5 to 6 feet tall.

Aluminum plant
(*Pilea* spp.)

More than 600 species belong to the genus *Pilea*. Those best suited to indoor gardening are 6 to 12 inches tall with variously colored and textured foliage. They're attractive enough to stand alone, but contrasting species work beautifully in groupings. The plants also appeal because they grow so easily.

Best site

Provide this tropical plant with medium to bright, indirect light in an east- or west-facing window. Overly strong light will burn the leaves; too little light results in spindly growth. The plants prefer a warm to high temperature, 60°F to 70°F. Cold air and cold water damage the leaves. Pileas will not thrive if exposed to cold drafts, drying winds, or low humidity.

Growing

The dark green leaves of aluminum plant (*P. cadierei*) appear to be painted with streaks of silver. The leaves of other species are splashed in copper or red and may have a quilted appearance. Some grow upright and are adapted to terrarium culture; others creep or trail, making them useful in hanging baskets. Let the soil begin to dry out slightly between waterings, but not so dry that the plants wilt or become droopy.

Reduce watering during the winter. The plants have small root systems and rarely need repotting. Good drainage is essential. Fertilize plants regularly from spring to fall, then lay off the plant food through the winter. Aluminum plant and its relatives are most attractive as young plants. Pinching or trimming the stem tips periodically helps keep a plant lush and bushy. Start new plants from stem cuttings—they grow easily.

Special notes

Sometimes aluminum plant is considered short-lived. But if you pinch off the stem tips and start new plants from the cuttings, you'll be rewarded with new branching on older plants as well as vigorous young ones. When humidity is low, spider mites may develop, causing the leaf edges to brown. Mealybugs and scale may also appear. Artillery plant can become a nuisance by sending its seeds flying into the soil of nearby plants; prevent overpopulation by keeping it isolated.

varieties:

1. **ALUMINUM PLANT** (*P. cadierei*) leaves are splashed with silvery markings.
2. **'MOON VALLEY'** (*P. involucrata*) has deeply corrugated and dramatically colored leaves.
3. **'NORFOLK'** (*P. spruceana*) is distinguished by bronze-green foliage with silver bands. The oval leaves have a quilted surface.
4. **CREEPING PILEA** (*P. nummularifolia*) has bristly, corrugated leaves on a vining plant.
5. **ARTILLERY PLANT** (*P. microphylla*) has tiny leaves on a branching, bushy plant.

YOU SHOULD KNOW
Creeping pilea (*P. nummulariifolia*) is also known as creeping charlie. But this plant should not be confused with the common weed in lawns also called creeping charlie (*Glechoma hederacea*).

Aralia
(*Polyscias* spp.)

This group of about 40 species of trees and woody shrubs has varied appearances but similar needs. Most have interesting foliage and stem textures. Aralias have a reputation for being difficult to grow indoors, but the plants can be successful and rewarding if you provide the right environmental conditions.

YOU SHOULD KNOW
Like true aralias, but not related to them, false aralia (*Schefflera elegantissima*) has interesting, textural foliage and can grow to 8 feet tall.

Best site

Provide aralias with medium to bright, indirect light. Low light causes spindly growth. Aralias insist on warm temperatures (60°F–85°F) and high humidity (65 percent). Without these conditions, the plants will drop their leaves. Placing an aralia on a bed of wet pebbles helps boost humidity. Keep the plants away from cold drafts and avoid letting the temperature drop below 50°F at night.

Growing

Let the potting mix dry slightly between waterings. Water the plant less during the winter. Aralias grow somewhat slowly and don't often need repotting. But a plant will let you know when it needs a larger pot: It will no longer take up water. During the growing season, fertilize every three weeks, using an all-purpose plant food. Prune as needed to maintain an aralia's

overall size and shape. If your plant drops many of its leaves over the winter, it will start to fill in during the spring if you trim the plant a bit and set it in a place where it will receive more light.

Special notes

Aralias grow to 8 feet tall and 3 feet wide indoors. Some types can be kept smaller with regular pruning. They can even be trained into beautiful bonsai. Leaf drop and leaf-edge browning are signs of inadequate humidity. Although aralias require high humidity, they are sensitive to overwatering. At first, overwatering causes shiny dark spots on the backs of the leaves, which will then turn yellow and fall off. The plant may wilt if it is being kept too wet. Aralias are also prone to root rot from overwatering. They are not usually prone to insect invasion, but spider mites, mealybugs, and scale insects may become problems. Treat them with horticultural oil. Aralias are poisonous. Children or pets can become ill if they chew or eat aralia leaves.

varieties:

1. **MING ARALIA** (*P. fruticosa*) has feathery leaves and a textured trunk. It develops a treelike form, even at a young age. Group several in one pot to create a shrubby plant.
2. **BALFOUR ARALIA** (*P. scutellaria* 'Balfourii') is a woody plant with glossy, scalloped leaves.
3. **VARIEGATED BALFOUR ARALIA** (*P. scutellaria* 'Balfourii Variegata') offers round, deeply veined, variegated leaves. It grows to 8 feet tall.

Arrowhead plant
(Syngonium podophyllum)

Also called arrowhead vine, this tropical trailing plant grows easily indoors, whether in its own pot or in a mixed planting. As the plant matures, its leaves become more deeply lobed and some of the compact stems change to vines. The leaves may be deep green, white-variegated, or tinged metallic pink.

YOU SHOULD KNOW
Arrowhead plant is toxic if chewed or eaten. Keep it away from kids and pets.

Best site

The native region of arrowhead plant ranges from Mexico to Central America. The popularity of this plant has propelled intensive hybridizing, and now compacter forms of *Syngonium* are available. Newer varieties also boast unusual coloring (bronze or pink hues) and increased disease resistance. Arrowhead plant will thrive, remaining compact and showing off its best color, in medium to bright, indirect light. This attractive foliage plant tolerates various indoor conditions, with the exception of direct sun and very low light. Too much sunlight will burn or bleach the leaves; too little light prompts spindly, weak, and pale growth. Most humidity levels and average temperatures suffice, as long as the plant is not exposed to cold drafts. Temperatures of 60°F to 75°F are ideal.

Growing

When arrowhead plant matures and develops its vining characteristics, it can reach from 4 to 10 feet tall. A juvenile plant and one kept from vining by pruning will be about 1 foot tall. Repot your arrowhead plant each spring in fresh potting mix enriched with compost. Fertilize monthly from spring through fall. When watering, aim for even moisture—not too wet and not too dry. It won't hurt if the soil starts to dry a little between waterings. Avoid overwatering. The plant will rot in soggy soil. Propagate an arrowhead plant from cuttings of pencil-size stem ends.

Special notes

Arrowhead plant is an excellent candidate for a hanging planter or a pot placed on a pedestal. Give an older plant grown in a pot an upright support—a moss-filled pole works best—to help it climb, or snip off the vining stems to keep the plant more compact. When training a plant to a moss pole, pin the stems with stubby aerial roots to the pole and keep the moss damp. A monthly shower helps prevent spider mites. Also watch for scale and mealybugs.

varieties:

1 **'PINK ALLUSION'** is one of the decorative Allusion Series characterized by pink veining or pink-blushed leaves.

2 **'LEMON LIME'** is among dozens of newer cultivars that has vivid lime-green leaves marked by white veins that fade to a whiter leaf over time.

3 **'HOLIDAY'** stands out with its ornamental foliage distinguished by berry-pink veins.

Baby's tears
(*Soleirolia solerolii*)

A delicate, creeping plant with tiny foliage and fine stems, baby's tears grows well in a shallow pot. The 2-inch-tall groundcover spreads quickly in a terrarium. Plant it in a hanging container, where it will trail over the pot's edges, or as living mulch in the pot of a larger plant.

Best site

Baby's tears does best in bright, indirect light but it will also grow in medium light. Provide average room temperatures, from 60°F to 75°F. High humidity is essential.

Growing

Add coarse sand to the potting mix to boost drainage. Keep the potting medium evenly damp, but not soggy. Allowing the soil to dry out damages the plant's roots and causes dieback.

Special notes

Gently divide or prune the plant periodically to keep it under control. If the plant dies back due to less-than-ideal conditions, trim off the damaged portion. Baby's tears will regenerate from the remaining healthy roots.

Bloodleaf
(*Iresine herbstii*)

This ornamental plant gets its common name from the intensely colored foliage. Given adequate light, the dark purple leaves of bloodleaf have crimson veins and pink stems. Other varieties have different coloring such as lime-green leaves with yellow veining. This native of Brazil grows upright and reaches 2 feet tall.

Best site

Set the plant in bright, indirect light. Provide average warmth (60°F–75°F) and cooler (not below 55°F) conditions in winter, with average to high humidity (above 30 percent).

Growing

During the growing season, keep the soil evenly damp and fertilize monthly. In winter, cut back on watering to prevent root rot. Snip off the stem tips often to promote dense growth. Propagate by stem cuttings.

Special notes

Leaves tend to fade if the light is not bright enough. The light must be indirect or filtered, or the leaves will bleach out and the edges will brown.

YOU SHOULD KNOW Baby's tears grows happily outdoors in shade, but it is hardy only to 25°F. Bring it back indoors in late summer.

YOU SHOULD KNOW The leaves of bloodleaf fade and become dull if the light is not bright enough. An east- or west-facing window provides the bright, indirect light this plant prefers.

Cast-iron plant
(*Aspidistra elatior*)

Aptly named for its durable constitution, this plain-but-popular houseplant grows in almost any conditions. Cast-iron plant has leathery oblong leaves that reach about 2 feet tall. They're usually dark green, but you might find a variegated plant. The plant grows slowly, and it can remain in the same pot for years.

Best site

Thanks to its tough-as-nails nature, this plant will survive low light and extremes of humidity. But it responds to good care and medium to bright, indirect light by producing shiny, healthy leaves. It's a good choice for a home or office where a spot of green is needed, but natural light is limited—the plant responds well to artificial lighting. Cast-iron plant is not at all fussy about temperature or humidity, but it will be most content between 50°F and 80°F.

Growing

Allow the soil to dry somewhat between waterings. Cast-iron plant tolerates the occasional missed watering, but it won't cope well with overwatering. The plant grows from a rhizome that can rot if overly saturated. Unlike most plants, it resents being transplanted.

Because cast-iron plant grows so slowly, start with a large plant if you want its full effect. Unless you start with a large plant, wait for the plant to fill its pot before repotting. When repotting, also divide the rhizome if you want more plants. Each division should have at least three leaves attached to it. A monthly shower will rinse dust off the leaves. Snip off any yellowed leaves. Fertilize every three or four months with half-strength plant food for foliage plants. Fertilize variegated plants less often to maintain their variegation.

Special notes

The plant will rot in soggy soil. If fungal leaf spots become a problem, cut out the damaged leaves and cut back on watering. Spider mites can proliferate on the undersides of a cast-iron plant's leaves in dry situations. Mealybugs can also be problematic.

YOU SHOULD KNOW
The leaves of cast-iron plant add sleek greenery to floral arrangements. Cutting stems at their base also prompts new growth.

varieties:

1 **'MARY SIZEMORE'** is a dwarf plant that grows to 18 inches tall and has dark emerald green leaves with white spots.

2 **'ASAHI'** shows off 20-inch-long, pale green leaves. The upper third of the leaves develop an airbrushed white variegation as they mature.

Chinese evergreen
(*Aglaonema* spp.)

One of the most durable and attractive foliage plants, Chinese evergreen grows upright with nonbranching stems and leathery, spear-shape leaves. Foliage color and size differ widely by variety. This slow-growing plant can cope with low-light conditions. Newer varieties sport red- or pink-variegated foliage.

YOU SHOULD KNOW
In parts of Asia, it is considered good luck to grow a Chinese evergreen. In Thailand, the plants are called "smiles of fortune plants."

Best site

An especially pleasing green plant for poorly lit places, Chinese evergreen's silver-, white-, and yellow-variegated forms show off their best coloring when grown in medium light. This native of South Vietnam and the Philippines prefers warm temperatures (60°F–80°F) and high humidity. Protect it from cold drafts and drying winds.

Growing

Place several plants in a shallow and wide pot for a bushy appearance. Repotting is seldom needed and the plant likes to be pot-bound. Repot only when the roots have filled the pot. Allow the soil to dry slightly because the roots are prone to rotting. Shower the plant monthly with warm water to clean dusty foliage. If you grow Chinese evergreen in low light, fertilize the plant only once or twice a year, using an all-purpose plant food. A plant grown in brighter light should

be fed monthly in summer. Propagate Chinese evergreen by dividing the root ball: Cut the root ball in half and pot each division. Chinese evergreen blooms occasionally indoors, but the flowers are insignificant. Long-lasting, bright red berries follow. You can sow the seeds from the berries to propagate new plants.

Special notes

Chinese evergreen leaf edges turn brown in cold or dry air or if mineral salts build up from fertilizing or watering. An older plant may lose its lower leaves over time, exposing a short, bare woody stem. To hide this stem and revitalize the plant, cut off the bottom of the root ball and then repot the plant, covering the bare base of the stems. New roots will grow from the buried portion. Chinese evergreen sap contains oxalic acid, which can irritate the skin, mouth, tongue, and throat if chewed.

varieties:

1. **'SILVER QUEEN'** is characterized by lance-shape leaves with silver markings. This compact grower reaches 1 to 2 feet tall.
2. **'WHITE LANCE'** has especially slender leaf blades that are mostly silver with a green margin. It grows densely up to 42 inches tall.
3. **'VALENTINE'** wins hearts with its especially colorful pink-splashed, dark green foliage. This slow-growing cultivar was hybridized in Thailand.
4. **'EMERALD BAY'** is one of the easy-to-grow Bay Series. It sports silvery-gray leaves that are variegated green along the leaf perimeter.
5. **'SIAM AURORA'** is another hybrid from Thailand. It has stunning magenta stems and leaf edges contrasted with chartreuse green leaf blades.

Clivia
(Clivia miniata)

Also known as Kaffir lily, this exotic cousin of amaryllis grows from a crown with thick roots. Known for its strappy, glossy evergreen leaves, clivia has clusters of trumpet-shape flowers on stiff stalks from late winter through early summer. The plant needs a winter rest to ensure rebloom.

Best site
The bright, indirect light from an east window suits clivia. Throughout fall and into winter, clivia must rest in a cool (40°F–50°F) room to prepare for its next bloom cycle.

Growing
Plant top-heavy clivia in a pot large enough to keep it from tipping over. Crowded roots left undisturbed produce the best blooms. Let soil dry between waterings. Water just enough during the rest period to keep leaves hydrated. Fertilize monthly during spring and summer.

Special notes
Give the plant plenty of room to grow. In the landscape, clivia forms a large, spreading clump. In a container, new offsets need room to develop so choose a sizable pot for your plant. Peel off the lower leaves as they turn yellow and shrivel. Snip off spent flower stalks.

Coffee plant
(Coffea arabica)

Coffee plant is a dark green shrub that grows to 6 feet tall. Less demanding than many other exotic plants, coffee plant matures in five years or so, and may produce fragrant flowers and red berries or beans—maybe enough for a cuppa. It has potential as a long-lived and entertaining plant.

Best site
Coffee plant grows best in the bright light of a south-facing window, but prefers some shade in summer. Temperatures between 65°F and 75°F, and high humidity (65 percent or higher) are ideal. Keep the plant out of cold drafts and wind.

Growing
Water the plant generously throughout spring and summer to keep the soil evenly damp. Ease off watering slightly in fall and winter. Feed every two weeks during the growing season with half-strength fertilizer formulated for acid-loving plants.

Special notes
Pinch off the growing tips of coffee plant periodically to encourage shrubby growth. Watch out for spider mites and mealybugs. Transplant only when the plant's roots have filled the pot.

YOU SHOULD KNOW Clivia needs well-draining soil. Amend the potting mix with compost, perlite, and grit. Repot only when the plant begins pushing out of the pot.

YOU SHOULD KNOW A coffee plant may not flower and fruit indoors, but the dark, wavy foliage is reason enough to grow the evergreen shrub.

Croton
(*Codiaeum variegatum pictum*)

Croton is valued for its vivid foliage. Leathery and stiff, the leaves vary in size, shape, and variegation. The red, yellow, and green color markings vary among leaves on the same plant. Crotons grow upright and are often potted in multiples to create a bushier form.

YOU SHOULD KNOW
Croton is poisonous and should be kept away from children and pets.

Best site

Croton does best in bright light, especially during winter. Given less than bright light, the plants' leaf colors fade and lower leaves drop. Young plants can adapt to lower light and drier air. Once settled, the plants reach full height (typically 4 feet). Many crotons sold throughout North America are taken from a sunny southern state, packed in trucks, and shipped to stores where they're immediately put on sale. But mature plants can react badly if moved from their usual growing location, losing leaves en masse and even dying. If your home has an environment unlike Florida's, start with a small plant. If you buy a full-size specimen, ask for a well-acclimated plant that has been in a local greenhouse for at least two months. Croton requires temperatures above 60°F and high humidity (65 percent). Protect the plant from cold drafts. If the leaf edges turn brown, the temperature may be too low.

Growing

Keep the potting mix damp—neither soggy nor dry. If a croton's leaf tips turn brown, the potting mix is not damp enough or the humidity is too low. Fertilize croton monthly during the growing season with all-purpose plant food; stop feeding over the winter. Propagate croton from stem cuttings in early summer, removing all the leaves except the top two from the stem. Crotons can also be propagated by air layering. This plant benefits from summering outdoors.

Special notes

Showering the plant monthly keeps the leaves shiny and dust-free, and helps prevent spider mites. Watch for mealybugs and scale. Pinch off the stem ends occasionally to stimulate branching. Croton doesn't often need pruning, but you can cut it back by one third to one half to revitalize the plant, if necessary. The plant's sap stains, so be cautious when pruning.

varieties:

1. **PETRA CROTON**, otherwise known as autumn plant, hails from India, Malaysia, and some South Pacific Islands.
2. **'MAMMEY'**, or fire croton, is known for its elongate, slender, and slightly spiraled leaves.
3. **'GOLD DUST'** features golden-yellow speckles all over the lance-shape leaves and grows to 3 feet tall.
4. **'TETRA'** is a newer cultivar that boasts brilliant markings. As the young, greener leaves mature, they develop bright hues of pink and yellow.
5. **'MANGO'** sports top leaves that are bright yellow whereas the bottom leaves range from dark orange to almost black.

Dieffenbachia
(*Dieffenbachia* hybrids)

Native to Central and South America, this striking foliage plant has an architectural presence. Also called dumb cane, it grows 4 to 6 feet tall, and can be planted in a group for a shrublike effect, or singly and treelike. Ingested sap from the plant stem causes temporary speechlessness and much pain, hence its common name.

Best site

Grow dieffenbachia in medium light. Inadequate light causes the plant to lose its lower leaves. Ideal conditions include average humidity (30–65 percent) and warm temperatures from 80°F during the day to 60°F at night. Keep the plant out of cold drafts.

Growing

Plant several young dieffenbachias in one pot to disguise their canes or stems and create a shrubbier appearance. As a dieffenbachia grows, it sends up the thick canes from which the variegated leaves unfurl. It naturally drops its lower leaves as it ages. Mature plants may eventually reach ceiling height. They can be cut back to stimulate new growth and propagated by stem cutting or air layering. Cut the plant back to its base when it becomes overly leggy. Use the upper, leafy portion as a cutting and let the stump regenerate. A new plant will also develop from a leafless, 3-inch-long section of stem laid on its side and half-covered with potting mix. Wear gloves and handle cuttings with care to avoid ingesting the sap. Allow the potting mix to dry slightly before watering, but be aware that allowing the plant to wilt can cause severe leaf drop. Fertilize only monthly during the summer, using a diluted plant food. Wipe the leaves with a damp cloth every other month to remove dust. Remove faded or damaged leaves.

Special notes

Poor drainage and standing water cause root rot. If the conditions are too dry, the leaf tips turn brown. Leaves develop a washed-out appearance when the plant is exposed to excessively bright light. Spider mites, aphids, mealybugs, and scale are possible pests. This is not a good plant to have in the same household with young children or chewing pets. But it is an outstanding choice for indoor displays, starring independently or adding tropical appeal to a grouping.

ⓘ YOU SHOULD KNOW Double-potting a dieffenbachia helps prevent a top-heavy plant from tipping over. Set the plant's pot inside a larger heavy one.

varieties:

❶ **'TROPIC MARIANNE'** is a hybrid in the *D. amoena* Tropic Series. It has nearly variegated leaves that are almost entirely white.

❷ **'DELILAH'** has especially thick silvery leaves and the ability to survive in lower humidity conditions that are typical indoors.

❸ **STAR BRIGHT** is known for its narrow (half the width of most varieties), slightly arching leaves with bright creamy white markings.

❹ **'CAMILLE'** is a compact plant that grows 2 to 4 feet tall. The leaves have creamy variegation with a narrow band of green on the leaf edge.

❺ **'TROPIC SNOW'** is another hybrid in the Tropic Series. It has pale green and cream variegation on extra-large leaves with a lot of substance.

Dracaena (*Dracaena* spp.)

This large group of plants is extremely popular for its wide variety. Many dracaenas have tall, thick stems topped with tufts of narrow swordlike leaves. Some grow into large treelike plants. They may reach 10 feet or even taller and serve as imposing pieces of living artwork indoors. Other varieties grow shrubbier and have wider, arching leaves. Most dracaenas are chosen for their foliage traits, whether multicolored, striped, speckled, or banded with contrasting margins.

Best site

Medium light suits most dracaenas, but the plants are typically sturdy and adaptable. Most varieties can tolerate lower light, but their growth will be very slow, and variegated ones can lose the brightness of their coloring. Bright, indirect light in winter pleases the Madagascar dragon tree (*D. marginata*) but direct, full sun is too much for all dracaenas grown indoors. During the growing season, dracaenas grow best in average temperatures between 60°F and 80°F. In the winter, the plants adjust to cooler conditions (55°F).

Most varieties need average humidity (35–65 percent) and they benefit from the increased humidity that comes from grouping plants. Here again, Madagascar dragon tree is an exception—it can grow well in drier conditions, but extremely low humidity or too-dry potting mix can prompt the plant to shed its lower leaves. If humidity is too low, dracaena leaves commonly develop brown tips and yellow margins. The leaves may become soft and curled with brown edges if the plant is situated too close to a cold, drafty window during the winter.

Growing

In general, dracaenas grow slowly. They remain attractive for many years, and their leaves are long-lived until they lose most of the lower leaves. When that happens, start the plants over again from cuttings or air-layer them. Taller and tree-form varieties must be cut back occasionally, such as the corn plant (*D. fragrans*), which can reach 20 feet. 'Song of India', the best known pleomele (*D. reflexa*) tends to grow at odd angles and must be pruned to keep it under control. It can become tree-size (4 to 8 feet) or trimmed within bounds. Madagascar dragon tree also eventually grows too tall for indoor use and must be cut back or rerooted. Most dracaenas need repotting periodically to give the roots more growing room.

Allow the top inch of potting mix to dry before watering dracaena. Pleomele benefits from more evenly damp soil than other dracaenas. Lucky bamboo (*D. sanderiana*) is often grown in water, held up by decorative stones—clearly, it would also appreciate moist soil. Reduce watering of all varieties somewhat during the winter, but do not let the potting mix dry completely. Feed dracaenas using half-strength all-purpose fertilizer every other month during the growing season. Do not fertilize when growing the plants in low light. Excess fluoride and mineral salts buildup cause brown leaf tips, so use rainwater whenever possible.

Special notes

Spider mites can be a problem in low humidity, but a monthly shower or wiping the plant's leaves with a damp cloth will control the pests. Mealybugs and scale are less common problems. Over time, dracaenas lose their lower leaves and can become gangly. Grouping plants of different sizes helps minimize their bare stems.

canelike varieties:

1 MADAGASCAR DRAGON TREE (*D. marginata*), or red-edge dracaena, often has leaves with lengthwise stripes and bent or twisted stems.

2 'LEMON LIME' (*D. deremensis*) has striped green, gray, and white foliage with chartreuse leaf margins.

3 'ART' (*D. deremensis*) bears straplike deep green leaves with creamy yellow margins.

4 'LIMELIGHT' (*D. deremensis*) produces lime-green leaves on tall, canelike stems.

5 'MASSANGEANA' (*D. fragrans*), also called variegated corn plant, occasionally produces sweetly scented blossoms indoors, given ideal conditions.

shrubby varieties:

6 LUCKY BAMBOO (*D. sanderiana*) grows in water or soil. The stems can be trained to loop, braid, or twist.

7 'SONG OF INDIA' PLEOMELE (*D. reflexa*) has boldly variegated leaves and needs regular pruning to maintain a pleasing shape.

8 'FLORIDA BEAUTY' (*D. surculosa*), or gold dust dracaena, has wiry stems different from most dracaenas. It reaches 2 feet tall.

Fig (*Ficus* spp.)

This diverse genus of more than 800 species is native to tropical and subtropical regions worldwide. The group includes trees, shrubs, and climbing or creeping vines. Most of the stately trees, from the ever-popular rubber tree (*F. elastica*) to edible fig (*F. carica*) can be kept 3 to 8 feet tall indoors. Most shrubby varieties grow up to 4 feet tall. Vines can be trained up trellises, used as groundcover, or grown as hanging plants.

Best site

Figs are among the most useful evergreen plants for leaf interest and tropical effect. Display a plant where you will get the best effect from its presence. Light requirements vary by the variety, but most figs prefer medium light in spring and summer and bright light in fall and winter. Exceptions include the groundcover oakleaf fig (*F. montana*) and creeping fig (*F. pumila*); provide them with medium to low light. Figs are notorious for dropping their leaves if they don't receive enough light. They also react this way to sudden changes in the environment, cold drafts, and low winter temperatures, as well as too much water or fertilizer. If you're worried about your plant dropping its leaves, don't move it outside for the summer. Figs need consistent temperatures between 60°F and 80°F. Most varieties are content with average humidity (30–60 percent). High humidity is essential for vining figs.

Growing

Plant figs in compost-rich, well-draining potting mix. Small plants do best if repotted annually in a slightly larger pot. Larger plants can be kept in the same pot by changing the soil and pruning the roots. In general, figs need evenly damp soil during the growing season. Allow the soil to dry slightly between soakings during winter. Vining types require more frequent waterings. Fertilize a fig monthly throughout the growing season, using an all-purpose plant food. Most figs benefit from occasional pruning to maintain their form or keep them smaller and within bounds. In general, propagate plants by stem cuttings, providing rooting hormone powder and humidity, or by air layering. It is natural for older shrub- or tree-type figs to shed their lower leaves gradually. Cut the bare stem of a rubber plant back to its base, and propagate the leafy tip to make a new plant. If a fiddleleaf fig (*F. lyrata*) loses its lower leaves, propagate stem cuttings or air-layer the plant. Prune wayward branches and trim stem ends to shape a weeping fig (*F. benjamina*), narrowleaf fig (*F. maclellandii*), or Indian laurel fig (*F. microcarpa*). These plants can be cut back by one third each year to keep them in good form.

Special notes

Wear gloves when cutting figs—the sap irritates the skin and eyes and can cause allergies. It is also slightly toxic, so keep plants away from children and pets. Scale insects are a common problem for figs. Mealybugs and spider mites may also become problems. Avoid using leaf polishes. Instead, dust leaves with a damp cloth. When bringing home a new plant, minimize the shock of a change to lower light conditions by draping the plant with a sheet of lightweight clear plastic for a few weeks. This raises the humidity until the plant adapts to the new setting.

treelike varieties:

① **WEEPING FIG** (*F. benjamina*) varies from small tabletop-size varieties to large floor plants. 'Starlight', pictured here, has green-and-white variegated leaves and arching branches.

② **'ROBUSTA' RUBBER TREE** (*F. elastica*) has extra-large burgundy leaves up to 18 inches long.

③ **MISTLETOE FIG** (*F. deltoidea*) grows to 15 feet tall. It has spoon-shape leaves with reddish undersides and tiny fruits.

④ **'BREEZE VARIEGATED' WEEPING FIG** (*F. benjamina*) is noted for its resistance to leaf drop. This variety features small, glossy leaves edged in white.

⑤ **'AMSTEL KING'** (*F. maclellandii*) impresses with its glossy, pinkish-reddish foliage on an upright, treelike plant form.

vining varieties:

⑥ **CREEPING FIG** (*F. pumila*) is a woody, evergreen vine with 1- to 1½-inch-long, leathery leaves, perfect as a groundcover or for covering a topiary form.

⑦ **VARIEGATED CREEPING FIG** (*F. pumila* 'Variegata') has white leaf edges that contrast with the green of its foliage. Pair it with a Norfolk Island pine or grow it in a terrarium.

⑧ **VARIEGATED TRAILING FIG** (*F. radicans*) is a small, trailing vine with white-splashed 2-inch-long leaves. It needs more frequent watering than most other figs.

Flamingo flower
(*Anthurium andreanum*)

Hundreds of species and hybrids of flamingo flower include both flowering and foliage plants. They bring tropical flair to the indoors. The best-known blossoming types produce a floral spike (spadix) and a colorful, heart-shape leaflike bract (spathe).

YOU SHOULD KNOW
Blooming varieties of flamingo flower may be more widely available in local markets around Valentine's Day. They are a popular gift plant.

Best site

Flamingo flower blooms can last for months, and many species are repeat-bloomers when grown in bright light. Provide medium to bright light for flowering plants; foliage plants adapt to lower light. Hybrid flowering types have been developed for the average conditions of most homes, and they are not difficult to maintain even in low light. Average to high humidity (up to 75 percent) is necessary for most flamingo flowers to survive indoors; some varieties require very high humidity (80 percent) and will not bloom well without it. Thin-leaf varieties need high humidity; leathery-leaf ones can cope with drier air. Research a variety to determine its needs. Maintain temperatures of at least 60°F at night and 70°F during the day. Keep the plants away from cold drafts and high-traffic areas—the exotic leaves and flowers are easily damaged.

Growing

The largest group of anthuriums are epiphytes with aerial roots. They need a coarse, fast-draining medium such as bark chips. The roots can then be covered with sphagnum moss. For other types, use a mixture of half potting mix and half small bark chips to make a well-draining medium. Repot the plant every other year or when the stems crowd the pot. Fertilize in summer only, using food formulated for flowering plants. Water the potting medium thoroughly, then let it dry slightly before the next watering.

Special notes

Propagate plants by division. Give your flamingo flower an occasional shower to prevent spider mites. Prune only to remove old flowers and leaves. Excess mineral salts cause the leaf tips to brown and the stems to die back. When repotting, place the crown high in the pot to help water drain easily away from the plant and prevent root rot.

varieties:

1. **'SARA'** (*A. andreanum*) has pale salmon-pink flowers four times the size of most varieties. It was first developed for the cut-flower industry.
2. **'RED ROCKET'** (*A. andreanum*) is graced with dark red flowers and a white spadix. This blooming plant has good disease resistance.
3. **'WHITE HEART'** (*A. andreanum*) combines large flower size with disease resistance. The white spathe contrasts with a pink spadix.
4. **'KERRICH RUBY'** (*A. andreanum*) is known for its bright red spathe and spadix. Watch for this and other varieties in stores around Valentine's Day, Easter, and Mother's Day.

Flowering maple
(*Abutilon* hybrids)

This adaptable plant grows easily and vigorously, up to 3 feet per year. Different varieties have varying forms, from upright plants (shrubs or trees) that reach 4 to 5 feet, to trailing, wiry-stem ones that star in hanging baskets. Most have maplelike leaves and showy, cupped flowers in assorted colors.

Best site
Blooming occurs much of the year when light is medium to bright, but flowering is often most intense during spring and summer. The plants stretch and stop blooming in low-light situations. Set flowering maple outdoors for the summer, situated where it is shaded from midday and afternoon sun. The plants fare best in average temperatures (60°F–75°F) and no less than 50°F at night; they grow well in a cooler winter setting. Average to high humidity is ideal. Give the plants plenty of room to grow with good air circulation.

Growing
Flowering maple blooms best when somewhat pot-bound. The roots fill a pot quickly, so a plant may need repotting annually if it is ideally situated. Repot in winter or early spring to avoid disrupting the bloom cycle. Keep the potting mix evenly moist during the flowering season.

Reduce water in winter, allowing the top 2 inches of potting mix to dry between waterings. Feed flowering maple monthly from spring through summer with a plant food formulated for blooming plants.

Special notes
Propagate flowering maple from stem cuttings or seeds. The plants grow quickly from seeds and this is a good way to get the cultivar you want. Remove spent flowers and yellowed leaves regularly. If you have a shrub- or tree-type plant, cut it back to half its size in fall to ensure a bushy, full plant the following year. Otherwise, cut the stem tips back slightly in winter to shape the plant and encourage it to flower abundantly. Whiteflies and mealybugs are the most common pests to plague flowering maple. If your flowering maple doesn't bloom, set it in a place where it receives bright light for at least five hours each day.

YOU SHOULD KNOW
Grow cultivars of flowering maple with white variegation as foliage plants—they rarely bloom indoors.

varieties:

1. **VARIEGATED ABUTILON** (*A. pictum*) is a colorful plant that has light orange bell-shape flowers and spring-green leaves heavily variegated with yellow.
2. **'MARILYN'S CHOICE'** is a large, 4-foot-tall shrub that displays 2-inch-long, bell-shape blooms with red calyxes (blouses) on top of yellow-orange petals (petticoats).
3. **'NABOB'** is noted for its nodding, deep crimson blooms which are part of the charm of this 6-foot-tall hybrid shrub.
4. **'LUCKY LANTERN WHITE'** is part of the Lucky Lantern Series of flowering maples. This dwarf plant features a compact, bushy 12-inch-tall form and pure white blooms.

Grape ivy
(*Cissus* spp.)

This fast-growing relative of grape shares the same habit of climbing via tendrils. Often grown in a hanging basket or trained up a trellis, grape ivy (*C. rhombifolia*) has long been a favorite indoor plant because it flourishes in a wide range of conditions. The dark green leaves add to the plant's lush appearance.

Best site

Place grape ivy in bright light during the winter and medium (indirect, bright) light the rest of the year. It also tolerates low light for extended periods, but pinch the vine ends frequently to keep the plant lush. Average humidity and temperatures of 60°F–80°F are best, although grape ivy also adapts to cooler conditions (no less than 50°F). Ensure good air circulation to prevent powdery mildew, a fungal disease, and white flies, a common pest.

Growing

Grape ivy has a minimal root system and seldom needs repotting. When the plant cannot take up water, it's time to repot. Let the potting mix dry a little between waterings. The leaves will shrivel and die if the soil is too dry or too wet. Provide an all-purpose fertilizer during the growing season. Start new plants by making stem cuttings anywhere along the stems. Remove the leaves from the bottom of the cutting and root it in water or a soilless mix. Or propagate by layering. To rejuvenate a lanky plant, cut back about one third of the vines to 6 inches long in late winter or early spring. One year later, cut back another one third of the plant's older vines; repeat the following year to complete the process. Practice this pruning regimen annually, cutting off no more than one third of the older vines to maintain a dense plant.

Special notes

Grape ivy also makes an attractive groundcover for a large potted plant, such as a Norfolk Island pine or weeping fig. Show off grape ivy by setting the potted plant on a pedestal, or training the vines onto a topiary frame and tying them in place with short lengths of soft twine. Shower the plant monthly to ward off spider mites. Keep an eye out for mealybugs, another common pest.

varieties:

1. **GRAPE IVY** (*C. rhombifolia*) grows as a vine well-suited to hanging baskets or as a specimen plant set on a pedestal.
2. **'ELLEN DANICA' OAKLEAF IVY** (*C. rhombifolia*) has deeply cut leaves resembling those of an oak tree. It has a compact form.
3. **REX BEGONIA VINE** (*C. discolor*) has silver-patterned leaves with red undersides comparable to a fancy-leaf begonia. It needs constant warmth and high humidity.

Hibiscus
(*Hibiscus rosa-sinensis*)

Known as Chinese hibiscus and rose mallow, this woody shrub is a reliable and long-lasting flowering indoor plant. Hundreds of cultivars are available in different leaf sizes and shapes—some are variegated. The intensely colored, short-lived flowers have single or double petals. The plant blossoms for months.

Best site

Hibiscus craves at least a few hours of direct sun each day. The more bright light it gets, especially during the winter, the better it will bloom. In the summer, move the plant outdoors where it can bask in sun early in the day. Protect the plant from drying winds, cold drafts, and frost. It grows best in cool to average temperatures (55°F–70°F) and needs high humidity to keep the buds from dropping. Conditions that are too dry, too damp, or too cold cause leaf drop.

Growing

Water just enough to keep the soil from drying out during the winter. In summer, keep the soil evenly moist. Fertilize every other week throughout spring and summer, using plant food formulated for flowering plants. Repot your hibiscus when roots start to grow out of the bottom of the pot. Propagate by taking stem cuttings in summer. Establish three or four main branches and remove all others at the base. Cut back the main branches by one third in late winter to promote new growth, lushness, and blooms. The plant blooms on new wood, so avoid pruning off new growth or you will lose the flower buds. Hibiscus can be shrubby, with multiple stems, or a single-stem tree form. The plant grows from 2 to 10 feet tall and 2 to 8 feet wide, depending on the variety and the extent of pruning it receives.

Special notes

Hibiscus drops its leaves if conditions change, but the plant will regenerate leaves on old stems. Spider mites can become a problem in dry air, causing leaves and buds to yellow and drop off. A weekly shower helps keep the pests at bay. Whiteflies, aphids, mealybugs, and scale are also potential pests. Yellow leaves may indicate low nitrogen—adding compost to the potting mix will help fix the problem.

YOU SHOULD KNOW
The flowers, buds, and young leaves of *Hibiscus rosa-sinensis* are edible. All add color and texture to salads.

varieties:

1. **LUAU LILIKOI YELLOW** has vibrant, sunny flowers on a compact, 3-foot-tall shrub, spreading cheer throughout the summer.
2. **'TONGA WIND'** bears bright red, 6-inch-diameter flowers that contrast with the shrub's dark green foliage.
3. **'MANDARIN WIND',** one of the Tradewind Series of hibiscus, is suited to a large pot and outdoor living as well as colorful indoor display.
4. **'TIKI TEMPTATION'** has showy oversized flowers that bloom twice as long as traditional hibiscus varieties.

Japanese aralia
(*Fatsia japonica*)

Popular since Victorian times, this large-leaf shrub reaches 6 feet or more. It is fast growing, durable, and tolerant of various environments. The naturally large plant can be kept smaller by regularly pruning long shoots that develop. Compact and white-variegated forms of Japanese aralia are available.

Best site
Japanese aralia is especially easy to grow in a cool, well-ventilated—even drafty—location indoors. It grows vigorously in medium to indirect, bright light, but also tolerates low-light conditions.

Growing
Allow the soil to dry out between waterings for a plant grown in low light; keep the soil more evenly moist in medium or bright light. Water less during winter. Pinch off the stem tips to promote branching; prune to keep the plant 3 to 4 feet tall.

Special notes
Leaves turn pale green and develop brown edges if the plant is underwatered. Overwatering rots the plant's roots. Propagate by stem cuttings.

Lipstick plant
(*Aeschynanthus* spp.)

The scarlet flowers of lipstick plant unfurl like lipsticks rolled out of their tubes. The plant usually blooms most in fall and then sporadically throughout the year. Lipstick plant has thick, glossy leaves and gently arching stems. A hanging basket or pedestal provides an ideal way to display it.

Best site
Provide medium to bright light but not direct sun, average to warm temperatures (60°F–80°F), and high humidity (65 percent). Let the plant rest after blooming, cutting back on water, reducing temperature, and lowering humidity.

Growing
Allow the soil to dry slightly between waterings, but let it dry more during the winter rest period. Feed every two weeks during bloom time with a formula for flowering plants.

Special notes
Lipstick plant may shed its leaves if it is too cold; the leaves may turn brown when humidity is too low. The vines reach 2 to 3 feet long. Cut them to 6 inches if they become scraggly.

YOU SHOULD KNOW
Give Japanese aralia a monthly shower to keep the large, shapely leaves looking their best and to control spider mite populations.

YOU SHOULD KNOW
Grow new lipstick plants from stem cuttings taken in spring. Any variety makes a striking plant, even without flowers.

Nerve plant
(Fittonia albivenis)

The intricately veined leaves of this spreading 6-inch-tall plant inspire another name: mosaic plant. Varieties feature red, pink, or white veining on the oval leaves. All varieties, including a dwarf form, add color and structural interest to terrariums and dish gardens, where the conditions promote their health.

Best site

The plant does best in a warm and moist environment. Place it in medium, well-diffused light; direct sun burns the leaves. Temperatures above 65°F and humidity above 60 percent are ideal. For these reasons, it is a popular terrarium plant. It combines well in mixed baskets and groupings with other plants that require high humidity and soil moisture, such as small ferns and prayer plant. Place nerve plant at the edge of a container, where it will grow upright at first and then begin to spill over the edge.

Growing

Nerve plant grows well if placed under a fluorescent light. It also adapts well to growing in an enclosed container such as a cloche. Use a peaty potting soil that holds moisture well.

Provide an even supply of moisture—not soaking wet—tapering off somewhat during the winter months and allowing the soil to dry a little between waterings. Fertilize monthly with all-purpose plant food.

Special notes

Pinch the stem ends regularly to keep nerve plant growing densely. When older plants lose their attractiveness, take stem tip cuttings and root them to make new plants. You can also propagate it by layering the stems. Sometimes the stems self-layer, forming roots where they touch the soil surface. Fungus gnats, mealybugs, and aphids are possible pests and root rot a potential disease of nerve plant.

YOU SHOULD KNOW

If you grow nerve plant in a wide pot, the low-growing stems will spread and root naturally, eventually filling the pot. This plant doesn't often need repotting.

varieties:

1. **'RED ANNE'** foliage has wide pinkish-red veins set apart by olive green leaves, giving the plant an overall appearance of pinkish-red foliage.
2. **VERSCHAFELTII** also known as painted net leaf, adds its showy oval leaves with bright pink veins to any plant display.
3. **ARGYRONEURA** is a group of nerve plants that feature silver or white vein patterns on the olive green leaves.
4. **'MINI'** has smaller leaves and a dwarf stature that make it an ideal plant for the confined spaces of a terrarium.

Palm (various genera)

Undemanding and adaptive, palms have long been favored as indoor plants. Many flourish indoors for decades, providing a lush, tropical backdrop. Their graceful leaves, called fronds, are either fan-shape or pinnate (feathery). Most palms grown indoors have a trunk, but others are clumping or stemless. Fronds range from 6 inches to many feet long. Your choice of plants depends on the shape and potential size that appeal to you.

Best site

Palms team up beautifully with other tropicals. Underplant a palm with low-growing, colorful houseplants for a pretty effect. Although palms are among the world's most easily recognized plants, it is often mistakenly assumed that the plants require desert conditions with direct sun and dry heat. This family of plants that evolved millions of years ago includes thousands of species within different genera, so few generalities apply. However, most palms will grow best in medium or indirect, bright light. The few that thrive in low light include lady palm (*Rhapsis excelsa*), parlor palm (*Chamaedorea elegans*), and Kentia palm (*Howea forsteriana*). Typically, palms grow well in warm temperatures (75°F or higher) and high humidity (65 percent or higher), but many types can adapt to average temperatures and lower humidity. Very low humidity can cause frond tips to turn brown. Palms should not be situated in cold drafts. If you move a palm outdoors for the summer, keep it in a spot where it is shaded most of the day.

Growing

Usually slow growing, palms' needs vary. For best results, research the species of plant you want and address its particular needs accordingly. During spring and summer, water liberally to keep the potting mix evenly damp. Most palms will benefit from allowing the surface of the potting mix to dry out before watering during the winter. The potting mix should drain well. Palms vary in their needs for repotting. When the plant's roots fill the pot, move it into a somewhat larger pot with fresh potting mix. If a year or two goes by and the plant does not need repotting, replace the top 2 or 3 inches of potting mix with fresh mix. Palms do well in most potting mixes, but they'll grow better if you amend the usual mix with small pine bark and coarse sand or use a specialized palm potting mix. Fertilize palms monthly during the summer, using a plant food formulated for houseplants. Palms thrive and develop a rich green color when spending the summer outdoors in a shaded spot. Shelter your palm from wind to prevent damage to the fronds.

Special notes

Allow plenty of room for palms. They can be damaged easily. Snip off any damaged or dead fronds, but never cut off the top of a plant. Unlike most plants, palms produce new growth only from the tip, so removing its growing point kills the stem—and the whole plant. Some palms draw nutrients from old fronds (yellow or brown), so remove them judiciously and avoid taking off too many fronds, which will weaken the plant. Palms can be grown from seed, but most grow so slowly it makes sense to buy a palm the size you need. Shower the plant regularly, especially when the air is dry, to help prevent spider mites. Whiteflies, mealybugs, and scale may also present problems. Palms are sensitive to mineral salts accumulation in soil, from the local water supply or fertilizer. Use rainwater to hydrate a palm and help prevent this problem.

treelike varieties:

1. **MAJESTY PALM** (*Ravenea rivularis*) needs plenty of water, light, and fertilizer. It grows along rivers in nature. Spider mites can become problematic if humidity and moisture are lacking.
2. **BAMBOO PALM** (*Chamaedorea seifrizii, C. erumpens*), or reed palm, has a thick canopy. It likes uniformly damp but not wet soil.
3. **CHINESE FAN PALM** (*Livistona chinensis*) often grows as wide as it is tall. Give it bright, indirect light.
4. **LADY PALM** (*Rhapis excelsa*) is a slow grower that eventually may reach 10 feet tall. With its fan-shape leaves and multiple stems, it resembles bamboo.
5. **KENTIA PALM** (*Howea forsteriana*), or sentry palm, carries more fronds if kept in medium, indirect light.

shrubby varieties:

6. **PYGMY DATE PALM** (*Phoenix roebelinii*) is a slow grower that reaches 3 or 4 feet indoors and tolerates less-than-ideal conditions. It likes warmth and bright light.
7. **ARECA PALM** (*Dypsis lutescens*) produces yellow to yellow-orange lower stems. Give it bright light, high humidity, and consistent warmth.
8. **PARLOR PALM** (*Chamaedorea elegans*) prefers warm temperatures, but is not as fussy about high light and humidity as are many other palms.

Peace lily
(*Spathiphyllum wallisii*)

The peace lily gets its common name from its distinctive bloom—a bract—that resembles a white flag. The plant has become popular for its glossy arching foliage and adaptable nature. Dozens of cultivars exist in varied sizes: dwarf (1 foot tall); medium (2 feet); and large (3 feet).

YOU SHOULD KNOW

Peace lilies are considered excellent air-cleaning plants, absorbing contaminants such as benzene and formaldehyde. Even without flowers, the peace lily makes an attractive foliage plant. Over time, a single plant slowly produces offsets, creating a pot full of verdant leaves.

Best site

Peace lily is commonly used in commercial settings because it tolerates most indoor conditions. The plant grows best in medium to indirect or filtered, bright light. Light that is too intense yellows the leaves. Peace lily tolerates lower light but usually needs bright light to bloom. As long as the plant is kept out of cold drafts, it can cope with a range of temperatures (60°F–80°F). Placing the plant on a chilly windowsill (below 55°F) can damage it. The higher the humidity, the better, although peace lily is forgiving about this too.

Growing

If you grow peace lily in bright light, keep the soil damp. The lower the light, the drier the soil should be—especially in winter. The soil should not dry out completely, allowing the plant to wilt. If water is too scarce, the leaf tips may turn brown. Fertilize monthly in summer, using an all-purpose plant food. Overfertilizing will prevent flowering and cause brown spots on the leaves. Pot a peace lily in good-quality potting mix and repot rarely, when the roots have filled the pot. This is also a good time to divide the plant and pot the divisions in fresh soil.

Special notes

The plant typically blooms in spring and sometimes in fall. But many varieties, especially newer ones, have been bred to produce flowers more frequently. They may bloom sporadically throughout the year. Dust or shower the plant monthly. Most plants begin flowering only when they are more than a year old. Snip off yellow leaves and spent flowers. Insect pests are rare, but keep an eye out for potential problems, including mealybugs, spider mites, and scale. Overwatering and setting the plant too low in the pot can cause a peace lily's crown (raised center) to rot.

varieties:

1. **'DOMINO'** variegated peace lily is a compact plant that works well on a tabletop, where its white streaks can be appreciated up close. It grows 18 to 24 inches tall.
2. **'JETTYSTAR'** is a new cultivar with glossy, smooth, broad green leaves, clear white blooms, and compact growth suited for containers 8 to 10 inches in diameter.
3. **'SENSATION'** is a massive cultivar that grows to 5 feet tall and 4 feet wide. The tough leaves have a ribbed texture.

Peacock plant
(*Calathea* spp.)

This genus includes hundreds of beautiful foliage plants—some are challenging to grow indoors. Once you've had success with one, their appeal is strong. Peacock plants have ornately patterned leaves, marbled with pink, red, silver, or white. They mix well with ferns and other plants that thrive in humid conditions.

Best site

Peacock plant can be difficult to maintain without high humidity. Try grouping one—or several—with ferns in a bathroom. Use a humidifier to create ideal conditions (60 percent or higher humidity) and discover how other plants will benefit too. Or grow peacock plant in a tabletop conservatory or large terrarium. The plant grows best in medium light or diffused, bright light, but it can tolerate lower light when supplemented with artificial light. The coloring and patterning of peacock plant is most appreciable when lit from behind; the markings can fade in too-bright light. Many varieties have lacy, papery foliage or leaves with pale marbling set off by dark veins—reminiscent of stained glass. Provide warm temperatures (70°F–85°F); keep the plant out of cold drafts.

Growing

Keep the potting mix evenly damp from spring through fall. Use warm or room-temperature water. Fertilize monthly in summer, using an all-purpose plant food. Growth slows as winter comes, preparing the plant for a rest period. Continue to keep the humidity high, but reduce watering. Remove any dead leaves. Pinch off ragged leaves in late winter. Leaves will be replaced by new growth in spring. Divide the root ball every two or three years in spring or early summer and pot the divisions in well-draining potting mix to create new plants, if you wish. Shower the plant occasionally to remove dust; do not use leaf polish. Peacock plant grows from 1 to 2 feet tall, depending on the variety.

Special notes

Your peacock plant may produce insignificant flowers, but dramatic foliage is the plant's greatest asset. Possible pests include spider mites, mealybugs, and aphids. Excess mineral salts cause leaf tip browning and stem dieback.

YOU SHOULD KNOW
Check a peacock plant's roots each spring. If they have filled the pot, it's time to give the plant a more spacious container with fresh potting mix.

varieties:

- **'HOLIDAY'** (*C. roseopicta*) is a spectacular plant with white-patterned green leaves with purplish undersides and pinkish-red flowers if grown in bright light.
- **'ROYAL STANDARD'** is a new hybrid variety with silvery leaves surrounded by a deep green margin. In bright light it may develop pink flowers.
- **CONCINNA PRAYER PLANT** (*C. concinna*) has showy leaves that display a pattern of light and dark green. Small white flowers may appear at the base of the plant.
- **LANCELEAF CALATHEA** (*C. lancifolia*), native to Brazil, grows to 30 inches tall with lance-shape leaves that have bold markings, purple undersides, and wavy edges.

Peperomia (*Peperomia* spp.)

This extremely varied genus offers an amazing array of plants with different leaf forms, colors, and growth habits. Some peperomias grow upright, others trail, but most are compact and clumping. Some have flat, glistening leaves; others appear corrugated. Many have off-white flower spikes that resemble rat tails. These interesting plants display so much variety, an entire indoor garden could be created using peperomias alone.

Best site

Situate peperomias in medium or indirect, bright light. They usually grow well in a north- or east-facing window, or in a west window with a sheer curtain. Direct sunlight is too intense, but many varieties adapt to low-light conditions. They're ideal for a desktop or a dish garden. Variegated peperomias are less colorful in low light. As natives of the tropics and subtropics, peperomias fare best in temperatures between 60°F and 75°F, and should not be exposed to cold drafts or temperatures below 50°F. If leaf tips or edges turn brown, check the surroundings and move the plant away from a chilly windowsill, air-conditioning vent, or otherwise drafty spot.

Growing

The genus *Peperomia* includes more than a thousand species, although most of them are not widely grown. Nonetheless, this is a fun group to collect—see how many different varieties you can find. They grow without special care and reward you with lasting beauty. Depending on the type you choose—upright, trailing, or clumping—the plants grow 6 to 12 inches tall. Some peperomias have waxy, fleshy, succulent leaves; the leaves of others are attractively marked.

Most peperomias will flourish during the warm, humid weeks of summer. But these adaptable plants can also tolerate the dry atmosphere of a heated home or office. Peperomias benefit from occasional showers to keep their leaves pristine. What's more, the plants tolerate a bit of neglect, such as a missed watering, better than most plants. For best results, allow the soil surface to dry between waterings, and then water the plant from the bottom, avoiding wetting the leaves and the center or crown of the plant. Do this by filling the pot's saucer with water and allowing the potting mix and plant roots to draw up the moisture. Peperomias are sensitive to overwatering, which causes root rot especially if the plant grows in cool and moist conditions. Keep the soil barely damp from late fall until early spring. Peperomia has a minimal root system, so repotting is not often necessary. After several years, when a plant has become crowded in its container, move it into a slightly larger pot with new potting mix. Use a peat-based potting mix that drains well rather than heavy potting soil. Feed peperomia every other week in the summer only, using a half-strength solution of all-purpose plant food.

Special notes

If your peperomia elongates into a heightened, central crown, it's time to make divisions of the root ball or remove offsets for new plants. Trailing peperomias are also propagated by stem cuttings. Peperomia is impressively pest-free most of the time. Scale and mealybugs become problems once in a while. If the leaves of your peperomia wilt or become discolored, or the stems rot, chances are the plant is being overwatered. It may also be affected by ringspot, a viral disease marked by brown rings and deformed leaves. In any case, remove the damaged plant parts and cut back on watering. Ensure good air circulation around peperomia to help prevent disease.

smoothleaf varieties:

1. **WATERMELON PEPEROMIA** (*P. argyreia*) is a small species that grows to 6 or 8 inches with silver-striped leaves.
2. **VARIEGATED BABY RUBBER PLANT** (*P. obtusifolia* 'Variegata') has gold-and-white variegation on its glossy leaves. Try it in a terrarium.
3. **'PEPPY'** (*P. ferreyae*) has thick, lancelike leaves. It grows 8 inches tall and 12 inches wide.
4. **TEARDROP PEPEROMIA** (*P. orba*) is a compact and mounding plant that begins to trail as it matures. Its leaves are shaped like an elongated teardrop.
5. **RED-EDGE PEPEROMIA** (*P. clusiifolia* 'Tricolor') bears leaves that have broad white borders with a pink blush along the edge. Pinch the stem ends to encourage branching.

textured-foliage varieties:

6. **BURGUNDY** (*P. caperata*) is one of the most popular varieties. It comes from the rain forests of Brazil and grows well in a terrarium or Wardian case.
7. **'EMERALD RIPPLE'** (*P. caperata*) has heart-shape, dark green leaves with a wafflelike texture. It is a popular easy-to-grow, compact plant.
8. **SILVERLEAF PEPEROMIA** (*P. griseoargentea*) reaches 6 inches tall and has silvery green leaves with a slightly rippled texture.

Philodendron (*Philodendron* spp.)

It's no wonder these are among the most widely grown indoor plants, known for their tough nature and tolerance of low light. Philodendrons' adaptability to different settings, combined with a long life expectancy, makes them highly successful indoor plants. In the wild, they grow on the floor of South American rain forests as vines, shrubs, and trees. With a conducive indoor environment, they typically pose few problems.

Best site

Philodendrons are grouped according to their growth habits: climbing, tree, and clump-forming. The leaves of each are glossy and attractive—but different.

The most commonly grown climbing varieties do best in humid conditions and where they can attach themselves to a sturdy support, such as a moss pole or bark slab. Climbers also make excellent candidates trailing from hanging planters. Climbing philodendrons include spadeleaf (*P. domesticum*), splitleaf (*P. pertusum*), redleaf (*P. erubescens*), and heartleaf (*P. hederaceum oxycardium*, syn. *P. scandens*).

Tree philodendrons, in particular the cutleaf or lacy tree philodendron (*P. bipinnatifidum*), have a distinct trunk and can become very tall (6 to 8 feet). They usually produce aerial roots, which reach down into the soil to support the plant, and are especially suited to offices or large rooms with high ceilings.

The clump-forming philodendrons form ground-hugging rosettes that are often wider than tall. They rarely need staking and don't usually produce aerial roots, but some hybrids have climbing genes in their backgrounds and will eventually produce stems that begin to clamber. The clump-forming plants are handsome standing on a floor or a table.

Philodendrons prefer medium light, but some tolerate low light. The heartleaf climber grows best in low light; others can develop smaller leaves that form farther apart on a stem with insufficient light. Generally, philodendrons grow well in average temperatures (60°F–75°F) and humidity (65 percent). Keep the plants out of cold drafts.

Growing

Allow the soil to dry slightly between waterings, especially in low light. During the winter, let the plant rest: Water only enough to keep the potting mix from drying out completely. Rinse the leaves periodically to keep them clean and glossy. To encourage growth, feed the plant monthly in summer, using an all-purpose fertilizer. Otherwise, feed the plant only once a year. Repot a philodendron only when the roots have filled the pot and the plant can no longer take up water. Do not use overly large pots or planters; philodendrons benefit from crowding. Use an average, well-draining potting mix. Cut back vigorous plants to control their size as you like, and snip off occasional faded leaves. Give climbing varieties adequate support with a moss pole—kept damp—or let them trail from a suspended container, and cut back the stems regularly to keep the plant lush.

Special notes

Propagate a philodendron from stem cuttings in summer. Keep the cuttings warm to promote rooting. Climbing varieties propagate well by layering the lengthy stems in soil. If a climbing plant becomes leggy or bare at its base, prune the stems to rejuvenate the plant and encourage new growth. Clump-forming plants may also become lanky over time. Cut them back by at least one third and up to two thirds—they'll return to their dense form eventually. Philodendrons are not ordinarily bothered by pests or diseases. If conditions are too dry, spider mites may proliferate. Mealybugs may also appear. All parts of a philodendron are toxic, and the sap irritates skin, so keep plants out of the reach of children and wear gloves.

climbing and trailing varieties:

① **'BRASIL'** has glossy leaves splashed with yellow and light green markings. This trailing plant reaches 4 feet long.

② **HEARTLEAF PHILODENDRON** (*P. hederaceum oxycardium*, *P. scandens*) can be trained to a support or allowed to form a mounding plant.

③ **VELVETLEAF PHILODENDRON** (*P. hederaceum hederaceum*) is a graceful plant with a velvety leaf texture and bronze hues in the new foliage.

④ **FIDDLELEAF PHILODENDRON** (*P. bipennifolium*) needs medium light and high humidity. It will climb if you let it.

⑤ **'PINK PRINCESS' REDLEAF PHILODENDRON** (*P. erubescens*) has black to burgundy foliage splashed with white and bright pink.

shrubby varieties:

⑥ **'CONGO'** has large, spade-like medium green leaves with lighter midribs. It withstands moderate light conditions. 'Rojo Congo' is similar, but with burgundy foliage.

⑦ **'PRINCE OF ORANGE'** is a hybrid with coppery-orange new foliage. Leaves turn green as they age, but retain a pinkish midrib.

⑧ **'GOLDEN XANADU'** has deeply lobed yellow-green foliage that forms a mounding plant up to 18 inches tall and wide.

Piggyback plant
(*Tolmeia menziesii*)

Piggyback plant has fuzzy pale green leaves that often support little plantlets piggyback-style. The arching stems of this mounding plant grow to 12 inches tall and can quickly fill a hanging planter with an attractive mass of soft foliage. It is also handsomely displayed on a pedestal or open shelving.

Best site

Place this plant in medium to bright light, but not direct sunlight. It tolerates low light. Cool to average temperatures (50°F–75°F) and average humidity (30–60 percent) are best. Leaf edges brown when humidity is too low.

Growing

Let the soil dry a bit when growing piggyback plant in medium light; keep it moister in brighter light. Monthly feeding in summer suffices.

Special notes

Rinse the foliage or use a soft brush to remove dust. Propagate new plants by snipping leaves with "piglets" and potting them in small pots. Excess mineral salts damage the roots and cause the plant to die back. Cultivars of piggyback plant with bright chartreuse or golden-variegated leaves are available.

Ponytail palm
(*Beaucarnia recurvata*)

The popular plant known as ponytail palm or elephant's foot is not a true palm but an agave family member, more closely related to dracaena and yucca. It resembles a ponytail, with narrow, dark green leaves that often reach down the full length of the trunk. It grows to 12 feet tall indoors.

Best site

This native of the semideserts of Mexico is impressively adaptable indoors, thriving in medium or bright light, dry air, and cold or heat.

Growing

If this plant is flawed in any way, it is extremely slow growing. Water thoroughly, then let the potting mix dry between waterings. The plant stores water in its bulbous base. An established plant can go several weeks or longer without watering, especially when grown in cool conditions. The plant rarely needs repotting or fertilizing.

Special notes

Ponytail palm rots when overwatered. Use a damp cloth to clean foliage monthly. Watch for spider mites, scale, and mealybugs.

YOU SHOULD KNOW
Ponytail palm naturally sheds its long, strappy leaves as it grows. Otherwise, snip off any spent foliage as it turns brown.

Pothos
(*Epipremnum aureum*)

Native to Southeast Asia, pothos is a vining plant widely used in hanging baskets or trained on moss stakes. Its heart-shape leaves are shiny green and often marked with yellow, white, or silver variegation. Pothos withstands neglect, low light, and poor watering practices. It's a good plant for novice gardeners.

Best site

Provide medium or indirect, bright light for best results. Direct sun will scorch the leaves. In lower light, the plant's variegation may be lost. Pothos prefers average temperatures (60°F–75°F), but will tolerate cooler periods. It is not so forgiving of cold drafts. High humidity (60–70 percent) is important. The leaf tips will turn brown and shrivel if the humidity is too low. When you grow pothos on a bark slab or moss pole, water the slab or pole to help the aerial roots hold on and provide more ambient humidity. To train pothos onto a moss pole or bark slab, insert the pole next to the root ball and drape the vines on it. You may need to occasionally pinch and reattach vines, but once the aerial roots form, the plant will keep itself upright.

Growing

Pothos may grow, as it does in the wild, as a climber. Its aerial roots cling to all but the smoothest surfaces, even on interior walls. Allow the potting mix to dry after being thoroughly soaked. Yellow and fallen leaves and rotting stems are indicators of overwatering. Feed pothos only once or twice a year with an all-purpose plant food. Repot every two or three years, when the plant's roots have filled the pot. Use a peat-based potting mix amended with coarse sand and perlite. Pinch off the plant's tips frequently to keep it lush. Prune pothos as needed periodically to maintain a full, symmetrical plant.

Special notes

Propagate pothos from stem cuttings taken in spring or summer. Root the cuttings in potting mix or water. You can also layer the stems (vines) to make new plants. Use 5-inch-long stem ends with remaining leaves to propagate new plants.

YOU SHOULD KNOW
An old pothos plant may become too large for its space or leggy (when long vines shed leaves and become bare with only foliage remaining at the tips). When this happens, prune the plant back severely, to within an inch or two of the base.

varieties:

1. **COMMON POTHOS** has deep green heart-shape leaves with splashes of gold.
2. **'NEON'** is a trailing plant with bright chartreuse leaves. Because this variety grows to 2 feet or longer, it's an ideal candidate for a hanging basket in bright light.
3. **'PEARLS AND JADE'** has gray-green leaves with white splotches and a slightly smaller size (1 to 2 inches long and wide) than most other cultivars. It trails to 2 feet long.
4. **'MARBLE QUEEN'** leaves are heavily variegated with creamy white. This variety needs a bit more light than others or it will lose its variegation and revert to green.

Prayer plant
(*Maranta leuconeura*)

Here's a must-have for a foliage plant collection, due to its leaves' unusual coloration and habit of folding up at night. Various cultivars boast different colorful markings. The undersides of the leaves are usually maroon. Prayer plant grows about 12 inches tall and wide and is well-displayed in a hanging basket.

Best site

Prayer plant grows best with medium light and average temperatures (60°F–75°F). It can handle less light, but in excessively bright light the leaves brown along the edges and become pale. Protect the plant from cold drafts and keep the humidity high.

Growing

Evenly damp soil is ideal. Overwatering causes root rot, especially in winter. Fertilize monthly during the growing season with all-purpose plant food. Repot only when the plant fills its pot. Use well-draining, compost-rich potting mix.

Special notes

Rinse the plant monthly to remove dust and spider mites. Most prayer plant varieties can be propagated by division or stem cuttings.

Purple passion plant
(*Gynura aurantiaca*)

The velvety leaves of purple passion plant are densely covered with fuzzy purple hairs. New leaves are especially colorful. The fast-growing plant starts out growing upright. As it matures, the stems trail and reach 20 to 30 inches long. Purple passion plant provides a showy option for a hanging planter.

Best site

Give the plant bright light during winter and medium light the rest of the year. Purple passion plant becomes leggy in low light. The plant does well with average temperatures (55°F–65°F) and humidity (30–60 percent).

Growing

Evenly damp soil is best; soggy soil rots the plant's roots. Purple passion plant can do without fertilizing and repotting. A happy, healthy plant produces clusters of yellow-orange flowers. Pinch off the flower buds because the flowers have an unpleasant odor and a mature plant declines after flowering.

Special notes

Make new plants from stem cuttings, which root easily in water or soil.

(i) YOU SHOULD KNOW Prayer plant may stop growing and take a rest (go dormant) during winter. When it perks up in spring and resumes growing, remove dead leaves.

(i) YOU SHOULD KNOW Regularly pinch out the stem tips of purple passion plant to promote branching and compact, lush growth.

Purple waffle plant
(*Hemigraphis alternata* 'Exotica')

This low-growing, spreading plant reaches 6 inches tall and has deeply puckered leaves. The colorful foliage has a purple sheen and reddish undersides. The plant occasionally produces clusters of tiny white flowers. Display it in a hanging basket, as a groundcover for a large plant, or in a terrarium.

Best site
Grow purple waffle plant in medium light. Average to high temperatures (60°F and higher) and medium to high humidity (30 percent or higher) are best. Keep the plant out of winds and cold drafts.

Growing
The soil should be evenly damp. If it is allowed to dry, the leaves will turn brown and crispy; overwatering will cause the plant to rot. Repot annually in compost-rich potting mix. Feed monthly during the growing season with half-strength all-purpose plant food.

Special notes
Regularly pinching off the stem tips promotes dense growth and a well-balanced appearance. Root new plants from stem cuttings or by layering the stems in soil.

Sago palm
(*Cycas revoluta*)

Although it resembles a palm tree, sago palm is more closely related to modern evergreens. Over time, the slow-growing plant develops a rough, thick trunk. The arching fronds are shiny and extremely stiff. Sago palm is a long-lived plant that grows to 6 feet tall.

Best site
Situate a sago palm in medium light year-round. If you move it outdoors for the summer, let it have morning sun and afternoon shade. Average indoor temperatures and humidity are fine.

Growing
Let the surface of the potting mix dry between waterings. Avoid allowing the soil to dry completely. This plant does not indicate when it is dry, but the leaves will turn yellow if overwatered. Feed only once in spring and once in summer using half-strength fertilizer. Repotting is seldom needed.

Special notes
The plant is toxic. The spiny fronds are easily damaged. Display the plant away from children's reach but below eye level to appreciate the plant's unique architectural features.

 YOU SHOULD KNOW Red flame ivy (*Hemigraphis alternata*) is a parent of purple waffle plant. It has similar characteristics and needs.

YOU SHOULD KNOW Avoid using pesticides on a sago palm. Many of them damage it. If necessary, turn to nontoxic pest control solutions instead.

Schefflera
(*Schefflera* spp.)

The easy-care tropical plant, also known as umbrella tree, grows upright indoors, producing glossy leaflets on slender stems resembling small umbrellas. Indoors it grows to 8 feet but rarely blooms. As one of the most reliable, forgiving houseplants, schefflera can be a long-term evergreen resident.

YOU SHOULD KNOW

If you want to house a schefflera but are concerned about space limitations, dwarf umbrella plant is smaller in leaf size (7 inches in diameter) but grows to more than 6 feet tall. Pruning helps minimize plant size.

Best site

Medium light produces the best growth, although schefflera can tolerate less light. It copes with high temperatures, but the plant will drop leaves if it gets too cold and grow spindly if the light level is too low. Average home temperatures (60°F–75°F) are ideal. Schefflera needs only average humidity (30–60 percent). Keep it out of drying winds and cold drafts.

Growing

Water regularly during the growing season to keep the soil mix evenly damp. Overwatering leads to leaf loss or root rot. In winter, water sparingly—just enough to prevent the soil from drying out completely. Fertilize monthly in summer; feeding more than that will spur an already vigorous plant and could translate into annual repotting. Adopt a schefflera only if you have room for one. To keep the plant smaller than a small tree, pot it in a container no larger than 8 inches in diameter. You may need to prune the plant's roots periodically. Replenish some of the soil annually. To keep schefflera looking its best, wipe the leaves regularly with a dry, soft cloth. It is slow to propagate from stem cuttings; air-layering presents another option.

Special notes

Schefflera is often sold as several small plants in one pot—a good start for a more lush appearance. The palmlike leaflets are small when young, but can grow to 10 inches across. As the plant grows, you can shape it by pruning. A plant that becomes top-heavy should be pruned back to a more desirable shape. Remove wayward branches and faded leaves from time to time. Watch out for mealybugs, scale, and spider mites. Give your schefflera a summer vacation outdoors, helping it adjust by exposing it gradually to the elements in a sheltered and shaded location.

varieties:

1. **'AMATE SOLEIL' UMBRELLA PLANT** (*S. actinophylla*) is an improved variety with bright chartreuse foliage and resistance to leaf spot and spider mites.
2. **UMBRELLA PLANT** (*S. actinophylla*) has treelike foliage consisting of 10-inch-long leaflets, attached to the stem like the sections of an umbrella.
3. **'HAWAIIAN ELF' DWARF UMBRELLA PLANT** (*S. arboricola*) is a common indoor plant with dark green, shiny leaves. It is smaller in all dimensions than umbrella plant.
4. **FALSE ARALIA** (*S. elegantissima*, syn. *Dizygotheca elegantissima*) has a much finer leaf texture than other scheffleras.
5. **'GALAXY' FALSE ARALIA** (*S. elegantissima*) is a brightly colored form of false aralia with creamy leaf edges.

Snake plant

(*Sansevieria* spp.)

A strong accent plant, snake plant is prized for its ability to withstand low light, stifling heat, and even months of neglect. But it does better with proper care, a bright location, and regular watering. The tough, succulent leaves grow from a rhizome, stretching to 5 feet tall.

Best site

Although snake plant can tolerate low light for extended periods, it performs best in medium or bright light. This succulent plant thrives in the average humidity (30–60 percent) and temperatures (60°F–75°F) of most homes, but it can cope with dry, hot conditions too. Snake plant even tolerates air conditioning, but it will be happier to sit outdoors and bask in summer heat. During the winter, a minimum temperature of 50°F is essential to keep the plant going. Given bright enough light, the plant may produce a tall stalk of tubular, greenish flowers that exude a heavenly scent at night.

Growing

Let the soil dry between waterings. The plant rots easily if overwatered, especially in low-light situations. Water sparingly during winter. Grow snake plant in well-draining soil, amended with sand and pea gravel or perlite, and repot only when the plant fills the pot. Place more than one plant in a shallow, heavy, terra-cotta pot for a more effective display of contented plants. Fertilize only once a year, using an all-purpose plant food.

Special notes

Snake plant's leaves break easily. If a leaf becomes damaged, selectively prune it out. Propagate snake plant by division, leaf cuttings, or leaf-section cuttings. Cut 3-inch-long leaf sections and stand a cut end in potting mix or vermiculite to root the cuttings. New plants started from leaf cuttings lose their variegation. Offsets or new plants also form at soil level and can be separated from the mother plant and transplanted. When dividing snake plant, cut a portion of rhizome with attached foliage. This is the surest way to reproduce variegated forms of the plant. Clean the leaves monthly to remove dust and help keep them growing well. Remove any spent flowers. Pests rarely bother this plant.

varieties:

① **SNAKE PLANT** (*S. trifasciata*) has stiff sword-shape leaves that reach 4 feet and have gray horizontal markings resembling snakeskin.

② **VARIEGATED SNAKE PLANT** (*S. trifasciata* 'Laurentii') is a popular variety with creamy yellow leaf margins. It grows 2 to 3 feet tall.

③ **'SILVER QUEEN'** (*S. trifasciata*) is a cultivar with silvery gray foliage. In low-light conditions, the leaves become darker green.

④ **'HAHNII'** (*S. trifasciata*) is a compact variety that produces rosettes with 4-inch-long leaves with horizontal stripes.

⑤ **CYLINDER SNAKE PLANT** (*S. cylindrica*) produces round, rigid leaves arching out from a central crown, eventually reaching 5 feet long and more than an inch in diameter.

YOU SHOULD KNOW
A wide variety of snake plant cultivars are available. Some have leaf markings with white, off-white, yellow, or chartreuse; others are green only. Some are compact; others are strongly upright.

Spider plant
(*Chlorophytum* spp.)

One of the easiest and most popular indoor plants, spider plant grows quickly and adapts to cool or hot rooms, shade or sun. A hanging basket shows off the strappy, variegated foliage and long, wiry stems with attached, dangling plantlets. Starry white flowers are a bonus of this South African native.

YOU SHOULD KNOW
Spider mites and scale occasionally bother spider plant. Typically a vigorously growing plant will not become infested.

Best site

The plant will survive but not bloom or produce plantlets in very low light. It prefers indirect, bright light and may sunburn in direct sunlight. Spider plant grows vigorously when situated outdoors over the summer in a mostly shaded spot. Average temperatures (55°F–75°F) indoors suit the plant, with a winter minimum of 45°F. Average humidity suffices. If brown streaks appear on the leaves, the conditions are too cool and wet. Limp, pale leaves indicate too much heat and too little light in winter. The plant will improve in adjusted conditions.

Growing

Spider plant revels in regular showers. During the growing season, allow the soil to dry a bit, and then soak it thoroughly. In winter, water sparingly. Fertilize spider plant every other month, using half-strength all-purpose plant food. This plant produces bulky, fleshy tuberous roots that are capable of storing water and enabling the plant to survive neglect. The roots can quickly fill a pot and make watering a challenge—water will run straight through the pot. Allowing the pot to soak up water from a deep saucer works well; pour off any excess after watering.

Special notes

Repot in spring, if needed. If excess mineral salts or fluoride causes the leaf tips to brown, repot the plant in fresh potting mix. Snip off the brown leaf tips. Starting new spider plants is easy. First, situate small pots full of potting mix next to the mother plant. Snuggle one or two plantlets into each pot. When the plantlets have rooted, cut the wiry stem to let the plantlets become fully independent. You can also divide a mature spider plant. Spring is an ideal time for propagating spider plant. A compost-and-peat blend works best for potting the plant; steer clear of a soil mix that contains perlite.

varieties:

① **'VARIEGATUM' SPIDER PLANT** (*C. comosum*) is among the easiest indoor plants to grow. This variegated type has ribbonlike green leaves with creamy white margins.

② **'VITTATUM' SPIDER PLANT** (*C. comosum*) is a common cultivar with the reverse variegation of 'Variegatum'. It develops a central white stripe and green edges.

③ **GREEN SPIDER PLANT** (*C. comosum*), the plain species, has dark green, satiny leaves and is not as common as the variegated forms.

④ **'GREEN ORANGE' SPIDER PLANT** (*C. orchidastrum*, syn. *C. orchidantheroides*, *C. amaniense*) has broad foliage with orange petioles, which distinguishes it from its more common relatives.

Strawberry begonia
(*Saxifraga stolonifera*)

Not a begonia at all, this trailer produces scalloped, silver-veined leaves and scads of plantlets. The leaves have red-tinged undersides. The delicate plant makes a pretty display in a hanging planter or perched on a pedestal. It reaches 9 to 12 inches tall, plus 12 inches of trailing stems and plantlets.

Best site

Medium to bright light brings out the best coloring in the fuzzy leaves of strawberry begonia. Give the plant bright light in winter and medium light the rest of the year. Cool temperatures (to 40°F) at night and average to high humidity (30–70 percent) are ideal.

Growing

Strawberry begonia grows best in evenly damp soil with monthly doses of fertilizer throughout spring and summer. During the winter, allow the soil to dry more and let the plant rest.

Special notes

Repot annually in well-draining potting mix. Strawberry begonia almost propagates itself with its tiny plants hung on delicate pink stolons. Give the plantlets moist soil on which to sit and they will root. Low light causes spindly growth. Dry air and hot temperatures cause leaf dieback.

Stromanthe
(*Stromanthe sanguinea* 'Tricolor')

The bold coloring of this little-known plant gives it strong appeal for indoor gardens. Rich, emerald green- and ivory-streaked foliage folds up at night and reveals intense red undersides. The stems rise up in a tight clump that fans out, reaching 12 to 18 inches tall.

Best site

Situate stromanthe in medium light, such as an east window, or indirect, bright light near a south- or west-facing window. Get best results in average temperatures (60°F–70°F) and average to high humidity (30–70 percent).

Growing

This plant needs evenly damp soil throughout the growing season. Ease up on watering in winter, allowing the soil surface to dry between waterings. Rinse the plant monthly to help keep it healthy and dust-free. Use an all-purpose fertilizer monthly in summer.

Special notes

Overly dry soil invites mealybug infestation. Overwatering causes stems and leaves to collapse or become diseased. Divide the plant to propagate it.

YOU SHOULD KNOW To promote stromanthe's best form, keep in mind that higher temperatures require high humidity to prevent leaf browning.

Swedish ivy
(*Plectranthus* spp.)

This fast-growing trailing plant is a member of the mint family—not an ivy. The stems drape well from a hanging basket and reach several feet long if left unpinched. Swedish ivy produces a scent when the leaves are bruised or stems are cut. It develops spikes of tiny white or blue flowers.

YOU SHOULD KNOW
You'll find numerous varieties of plectranthus widely prized as ornamental plants for indoor and outdoor gardens. In India, southeast Asia, and Africa, several varieties are grown for their edible leaves.

Best site

Place Swedish ivy in bright light during the winter and medium light the rest of the year. It thrives outdoors during the growing season and will do best in a location with afternoon shade. Indoors, it prefers average temperatures (60°F–75°F) and humidity (30–60 percent). The plant can handle cooler temperatures too, but it must be protected from freezing. Many gardeners use cuttings from their indoor plants to provide outdoor plants for hanging baskets and other containers.

Growing

Swedish ivy grows well when the potting mix is kept evenly damp. Although it can survive drier conditions, long periods of dryness will cause the plant to produce smaller leaves. Fertilize monthly or less in summer, using a half-strength plant food. Give the plant plenty of room to grow in a spacious pot from the start and it will seldom need repotting. Use a compost-rich potting mix. By the time a plant outgrows its pot, it will likely be mature and no longer in top form—time to compost it. If you regularly start new plants from stem cuttings in soil or water, you'll always have attractive plants. They root and grow easily. Take cuttings or pinch off stem ends often to create a dense and compact plant.

Special notes

Most Swedish ivies grow upright at first, and then arch over and eventually trail. Besides being ideal for hanging baskets, they also make a pretty display for a mantel, open shelf, window box, or mixed planting. Grow Swedish ivy as an understory to a large potted tree or train your plant into a lush topiary. A sturdy plant that grows so readily from cuttings, Swedish ivy gives you even more pleasure when you share it and pass along pieces to friends and family. It is susceptible to whiteflies and mealybugs.

varieties:

1. **SWEDISH IVY** (*P. verticillatus*) is a traditional indoor plant adapted to container gardening.
2. **VARIEGATED PLECTRANTHUS** (*P. coleoides* 'Variegata') pleases with its creamy white leaf edges. It is widely grown as an annual outdoors, adding its trailing form to container gardens.
3. **'CERVEZA 'N LIME'** is a hybrid plectranthus with fuzzy, succulent chartreuse foliage and a citrusy fragrance.
4. **CUBAN OREGANO** (*P. amboinicus*) also has succulent, velvety leaves with scalloped edges. This species has a sharp scent. It is valued as a culinary plant in some countries.
5. **'LIMELIGHT'** (*P. oertendahlii*) is another easy-to-grow plant, characterized by its colorful foliage. The golden leaves are variegated with dark green and burgundy.

Swiss cheese plant
(*Monstera deliciosa*)

Easy to grow and durable, Swiss cheese plant is a dramatic addition to the indoor garden. The dark green, leathery, heart-shape leaves of a mature plant reach 3 feet across and have deep slashes and perforations. Aerial roots attach to a support and help the plant climb 10 to 15 feet. Its fruits are delicous.

Best site
Medium to indirect, bright light is best. The plant produces smaller leaves without holes in lower light. Ensure average warmth and humidity.

Growing
Let the top inch of potting mix dry between waterings. Water less in winter. Feed the plant monthly in summer. Repot infrequently in compost-enriched potting mix; top off the potting mix with an inch or two of compost annually. Give the plant room to grow and a strong support such as a moss pole.

Special notes
Clean the leaves regularly, using a damp cloth. Brown, brittle leaf edges indicate that humidity is too low; brown edges of yellowed leaves is symptomatic of overwatering. Propagate the plant by tip cuttings or air layering. All parts of the plant are toxic except the ripe fruit.

Ti plant
(*Cordyline fruticosa*, syn. *C. terminalis*)

Also known as the good-luck plant, this sturdy tropical shrub grows upright with woody stems, and reaches 3 to 6 feet tall indoors. The green or red leaves have pink or white variegations or margins, depending on the variety. The leaf color intensifies with age.

Best site
Indirect, bright light helps keep ti plant healthy. Direct sunlight scorches the leaves. High humidity is essential; use a humidifier during the winter and whenever the air is dry. Average temperatures (60°F–75°F) suffice.

Growing
Keep the soil evenly damp using rainwater, and allow the soil surface to dry between waterings. Apply all-purpose fertilizer monthly during the summer.

Special notes
Include several plants in a pot for a fuller appearance. Although ti plant is not usually bothered by pests, help prevent them by showering the plant monthly and removing yellow leaves. Brown leaf tips indicate low humidity or excess mineral salts or fluoride.

 YOU SHOULD KNOW Propagate ti plant by air layering or placing 2- to 3-inch-long pieces of stem cuttings in damp potting mix. Cover with plastic until the pieces sprout.

Tradescantia
(*Tradescantia* spp.)

Few indoor plants are easier to grow or better suited for a hanging container. Tradescantia's foliage brightens an indoor garden almost as effectively as do flowers. This plant blooms, although the flowers are subtle. Tradescantia is mostly grown for its colorful leaves, trailing form, and ease of propagation.

YOU SHOULD KNOW
A multitude of tradescantia cultivars boast foliage striped with different hues of green, purple, white, or silver. Many are common, easy-growing plants shared among generations of families and friends.

Best site
Although tradescantia tolerates medium light, it grows well and maintains the best leaf color in indirect, bright light. If the light is too bright, the leaf color bleaches out; in low light, the leaf coloring can fade to green and the plant becomes leggy. Cool to average temperatures (55°F–75°F) help keep tradescantia more compact. Humidity of 30 percent or higher prevents the leaf edges from browning.

Growing
Tradescantia makes an attractive groundcover for larger houseplants, or the trailing element in a mixed planting with an upright plant and a midrange filler. You can perch the plant on a pedestal or shelf, as long as the stems can trail freely. Water enough to keep the soil evenly damp. Potting mix that is too wet or too dry causes the stems to deteriorate. Pot in an all-purpose, well-draining potting mix and repot only when the plant fills the pot with roots.

During the growing season, fertilize monthly with half-strength plant food. Pinch the growing tips regularly to keep the plant compact and lush. Tradescantia does not age gracefully. Cut it back regularly and root the cuttings to provide a continuing source of new plants. When you take cuttings, tuck the cut stems into the same pot as the mother plant to make a fuller display, or root them in another pot.

Special notes
Tradescantia needs regular grooming to remove dead leaves and leggy stems and to encourage new, dense growth. Shower the plant to remove dust. Control mealybugs and spider mites; other pests are not common. Temperatures below 50°F will harm the plant; protect it from cold drafts. If the leaf tips or edges turn brown, check the humidity level and look for spider mites. Cut off stems with browned foliage.

varieties:
- **WANDERING JEW** (*T. zebrina*) is a traditional easy-care trailing plant bearing olive green foliage with silvery stripes and purple undersides.
- **PURPLE HEART** (*T. pallida* 'Purpurea', syn. *Setcreasea pallida*) is slow growing and requires less pinching than other species. It needs brighter light to bring out the deep purple leaf color.
- **STRIPED INCH PLANT** (*T. fluminensis*) is a fast-growing, trailing plant that forms a dense mass of shiny green-and-white foliage.
- **'TRICOLOR' BOAT LILY** (*T. spathacea*) is a striking white-, magenta-, and green-variegated form of boat lily with a finer texture.
- **BOAT LILY** (*T. spathacea*) is a species that forms clumps of shiny green leaves with purple to maroon undersides.

Wax plant
(*Hoya* spp.)

H. carnosa is the best-known member of this tropical plant genus. It is a climber with vining stems and waxy leaves. The growth habit, leaf shape, color, and size of each species differ. Some wax plants are compact; others are shrubby. Most have smooth, shiny leaves; others bear fuzzy foliage.

Best site

Wax plant rewards those who ensure it gets adequate light by producing fragrant blossoms. Train the plant on a trellis or grow it in a hanging pot. The vines can grow to 4 feet, but you can double them back on a support to give the plant a denser appearance. Place wax plant in indirect, bright light. Direct sun discourages flowering. The plant benefits from growing outdoors over the summer, as long as it is kept in partial shade or filtered light. Cool to average temperatures (45–75°F) will help the plant grow its best. Average humidity (30–60 percent) will do, but higher humidity helps prompt the annual flowering. Situate the plant where you can enjoy the fragrance of the night-blooming flowers; avoid moving the plant once buds appear.

Growing

During the growing season, water wax plant only after the top ½ inch of soil has dried. In winter, when the plant is resting, water less but don't let the soil dry out completely. Repot the plant infrequently. It has a minimal root system and will bloom better if it is pot-bound. This plant does not withstand the stress of repotting very well. Use an average soil that drains well and repot during mid- to late winter when the plant is resting. Fertilize monthly in summer with an all-purpose plant food.

Special notes

Overwatering causes the leaves to drop off. After the plant blooms, allow the faded flowers to fall off, but don't remove the flower stalk. Wax plant reblooms each year on the same stalk. Propagate by stem cuttings or layering the stems in soil. When cut the stems of wax plant exude a milky sap, which can attract insects. Keep an eye out for scale, mealybugs, and spider mites.

varieties:

1. **VARIEGATED WAX PLANT** (*H. carnosa rubra*) is distinguished by its variegated leaves with green edges and creamy centers. This species produces pink flowers.
2. **'TRICOLOR' WAX PLANT** (*H. carnosa*) has pinkish-purple stems and leaves variegated with pink, purple, and creamy white. Pink flowers typically appear in summer.
3. **HINDU ROPE VINE** (*H. carnosa* 'Crispa') has curled and twisted leaves packed tightly along the trailing stems.
4. **'ROYAL FLUSH' WAX PLANT** (*H. lacunosa*) has elongated, flattened foliage heavily speckled with pale, silvery-green spots. New growth is purple, and it bears star-shape white flowers.

Zebra plant
(*Aphelandra squarrosa*)

This is grown mostly as a dramatic foliage plant with boldly striped, shiny leaves. In fall, it produces a bright yellow bract that lasts for months and shorter-lived tubular flowers in a similar hue. Compact, modern cultivars grow to 15 inches tall. The flowering spike adds several inches.

Best site

Zebra plant grows well in medium light from spring through fall and in bright light during the winter. It needs constant warmth (65°F or more) and high humidity (65 percent or more) to thrive. Cold, dry air scorches the leaves.

Growing

Keep the soil damp, but not soggy. Water less in winter, when the plant rests. Feed only monthly during the summer, using half-strength fertilizer. When roots fill the pot, repot in spring.

Special notes

Zebra plant's leaves fall off if the soil is too dry or too wet; or if the air is too dry or too cold. Adjust the environment and new leaves will develop to replace those lost to unfavorable conditions. The plant needs ideal growing conditions to rebloom, but the variegated foliage is attractive on its own.

Zeezee plant
(*Zamioculcus zamiifolia*)

This plant is popular because it tolerates average household conditions and some neglect, yet keeps its attractive, glossy dark-green foliage. A distant relative of philodendron, it grows upright and forms a rosette of fleshy leafstalks. With time, it produces offsets and fills up its pot with foliage.

Best site

Choose a location for the plant where it has room to grow and spread to its mature size: 3 feet tall and wide. It grows best in indirect, bright light, but can tolerate low light. Zeezee plant needs temperatures above 40°F and low humidity (30 percent).

Growing

Keep the soil damper in bright light; let it dry between waterings in lower light. Overwatering results in yellow leaves. Fertilize monthly in summer. Repot when roots fill the pot.

Special notes

Move zeezee plant outdoors to a shaded place for the summer. Shower the plant regularly or wipe the leaves with a damp cloth to remove dust. Propagate it from leaf cuttings. Be sure to take a full leaf rather than a leaflet for the cutting.

YOU SHOULD KNOW
Zebra plant is often widely available in fall when it is blooming. The plant may not rebloom unless it is grown in ideal conditions.

YOU SHOULD KNOW
Zeezee plant is toxic, so keep it away from pets and children.

Bulbs, Plants, and Seeds

AIR PLANTS, EPIPHYTES, AND *TILLANDSIAS*

Airplants4U/ John McKenzie
P.O. Box 1359
Maglia, CA 95954
530/873-6730
airplants4u.com

BONNIE PLANTS

Bonnie Plant Farm
1727 Highway 223
Union Springs, AL 36089
334/738-3104
bonnieplants.com

BRENT AND BECKY'S BULBS

7900 Daffodil Lane
Gloucester, VA 23061
877/661-2852
brentandbeckysbulbs.com

COSTA FARMS, LLC

costafarms.com

FUNGI PERFECTI, LLC

P. O. Box 7634
Olympia, WA 98507
800/780-9126
fungi.com

HINES GROWERS

hineshort.com

LOGEE'S GREENHOUSES

141 North Street
Danielson, CT 06239
888/330-8038
logees.com

RENEES GARDEN SEEDS

6060 Graham Hill Road
Felton, CA 95018
888/880-7228
reneesgarden.com

RUSSELL'S BROMELIADS

15100 Lost Lake Rd.
Clermont, FL 34711
800/832-5632
russelsairplants.com

WHITE FLOWER FARM

P.O. Box 50, Route 63
Litchfield, CT 06759
800/420-2852
whiteflowerfarm.com

Containers

CRAFTWARE POTTERY & BASKETS

6606 Grover St.
Omaha, NE 68106
800/311-7491
craftwareusa.com

LECHUZA PLANTERS

877/532-4892
lechuza.us

SCHEURICH USA, INC.

www.scheurich.de

SIMPLE GARDEN JR.

877/883-2784
fertileearth.com

Tools and Specialty Supplies

BLACK GOLD SOIL PRODUCTS

blackgold.bz

GARDENERS SUPPLY CO.

128 Intervale Road
Burlington, VT 05401
800/876-5520
gardeners.com

JAMALI GARDEN

149 W. 28th St.
New York, NY 10009
212/996-5534
jamaligarden.com

LEE VALLEY TOOLS

P.O. Box 1780
Ogdensburg, NY 13669-6780
800/267-8735
leevalley.com

index

index

Looking for more gardening inspiration?

See what the experts at *Better Homes and Gardens* have to offer.

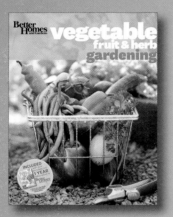

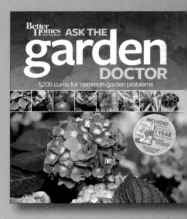

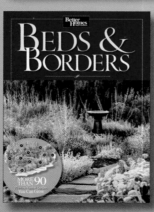

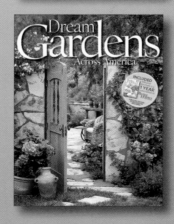

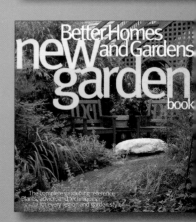

Available where all great books are sold.

WILEY